POPULAR EUGENICS

National
Efficiency and
American Mass
Culture in the 1930s

Popular
Eugenics

Edited by Susan Currell and Christina Cogdell

Ohio University Press
Athens

Ohio University Press, Athens, Ohio 45701
www.ohio.edu/oupress
© 2006 by Ohio University Press

Printed in the United States of America

Ohio University Press books are printed on acid-free paper ⊗ ™

13 12 11 10 09 08 07 06   5 4 3 2 1

Library of Congress Cataloging-in-Publication Data

Popular eugenics : national efficiency and American mass culture in the 1930s / edited by
Susan Currell and Christina Cogdell.
    p. cm.
Includes bibliographical references and index.
ISBN-13: 978-0-8214-1691-4 (hardcover : alk. paper)
ISBN-10: 0-8214-1691-X (hardcover : alk. paper)
ISBN-13: 978-0-8214-1692-1 (pbk. : alk. paper)
ISBN-10: 0-8214-1692-8 (pbk. : alk. paper)
    1. Eugenics—United States—History—20th century. 2. Eugenics—Social aspects—
United States. 3. Popular culture—United States—History—20th century. 4. Eugenics
in literature. 5. Eugenics in motion pictures. 6. United States—History—1919–1933.
7. United States—History—1933–1945. I. Currell, Susan. II. Cogdell, Christina.
HQ755.5.U5P66 2006
    363.9′2097309043—dc22

                                    2006017473

CONTENTS

v

PART TWO: VISUAL CULTURE AND EUGENICS

ILLUSTRATIONS

ACKNOWLEDGMENTS

Editors Susan Currell and Christina Cogdell would like to thank Gillian Berchowitz and the staff at Ohio University Press for making this anthology possible, as well as Greg Dorr and the anonymous reviewer for the collection. We would also like to thank all the organizations that granted us permission to publish the images in this volume and acknowledge the funding provided by the Research Fund of the School of Humanities at the University of Sussex and the Thaw Art History Center at the College of Santa Fe. In addition, we thank the University of California Press at Berkeley for allowing us to reprint Wendy Kline's chapter, "A New Deal for the Child: Ann Cooper Hewitt and Sterilization in the 1930s," which originally appeared in her book *Building a Better Race: Gender, Sexuality, and Eugenics from the Turn of the Century to the Baby Boom* (2001), and the University of Pennsylvania Press for allowing us to reprint Cogdell's chapter "Smooth Flow: Biological Efficiency and Streamline Design," which originally appeared in her book *Eugenic Design: Streamlining America in the 1930s* (2004). Finally, we would like to thank all of the contributors for their patience, suggestions, and cooperation.

Individual acknowledgments are as follows:

Susan Currell would like to thank Christina Cogdell, the Leverhulme Foundation, and Nottingham University, England, and Warren Pleece.

Betsy Nies would like to thank the editors as well as the anonymous reviewer for Ohio University Press for their helpful comments and suggestions, which spurred content revisions at various stages of her chapter's development. She would also like to acknowledge Marnie Jones of the University of North Florida for her fine reading of the chapter; her thoughtful responses helped stimulate the final stages of revision.

Stephen Fender would like to thank the librarians of the Southern Historical Collection—and especially John White and Bob Antony—at the University of North Carolina Library, Chapel Hill; the many helpful librarians in the Library of Congress Manuscript Division; and the Leverhulme Trust for financial support to fund the research behind his chapter.

Acknowledgments

Christina Cogdell would like that thank Sue Currell; Rick Watson and the librarians in the reading room at the Harry Ransom Humanities Research Center, University of Texas, Austin; Christian Dupont and the research librarians at the Special Collections Research Center, Syracuse University; Robert Cox, Valerie Lutz, and others at the American Philosophical Society, where the research for this chapter was first done; Jill Bloomer and others at the Cooper-Hewitt National Design Museum, Smithsonian Institution; the American Council of Learned Societies; Gene Thaw and the Thaw Art History Center at the College of Santa Fe; and her husband, Todd Gogulski.

Nicole Hahn Rafter would like to thank Robert Hahn and the Peabody Museum, Harvard University.

Karen A. Keely would like to thank the editors, Martha Banta, Peter Dorsey, Gregory S. Jackson, and Michelle McEvoy for reading and making suggestions on the various incarnations of her chapter. A reviewer for Ohio University Press also gave thoughtful feedback that improved the essay. Carol L. Hinds of Mount Saint Mary's University generously provided funding to reproduce the film publicity stills in this chapter. Keely presented an earlier version of this essay at the 2000 meeting of the American Association for the History of Medicine. She would also like to thank her partner, Dylan Breuer, who has, as always, been supportive of and interested in her quirky research.

Angela Smith would like to thank the editors and the anonymous reviewers of the manuscript for Ohio University Press for their comments on earlier versions of her chapter; Kel and Marilyn Smith for putting a roof over her head while she revised the essay; and Matt Basso, for daily inspiration.

Robert Rydell, Mark Largent, and Christina Cogdell would like to thank Professor David C. Large at Montana State University for help with German translations. They are also indebted to Jim Edmundson and Jennifer Nieves at the Dittrick Medical History Library, Claire Cronin at the U.S. Holocaust Memorial Museum, Kevin Knox at the Cal Tech Archives, Ernst Both at the Buffalo Museum of Science, and Gay Walker of Special Collections at Reed College.

Introduction

Susan Currell

Published in 1929, the year of the economic crash that heralded the onset of the Great Depression, Southern writer Erskine Caldwell's short novel *The Bastard* follows the downward spiral of the dysgenic life of Gene Morgan. Gene is the bastard child of a hoochie-coochie dancer and an unknown father. Illustrating the evils of dysgenia, his fictional world epitomizes the random, violent, and diseased life that propelled eugenicists' fears of the era. Gene proceeds to drink, mutilate women, have sexual intercourse with his mother (who does not recognize him), rape a child, have sexual intercourse with a black woman who shares his surname, contract syphilis, and casually murder and mutilate a black co-worker. Finally, Gene falls in love with a decent girl and marries poor but "clean" Myra Morgan. The match, however, hints of inbreeding (she, too, shares his surname), and Gene's dysgenic past returns to haunt him. The baby they produce is a "freak," a monstrous, hairy epileptic who fails to grow but also will not die. The doctor tells Myra that she should not have any more children, that "there was something wrong somewhere."[1] Unable to escape his diseased inheritance, Gene kills the child and returns to the brothel and his old ways.

The Bastard shows, in barely disguised form, how some popular literature engaged with the issues of eugenics at the start of the Great Depression.

The novel ushered in Caldwell's literary career and a continued fascination on his part with degeneracy and decline as depicted in subsequent novels such as *Tobacco Road* (1932) and *God's Little Acre* (1933)—through which he became one of the most celebrated and popular writers of the 1930s. Despite the presence of these ideas in his books, virtually all criticism of Caldwell has ignored the presence of eugenics in his work.[2] Just as he repressed his first novel, later claiming that his debut novel was *Tobacco Road,* critics of American culture in the 1930s have failed to address the influence of eugenics on the cultural productions of the era. It is not easy to say why this should be—like the ugly, extreme, Gothic tale of Gene and his monstrous progeny that was repressed and censored by both Caldwell himself and the censors at the time, the history of eugenics has become a twentieth-century horror story that does not fit neatly or clearly into liberal paradigms of the past or historical representations of the Great Depression. Characterized as a period of social reform in which cultural workers strove to highlight societal problems and document images of poverty, the 1930s have not been fully examined for vestiges of the eugenic movement that were clearly part of the intellectual climate of the time.

By the 1920s, eugenic thought permeated modern cultures and societies on a global scale. It affected the way that national identities were constructed and represented in many countries. As a *scientifically* acceptable theory and method for genetic reform, eugenics had already passed its heyday by the time Adolf Hitler gained power in 1933. Yet despite the scientific questioning of its methods, eugenics had become an international ideological construct by that point, as well as the scientific discourse through which the Nazis justified their state and foreign policies to the rest of the world. Until recently, many scholars have presumed that by the early 1930s, eugenics in the United States had gone into decline.[3] Contrary to established historical opinion, however, as historian Edward Larson has pointed out, "the 1930s represented the pivotal decade for compulsory eugenic sterilization in the United States." And because of Supreme Court approval in 1927, more legal eugenic sterilizations took place during the 1930s than in any other decade in U.S. history.[4] Sterilization rates climbed throughout the 1930s and reached record numbers, even though eugenic beliefs were supposedly on the wane.[5] By the thirties, then, the concerns of earlier decades—that hereditary defects caused crime, mental illness, and disease—had "resulted in an intensive campaign for custodial care and sterilization of the unfit."[6] The essays in this volume therefore concentrate on a variety of representations of eugenics in the 1930s to illustrate the fact that eugenics was a continuing presence in the public psyche. Though not contending that eugenic thought was as scientifically popular in the United States as it had been in the 1920s, the contributions here illustrate an open engagement with eugenics in the realm of popular culture that has been overlooked.

In the thirties, many observers connected the visible decay of the social fabric resulting from the economic crash to the ongoing genetic decline of the multiethnic American population. The decline and descent of humankind that had been predicted by eugenicists for so long appeared to have reached its apotheosis in the manifest degeneration of culture and society at the start of the Great Depression.[7] During that time, the physical health and eugenics movements gained increased momentum due to intensified fears of racial decline, male passivity, low levels of intelligence, moral and physical degeneracy, and low fertility. These concerns were manifested in contemporary culture in prominent public discussions about high divorce rates, low marriage rates, low birthrates, low literacy levels, high mental illness rates, and the causes and effects of widespread poverty. Hopes for the future strength of the nation were often linked to hopes for stronger and more robust mental and physical responses to the challenges of the era, on a personal as well as a political scale. The contributors to this book contend that those popular debates channeled ideas about eugenics in the thirties, revealing a shifting trend in eugenic thought as well as a more lively interaction with eugenic theory than has previously been discerned. After two decades of popular promotion, it is perhaps not surprising that ideas about eugenics had filtered into the rhetoric of decline and recovery that dominated discussions about the future of U.S. society at the start of the New Deal. What is surprising, however, is that the historical discourse surrounding "official" eugenic theory in the realm of the popular has been almost entirely ignored.

By 1932, concerns over the future recovery of U.S. society reflected the widespread belief that the country was not just economically depressed but also "diseased" in some way. This belief was fueled by the production of popular texts that indicated cultural stagnation and stasis on a broad scale. Eleanor Wembridge's *Life among the Lowbrows* (1931), for example, offered a contemporary tour of "Moronia," where 5 to 10 percent of the people were verbal and financial illiterates; "they and their pale babies are recognized as disasters," she claimed.[8] As in the economic Depression (another disaster of imbeciles, according to one writer), the parallel between personal and political stagnation was apparent.[9] At a time of increasing welfare costs and decreasing state revenues, the nation appeared to be facing bankruptcy unless it could improve its stock of human beings. In many states, sterilization of those deemed unfit was seen as one way that welfare costs could be cut, for "degenerates" could be released into the community without fear that their offspring would be returned to state institutions and further swell the burgeoning welfare budget.[10] At the same time, the Depression created an awareness of extreme poverty and social problems that fueled reformers' adoption of eugenic beliefs. Edward Larson, in fact, has claimed that contact with squalid conditions for the first time during the Depression via relief work led many prosperous women to champion eugenics as a way of ending poverty and squalor.[11]

The essays in this volume push forward the contention that rather than killing off eugenic thought, the Depression extended and transformed it. In that period, the popular press disseminated a version of eugenics to readers that cast it as a renewed topic for social debate. As Wendy Kline indicates in the first essay of this collection, popular debates over the "right" and "wrong" uses of eugenics were hashed out in the mass media and contributed to a widespread discourse on modernity that focused on the social and political uses of the American body. Kline's study of the Cooper Hewitt trial of 1936 illustrates the shift into the new phase of eugenic strategies that characterized the movement in the 1930s, which emphasized the importance of motherhood and reproduction over genetic inheritance. The rise of reform eugenics, she argues, was a response to changing ideologies of social responsibility and welfare reform—an effective survival strategy for eugenicists during the period. Eugenics in the thirties thus figured not as a separate "scientific" discourse propagated by a few adherents but as a central, underlying feature of the modern state wherein recovery (economic, social, and personal) and reproductive control were inseparably linked.

To some observers, the Depression was a result of the unrestrained forces of capitalism, in which base instincts and greed had reigned without check. Others went further and paralleled the uncontrolled greed, individualism, and lust for profit of the business community with a lack of control over the willful libido. The perceived threat to the nation's health and financial well-being was not just the rhetoric of an extreme Right or of supporters of fascism; for reform eugenicists, capitalism itself was dysgenic by allowing the "race suicide" of an elite and producing at the same time an uncontrolled surplus of humans, made all too apparent by the bread-lines and dole queues.[12] Unprecedented middle-class poverty likewise posed the most serious threat yet to the project of positive eugenics, which had aimed to increase births among the educated and prevent the race suicide of the white middle classes for several decades.

By adding to the popular interest in sterilization an additional focus on self-improvement, mass leisure, and the family, eugenic ideals became broadly compatible with wider social ideals of the New Deal and the Popu-lar Front. The formation of the New Deal, the interaction of the modern citizen with the modern state, and personal interpretations of eugenics thus underlay much of the shift in eugenic discourse at that time. As this book indicates, the Depression necessitated new responses to social and political organization and personal choices. In 1932, then, as President Franklin D. Roosevelt was campaigning for election and the Third Interna-tional Congress of Eugenics was being held in New York, popular enter-tainment reflected awareness of the important eugenic role played by personal action. Popular dramas of eugenic promise and failure were played out in films that appeared on cinema screens that year. A good ex-ample is the movie *A Bill of Divorcement* (1932), in which Katharine Hepburn, as Sydney Fairfield, the daughter of a genetically insane father, breaks her engagement and vows not to marry or have children for fear of passing on this genetic inheritance. Her heroic actions can only be understood in re-lation to the common discourses surrounding popular eugenics at the time. As Angela Smith's essay in this collection also shows, popular hor-ror movies at the start of the Depression played out the repressions and anxieties surrounding eugenics in more Gothic ways.

A closer examination of these representations of hereditarian theories reveals that beneath the desires for economic and social rationalization that characterized the modern welfare state lay repressed fears of decline and debility that fit well with the earlier eugenic rhetoric of degeneracy. New Deal plans to regulate capitalism were thus also welcomed by some sup-porters of eugenics as part of the social planning that would control all li-bidinous excesses. Just as laissez-faire economic policy was coming under heavy criticism in 1932, laissez-faire, or unregulated, responses to personal decisions were perceived by many to be equally unacceptable; they were to be replaced by "self-insight, self-planning, and self-control," assisted by the insights of instructional manuals, educational texts, and popular science.[13] How humans would adapt to the modern environment and climate of political change was of paramount concern to sociologists in the early thirties, and that issue was the focus of Chicago sociologist William Ogburn's speech to the American Society of Naturalists in 1931. "The lower animals have a simple natural environment toward which to make an adaptation, as was also the case of early man," he stated. "But modern man has a huge cultural environment to which he must adapt himself, a huge culture that is whirling through time, gaining velocity as it goes."[14] Ogburn constantly stressed the importance of adapting to modernity, inventing the term *cultural lag* in the 1920s to describe the process by which humans biologically failed to keep pace with their inventions. As Susan Currell discusses in her essay on popular self-help and eugenic rhetoric, fitting in and adapting to changes related to Depression culture—to overcome cultural lag and "streamline" oneself for the future—was central to the notion of creating modern citizens who could cope with the vicissitudes of the age. This adaptation was addressed most commonly in the texts that were popular at the time, distributed in schools, popular journals, and the mass media.

Throughout the decade, educational and scientific discourses were permeated with eugenic rhetoric. In the pages ahead, Andrés Reggiani shows how the formulation of popular ideas about eugenics was taken up in the form of the best-seller *Man, the Unknown,* by Nobel Prize-winning scientist Alexis Carrel. Popular science explored modern social problems within a "biologizing" framework that often owed much to the eugenics movement of the twenties. Exploring common fantasies about the possibility of renovating and modernizing society, success literature, science fiction, comics, and films all employed eugenic discourses, even if the writers did not always agree with them or represent them with scientific accuracy. Utopian fiction, for example, prominently featured societies created by eugenic engineering and rationalized social planning. In *New Industrial Dawn* (1939) by A. T. Churchill, the protagonist—Fenton, a banker—falls into a drunken stupor in 1929 and awakens in the future to a eugenically streamlined, perfectly balanced, and rational society. As the United States prepared for a war against fascism in 1939, the New York World's Fair fetishized the "typical American family" in a display that, as Robert Rydell has illustrated, evolved directly from the eugenic "better babies" contests of the twenties. Eugenics was on display at the fair as one way to make the nation modern, as Rydell and Christina Cogdell have asserted in previous studies, and it cohabited neatly with the futuristic vision of fair planners and designers.[15]

How to adapt and survive in this brave new world became a subject that many writers addressed. As cultural historian Warren Susman has shown, the thirties saw an increased preoccupation with the problems of cultural lag and growing anxieties over the adaptation to modernity. Yet questions about how much this anxiety involved long-standing concerns over genetic inheritance and to what extent these ideas were disseminated in popular locations have not been addressed.[16] In his chapter, Michael Rembis reveals how the promotion of the eugenic textbook and the development of new school curricula based on eugenics expanded during the decade, illustrating that even though eugenics as a science may have been on the wane, it was reaching a huge audience of schoolchildren via a changing course of study. Instructional manuals, then, comprise a largely overlooked popular medium that provides a valuable alternative vision of the history of eugenic ideological diffusion. The eugenic influences in even more closely scrutinized writings, such as the canonical works of Southern literature, have been virtually ignored.

The fear that the human body and mind could not be made to fit in with modern times was most intense in the South, where the discourse of social and economic decline resulting from the Civil War still permeated mass culture and regional identity in the 1930s. The Depression merely heaped another disaster onto that earlier one, from which the South had never fully recovered. Fears of decay and degeneracy as well as cultural lag reappear over and over again in discourses about the South in the 1930s. The relationship between modernity, eugenics, and cultural production was proposed as early as 1915, when H. L. Mencken first published his call for a renaissance of Southern literature in his essay "The Sahara of the Bozart." Mencken claimed that "the South has not only lost its old capacity for producing ideas; it has also taken on the worst intolerance of ignorance and stupidity." The essay went on to describe the dysgenic conditions of the South that had led to this situation. "As for the cause of this unanimous torpor and doltishness, this curious and almost pathological estrangement from everything that makes for a civilized culture, I have hinted at it already, and now state it again. The south has simply been drained of all its best blood," he asserted. "The vast blood-letting of the Civil War half exterminated and wholly paralyzed the old aristocracy, and so left the land to the harsh mercies of the poor white trash, now its masters."[17] Explicitly associating what Mencken saw as a lack of modern culture and aesthetic progression with the genetic inheritance of bad blood, the essay was a call for cultural modernity in the literature and culture of the South. The call for a modern Southern aesthetic was met through the emergence of the Southern writers of the 1930s. But amazingly, the fact that Mencken's essay was almost wholly about the inability of the South to produce humans who were eugenic (or "wellborn") has barely been examined in studies of this Southern renaissance. Other Southern writers were not all such strong promoters of eugenic ideas as Mencken. Yet even where modern writers showed ambivalence to the inheritance of this genetic discourse, their reflection of the discourse itself still proved its ongoing influence on contemporary thought.

The essays on the South in this book explore this ambivalence and the inheritance of eugenic rhetoric as a repressed discourse that emerged at the level of narrative and structure within modern Southern writing. Betsy Nies examines characterizations of the South as dysgenic—and varied responses to those characterizations—through her analysis of the writings of Mencken, Caldwell, and other Southern Agrarian writers. According to Stephen Fender's contribution, the very drive to modernize the inhabitants of the South was imbued with unwitting eugenic discourse adopted from earlier sociological studies of "white trash." As these two essays illustrate, the interaction between the South and eugenics emerged in its literature and culture in complex ways, through the themes and narratives of decline and degeneracy that became so popular in the 1930s. Barbara Ladner's essay carries this analysis even further, showing that the tropes of William Faulkner's fiction are better understood within this context of eugenic discourse surrounding family histories and inheritance, phrased in a rhetoric critiquing the objectives of racial purity that characterized period sociological and scientific studies. Southern literature as a whole, then, indicated a more complex interaction with the so-called aesthetics of eugenics than the one depicted by Erskine Caldwell in *The Bastard*. By looking at the way the tropes of scientific discourse were taken up and rewritten in the cultural imagination, a more complex vision of eugenics in the thirties emerges— one that enables a transgressive and multilayered response not always available to straightforward analyses of scientific documents and historical records. Because such celebrated Southern writers developed their oeuvres at the height of eugenic theories and wrote during their most extensive implementation, it is important to reread these texts in the light of perceptions about eugenics in the 1930s.

The second section of this collection shifts from popular printed texts, whether scientific, educational, or literary, to a different locus of popular eugenic inscription: the modern aesthetics of visual culture, particularly with regard to the modern body. By reconfiguring and rearticulating notions of the modern American body, a few of the essays in this section illustrate that "fitting in" was not only a psychological, political, and intellectual demand but also a physical one. Mary Coffey's essay on the history of the sculptural exhibit of the "Average American" (Man) demonstrates that judging and assessing what was average became an obsession intertwined with eugenic ideas of success. This ideological thrust explains the popularity of exhibits of the "Average American," while at the same time indicating a shift in eugenic thought from the 1920s to the 1930s. As Christina Cogdell discusses in her essay on streamlining, the national concern with bodily efficiency and "smooth flow" illustrates how eugenics entered into the discourse of the body as well as the visual aesthetics of modern design at the time. Through these essays, then, we see a manifestation of eugenics as an unwritten text, visible within ideologies of the body that defined the average and ideal shapes that still remain central to Western culture.

According to Nicole Rafter's essay, this notion extended even to the discourse on American teeth, which to anthropologist Earnest Hooton represented the "softening of American bodies and the erosion of civilization" (260). Understanding the fears of cultural decline and decay is crucial to understanding the social and cultural climate of the 1930s. How such scientific information was channeled into expressions and ideologies of the body is also shown in Kerry Soper's study of popular imagery, in particular the *Dick Tracy* comic strip. Soper examines the ways in which visual metaphors of the body and face, derived from eugenic ethnic stereotypes, were used to express fears of genetic decline in the thirties. During the Depression, as he indicates, cartoons expressed prevalent concerns that the perceived crime wave was a result of dysgenic breeding and not just a result of desperation caused by widespread unemployment. His close analysis of the style and history of Chester Gould's comic strip shows that the popular culture of the era attempted to mediate and imagine the concerns of eugenicists of the earlier part of the century—putting them into a modern context and updating them for the masses. These essays illustrate the benefits of looking beyond the traditional "documents" of history and reading the nontextual or material environment for an engagement with eugenics, whether from an ambivalent, supportive, or critical position.

This engagement with eugenics is apparent in the films and popular exhibitions of the decade. The emergence of the eugenic movement in the late nineteenth century paralleled the emergence of the U.S. film industry, and by the 1930s, the representation of eugenics on the screen was a tried and tested way of promoting eugenic messages to a multilingual or illiterate audience. In her analysis of *College Holiday* (1936), Karen Keely establishes that by the 1930s, eugenics had also become a subject for madcap comedy, which both critiqued and colluded with eugenic ideology. Keely shows that simple or reductive readings of eugenics cannot be made in the realm of popular culture. Films, whether humorous or horrific, contained overt and repressed narratives of eugenics that attempted to subvert, as well as negotiate, the problematic heritage of a science of racial purity. For this reason, examining popular representations provides a new way of negotiating the problematic and often contradictory heritage of eugenics within U.S. culture during this period. Horror films, as Angela Smith addresses in her essay on the role of eugenic discourse in *Dracula* (1931) and *Frankenstein* (1932), also offered both a classic presentation of genetic inheritance and more subversive readings of the eugenic message—illustrating, for example, the dangers of scientific experimentation. The importance of readings such as those by Keely and Smith is that they allow us to see the influence of eugenic thought on the cultural imagination while still making room for the "rupture" of that discourse at the point of transmission and reception.

The final essay in this collection, by Robert Rydell, Christina Cogdell, and Mark Largent, illustrates, however, that monolithic eugenic theories of "race hygiene" were still being disseminated as scientific fact as late as 1943. While popular culture played with, reaffirmed, or dismantled eugenic ideas, an exhibition about Nazi eugenics toured the United States, providing allegedly factual underpinning to fictional ideas of race supremacy. This essay serves to remind us that although eugenics returned in repressed forms in the aesthetics and social and literary narratives of American mass culture, a real eugenics movement continued to operate and legitimate the widespread sterilization programs that took place during the 1930s. As a popular "road show," the eugenics exhibit had official and respected scientific and medical sponsors. Just as important, it became a popular "educational" show that transmitted a eugenic message in an unambivalent way to the masses of exhibit viewers.

The essays in this volume, then, all depict the multifarious ways that popular culture disseminated eugenic concepts over the 1930s, illustrating that the impact of eugenics on U.S. cultural productions and public perceptions was far from over. Even as scientists and anthropologists began to divest their discourses of eugenics, the popular sector continued to advance these ideas, albeit in contradictory, piecemeal, ambivalent, and often erroneous ways. For this reason, the ways in which the essays register eugenics are not always consistent or identical. These readings reflect the contradictions and internal inconsistencies of the eugenic movement out of which the representations came. Some cultural sectors relied more heavily on late-nineteenth-century criminology (influenced by the criminologist Cesare Lombroso), for instance, whereas others were more conversant with the reforms taking place among eugenicists in the 1930s. And some merely adapted and distorted key concepts from eugenics (an interest in norms or ideals, ideas of race and environment, or concerns over natural reproduction), dispensing with other aspects of the discourse that would have complicated their agendas. The essays illustrate that even though eugenics coexisted with popular perceptions of the modern subject, these ideas were never monolithic, and they therefore serve to reflect this contradictory popular uptake of what was never a fully scientific or rational discourse anyway.

While showing the divergent ways that eugenics was manifested in the popular imagination, as well as the ways that eugenic ideas were dismantled or deflated by culture, this book illustrates how fundamental eugenics is to an understanding of mass culture of the thirties. By repressing the eugenics component, previous scholars have misunderstood a key aspect of the history of eugenics that existed outside of mainstream scientific discourse. But here, by documenting the influence of eugenic ideology on U.S. culture and society during the 1930s, the authors have closely examined instances in which such tendencies emerged within the rhetoric, ideology, and visual aesthetics of mass culture. Often, this investigation has meant looking at trivial or forgotten cultural sites—teeth and toilets rather than science and politics. Yet the apparent triviality is all the more significant for demonstrating not only how pervasive eugenic precepts were in U.S. culture but also the extent to which the concepts eugenics linked (beauty, biology, environment, race, class, ability, and gender norms) touched nearly every aspect of American life. This very pervasiveness and diffusion demonstrates how broad the effects of eugenics were on the development of a modern U.S. culture. And however much we would like to limit its effects to a few pseudoscientists in the 1910s and 1920s, to do so would obscure not only the past but also the extent to which its legacy is still with us.

Consequently, this book makes an original contribution to our understanding of the workings of eugenic ideology as it permeated debates in the arenas of popular literature, science, art, and film. In the process, it furthers discussion on the ways that eugenic discourses were reconfigured in the 1930s and how they negotiated the shock of the Great Depression and the proliferation of popular mass media. Furthermore, it shows that the notions of modernity and progress that characterized much of the 1930s were often informed by eugenic theory and that a heightening of eugenic thinking at that time was, in many ways, a response to the national problems encountered and made visible by the Depression.

Notes

1. Erskine Caldwell, *The Bastard* (New York: Heron Press, 1929), 67.

2. The exception is Karen Keely, who has examined Caldwell's relationship to eugenics in her essay "Poverty, Sterilization, and Eugenics in Erskine Caldwell's *Tobacco Road*," *Journal of American Studies* 36, no. 1 (2002): 23–42.

3. Although Diane Paul, in *Controlling Human Heredity, 1865 to the Present* (Atlantic Highlands, NJ: Humanities Press, 1995), and Daniel Kevles, in *In the Name of Eugenics: Genetics and the Uses of Human Heredity* (Cambridge, MA: Harvard University Press, 1985), have examined the ways in which eugenic ideals influenced the politics and research of the scientific community in the interwar period and beyond, few related studies have looked at how these ideals reemerged within popular culture. Similarly, although studies by Steven Selden, Martin Pernick, Nicole Hahn Rafter, and Betsy Nies have indicated the ongoing popularity of eugenics into the 1930s, the primary focus of such works has been on the 1920s and earlier years. Few studies have focused on eugenics in its

popular manifestations during the Depression era. Those that have—Stefan Kühl's on politics, Robert Rydell's on world's fairs, Wendy Kline's on sexuality and motherhood, and Christina Cogdell's on streamline design—have been all too rare. In her article "The Futurama Recontextualized," *American Quarterly* 52, no. 2 (June 2000): 193–246, for example, Cogdell noted that "eugenics experienced a resurgence during the 1930s in the realm of popular culture" (202) and that "eugenic thinking in the U.S and abroad underwrote key legislation, hotly debated social issues, basic high school education, and various facets of popular culture" (205). There are a number of excellent books on the history of eugenics in U.S. culture. See, for instance: Cogdell, *Eugenic Design: Streamlining America in the 1930s* (Philadelphia: University of Pennsylvania Press, 2004); Ian Robert Dowbiggin, *Keeping America Sane: Psychiatry and Eugenics in the United States and Canada, 1880–1940* (Ithaca, NY: Cornell University Press, 1997); Nicole Hahn Rafter, ed., *White Trash: The Eugenic Family Studies, 1877–1919* (Boston: Northeastern University Press, 1988); Mark H. Haller, *Eugenics: Hereditarian Attitudes in American Thought* (New Brunswick, NJ: Rutgers University Press, 1963); Kevles, "Eugenics in North America," in *Essays in the History of Eugenics,* ed. Robert A. Peel (London: Galton Institute, 1998), 208–25, and *In the Name of Eugenics*; Wendy Kline, *Building a Better Race: Gender, Sexuality, and Eugenics from the Turn of the Century to the Baby Boom* (Berkeley: University of California Press, 2001); Edward J. Larson, *Sex, Race and Science: Eugenics in the Deep South* (Baltimore, MD: Johns Hopkins University Press, 1995); Nancy Ordover, *American Eugenics: Race, Queer Anatomy, and the Science of Nationalism* (Minneapolis: University of Minnesota Press, 2003); Martin Pernick, *The Black Stork: Eugenics and the Death of "Defective" Babies in American Medicine and Motion Pictures since 1915* (New York: Oxford University Press, 1996); Mark Pittenger, *American Socialists and Evolutionary Thought, 1870–1920* (Madison: University of Wisconsin Press, 1993); Robert Rydell, *World of Fairs: The Century-of-Progress Expositions* (Chicago: University of Chicago Press, 1993); Steven Selden, *Inheriting Shame: The Story of Eugenics and Racism in America* (New York: Teacher's College Press, 1999); Stefan Kühl, *The Nazi Connection: Eugenics, American Racism, and German National Socialism* (Oxford: Oxford University Press, 1994); and Betsy Nies, *Eugenic Fantasies: Racial Ideology in the Literature and Popular Culture of the 1920's* (New York: Routledge, 2001).

4. Larson, *Sex, Race and Science,* 119.

5. Ibid., 120; Kevles, "Eugenics in North America," 220.

6. Haller, *Eugenics,* 92.

7. This idea is discussed in more detail in Susan Currell's *The March of Spare Time: The Problem and Promise of Leisure in the Great Depression* (Philadelphia: University of Pennsylvania Press, 2005).

8. Eleanor Wembridge, *Life among the Lowbrows* (New York: Houghton Mifflin, 1931), 21.

9. Walter B. Pitkin, *A Short Introduction to the History of Human Stupidity* (New York: Simon and Schuster, 1932).

10. This terminology comes from the publications of the era and is not my own, but hereafter, the authors of this volume will not use quotes around terms such as *degenerate*.

11. Larson, *Sex, Race and Science*, 132.

12. See Diane Paul, "Eugenics and the Left," *Journal of the History of Ideas* 45, no. 4 (Fall 1984): 568.

13. Walter B. Pitkin, *Life Begins at Forty* (New York: McGraw-Hill, 1932), 89.

14. William Fielding Ogburn, *How Man Will Live in the Future* (Girard, KS: Haldeman-Julius Publications, 1931).

15. Rydell, *World of Fairs*, 38–61. Cogdell, in *Eugenic Design*, 111–27, addresses numerous other exhibits at the Chicago and New York World's Fairs that included eugenic ideas in the visions of the future.

16. Warren Susman, *Culture as History: The Transformation of American Society in the Twentieth Century* (New York: Pantheon, 1984), 156.

17. H. L. Mencken, *Prejudices: A Selection*, ed. James T. Farrell (New York: Vintage Books, 1955), 74.

PART ONE

POPULAR WRITING
AND EUGENICS

ONE

A New Deal for the Child

Ann Cooper Hewitt and
Sterilization in the 1930s

Wendy Kline

ABSTRACT

Wendy Kline's essay on the Ann Cooper Hewitt sterilization trial of
1936—excerpted from her book *Building a Better Race: Gender, Sexuality, and Eugenics from the Turn of the Century to the Baby Boom* (2001)
and reprinted here in shorter form, with permission from the University of California Press at Berkeley—highlights a number of themes
that run throughout the chapters in this volume. In her discussion of
federal debates about child welfare and the details of the case itself,
Kline shows that in the 1930s, a general mood spurred by the stringencies of the Depression tilted public opinion decidedly in the direction
of eugenic social control, regardless of race and class distinctions. The
ruling in the case de facto extended the right to sterilize "unfit" individuals into the realm of private practice, where wealthier families often
sought care; public wards of many states were already subjected to the
practice. Yet just who was considered unfit in this case was not clear:
was it the wealthy white mother or her daughter?

Media coverage played it both ways and, in doing so, revealed that
eugenic arguments were open to interpretation. "Fitness" was believed
to be genetically determined ("high-grade moronity," as debated in Ann's
case, was thought to be hereditary) but still strongly influenced by the
environment in which a child was raised, to the extent that environmental context arguably determined whether the child was able to realize
the full potential of her inherent genetic capacity. Hence, the case emphasized the necessity of having "fit" mothers, an emphasis that not only
reaffirmed traditional gender roles but also revealed the strong public

pressure on individuals (in this instance, women) to sacrifice their individual rights and desires in order to conform to the broader, eugenic principles of responsible procreation for the good of society as a whole.

From January through August of 1936, the *New York Times* offered readers nearly fifty articles on a sensational court case taking place twenty-five hundred miles away in the city of San Francisco. In this case, which received coverage around the globe, twenty-one-year-old Ann Cooper Hewitt, heiress to millions from her late father, Peter Cooper Hewitt, sued her mother and two surgeons for surgically sterilizing her without her knowledge. At stake was not only the legality of sterilization but also the meaning of eugenics and the appropriate balance of power between mothers and daughters in 1930s America. The Cooper Hewitt trial signaled a new phase in eugenic strategies, which focused on the importance of motherhood and family to the future of the race. In addition, the widespread coverage of the trial moved eugenics more directly into the public eye, generating greater discussion and acceptance of sterilization as a social stabilizer in a turbulent decade. During the 1930s, eugenics played a formative role in the transition from a culture of individualism to a culture of responsibility by offering sterilization as a way to strengthen the American family.[1] The Cooper Hewitt story helps to explain how eugenics actually gained influence in a decade in which the movement was previously believed to have been dismantled.

Redefining Eugenics in the 1930s

A newfound emphasis on environment over heredity in the social sciences has misled many historians to dismiss the role of eugenics in the 1930s. Assuming that eugenicists were concerned exclusively with heredity and disregarded the role of environment, scholars have concluded that eugenics lost all scientific and academic credibility and support in the 1930s. An influential authority in the history of eugenics declared in 1963 that "the most significant development in eugenics after 1930 was its rapid decline in popularity and prestige," a claim that has, until recently, remained largely unchallenged.[2]

As a result, U.S. historians have ignored the role of eugenics in a significant decade, one in which eugenicists promoted sterilization as a panacea for the problems of the family. Specifically, eugenicists popularized a doctrine of reproductive morality that countered selfish individualism with social responsibility. They transformed the politics of reproduction from a private matter of personal liberty to a public issue of racial health and, with the assistance of the widely publicized Cooper Hewitt trial, convinced the public that sacrificing reproductive freedom for the sake of stabilizing the American family was well worth it. In this sense, eugenic sterilization became the social security of American civilization: it guaranteed a healthy and stable future citizenry. It promoted the idea of increasing state intervention in and regulation of previously private matters for the protection and stabilization of social institutions—the very model on which Franklin Roosevelt would construct his New Deal policies. The familial language that eugenicists appropriated in the 1930s proved potent. The combined ideal of strengthening the race and preserving the family held great public appeal and paved the way for public acceptance of New Deal social liberalism and its "sacrifice of liberty for the sake of stability."[3]

In the face of social changes, sterilization advocates creatively adapted their definition of eugenics. No longer pitting nature against nurture, they combined both in their new formula, which was centered on the importance of motherhood and the family. In order to maintain scientific legitimacy, they emphasized the importance of the home environment for child development. This new strategy, which shifted the emphasis from heredity to maternal care, worked to strengthen and consolidate their movement. For example, though the superintendent of the Sonoma State Home for the Feebleminded, Fred Butler, had previously considered "the hereditary type of individuals" first when deciding which cases to accept, he noted that by 1930, "we [had] reached the point where we *practically disregard[ed]* whether they are the hereditary or nonhereditary type" (emphasis added). In either case, the patient would not make a suitable mother because she would not care for a child properly. "The saddest of them all, in my opinion," he wrote in 1931, "is a feebleminded mother trying to care for normal children."[4] Regardless of what ailed his patients, they could never be acceptable mothers.

By emphasizing environment rather than heredity, the eugenics movement survived attacks by geneticists and social scientists and flourished in a society in search of immediate and effective solutions to severe economic and social problems as well as for ways to stabilize the family. Touting sterilization as a cost-effective strategy for the production of "better" children and the rehabilitation of the American family, eugenicists attained a greater degree of cultural authority than ever before. The creation of a better race would come from the production of better children, they argued in the 1930s, a catchy idea that inspired many, including President Herbert Hoover, to pay increased attention to eugenics. "There shall be no child in America," Hoover declared, "that has not the complete birthright of a sound mind in a sound body." (This statement, part of the American Child Health Association's Child's Bill of Rights, inspired the name of a national sterilization organization, Birthright.)[5]

This new focus on tomorrow's children rather than on today's "misfits" was an attempt to modernize the movement and thereby enhance its appeal. Because children and family gained media coverage as well as public and professional interest during the Depression years, eugenicists incorporated these popular family issues into their public appeal to stabilize the race.

Eugenicists had the opportunity to influence popular attitudes and public policy toward children beginning in 1930, when they played a leading role in President Hoover's White House Conference on Child Health and Protection, the first executive-inspired event on child development since 1909.[6] Four thousand professionals attended the Washington conference, which presented the investigative work of twelve hundred specialists, including physicians, psychologists, home economists, sociologists, and eugenicists. In all, 175 committees issued a total of 141 reports on "every angle" of the well-being of the child, from public health, education, and child labor to treatment of the mentally deficient and delinquent. Significantly, the conference chair, Secretary of the Interior Ray Lyman Wilbur, was an active member of the American Eugenics Society (AES). He declared the conference a "far-seeing move in the interest of our future citizenry." Applying eugenic language to the issue of child welfare, Wilbur explained that the conference's ultimate goal was "making this a fitter country in which to bring up children."[7]

President Hoover's vision of the future also incorporated a eugenic message. On November 19, in a live radio address, Hoover confronted the nation about the need for healthy children to stand up under the "increasing pressure of life." He used the image of the physically and mentally strong child as a symbol of the nation's potential. Addressing the "unseen millions listening in their homes" (more than twelve million families owned radio sets in 1929), he explained that the purpose of the White House conference was to provide parents with information and safeguards to ensure their children's "health in mind and body," a measure designed to guarantee future success. "If we could have but one generation of properly born, trained, educated and happy children," he explained to families listening at home, "a thousand other problems of government would vanish. We would assure ourselves of healthier minds in more vigorous bodies, to direct the energies of our nation to yet greater heights of achievement."[8] Implicit in this statement was the necessity to eliminate the unhealthy, whose burdens stood in the way of cultural progress.

In stark contrast to this image of physical and mental perfection, Hoover cited statistics intended to shock his listeners. Of the nation's forty-five million children, ten million suffered some sort of mental or physical deficiency and therefore hindered human progress. It was not the poverty of the Depression that prevented America's children from embodying physical and mental ideals, Hoover argued, but "ignorant parents" and "ill-instructed children." As the journal *Survey* argued the following year, the White House conference had "put the parents of the United States on trial."[9]

The Committee on Mental Deficiency at the White House conference suggested a two-pronged approach to the problem: foster increased social responsibility for the mentally deficient and promote sterilization of the unfit.[10] The committee convinced the conference to go "squarely on record in favor of sterilization."[11] Hoover's White House conference and the conclusions of its Committee on Mental Deficiency thus promoted sterilization as a social stabilizer to the American public. As Hoover suggested, civilization and the family would only march forward "on the feet of healthy children."[12] If reproduction were restricted in the name of social responsibility, healthy children would ensue.

Three years after Hoover's conference drew national attention to the problem of "defective" children, sterilization achieved international repute. In 1933, shortly after Adolf Hitler rose to power, the Nazis enacted a eugenic-sterilization law that targeted the mentally and physically deficient and ultimately resulted in the sterilization of more than 350,000 individuals.[13] Initially, American eugenicists defended the German law. In both private correspondence and publications, Paul Popenoe, a specialist in heredity and eugenics, emphasized that the law was "not [a] hasty improvisation of the Nazi regime" but the product of years of sterilization practice and research.[14] In an article published in the *Journal of Heredity*, Popenoe praised the German government for developing a solid eugenic policy that appeared to "accord with the best thoughts of eugenists in all civilized countries." In his estimation, Hitler's ideas about human progress and the advancement of civilization were no different from those popularly expressed in the United States. Drawing from Hitler's *Mein Kampf* (1923), he quoted a passage remarkably similar to Hoover's Child's Bill of Rights. "He who is not sound and worthy in body and mind should not perpetuate his handicaps in the bodies of his children," declared Hitler in the volume.[15]

By 1936, eugenicists recognized that Hitler's persecution of the Jews might undermine the credibility and support of eugenics. Some continued to believe, however, that Hitler would be remembered not for his "political high crimes" (which would soon be forgotten) "but as the first head of a modern government who enforced legislation for the elimination of the unfit for the biological improvement of the race." *Los Angeles Times* columnist Fred Hogue quoted a "venerable student of history of international repute" as saying that "the evolutionary development of the race is much more important than passing political and social revolutions."[16] But by the end of the decade, many wanted to avoid any associations with Hitler, who had little popularity in the United States. They avoided the racial categories he used and suggested that sterilization in the United States would be employed selectively rather than on large groups.

Hitler was not the only inspiration for the new terminology of *selective sterilization* in the American eugenics movement. The growth of mass culture was blurring racial distinctions by the 1930s. Mass consumption and the development of national chain stores, brand names, and mail-order catalogs, as well as new forms of communication, forged a new era of cultural homogeneity that glossed over the previous era's emphasis on racial differences. Though the United States was more culturally diverse in the 1930s than in any previous decade as a result of massive immigration between the 1880s and 1920s, modern mass culture exposed the population "to unprecedented pressures toward cultural uniformity."[17] In this modern culture, normality—that is, the concept of a culturally constructed, gender-specific standard of behavior, ability, and appearance—became increasingly prevalent as a key principle in society. Abnormality, rather than race, class, or ethnicity, differentiated those who, from a eugenic perspective, should not reproduce from those who should.

As a result, eugenicists used the term *selective sterilization* to explain the goal of eugenics: civilization would improve when only those considered "normal" were allowed to reproduce. Sterilization promised "sound minds in sound bodies" to fit the images promoted in Hoover's political speeches, as well as the increasingly rigid and standardized images of beauty promoted by mass culture.[18] Dismissing explicit racial categories, selective sterilization targeted abnormality as a flexible category of physical and mental traits that allowed for both hereditary and environmental causes of difference.[19]

Beginning in the 1930s, then, eugenicists who had previously established their careers on the principles of heredity seemingly contradicted themselves by inviting environmental factors to come into play, a move that previous historians have interpreted as an indication of eugenic defeat. But ultimately, this was a smart tactic. It saved the movement from extinction, and it also widened eugenicists' sphere of influence and further popularized their goal of improving civilization by making reproduction a social and medical responsibility rather than an individual right.

As a result, sterilization gained supporters in the 1930s. Incorporating an environmental justification for sterilization paved the way for its increased use. Dr. Gladys Schwesinger, addressing the New Jersey Health and Sanitary Association in 1937, emphasized the "right of every child to have competent parents." Playing on Roosevelt's New Deal policies, she argued that sterilization played a critical role in "procuring a better deal for the child." Children should not be entrusted to just anyone; the same supervisory control should be administered over parenthood as over teaching, nursing, and other services. Given that a child's personality could be "made or marred" at home, it was all the more important to protect children from "the wrong kind of parents." Sterilization would spare "many unborn children the affliction of being born to unqualified parents." Echoing the eugenic emphasis on reproductive morality as an essential component of modern society, Schwesinger pleaded for Americans to heed the call of social responsibility. "It is society's obligation," she argued, "to encourage the burden and responsibility of parenthood in the best and withhold it from the worst individuals of each generation."[20]

Schwesinger's call for social responsibility reinforced a central aspect of Roosevelt's New Deal policy that was established when he assumed the presidency in 1933. For the first time in American history, the federal government assumed responsibility for family welfare. Whereas Hoover had intimated that mothers needed the aid of experts in raising physically and mentally healthy children, Roosevelt suggested that the federal government itself should become more involved than it had been in the lives and welfare of the American family.[21]

Even prior to New Deal politics, eugenicists had announced that it was time for the government to aid their cause. "Race Degeneration Seen for America," the *New York Times* announced in June 1932, referring to a paper presented at the American Association for the Advancement of Science. If the government did not intervene, eighteen million people burdened by disease or mental defect would become a charge and burden on the rest of the population, the authors declared. Emphasizing the importance of collective health over individual rights, the directors of the Human Betterment Foundation demanded that the government take an increasingly active role in regulating fertility. "The law of self-preservation is as necessary for a nation as an individual," they announced.[22]

Legislators heeded the eugenicists' call. Between 1931 and 1939, over twenty thousand institutionalized patients were sterilized, nearly triple the number sterilized between 1920 and 1929.[23] Seventeen states enacted or revised sterilization laws during a four-year period after the Supreme Court upheld the constitutionality of Virginia's involuntary sterilization law in the case of *Buck v. Bell* in 1927.[24] By 1936, eight states had expanded their statutes to allow the sterilization of mentally deficient individuals who were not institutionalized. Nebraska enacted a law in 1935 requiring the registration of all feebleminded people in the state and denying a marriage license to any such person without proof of sterilization. As legal analysts underscored, heredity was no longer a necessary element of eugenic sterilization laws. Nebraska's law was "based mainly on a consideration of feeblemindedness from the social point of view," Popenoe observed: "No mention is made of any considerations regarding the transmission of defective genes to offspring." Parenthood was becoming an increasingly exclusive privilege; as Popenoe noted of the Nebraska law, "Though some feebleminded parents might produce a small proportion of normal children, the Nebraska legislators evidently did not think it desirable to have even normal children brought up by feebleminded parents."[25] Thus, laws originally intended to prevent the hereditary transmission of unfavorable genetic traits were bolstered and more widely utilized after belief in their original purpose had virtually disappeared.

In this climate of diffuse anxiety about the future of tomorrow's children, a court case erupted that would change the way many Americans thought about sterilization and family politics. When the wealthy Ann Cooper Hewitt took the stand in San Francisco in 1936 to testify that she had been sterilized without her knowledge or consent, Americans followed her story with fascination. She was not an institutional inmate, and she was far from poor. Her case symbolized the new role that sterilization played in the 1930s as a way to strengthen the American family.

The *Literary Digest* labeled the case the "daughter-versus-mother drama."[26] Unlike any sterilization-related event before it, the Cooper Hewitt trial riveted the American public. Even the well-known *Buck v. Bell* Supreme Court case (upholding the constitutionality of eugenic sterilization), which historians point to as a highly significant episode in the history of eugenics, failed to capture public attention, and it stimulated no editorial comment; the *New York Times* did not print a single article on the case.[27] Ann's story, however, succeeded in capturing public attention because it addressed the very issues eugenicists had put forward in their campaign of the 1930s: the relevance and legitimacy of environmental factors in determining who should be sterilized and the importance of protecting the child and preserving the family.

In addition, the trial drew public attention because of the legal questions it raised about both sterilization and sexuality. Because Cooper Hewitt was sterilized by a private physician rather than an institution, her case hinged on the legality of sterilization in private medical practice. The California sterilization law did not specify whether such a procedure was allowable, and no previous court decisions had established a precedent, so eugenicists hoped that the Cooper Hewitt case would clarify the law and increase the number of sterilizations performed in private practice. Female sexuality was also on trial in the case; legal analysts debated whether the primary function of sexuality for women was procreation or pleasure. The surgeons who conducted Ann's sterilization were charged with "conspiracy to commit mayhem" on the grounds that sterilization fell into this criminal category. The crime of mayhem generally consisted of illegally and intently rendering part of a human body useless or removing it.[28] Yet, as eugenicists effectively argued, sterilization did not "unsex" the patient, as she could still experience sexual pleasure. Also central to the case, then, was the lingering question of the meaning of female sexuality in American society. The Cooper Hewitt story, debated by legal experts, sensationalized by journalists, and followed by millions, introduced sterilization as a family-centered solution to the problem of female sexuality.

Sterilization on Trial

On January 6, 1936, in the city of San Francisco, Ann Cooper Hewitt filed a $500,000 damage suit against her mother and two surgeons who had sterilized her without her knowledge in August 1934. She had entered the hospital just eleven months short of her twenty-first birthday for an emergency appendectomy, but, after the administration of a mental test that labeled her a moron and at the request of her mother, she received a salpingectomy as well. Charging that the operation was part of a plot to deprive her of her inheritance, she sought remuneration from those responsible. In the will of her late father, Peter Cooper Hewitt, Ann was to receive two-thirds of the millionaire's estate, but if she died childless, the estate would revert to her mother. She believed, therefore, that her mother had requested the operation in order to ensure that Ann would lose her fortune. Though the case initially appeared to be concerned with financial matters, it was quickly shaped into a story about sterilization and the family.

Ann's charges led to a criminal investigation the following day, and the case quickly took on increased significance as it raised questions about the California sterilization law and about parental power over minors. Based on Ann's testimony, the San Francisco municipal court charged her mother and the two surgeons with conspiracy to commit mayhem and issued arrest warrants based on invasion of personal rights.[29]

After filing an affidavit denying any wrongdoing, Ann's mother fled to New Jersey, attempted suicide, and spent five months in the psychopathic ward of the Jersey City Medical Center, distraught over her daughter's accusations. Though she was indicted, the charges were informally dismissed by the San Francisco district attorney in December 1936 because of Ann's reluctance to testify against her mother.

California surgeons Tilton E. Tillman and Samuel G. Boyd did not escape a trial, however. After months of discussion and preparation, the case went before Superior Court Judge Raglan Tuttle in August 1936. For six days, a jury listened to family members, expert witnesses, and the arguments of prosecution and defense attorneys. Finally, Tuttle dismissed the case and all charges against the physicians on the grounds that sterilization was perfectly legal and that mayhem had not been committed. Though the prosecution filed an appeal, the state supreme court declined to reopen the case. To the delight of sterilization advocates, the Cooper Hewitt case ended in their favor by validating the use of sterilization in private practice even without the consent of the patient.

Though Ann's mother was noticeably absent from the August proceedings involving Tillman and Boyd, coverage of the case still centered on her and her relationship with Ann. Between January and August of 1936, family members, health professionals, hospital attendants, and other witnesses, along with the press, constructed two competing narratives of the mother-daughter relationship. In one, Mrs. Hewitt was a conscientious, indulgent, and loving mother who sought only to protect society and a "dangerously oversexed" daughter from her own mental and moral incompetence. In the other, Mrs. Hewitt, a five-time divorcée, was an abusive mother who had deprived her neglected but otherwise normal daughter of love, education, and her right to reproduce. The conflicting narratives engaged the public because each offered a villain who possessed the symbolic power to destroy the American family: either an oversexed daughter or an abusive mother needed to be reckoned with. By focusing on the construction and use of these competing narratives, we can explore the multiple meanings of the trial to those involved in and witnessing the drama.

In a sense, both women were on trial for the same crime: the incapacity to mother. While the prosecution cited evidence that Mrs. Hewitt's inability to control Ann stemmed from her failure as a mother, the defense charged that Ann herself would never be a "desirable" or "competent" mother, thus justifying her sterilization. To fashion narratives they believed would most likely appeal to a jury of ordinary Americans, both sides placed their protagonists within the context of the family. As the case underscored, family pathology was not just a problem of the Depression era poor. The real problem was not financial but feminine: both mother and daughter had deserted domesticity, violating their prescribed gender roles at a time when such prescriptions were deemed crucial to social survival.

When Ann's lawyer, Russell P. Tyler, announced in January 1936 that Ann was suing her mother, he called the mother's reputation into question by using her full name. The suit, he declared, "will be against Miss Hewitt's mother, Mrs. Maryon Bruguiere-Denning-Hewitt-D'Erlanger-McCarter."[30] The press consistently printed her full string of names, thus emphasizing her five failed marriages. Though her marriages placed her in a position of great affluence and made her a socialite known in San Francisco, New York, London, and Paris, she had ultimately failed as a wife.[31]

In Tyler's portrayal of Mrs. Bruguiere-Denning-Hewitt-D'Erlanger-McCarter, she was no better at motherhood than she was at marriage. He charged that throughout Ann's childhood, she had "failed in her duty as a mother and guardian" and "shamefully neglected" her daughter's education. Though one of the wealthiest women in the United States, she deprived Ann of everything to which a financially privileged child was entitled. As a result, Ann was "virtually the prisoner of her mother," Tyler declared, "a victim of cruelty, forced to live with hardly more than the bare necessities or comforts of a poorhouse waif."[32]

In this narrative, Mrs. Hewitt's greatest transgression was the neglect of her child. During the Depression, sensitivity toward and public awareness of child neglect were on the increase. In an era that witnessed a return to traditional gender roles, "neglect became *by definition* a female form of mistreatment"[33] (emphasis in original). Neglected children signaled neglected domesticity, and in the case of Ann's mother, evidence of one suggested the presence of the other. She was thus allegedly a failure as both wife and mother.

In a public statement made immediately after filing suit, Ann reinforced Tyler's portrait of her childhood. "I had no dolls when I was little," she began, "and I'll have no children when I'm old. That's my story." Described as "timid and nervous," she confessed to an unhappy childhood in which her mother frequently kept her "locked up" and called her an "imbecile."[34] Instead of being nurtured by her mother, she watched much of her fortune disappear, she claimed, as her mother had "squandered hundreds of thousands of dollars" of Ann's money at gambling resorts around the world.[35]

Three nurses who had attended her after the sterilization operation validated Ann's claims of abuse. Grace Wilkins recalled that when hired to take care of Ann, she was told that the young woman was a "mental case." Yet after only a half hour in attendance, she judged that Ann suffered not from mental deficiency but from abuse. Over a period of three months, Wilkins witnessed Ann's letters and phone calls being censored by her controlling mother.[36] A second nurse, Anne Lindsay, assisted in Ann's sterilization but also found her to be "entirely normal."[37] Sarah Bradford, who cared for Ann during her month of convalescence, testified that her mother was "cruel, inhuman, unnatural and inconsiderate." Describing Mrs. Hewitt's "late night drinking parties," Bradford noted that she "did not conduct herself as a *normal* mother would."[38]

The sworn affidavits of Ann, her lawyer, and three attendants who had witnessed the mother-daughter relationship firsthand portrayed Ann as a timid, undeserving victim of her mother's greed and wrath. Emphasizing that Ann herself was "normal," they constructed a portrait of her mother as monstrous and inhuman, incapable of performing the duties of mother-hood. Maryon Hewitt symbolized the poisonous effect of the 1920s culture of individualism on the American family. As an independent woman, trav-eler, drinker, and gambler who gave birth to her daughter out of wedlock (only afterward marrying Ann's father), she demonstrated to eugenicists and other social critics that the widespread desertion of domesticity in the 1920s had severe ramifications for the American family in the 1930s. In this narrative, it was she, not Ann, who posed the greater threat to the fam-ily's survival.

Though witnesses testified to Ann's normality, they lacked the scientific expertise to free her from accusations of abnormality. As eugenicists had argued since the turn of the twentieth century, the real danger of high-grade morons (as experts labeled Ann) was that they could pass as normal. Ann may have been able to fool those around her into thinking that she possessed normal mental faculties, skeptics contended. Evidence of her pathology stemmed from the report of psychologist Mary Scally, head of the Division of Mental Hygiene of the Board of Health of San Francisco. Hours before Ann's sterilization, Scally diagnosed her as a moron with a mental age of ten years and eleven months. "Had she applied herself more persistently to the tasks presented she might have scored a few points higher," Scally admitted. "However, my impression from these tests," she continued, "is that she will never develop intellectually beyond the level of a high grade moron."[39]

How could those constructing the narrative of Ann as normal counter such damning scientific evidence? Needing a medical expert to endorse their claim, they found psychiatrist Lawrence Collins, senior resident physi-cian at the New Jersey State Hospital for the Insane. On January 8, while lawyers for Mrs. Maryon Hewitt McCarter declared they would produce ex-pert testimony proving that Ann was feebleminded, Collins certified that the young woman was "mentally sound."

In his statement, Collins declared that after an examination of Ann, he found her to be "perfectly normal in every respect." He based his con-clusion not on mental test scores but on her social abilities. He found her widely read (familiar with Shakespeare and Dickens), fluent in French and Italian, and possessing a wide range of interests. If she lacked anything, he argued, it was due to an "unwholesome environment" rather than any "pathological defect."[40] As eugenicists were beginning to argue in the 1930s, an inadequate environment—not just a pathological defect—could and did damage a child. Yet Collins used this evidence not to justify sterilization of the child but to condemn an allegedly incapable mother.

Collins's analysis, along with the testimony of Ann and her three nurses, was enough to convince Municipal Court Judge Sylvain Lazarus that criminal charges should be filed against Ann's mother and the two surgeons. After hearing Ann testify in front of hundreds of curious onlookers, Lazarus addressed her with sympathy and respect, apparently persuaded by her story. For example, when Ann described Scally's testing procedures, she reported that she had asked Scally in disgust, "Why are you asking me these asinine questions?" Lazarus turned to her with a smile, duly impressed, and asked, "Did you really say asinine?"[41] When she mentioned she had corrected Scally's French pronunciation during another part of her questioning, the judge remarked, "Never dispute a psychiatrist. She probably marked you down a couple of points for that."[42] In his closing, he assured Ann, "You have been a wonderful witness. I know very few who think as clearly as you do."[43]

The discrepancy between Collins's and Scally's psychological evaluations led Lazarus to question the validity of mental testing. He asked Scally to give him a mental exam. She concluded, based on his answers, that he had a mental age of twelve. Lazarus facetiously responded, "I thought it was nearer eight."[44] Those in the courtroom, which was "crowded to capacity," burst out laughing, while the judge concluded that the whole thing was "too silly for words."[45] In an apparent blow to the reputation of psychiatric testing, he dismissed the procedure as useless, calling into question the idea that intelligence was an easily measured genetic trait. The real issue, he believed, was not whether Ann was feebleminded but whether mothers should have the power to determine their children's fertility. "The necessity and the desire to bear children is something not idly to be interfered with," he warned.[46] He signed a warrant for the arrest of Ann's mother and the two surgeons, satisfied that mayhem had been committed by the three.

Had the story ended there, the case would have been a hindrance rather than a help to the eugenics movement. As the media emphasized, Judge

Lazarus believed that Ann's individual rights had been violated. But in the 1930s, concern over individual rights had to compete with concern for the health and stability of the country as a collective body. In a time of crisis, eugenicists argued, personal rights had to be sacrificed for the common good, and they convinced many that the 1930s was such a time. They succeeded by emphasizing that eugenic sterilization was a "better deal for the child"—that all children should have the birthright of a sound mind in a sound body—and that such sterilization would ultimately preserve and strengthen the American family as a social institution.

In the only historical analysis of the Cooper Hewitt case, Daniel Kevles argues in a footnote that it "may have raised the general public's sensitivity to the misuses of sterilization."[47] But he does not discuss the powerful counternarrative in the case, which was influenced by the updated campaign strategies of eugenicists in the 1930s. Supporters of Mrs. Hewitt reversed the charges, suggesting that it was Ann, not her mother, who suffered severe abnormalities. Ultimately, this narrative held greater sway with the presiding judge, as well as with public opinion.

Mrs. Hewitt, as her lawyer insisted on calling her, presented herself as a concerned mother. She declared that her treatment of her daughter had been "only what a kind mother would do for a daughter to whom she has been devoted."[48] From the moment of Ann's birth, her mother testified, she struggled unsuccessfully to raise her as a normal child. Mrs. Hewitt's close friend, Dr. I. L. Hill, testified that Ann's birth was premature (she weighed only three and a half pounds) and that, as a result, her physical and mental development was slow. Because premature babies usually survived only with careful nursing, he argued that Ann's survival was itself proof of Mrs. Hewitt's "exceptional motherly care."[49] For her part, Mrs. Hewitt explained that she tried to give her daughter a good education and sent her to the "best of schools," but unfortunately, Ann was not interested in furthering her education and had to be withdrawn.

Though Ann's lawyer argued that the daughter lived like a "poor-house waif," Mrs. Hewitt argued that she had lavished expensive clothing and gifts on Ann. Embellishing this portrait, Ann's stepbrother came forward to defend Mrs. Hewitt. He declared that she had bought Ann forty pairs of shoes, one dozen evening gowns, and thirty hats. In addition, he claimed that she had made trips twice in "special railroad cars to insure privacy for her [Ann's] pet dog."[50] His testimony was supported by Helen Johnston, a buyer for the New York firm of J. M. Gidding and Co., who claimed that Mrs. Hewitt spent $35,000 a year on clothing for her daughter. Her purchases included expensive furs ("coats of ermine and chinchilla"), imported lingerie, and the "most expensive articles" in children's dresses.[51]

As evidence of the hardship she experienced in raising an obviously "backward" child, Mrs. Hewitt presented records of doctors' reports dating from a trip to the south of France in 1924. Two different doctors determined after examination that Ann suffered from "retarded growth" and "arrested mental development," which had led to "instability of mind and impulsive tendencies."[52] Along with Scally's conclusion that Ann's mind would never develop beyond that of a "high grade moron," Mrs. Hewitt used these medical reports to prove that she had Ann sterilized not out of personal greed but out of maternal concern. It was not that she did not want Ann to have children, she explained, but that she feared her mental condition would lead her into "moral difficulties."[53]

The operation, her lawyer explained, was performed both for Ann's own protection and for "society's sake." The girl's "erotic tendencies" had led her into a great deal of trouble. In 1932, she had become "infatuated" with a chauffeur and planned to run away with him. Her mother found love letters written by Ann that "justified their immediate destruction," and she paid thousands of dollars to ensure that they were destroyed. One particularly ardent letter contained locks of hair from Ann's head and her pubic region (a fact Mrs. Hewitt disclosed only to the surgeons when requesting the operation; she refused to include this sexually explicit evidence in her affidavit). In addition, Mrs. Hewitt believed her daughter to be "easily infatuated by men in uniform," addicted to masturbation, and "familiar" with a hotel bellboy and a "negro porter on a train."[54] Ann's mother had spent years monitoring her daughter's actions, trying to block the girl's infatuations from developing into something more serious.[55] In this narrative, it was Ann, not her mother, who posed a threat to family and society; based on her actions, eugenicists believed she would not make a "desirable mother."[56]

Clearly, Mrs. Hewitt's distress at her daughter's actions stemmed from the fact that Ann threatened her mother's rigid boundaries of class and race, as well as propriety. Ann challenged her mother's authority by independently asserting herself in relationships with men outside her own class and race. In the 1930s, such youthful rebellion was not new or uncom-

mon. What *was* new in the 1930s and clearly articulated in the Cooper Hewitt case was the use of eugenic sterilization as a family-centered solution
to the problem of female sexuality. Sterilization had become the private
decision of a mother who sought control of her child's habits. Completely
divorced from its institutional setting, sterilization offered Mrs. Hewitt a
way to enforce a standard of reproductive morality in her daughter. In the
process, it raised the stakes of combining eugenic ideology with reproductive technology. Without the barriers of institutional commitment or professional certification, sterilization could become a private family matter.
If used conscientiously, as sterilization advocates hoped it would be, this
family model could have a far greater effect on improving civilization than
any public institutional model would. As E. S. Gosney commented in reference to the Hewitt case, "Voluntary sterilization in private practice is of
great value. Many students of the subject are convinced that during the
next generation the great bulk of sterilizations in the United States will be
of the voluntary [that is, extrainstitutional] type."[57] Their assumption was
correct; beginning in the 1960s, hundreds of thousands of women (primarily black, Native American, and Puerto Rican) were "voluntarily" sterilized
in private hospitals, often allegedly by doctors offended by their fertility
patterns.[58]

Mrs. Hewitt's case had the full support of the surgeons who had agreed
to perform the operation. Tillman justified Mrs. Hewitt's actions as those
of a caring mother, claiming he would have done the same thing "had it
been my own daughter." The doctor, who was also a member of the San
Francisco Lunacy Commission, acknowledged that Ann's case was unusual in that she did not reside in an institution for the feebleminded, as
the law specified. But the situation was virtually the same, he argued:
"Where a family has sufficient means, the feebleminded person is taken
care of privately." Ann had escaped the asylum only because her mother
could afford to care for her at home. But she was just as solid a case for
sterilization as any. "I feel justified both from a moral and scientific standpoint," Tillman continued: "It is an injustice to all concerned to permit the
feeble minded to bring children into the world."[59]

Boyd, who assisted Tillman in the procedure, also supported Mrs. Hewitt's request. He noted in his surgeon's report that Ann had "never developed beyond eleven years."[60] Surprised at the accusation of mayhem, he
remarked that he had not worried about the legal aspects of the matter,

"figuring a mother had the right to request such an operation, since the girl then was a minor."[61] Though both doctors realized the California sterilization law did not explicitly give mothers the authority to have their daughters sterilized, they presumed it to be a "moral matter"; as Tillman said, "A mother is supposed to be acting for the best interest of her child."[62]

Tillman and Boyd were not the only ones confused about the boundaries of the law. Without legal precedent, the private sterilization based on a mother's consent (and therefore considered voluntary) raised widespread speculation about the purpose and limits of the California sterilization law. Assistant District Attorney August Fourtner, prosecutor in the Cooper Hewitt case, believed sterilization in private practice to be illegal, a belief that supported the claim that the doctors had committed mayhem. The doctors' defense attorney, I. M. Golden, argued the reverse.

In pursuit of an effective argument, Golden contacted Popenoe at the Pasadena-based Human Betterment Foundation for advice on the legal aspects of Ann's case and asked him to testify as an expert witness. "In your opinion," he asked Popenoe, "was it proper to sterilize her by removing the Fallopian tubes, as a matter of medical and scientific procedure?"[63] After consulting Butler at the Sonoma State Home, Popenoe responded, "I suppose we should all answer negatively the question whether a young woman such as you describe would be a desirable mother." Significantly, Popenoe was not concerned about whether Ann's reported abnormalities were hereditary; though this was his specialty, he did not believe it was "particularly the issue in this case."[64] Instead, he based his answer on her suitability as a mother.

Popenoe's comments reflected the changing strategies of eugenicists in the 1930s. In 1935, the American Eugenics Society recommended that sterilization be used "even in cases where there is no certainty that the traits of the parents will be passed on to their children through heredity."[65] The goal of eugenics, AES president Ellsworth Huntington argued, was to improve society at its source: the home.[66] The way to achieve this goal was to ensure that the largest possible percentage of children were born in homes "best fitted to develop their character and intelligence," while the smallest percentage were born in homes where "parents are unable or unwilling to provide good training both intellectually and morally." The most important factor, he explained, was the "character and vitality of the parents."[67] Based on these standards, in Popenoe's opinion, Ann did not make the cut. For this reason alone, he (along with surgeons Tillman and Boyd and, ultimately, the deciding superior court judge) found the sterilization to be justified.

After extensive correspondence with Popenoe, Golden appeared confident that he could argue for the surgeons' innocence based on the eugenic sterilization law. Like eugenicists in the 1930s, he was also careful to couch such an argument in terms that a jury would find meaningful by embedding it in family issues. As he confided to Popenoe before the case went to trial in August, "What I am going to try to prove is that, according to experience it is well, both for Society, for the individual and for the family group, that morons be sterilized."[68]

In his preparation, Golden probably studied a significant article published in the journal of the American Bar Association entitled "Liability of Physicians for Sterilization Operations." Authors Justin Miller and Gordon Dean, noting the rising number of sterilizations performed both in public institutions and in private practice, sought to determine the civil and criminal liability of physicians who performed them. A central question in their article, as in the Cooper Hewitt case, was whether doctors who performed sterilizations were guilty of mayhem. As mentioned, the crime of mayhem consisted of the "unlawful and malicious removal of a member of a human being or the disabling or disfiguring thereof or rendering it useless."[69] When applying this definition of mayhem to sterilization in the 1930s, legal analysts struggled to determine the primary function of the female sex organs. If reproduction was the primary function, then mayhem indeed could be applied. But if the primary function was the gratification of sexual desires, then sterilization did not render the organs useless.

The debate over the primary function of female sexuality—procreation or pleasure—was a result of the changing sexual morality of the 1920s. As women challenged the Victorian ideal of passionlessness and modern sexologists declared that sexual desire was a natural and normal characteristic of women as well as men, pleasure replaced procreation as the universal biological function of sex. Pleasure became a universal right, whereas procreation became an exclusive privilege. Thus, charging doctors who sterilized in private practice with mayhem rarely resulted in a conviction in the 1930s. The outcome depended on the interpretation of the phrase *rendering it useless* in the individual case. Shortly after the Cooper Hewitt proceedings, another legal analyst argued that the outcome also depended on the "attitude of the courts concerning the morality of sterilization." Hartley

Peart, a lawyer, noted in 1941 that "until recent years the attitude of all civic bodies, as well as the courts, was that sterilization was immoral in all aspects." But thanks to the work of sterilization advocates, "in California, and in many other states, public opinion has progressed to the point of approving sterilization for the purpose of rendering the unfit incapable of procreation."[70] Such approval was confirmed in the Cooper Hewitt case, where the charge of mayhem for sterilization was defeated.

After months of collecting evidence to sway the jury, defense attorney Golden and prosecuting attorney Fourtner came face to face in the courtroom of Superior Court Judge Tuttle to try the surgeons on August 14, 1936. They selected a jury of twelve individuals whose task was to determine whether the surgeons were justified in "depriving Ann Cooper Hewitt of the right to motherhood on medical, eugenic, or other compelling grounds." The state intended to show that the surgeons were not justified but rather acted "maliciously and feloniously." The defense planned to prove that the doctors acted "ethically and in good faith" and that Ann "had to be kept from motherhood" because of her mental and physical "unfitness."[71] Both intended to appeal to the jury by focusing on the family as a central theme in the case.

But Judge Tuttle never gave the jury a chance to make a decision, for after less than a week, he dismissed the case as a "useless expenditure of public funds." He believed that the prosecution, which had relied on the testimony of Ann, her attendants, and the surgeons, had failed to make a case against the defendants. Most significantly for the future of sterilization practice, Tuttle declared that sterilization was not a crime in California; he thus established a precedent, as this was the "first ruling on the right of doctors to sterilize minor persons at the request of the parents or guardians."[72] Though the prosecution attempted to appeal the dismissal, the state supreme court declined to reopen the case just one week later.

Sterilization advocates, relieved at the decision, recognized its significance. The widespread coverage, the focus on the family, and the judge's dismissal all served to popularize sterilization as a moral solution to the problem of female sexuality. Butler collected copies of the judge's decision to send to private physicians "who may wish to consider the operation on private individuals in their respective communities."[73] Popenoe, who had advised Golden on the case, argued that regardless of whether Ann suffered from a hereditary deficiency, sterilization was justified by her sexual transgressions, which indicated she would never make a "desirable" mother.[74] Excited by the judge's decision, which validated this argument, Popenoe wrote to Golden, "May I join my congratulations to the flood of them which I am sure you have been receiving for your smashing victory. . . . This case will be a milestone in the judicial history of sterilization in California."[75] Sterilization advocates were no longer required to provide proof of hereditary deficiency; questionable sexual behavior was justification enough for sterilization. The determining question was no longer, will she spread her genetic defect to her children? It was, will she make a desirable mother? This change paved the way for widespread use of sterilization as a way to regulate motherhood.

Though the case has been all but forgotten in the intervening years, the battle between Ann Cooper Hewitt and her mother familiarized Depression era Americans with sterilization as a social remedy. One popular magazine noted that the suit "evoked public interest in sterilization." Before the case, few realized that twenty-three thousand Americans had been sterilized, ten thousand of them in California.[76] Yet even after widespread coverage of the trial, no public uprising or protests against sterilization occurred. Convinced that personal liberty should be sacrificed for the common good in a time of crisis, many spoke in favor of the procedure. For example, in 1937, just one year after the Hewitt case, *Fortune* surveyed its readers on the issue and found that 66 percent favored compulsory sterilization of "mental defectives," whereas only 15 percent were opposed.[77]

Another indication of the increasing public interest in sterilization in the 1930s comes from Fred Hogue's weekly column, "Social Eugenics," in the *Los Angeles Times Sunday Magazine*. The *Times*, at the suggestion of E. S. Gosney (president of the Human Betterment Foundation), established the column in 1935 and continued it through 1940. Hogue introduced readers to a number of eugenic issues, stressing the need for eugenic sterilization in order to advance modern civilization, warning of race suicide, and updating readers on developments in the Cooper Hewitt case.

Hogue intended his column to evoke public interest in eugenics. "To appeal to the masses," he acknowledged, "one must speak in the language of the masses." As his column generated massive correspondence, he noted encouragingly the rise in public support for sterilization: "I am learning more about the actual reaction of the average person to the formulas of modern disciples of social eugenics from my correspondence than from all the books and lectures I have read on this subject."[78] In a column written four months after the Cooper Hewitt verdict, Hogue noted:

> In casting over my correspondence on Social Eugenics . . . I find there is a growing interest in a more extended enforcement of State sterilization laws. This increasing interest comes chiefly from women, most of whom are mothers. Many letters come from women who confide to me in confidence conditions of families in their immediate neighborhood. They see families of subnormals, both mentally and physically, increasing without let or hindrance and they write me that many of the mothers would be willing to submit to a surgical operation which would make sure that they would give birth to no more children mentally unequipped to care for themselves in the modern struggle for existence.[79]

His correspondents expressed concern over women they thought should not have children, revealing the existence of a widespread belief in reproductive morality in American society. "Reading your column," a thirty-year-old woman wrote, "I am amazed in this day and age right thinking people let imbeciles have children. Why, and when will a law be passed to stop this?"[80]

Along with the 1930 White House Conference on Child Health and the Cooper Hewitt case, the *Los Angeles Times*'s "Social Eugenics" column reinforced the eugenic argument that Depression era poverty was not the cause but only a symptom of a more deeply rooted family pathology. If the home environment shaped a child's personality and development, then it was all the more important, eugenicists concluded, to scrutinize the home. "Parents produce faulty children by bad rearing as well as by bad heredity," Roswell Johnson argued, while promoting an extension of the California sterilization law to authorize the operation on noninstitutionalized women at public expense.[81]

Newly packaged with enhanced appeal to a 1930s audience, eugenics addressed issues relevant to a majority of Americans: the survival and stability of the family as a social institution; the usefulness of "normality" as a central organizing concept; and the importance of environment, in addition to heredity, to human development. Portrayed in a eugenic narrative, fertility left unchecked had dangerous implications for both individual families and American civilization. By linking the personal to the larger social body in their campaign, eugenicists raised the stakes of procreation and drew Americans toward their doctrine of reproductive morality and its message of social responsibility.

Notes

1. For more on the shift in American society from individualism to social responsibility, see Alan Dawley, *Struggles for Justice: Social Responsibility and the Liberal State* (Cambridge, MA: Harvard University Press, 1991), 5.

2. Mark Haller, *Eugenics: Hereditarian Attitudes in American Thought* (New Brunswick, NJ: Rutgers University Press, 1963), 179.

3. Dawley, *Struggles for Justice*, 5.

4. Fred Butler, "Some Results of Selective Sterilization: Discussion," *Journal of Psycho-asthenics* 35 (1930): 336. For a detailed analysis of the Sonoma State Home for the Feebleminded, see Wendy Kline, *Building a Better Race: Gender, Sexuality, and Eugenics from the Turn of the Century to the Baby Boom* (Berkeley: University of California Press, 2001), chap. 2.

5. Hoover, quoted in James Hay Jr., "'A Wise Son Maketh a Glad Father': The President's November Conference on Child Health Will Work to Develop Our Greatest Asset," *World's Work* 59 (October 1930): 73.

6. Dawley, *Struggles for Justice*, 309.

7. Ray Lyman Wilbur, "Toward a Better Child Life," *Review of Reviews* 83 (January 1931): 55.

8. "President Hoover's Address on Nation's Children," *New York Times*, November 20, 1930, 2.

9. Haven Emerson, MD, "From Promoters to Parents: What Can We Expect from the White House Conference?" *Survey* 67 (November 1931): 191–92.

10. Ibid., 347.

11. "Annual Report of the Human Betterment Foundation," February 9, 1932, File SC 38, 2–13, Lewis Terman Papers, Department of Special Collections, Stanford University Library, Palo Alto, CA.

12. Hay, "'A Wise Son,'" 73.

13. Nancy Stepan, *The Hour of Eugenics: Race, Gender and Nation in Latin America* (Ithaca, NY: Cornell University Press, 1991), 195.

14. Paul Popenoe, "The German Sterilization Law," *Journal of Heredity* 25, no. 7 (July 1934): 257.

15. Ibid., 260, 257.

16. Fred Hogue, "Social Eugenics," *Los Angeles Times Sunday Magazine*, February 9, 1936, 31.

17. Nancy Cott, *The Grounding of Modern Feminism* (New Haven, CT: Yale University Press, 1987), 147.

18. See Joan Jacobs Brumberg, *The Body Project: An Intimate History of American Girls* (New York: Random House, 1997); Roland Marchand, *Advertising the American Dream: Making Way for Modernity, 1920–1940* (Berkeley: University of California Press, 1985).

19. See, for example, Frederick Osborn, "Implications of the New Studies in Population and Psychology for the Development of Eugenic Philosophy," *Eugenical News* 22, no. 6 (1937): 107.

20. Gladys Schwesinger, "Sterilization and the Child," extracts from a paper read at the Sixty-third Annual Meeting of the New Jersey Health and Sanitary Association, December 10, 1937, reprinted from *"Health Progress": Official Publication of the New Jersey Health and Sanitary Association, Inc.,* 1–2, in File 11.7, E. S. Gosney Papers, California Institute of Technology Archives, Pasadena (hereafter cited as Gosney Papers).

21. Steven Mintz and Susan Kellogg, *Domestic Revolutions: A Social History of the American Family* (New York: Free Press, 1988), 144–49.

22. "Race Degeneration Seen for America," *New York Times*, June 21, 1932, a copy of which is in Box 15, Folder 123, of the Association for Voluntary Sterilization (AVS) Papers, Social Welfare History Archives, University of Minnesota, Minneapolis (hereafter cited as AVS Papers).

23. Philip R. Reilly, *The Surgical Solution: A History of Involuntary Sterilization in the United States* (Baltimore, MD: Johns Hopkins University Press, 1991), 97.

24. Edward J. Larson, *Sex, Race, and Science: Eugenics in the Deep South* (Baltimore, MD: Johns Hopkins University Press, 1995), 119.

25. Paul Popenoe and Norman Fenton, "Sterilization as a Social Measure," *Journal of Psycho-asthenics* 41 (1936): 60–65.

26. "Sterilization: Ann Hewitt Brings Her Mother to Trial on Conspiracy Charge," *Literary Digest*, December 19, 1936, 13.

27. Daniel J. Kevles, *In the Name of Eugenics: Genetics and the Uses of Human Heredity* (Cambridge, MA: Harvard University Press, 1985), 112.

28. Herbert Ray, "The Law and the Surgeon's Liability in Human Sterilization Operations," June 8, 1935, 7, in the file "Human Betterment Foundation," AVS Papers.

29. "Three Warrants Issued in Ann Hewitt Case," *New York Times,* February 5, 1936, 3.

30. "Charges She Was Sterilized," *New York Sun,* January 6, 1936, in Box 14, Folder 120, AVS Papers.

31. Ibid.

32. Ibid.

33. Linda Gordon, *Heroes of Their Own Lives: The Politics and History of Family Violence* (New York: Penguin Books, 1988), 151–52.

34. "Police to Study Ann Hewitt's Operation Case," *New York Tribune,* January 8, 1936, in Box 14, Folder 120, AVS Papers.

35. "Hewitt Heiress Says Mother Had Her Sterilized to Get Estate," *New York Tribune,* January 7, 1936, in Box 14, Folder 120, AVS Papers.

36. "Calls Ann Hewitt Overly Romantic," *New York Times,* January 10, 1936, 2.

37. "Accuses Mother in Court," *New York Times,* January 24, 1936, 40.

38. "Mother Cites 'Erotic Letters' of Ann Hewitt," *New York Tribune,* January 10, 1936, in Box 14, Folder 120, AVS Papers (emphasis added).

39. A copy of the Scally report was enclosed in a letter to Popenoe from I. M. Golden, the San Francisco attorney who defended the surgeons in the August trial; it is dated May 23, 1936 and is in File 11.9, Gosney Papers.

40. "Alienists Line Up in Hewitt Contest," *New York Times,* January 9, 1936, 2.

41. "Judge Postpones Decision on Sterilization Charges," *Pasadena Post,* January 24, 1936, in File 11.9, Gosney Papers.

42. "Psychiatry Claims Another Victim," *Sacramento Bee,* January 27, 1936, in File 11.9, Gosney Papers.

43. "Judge Postpones Decision on Sterilization Charges," *Pasadena Post,* January 24, 1936, in File 11.9, Gosney Papers.

44. "Hewitt Case Judge Told His Mental Age Is 12," *New York Tribune,* February 19, 1936, in Box 14, Folder 120, AVS Papers.

45. "Judge Given Child Rating," *Los Angeles Times,* February 19, 1936, in File 11.9, Gosney Papers.

46. "Two Doctors Held in Ann Hewitt Case," *New York Times,* February 20, 1936, 3.

47. Kevles, *In the Name of Eugenics,* 345–46.

48. "Doctor Upholds Mental Fitness of Miss Hewitt," *Herald Tribune,* January 9, 1936, in Box 14, Folder 120, AVS Papers.

49. "$500,000 Operation," *Time,* January 20, 1936, 42–45.

50. "Stepbrother Denies Cruelty," *New York Times,* January 11, 1936.

51. "Tell of Hewitt Operation," *New York Sun,* January 9, 1936, in Box 14, Folder 120, AVS Papers.

52. Ibid.

53. "Charges She Was Sterilized," *New York Sun,* January 6, 1936, in Box 14, Folder 120, AVS Papers.

54. "Calls Ann Hewitt Overly Romantic," *New York Times,* January 10, 1936; letter from I. M. Golden to Paul Popenoe, May 23, 1936, in File 11.9, E. S. Gosney Papers.

55. "Tell of Hewitt Operation," *New York Sun,* January 9, 1936, in Box 14, Folder 120, AVS Papers.

56. Letter from Popenoe to Golden, May 126, 936, in File 11.9, Gosney Papers.

57. E. S. Gosney, quoted in Fred Hogue, "Social Eugenics," *Los Angeles Times Sunday Magazine,* March 1, 1936, 30.

58. John D'Emilio and Estelle Freedman, *Intimate Matters: A History of Sexuality in America* (New York: Harper and Row, 1988), 255; Helen Rodriguez-Trias, "Sterilization Abuse," in *Biological Woman—The Convenient Myth: A Collection of Feminist Essays and a Comprehensive Bibliography,* ed. Ruth Hubbard, Mary Sue Henifin, and Barbara Fried (Cambridge, MA: Schenkman Books, 1982). See also Johanna Schoen, *Choice and Coercion: Birth Control, Sterilization, and Abortion in Public Health and Welfare* (Chapel Hill: University of North Carolina Press, 2005). According to Angela Davis, 24 percent of all Native American women of childbearing age and 35 percent of Puerto Rican women of childbearing age had been sterilized by 1976; see Davis, *Women, Race, and Class* (New York: Vintage Books, 1983), 218–19. More recent scholarship, however, suggests the need to reevaluate the portrayal of sterilized women as merely victims of social control. See Kline, *Building a Better Race,* chap. 2; Laura Briggs, "Discourses of 'Forced Sterilization' in Puerto Rico: The Problem with the Speaking Subaltern," *Differences* 10 (1998): 30–66; Jennifer Nelson, *Women of Color and the Reproductive Rights Movement* (New York: New York University Press, 2003).

59. "Ann Cooper Hewitt Sues Her Mother," *New York Times,* January 7, 1936, 3.

60. "Dr. Boyd's Card," copy of surgeon's record enclosed in letter from Golden to Popenoe, May 23, 1936.

61. "$500,000 Operation," *Time,* January 20, 1936, 45.

62. "Ann Cooper Hewitt Sues Her Mother." The issue of parental rights in acting in the "best interest of the child" is still debated in California. The *San Jose Mercury News* of February 21, 1998, reported that a couple had paid two strangers to take their disobedient son out of the house in the middle of the night and ship him off for a year of disciplinary action at a Jamaican reform school. An Alameda County Superior Court judge ruled that they were acting within their parental rights, a ruling "consistent with decades of law that gives parents broad latitude in rearing their children as they see fit."

63. Letter from Golden to Popenoe, May 23, 1936.

64. Letter from Popenoe to Golden, May 26, 1936.

65. Barry Alan Mehler, "A History of the American Eugenics Society, 1921–1940" (PhD diss., University of Illinois at Urbana-Champaign, 1988), 260, a copy of which is in the American Eugenics Society Papers, American Philosophical Society, Philadelphia.

66. Ellsworth Huntington, *Tomorrow's Children: The Goal of Eugenics* (New York: John Wiley and Sons, 1935), 7.

67. Ibid., 63.

68. Letter from Golden to Popenoe, May 28, 1936, in File 11.9, Gosney Papers.

69. Justin Miller and Gordon Dean, "Liability of Physicians for Sterilization Operations," *Journal of the American Bar Association* (March 1930): 158–61, in File 19.6, Gosney Papers.

70. Hartley F. Peart, Esq., "Vasectomy and Salpingectomy under California Law," *California and Western Medicine* (May-June 1941), 6, in Box 73, Folder "California Department of Mental Hygiene," AVS Papers.

71. "Heiress Accuses Two San Francisco Doctors," *San Francisco Examiner*, August 14, 1936, in File 11.9, Gosney Papers.

72. "Hewitt Trial Plea Mapped," *San Francisco News*, August 20, 1936, in File 11.9, Gosney Papers.

73. Letter from Fred Butler to Gosney, January 30, 1939, in File 11.9, Gosney Papers.

74. Letter from Popenoe to Golden, May 26, 1936.

75. Letter from Popenoe to Golden, August 31, 1936, in File 11.9, Gosney Papers.

76. "Sterilization," *Literary Digest*, December 19, 1936, 13.

77. Reilly, *The Surgical Solution*, 125.

78. Fred Hogue, "Social Eugenics," *Los Angeles Times Sunday Magazine*, September 13, 1936, 31.

79. Fred Hogue, "Social Eugenics," *Los Angeles Times Sunday Magazine*, December 6, 1936, 31.

80. Fred Hogue, "Social Eugenics," *Los Angeles Times Sunday Magazine*, December 13, 1936, 29.

81. Roswell Johnson, "Comment on Dr. F. O. Butler's Paper at Railway Surgeon's Meeting, Los Angeles," October 7, 1938, in File 11.7, Gosney Papers.

TWO

Eugenic Decline and Recovery in Self-Improvement Literature of the Thirties

Susan Currell

ABSTRACT

In her essay on popular self-improvement literature from the 1930s, particularly the writings of Walter B. Pitkin, Susan Currell points to the rhetorical overlaps between the personal and the political in the arenas of decline and recovery. She intertwines three narratives in her argument: Franklin Delano Roosevelt's personal struggle with polio, so resolutely overcome to establish his fitness for the presidency; the lessons Roosevelt and many other Americans learned from physical fitness guru Bernarr Macfadden, lessons that strongly pushed eugenic principles; and Pitkin's personal eugenic beliefs and the ways that these infused his highly popular writings on self-improvement. In each of these narratives, the heavy emphasis on exterior environmental actions that one could perform for self-improvement seemed to overturn mainline eugenic emphases on the Mendelian genetics that was so prevalent in the 1920s, to the extent that traditional eugenic principles of controlling heredity became hidden. Yet as Currell, Kline, and others throughout this volume argue, eugenic assumptions still ran deep, serving as the foundation on which environmental contexts were built. Each of these three men, in their respective areas, assumed an inherent genetic potential—for themselves, for middle-class individuals, for the nation as a whole—that could be brought forth only through hard work and willpower. Currell's essay thus illuminates how fundamental eugenic beliefs became infused with and perhaps overshadowed by a heightened emphasis in the 1930s on environmental influences as the means to stem decline and spur recovery and a return to overall personal and national eugenic fitness.

You who are crossing forty may not know it,
but you are the luckiest generation ever. The
advantages you are about to enjoy will soon be
recited, with a sincere undertone of envy. The
whole world has been remodeled for your
greater glory. Ancient philosophies and rituals
are being demolished to clear the ground for
whatever you choose to erect upon their sites.

WALTER B. PITKIN, *Life Begins at Forty*[1]

At least one out of every eight [adults] deserves
biological suppression in some kindly and
painless manner because of low mentality
alone.

WALTER B. PITKIN, *A Short Introduction
to the History of Human Stupidity*[2]

Prior to Franklin D. Roosevelt's election in 1932, the Depression appeared to be a national disaster over which no one had any control.[3] The United States seemed stagnant, and the country's decline was conveyed in popular metaphors of national sickness and disease, symbolized by the very visible "forgotten man" who trudged the streets with a stoop that indicated he had little strength for recovery or productivity.[4] Lacking energy and vitality, the forgotten man appeared in the mass media as a symbol of the degeneracy resulting from war and the subsequent years of uncontrolled capitalism. Facing the enormous challenges of the Depression era, Roosevelt ran as the Democratic candidate for the presidency in 1932. In his now-famous "forgotton man speech," made while he was governor of New York in April that year, he argued for a social and economic restructuring that would take account of the "forgotten man at the bottom of the economic pyramid."[5] An anticapitalist symbol for many, the forgotten man was, at the same time, a sign of what was wrong with the United States; he symbolized a national weakness and debility that confirmed the need for strong leadership and change. Transforming this man, rebuilding his strength, and adjusting him to a new economic and social organization thus appeared vital to the enactment of national recovery.

To gain popular confidence in his anticipated social transformations, it was essential that Roosevelt show he had the strength and stamina for such a huge job. For a man who had been afflicted by paralysis due to polio since 1921, this may have seemed an insurmountable task. Yet in April 1932, *Physical Culture* magazine featured an article titled "Franklin Roosevelt's

Come-Back from Invalidism" that illustrated his determined conquest of the disease. His "strength and stamina today impress one as more than is possessed by most normal men ten years younger," journalist Earle Looker wrote, despite the fact that he appeared "more like a human being than a 'statesman.'" The text described the history of this everyman's success and his illness and treatment, and it was accompanied by a series of pictures of him at the various stages of his recovery, with the final image showing him sitting unaided and in apparent good health. Stressing Roosevelt's energy and stamina throughout, Looker concluded: "His impatience brought him back into public life when everyone said he was physically finished. It has accomplished a great deal for himself and more for others. How will he direct this powerful trait?"[6]

Advertisements accompanying the article addressed the listlessness of the modern citizen. "You can come back!" stated the ad for Borden's Richer Malted Milk, while iron supplement Food Ferrin's ad claimed that a child became "bright-eyed and rosy-cheeked, with an active brain in a strong body." "There is plenty of iron in her rich, red blood!" it added. So as Roosevelt's determined personality won the day, other afflicted Americans could follow in his wake—with the aid of food supplements and the latest health knowledge. The owner and publisher of *Physical Culture* magazine was the self-help physical fitness impresario Bernarr Macfadden, whose ideas on diet and exercise had led to a huge readership for the magazine. The combination of willpower and science had been a winning formula for *Physical Culture* since its inception in 1899, but the symbols it utilized became especially pertinent during the Great Depression, when illness and decay appeared to have infected the social fabric of the nation itself. In this context, Roosevelt was a particularly apt symbol of personal and political recovery from disease. His remarkable comeback illustrated his fitness to lead the country; it also provided a metaphor for the coming battle with the economic disease that had crippled the nation. Describing the Depression as an illness to be cured by "the killing of the bacteria in the system" rather than by treating the "external symptoms," Roosevelt sought—and gained—support for widespread economic reform.[7]

Others found Roosevelt's obvious inner strength, despite his physical handicaps, equally inspirational and symbolic of his fight for national recovery. Using rhetoric similar to Earle Looker's, *Time* magazine named Roosevelt the 1932 "Man of the Year," citing the recovery from paralysis as a reason for his newfound strength and worthiness for presidential election:

Man of the Year Roosevelt's climb to the Presidency represented a physical triumph of the first order. For a decade he had fought a dogged fight to regain control over his paralyzed legs. Today the President-elect can walk in his braces, without crutch, stick, or assisting arm, about 15 steps. Declares his wife: "If the paralysis couldn't kill him, I guess the Presidency won't." The Man of the Year's attitude toward his affliction is one of gallant unconcern. After his November election he went to Warm Springs where he addressed others there taking the cure: "We've shown that we people here have determined to get over the small physical handicaps which after all don't amount to a hill of beans."[8]

Roosevelt, it appeared, manifested the will to improve and recover that was so essential to repairing the nation. That the president was strong enough for the job and that he knew all about diseases and cures was thus established by such popular journalism.

Nonetheless, a question remained: were Americans equally fit for recovery? Indeed, to many, the crash of 1929 represented the ascendancy of the nitwits and the dysgenic, leading one sociologist to ask, "Are the American people breeding a stock with a lower inherited capacity to survive?"[9] In addition, with the growth of welfare provisions and the Social Security system to improve health, fears intensified that the cost of supporting the weak would mount inordinately as they survived longer and produced even more welfare recipients.

In this context of heightened fear over the strength and vitality of Americans, Macfadden reached the zenith of his fame, wealth, and success. He was renowned for his motto that linked strength with fighting disease: "Sickness is a sin; don't be a sinner. Weakness is a crime; don't be a criminal."[10] Showing that Roosevelt was no criminal in this respect, the report in *Physical Culture* indicated that his strength and willpower not only had been regained but also had been enhanced by his battle with disease. He and Macfadden were photographed together on a 1931 visit to Warm Springs, Georgia, where Roosevelt regularly received treatment for his paralysis (Figure 2.1).

The president and the health guru undertook exercise programs as part of a day-by-day personal plan for recovery from ill health, a plan with no apparent relationship to the eugenics movement that had been widely popular among intellectuals, reformers, and scientists in the previous two decades.

Fig. 2.1. Franklin D. Roosevelt and Bernarr Macfadden in Warm Springs, Georgia, 1931. Courtesy of the Franklin D. Roosevelt Library Digital Archives.

And on the national level, the long-term goals of eugenic breeding seemed to have little connection with the immediate and pressing adaptations to modernity that were being demanded of Americans. Yet a closer examination of the rhetoric of recovery and planning at that time shows that the self-improvement formula actually engaged closely with the eugenic thought of the 1930s. Roosevelt's battle with illness symbolized the possibility of turning adversity into advantage in a way that was central to the marketing and popularity of both the New Deal and the self-help formulas during the thirties.

Nearly all self-help books promoted "euthenics," or increasing human efficiency and health by improving the way humans interacted with and controlled their environment, but they only occasionally mentioned such long-range goals as the "controlled breeding" touted by eugenicists. But as a supporter of eugenics, Bernarr Macfadden emphasized the close connection between euthenic improvement and achieving eugenic goals in the future. In fact, he claimed, securing the proper euthenics—such as "healthful surroundings, proper food, education and business opportunities"—was the first step toward the wider implementation of eugenics. Self-improvement was central to the eugenic betterment of society, he asserted, for "no matter how strong the hereditary influence may be towards vigorous bodies, if people do nothing on their own initiative, through the idea they are so well born that they do not need to make any effort toward obtaining or maintaining health, much that has been gained through inheritance will be lost."[11] And Roosevelt, as a relative of the athletic President Theodore Roosevelt (who had been featured on the cover of *Physical Culture* in September 1904), was an ideal model for Macfadden to use in stressing the relationship between success and self-improvement and accomplishing the wider goals of the planned welfare state. No longer could the health and well-being of the nation be left to random chance and business flux.

So just as laissez-faire economic policy was coming under heavy criticism in 1932, laissez-faire responses to life were perceived as equally unacceptable; they were to be replaced by "self-insight, self-planning, and self-control," assisted by the wisdom of the self-improvement manual.[12] The flurry of how-to books that appeared in the thirties treated the problems of the national economy as a pathology and depicted the economic breakdown in terms of a psychological illness from which the patient sought recovery. Thus, in the same year that Roosevelt demonstrated his remarkable comeback, a Columbia University professor, Walter B. Pitkin, published the self-help best-seller *Life Begins at Forty*, offering a new start for Depression-weary citizens. His book offered the middle-class, middle-aged man a chance to come back himself, as Roosevelt had done, to emerge triumphantly from the ashes of a destroyed world by adopting a new psychological approach to life that accepted a total reorganization of American industrial culture. The rising popularity of the book coincided with wider social transformations that occurred in the same year. Charged with building a new world from the apparent ruins of laissez-faire capitalism, Roosevelt was elected president of the United States, and initiated the most significant revolution in political organization since the Civil War—the New Deal. How the new president would deal with the trauma of an ailing nation and, equally, how Americans would respond to his New Deal depended greatly, it seemed, on the ability of Americans to adjust to new ways of thinking and behaving.

Diminishing the optimism about a new experiment in social organization was the possibility that the experiment would fail, fueled by the fear that Americans had already fallen too far into decline. Such concerns were especially visible in the proliferation of adjustment, or self-help, literature in the aftermath of 1932. Self-help works provided a popular blueprint for coping with the new social and political demands of the era while also displaying an undercurrent of anxiety and pessimism permeated by the popular rhetoric of eugenic despair. Other manifestations of this anxiety over national decline and dysgenia were prevalent in mass culture as well, especially illustrated in the explosion of popular horror films that exhibited further concerns with vitality and heredity.[13] Of these early sound features, *Dr. Jekyll and Mr. Hyde* (1931), provided one of the most fitting metaphors of the possibilities and dangers of change and transformation. Roosevelt's claim in 1933 that "the only thing we have to fear is fear itself" touched on the paralyzing horror of possible failure that faced the American people, and it seemed to offer a choice: slide into atavism and demoralization or use all available willpower to create a civilized and healthy democracy.[14] As a cure for the economic disease afflicting Americans, the New Deal was welcomed as a potential way to counteract this apparent decline. And as the ultimate self-improvement story, Roosevelt's successful self-transformation in the face of disease provided all with a model of recovery. The transformation from a diseased to a healthy condition illustrated a possible reversal of the Jekyll and Hyde descent into a dysgenic, primitive chaos that apparently faced civilized Americans at the onset of the Depression.

Although they supported the general principle of eugenically improving the population, many social scientists at the time also realized that eugenic ideas were not sufficiently established scientifically to make future planning solely through eugenics an effective option even if it were desirable.[15] At the start of Roosevelt's term, for example, two population experts and members of the President's Research Committee on Social Trends, Warren Thompson and Pascal Whelpton, discussed the problems of scientific accuracy and the lack of consensus over implementing eugenics. They stated, "In the present state of knowledge there is bound to be violent disagreement as to those who are biologically 'undesirable'; hence, progress in their elimination will be slow." However, they reported, "eugenic sterilization laws and the segregation of certain groups of the mentally incompetent are making headway; and a national population policy would be inadequate which did not include plans for increasing the effectiveness of sound efforts to prevent births among the unfit."[16] At the same time, environment now featured more centrally in eugenic rhetoric, as the movement was starting to be reoriented toward more sociologically defined goals in which welfare and social improvements were perceived as highly complementary to the original goal of breeding a better race of Americans.[17] In a 1935 memorandum, for instance, the American Eugenics Society emphasized the importance of housing, health, and economic reform as a basis for a positive eugenics: "The American Eugenics Society has in the past been concerned mainly with those aspects of the birth-rate which affect genetic inheritance. It is now consciously enlarging its interests to include not only hereditary qualities, but also the environmental conditions which should influence size of family in homes of various types."[18]

To supporters of eugenic programs, then, the advent of the New Deal was an opportune moment to implement policies that would provide for a fitter populace that was able to cope with the demands of modernity. Roosevelt's euthenic quest for better health and fitness extended to the social body as a whole and was further played out in the public arena with the introduction of welfare and leisure programs on an unprecedented scale.[19] Simultaneously, the New Deal funded the most extensive program of public health reform ever seen in the United States, offering support for free school meals, nutritional education, mass vaccinations, medical care, and Social Security—all of which would contribute to a fitter and more secure society for every citizen.[20]

In line with New Deal policies, eugenics appeared to complement euthenic reforms that now seemed in keeping with ideas of democratic freedom of choice.[21] Thus, Frederick Osborn, secretary of the American Eugenics Society, argued in the *American Sociological Review* that economic reforms offering all classes of families more freedom of choice would function eugenically. "The eugenic philosophy which we have outlined would make eugenic selection a natural and voluntary process," he explained. "It is thus in full agreement with the concepts of individual liberty and of non-interference by government, which are so closely associated with the form of our democ- racy." Yet he went on to comment that administering intelligence, personality, and social tests to individuals would also help to establish social and genetic worth, giving couples a "parenthood rating" so that social scientists could establish "what forms of social control might be effectively employed to improve succeeding generations."[22] To Osborn, programs for environmental improvement correlated with eugenic improvements. In

1939, he went further, insisting on the democratic nature of the new "environmental" eugenics, but at the same time, he claimed that attempts to create a permanently improved environment would be "thwarted" without also implementing a eugenic program, for "the unequal handicaps attaching to parents with large families appear to exert their strongest dysgenic influence in those very environments which are generally considered the 'best' and which we are trying to extend to an increasing number of people."[23] Eugenic measures, in fact, would improve the environment in which children were raised, he asserted; without them, "our civilization may well fail to produce enough of those people who are able to take full advantage of the improved environment."[24] Ultimately, however, although some aspects of the movement were changed to better fit the times, the movement's leaders did not change their belief in the benefits of policies such as instituting mass sterilization programs. So, despite the fact that Osborn seemed to temper the extremism of the earlier movement with sociological and progressive language, there was little actual change in the ultimate goals and objectives of the American Eugenics Society at that time, regardless of this apparent switch to environmentalism.

Because of the remarketing of the movement, eugenic ideas appeared to be in step with modern times and the national adjustment to a welfare state. Antieugenicists thus appeared old-fashioned, backward, and out of step with modern medical thinking, as illustrated in a report to the director of the Works Progress Administration, Harry Hopkins, from journalist Martha Gellhorn. Describing the attitudes and procedures in one locality, she told him that "the medical set-up, from every point of view, in this area is tragic. In Gaston County there is not one county clinic or hospital; and only one health officer (appointed or elected?). This gentleman has held his job for more than a dozen years; and must have had droll medical training sometime during the last century. . . . He likewise refuses to sign sterilization warrants on imbeciles: grounds[—]'It's a man's prerogative to have children.'"[25]

It was ironic, therefore, that the quest for a healthier and more modern population also triggered intensified fears of further eugenic decay. As the building of a social security system to improve health and welfare provision progressed, many started to fear that, as weaker citizens lived longer and continued to reproduce, the cost of supporting them would only soar. Family sociologists reinforced this sense of social breakdown, commenting on the increases in mental health problems, divorces, alcoholism, and prostitution of mothers and wives as a direct result of the Depression. Ernest Groves, a sociologist at the University of North Carolina, stated that despite worries that the birthrate was in decline, "we find it highest where it has been stimulated by the dole." Equally, idleness and unemployment created by the Depression would only exacerbate the problem of overreproduction by the least fit: "Sex has become almost the only recreation for many, naturally leading, particularly in a group that largely lacks adequate contraceptive knowledge or is indifferent to it, to an increase of pregnancies. . . . There were never more unwanted children in the United States than at present."[26]

Such anxieties about the possible unplanned consequences of New Deal programs also led Harvard anthropology professor Earnest Hooton to announce, at the 1935 annual meeting of the American Association for the Advancement of Science, that the United States needed a "biological new deal" to prevent "a progressive deterioration of mankind as a result of the reckless and copious breeding of protected inferiors."[27] Others offered more headline-grabbing remedies for the problem of New Deal procreation. H. L. Mencken, literary critic and editor of the *American Mercury*, argued, "We have far too many clients of the New Deal in this country, and they multiply at a rate that must disquiet every solvent lover of the flag." He suggested paying the poor an "honorarium" of $100, $50, or even $25 to be voluntarily sterilized. "Certainly it is cheap at the price," he concluded, "immensely cheaper on all counts than supporting an ever-increasing herd of morons for all eternity."[28]

Popular concerns about improving the genetic stock of the nation thus increased during the thirties even as scientific skepticism about eugenic methods grew. Hereditarian beliefs still held sway over many social scientists who worried that "a shorter lived and less 'vital' race is being bred" because welfare prolonged the lives of the weak.[29] To restore balance to the diseased economic system, Thompson and Whelpton advised the President's Research Committee that population control should certainly play a strong part in welfare planning for the future: "The quantitative goal may well be to adjust numbers to national means so that a high standard of living can be maintained and the qualitative goal [may be] to forestall the increase of undesirable stock and stimulate that of desirable stock within the quantitative limits."[30]

In this context of changes in eugenic rhetoric and the development of welfare planning, the self-improvement formulas of the thirties became immensely popular. Books promoting these ideas came out of a long history of self-improvement literature in the United States, but by the 1880s, scientific and secular ideas, notably Darwinism, began to replace the formerly religious and moral preoccupations of early improvement manuals.[31] By the 1930s, evolutionary thought had become a bedrock on which many different formulas for social, political, and personal change were based.[32]

Pitkin's books often provided biological explanations for the deterioration of culture—blaming the chaos of the modern United States on the "influx of inferior stock," for example—but he made only brief explicit mention of eugenics.[33] This lack of concern with heredity on the surface of self-help literature was deceptive, however. Pitkin's books suggested social and personal changes that were entirely in keeping with the changes occurring within the eugenics movement as it moved toward environmentalism and adopted a greater variety of approaches to population problems. As Osborn noted, "Eugenic progress will only be made by attacking on many fronts."[34] By demolishing "ancient philosophies," Pitkin and others aimed to create a newly engineered future based not on religion and morality but on the science of psychology and large-scale social and industrial planning, both of which were heavily peppered with eugenic principles.

The use of self-help works as part of a eugenic program that attacked on all fronts—including the popular—did not go unnoticed by eugenicist and marriage counselor Paul Popenoe. In an article entitled "Mate Selection" in the *American Sociological Review,* he noted that in order to prevent the mating of "undesirable" partners and promote mating of "desirable" couples, "much can be done" in terms of choosing "more satisfactory partners" by consulting "some of the excellent books on the art of being popular, of making friends, and of achieving happiness, of which at least a dozen have been published during the last few years." "Some of the standard tests of temperament, personality, emotional qualities, and attitudes should be taken," he suggested, and the educated woman who encountered no marriageable men could "do much to meet the difficulty by studying the psychology of sex, improving her own personality, getting out of a rut, and devoting at least as much time and thought to marriage as she does to a career."[35] Self-improvement guides that enabled such relationships and personal change thus complemented the new social circumstances and the goal of eugenics to improve the race.

Pitkin, one of the most exemplary and prolific writers of such manuals in the thirties, was at the peak of his fame and fortune in 1932. In his books, he addressed the white male businessman or professional, treating his "problems" with modern culture as universal problems of civilization. The task he set before the man was to readjust to the new social order in order to be able to reassert his "natural" vigor and authority to become a leader rather than a failure. Pitkin's books were not just about individual adaptation to circumstance; they also presupposed "maladjustment" on such a wide scale that only corresponding social programs and massive scientific planning would enable the individual to achieve his highest potential. His concern with mental improvement, accelerated learning, and notions of success helped to redefine the role of American citizens in an era of rapid change. Significantly, his techniques and truisms are still promoted by accelerated-learning specialists, and today, the phrase *life begins at forty* is commonly used to signify the transformation toward successful maturity or a new phase of successful living.

Pitkin began developing theories for *Life Begins at Forty* while working with shell-shocked victims of World War I, whom he called "Misfits."[36] To Pitkin, modern life was a series of shell shocks, such as rapid urbanization, industrialization, and population changes via immigration. Following the war, the Great Depression was the quintessential cultural shock, and Pitkin found his experience with shell-shocked victims applicable to a confused audience anxious for advice. Rather than a return to agrarian simplicities (as promulgated by contemporaries such as the Southern Agrarian writers or the economist Stuart Chase), the book promised a new age of rationalization and machine-made leisure, where, freed from toil by technology, man would have time to improve civilization. Less manual work would leave more time to cultivate intellect, intelligence, and happiness— to master a "modern philosophy of life." "So you see," he claimed, "the great crash of 1929 appears to have been the luckiest event in American history; for it marked the beginning of a new era in which the nit-wits steadily lose ground to the Best Minds."[37]

Concerns about population underlay this description of the new era. With an aging population and a decreasing birthrate, Pitkin noted, the future relied on how the older citizens would adapt to changes and harness their new energies. The news was good, he insisted, for at forty, the brain had reached its optimum capacity and could be trained to master the vital energies that youth tended to dissipate, and the new leisure that came with the Depression offered the opportunity to cultivate this intelligence. Longevity, he stated, was directly related to intelligence and self-mastery;

thus, those over forty were promised that they could be "the truly civilized and happy of the land" even at a time of great material hardship.[38]

Pitkin's focus on euthenics and national planning was a logical corollary to New Deal moves to develop a healthier economy based on improved social and environmental conditions. As Macfadden had shown, there was indeed a strong connection between such environmental self-improvement ideologies and eugenicists' ideas for enhancing the gene pool.[39] One was meaningless without the other. Scientific efficiency and self-control with regard to one's personal habits, such as those promoted by Pitkin, were therefore integral to the philosophy of eugenics, which promoted full self-control over one's own sexuality for the betterment of the race.

Supporters of eugenics, including Pitkin, thus found the time was ripe for drawing connections between national planning and population planning. Overproduction in industry, most often perceived to be the main cause of the Depression at the time, was paralleled with uncontrolled reproduction in humans. "In a world where people breed like rats, the supply of workers is bound to exceed the demand," claimed Pitkin in 1935. Others put it less blatantly, but many shared his fears that without controls on reproduction, welfare would enable "low-grade people to multiply, at the expense of the high-grade" and that the "parasites" would drain the "strivers."[40]

Pitkin's many books complemented eugenic goals of the period because they offered euthenics and training for the individual that would move society toward the cultivation of elite Americans and allow a scientific assessment of those who impeded or were unable to contribute to this new phase of modernity. His books provided a way to establish intelligence, personality, and social ratings that would, he believed, enable true judgment of individual worth in a meritocratic society, leading to an elite culture of the "best" minds. This prospect was made most clear in his 1930 book, *The Psychology of Achievement*, written for the "Lords of Tomorrow"— "the four or five ablest Americans out of every hundred"—to allow them to "gauge their own aptitudes and direct their efforts with a well informed intelligence."[41] The book included charts of personality and energy patterns that would, it was said, create a future progressive society by finding "able youths" who were fit to lead, through what Pitkin called "euthenic psychology."[42] Euthenic psychology incorporated a scheme for grading intelligence and potential achievement that would provide information for the betterment of society through the proper selection of an elite. Pitkin noted natural limits to achievement, for "people's minds are graded by imperceptible degrees, all the way from idiocy up to genius; and each grade has its own insurmountable limits." Rather than attempting to overcome such limits, he suggested that successful living was more about finding a suitable place for oneself within a society engineered by experts and the elite. To Pitkin, success was never the result of "vast democratic movements" (which unfortunately enabled even the lowest in society to assume authority) but entailed maximizing the human potential with which one had been born. Self-help books such as Pitkin's aimed to help the reader find his or her proper place in this ranking system. The resulting society would be a meritocracy based on eugenic principles, in which the geniuses would lead the less able. There would be no major sociological shifts but merely the ascendancy of an elite that "roughly corresponds to the graduates of our better colleges [who are] upper middle class . . . [and] spring mainly from our professional classes of North European and Jewish stocks."[43]

Along with *Life Begins at Forty,* Pitkin published two other best-sellers in 1932—*The Consumer: His Nature and His Changing Habits* and *A Short Introduction to the History of Human Stupidity.* Collectively, his three books of that year summarized the failures and hopes of the new age being ushered in. Although he had started these books before the onset of the Depression, their successful publication hinged on the fact that many hoped that 1932 was a pivotal moment of transition from the old degenerate society to a new world of improved culture and civilization. As clarion calls to the middle classes to improve themselves and seize control over weakness and instability, Pitkin's works became immensely popular. *A Short Introduction* was translated into nineteen languages and went into several reprints, and *Life Begins at Forty* was widely regarded as the publishing phenomenon of 1933.

Pitkin's science of human efficiency shared many precepts with eugenic thought in its focus on intellectual ability and ways of nurturing an elite.[44] The numerous books Pitkin published over the twenties and thirties explored and advised on ways to cope with rapid changes in modernity and offered new models of social organization.[45] Concerns over education, intelligence quotient (IQ), and mental hygiene had underpinned eugenic programs of human betterment and social improvement since the introduction of mass intelligence testing during World War I.[46] Intelligence was considered pivotal to change and adjustment, but like Pitkin, a large number of psychologists believed that the human mind had not coped well with the transition to modernity. To many, the Great Depression was symbolic of the imbalance that modern science had created between the primitive and advanced elements of culture. Human mental development, it was claimed, was lagging behind the technological advances that had been achieved over the physical environment. To some, the fear and lack of direction among Americans in the early thirties was symptomatic of the mental decline and low IQ that presented "euthenic psychologists" with their biggest challenge yet. Intelligence, however, was closely connected to the adjustment to new social and political organization. "General intelligence" Pitkin claimed, "is the ability of the individual to adjust successfully to the new situation."[47] Intellectual immaturity, which was said to have characterized (and even caused) the crash, was therefore a concern for both individual and mass planning. Roosevelt provided an exemplary lead in emphasizing that intellectual as well as physical strength was needed, establishing his aptly named "brain trust"—a think tank of top-flight professors from Columbia University who provided direction to the elected leaders of the New Deal. To Pitkin, also at Columbia, this selection of top minds paralleled his own choice of the intelligent "over forties" to lead America out of the disarray. Propelled by the belief that an intelligent elite would guide the country away from disaster, Pitkin and Roosevelt had high hopes for intelligence in the early 1930s.

Self-improvement formulas emphasized that enhancing mental ability was comparable to physical recovery and that success would require mental training in addition to exercise to increase physical stamina. This euthenic psychology became part of other self-help books. According to author Ethel Cotton, in her *Keeping Mentally Alive,* books provided "mental vitamins" and a way of keeping the mind fit and healthy. To prevent the "fat" mind, she claimed, one had to develop "a mind so lithe it can bend over and touch its toes twenty times," for "the mind must be kept fit, as well as the body, if one hopes to adjust himself."[48] Dorothy Canfield Fisher, a fiction writer and educator, used a similar rhetoric in her book *Learn or Perish,* writing that "the scorn of the present physically active man of forty for people of his age who have allowed themselves to grow fat and sluggish and soft is exactly what we all hope may be the scorn of the man of forty in the future for people of his age who let their brains become fat and sluggish and soft." Fisher concluded that "the habit of study—not necessarily of books, but of conditions, of life—is the only one which can provide that improvement *in the quality of individual minds* which is the only way in which the quality of any national thinking can be improved."[49]

Although these books appeared to be concerned with individual success, the authors actually saw self-improvement and development of the IQ and intellect as complementary to wider social programs. Many of the books offered new cooperative standards for success rather than individual achievement and were about coping with "the crowd" as well as staying above it. Self-help books such as Cotton's *Keeping Mentally Alive* (1931) and Dale Carnegie's *How to Win Friends and Influence People* (1936) consequently emphasized the importance of social skills, empathy, and intelligence—not for personal use but for better social communication and rapport.[50]

Intelligence or stupidity functioned in Pitkin's writing as a way of explaining the problems of modernity. Most particularly, the notion of "cultural lag"—or the failure of the human mind to keep pace with technological change—explained the chaos of contemporary society, for he claimed that "as the modern world grows more complex, all men grow relatively more and more stupid toward it; for their sensitivities do not enlarge, broaden, and deepen apace with affairs."[51] To this, he added a new term, *social lag*, to describe how society slowed down to the speed of its slowest (least intelligent) members. Further, he employed the term *political lag*, or the lag between the needs of the people and the government's ability to respond quickly to them.

Eugenics played a part in his approach but did not address the problem as a whole, he claimed. Though both birth control and sterilization of the insane and feebleminded was deemed "admirable, if well managed,"[52] these procedures did not tackle the "simple dullness" of the common people. "Somehow we must stamp out the inferior types," he urged, and "somehow we must improve the neglected and mistrained."[53] To Pitkin, the curing of stupidity was comparable to the curing of any other illness; it would involve a combination of social programs and cultural evolution. The project was complex, and it necessitated several responses. First came the need to identify and accurately measure human stupidity (or intelligence); then, through scientifically planned community programs (including birth control, better medicine, better nutrition, and control of production and consumption) along with the proper use of leisure for self-improvement, mental inferiority would become a thing of the past. Like many other eugenic utopias at the time, Pitkin's "Tomorrow" featured a meritocracy based on the precise measurement of intelligence and a distinct upper class of the top minds. "This citizenry of Utopia," he claimed, "would be plagued with no slums, no morons, no criminal defectives, no insane, no crazy artists, no egomaniacs, no huge factory towns, no tenements."[54]

In 1932, many other social scientists, academics, and intellectuals also believed that deficiencies of the mind were inherited and that social programs should work to readjust and rebalance the mind and body in order to combat genetic tendencies toward feeblemindedness and weakness.[55] The rise of the mental hygiene movement, like euthenics and adjustment literature, incorporated ideals based on eugenic presuppositions of normality. Yet for many self-help writers, achieving normality was not enough, since streamlining oneself to fit with the demands of modernity involved rising above "native," or inborn, abilities. One way in which people could be sure to make the most of their genetic inheritance was to go beyond the so-called average. As Columbia University professor James Mursell argued in *Streamline Your Mind,* although the psychologist "cannot revise your heredity or make you over afresh, . . . he knows that if you really are the average man you are putting to productive use only a fraction of the power you possess." He continued, "You travel far more slowly and not nearly so far as you have a right to expect. You are throwing away much of your native energy in overcoming what the physical scientist calls 'parasitic drag.'"[56] In using the term *native energy,* Mursell showed that even though "inefficiency" might indeed be inherited, self-improvement and transformation could still take place, in spite of heredity. Consequently, in addition to supporting the eugenic rhetoric of inheritance, self-help achieved popularity by also addressing the "everyman," indicating that even those who were not so well born could increase their powers to rise above their station and "cure" natural weaknesses. Appealing in this multivalent way, self-help could attract a wide market without alienating those traditionally excluded by eugenic claims.

Nonetheless, *Life Begins at Forty* showed how the implementation of euthenic psychology, or "personal engineering," would lead to a utopian future that was overtly eugenic in design. In his chapter "The New World," Pitkin depicted a future United States consisting of scientifically organized towns where the decreasing population and the rising numbers of older and more intelligent citizens had resulted in a technologically enhanced world of abundance. In contrast to the poverty and idleness that surrounded Americans in the early years of the Depression, Pitkin's utopia was characterized by high living standards and leisure harnessed to the greater rationalization of society. "Utopia lies around the corner," he promised. This utopia, however, was not based on equal access to the benefits of technology or social equality. Once machinery could be used to replace "low-grade" workers, those who did not have the intelligence to adapt would be forced to migrate to separate communities:

> Already we begin to drive out the stupid, the unskilled, and the misplaced alien, not with whips or scorn but through the kindlier method of firing him for keeps. Watch the outbound stream of European and Mexican toilers, and you see this process in its first spurt. It must accelerate with the years, for the superior people are gaining *relatively* on the inferior. . . . Those who do not leave will be thrust farther and farther back into the lands of the hill-billy and the cracker. By 1975 the best quarter of a billion acres of America will hold none of their kind.[57] (Emphasis in original)

This supposedly utopian vision reappeared in his other books of the same year. By the end of *A Short Introduction to the History of Human Stupidity*, Pitkin called the inability of humans to progress in tandem with science a "plague of stupidity."[58] Again, he predicted that those with superior minds would eventually ascend, and he claimed that a superrace of intelligent individuals would devise ways of living separately from the inferior minds, if not extinguishing them altogether. The scientific measurement of IQ and intelligence would enable "a wholly new standard of normality" that "schools will use as the basis of their curricula."[59] Mostly, science was to reign supreme, overseeing an organic rise to rule of those deemed most intelligent and worthy. Above all other projects, he stated, the next major enterprise of the human race should be "self-analysis" so that society could learn from its mistakes and cultivate higher forms of living. Buying his self-help book, then, was the first step in reaching such echelons.

As historian Marouf Hasian has shown, "The most popular forms of eugenics . . . were not always the hard-line tales. . . . Rather, the interpretations of eugenics that were most common in the popular press seemed to be neo-Lamarckian in nature, where rhetors asked audiences to engage in a variety of social reforms that touched peoples' lives from 'the cradle' to 'the grave.'"[60] In 1932, self-help, like the New Deal, appealed in a broad way to socialists and libertarians as well as to those desiring greater social, individual, and even eugenic control. In the realm of popular literature, the rhetoric of the eugenics movement was highly influential in determining the perception of self-improvement and "recovery." The quest for political control and stability that appeared so important to national recovery in 1932 was thereby paralleled in self-help literature and popular culture with a sense that self-mastery would lead to collective social improvement.

Pitkin's books attempted to readjust Americans to a new social order so that they could reassert their "natural" vigor and authority over their mental and social inferiors. Adjustment by eliminating the irrational Hyde half of humanity was Pitkin's way of describing the route to full maturity, for in *Life Begins at Forty,* he claimed that "many of us pass through a long series of Jekyll and Hyde transformations, ending up with personalities in which mere vestiges of youth survive."[61] That the metaphor provided him with an apt psychological description for the problems of the nation is illustrated by its appearance in a chapter of his autobiography entitled "Dr. Jekyll and Mr. Hyde." Pitkin explained that the American melting pot had failed to blend nationalities and that it had instead created split or double personalities. The result was a schizophrenic citizenry of Jekyll and Hyde characters.[62]

Clearly, much of the rhetoric of political and eugenic recovery was recycled in such mass literature, yet at the same time, popular discourses contained a good deal of ambivalence beneath their apparent certainties. Only weeks after the close of 1932, Hitler emerged as the totalitarian leader in Germany, and the long shadow of Nazism fell over all allegedly democratic eugenic utopias.[63] "Fitting in" involved "improvements" that also had a more sinister side, as the film *Dr. Jekyll and Mr. Hyde* perhaps indicated.

On one level, the film provoked a simple horror at the apelike primitive Hyde, whose greedy sexual proclivities illustrated the base nature of all men when culture and intelligence were stripped away. But on another level, the cultured Jekyll began his scientific quest for his true self as a way of transforming a repressed and dissatisfied—overly modern—man. The release of his libidinous, primitive other half and his consequent battle with himself symbolized a scientific quest for perfection that had itself run out of control. The battle that ensued involved him in the murder of young women, and the ultimate result of his quest for "self-improvement" led to his death—for when the monster was shot, the cultured doctor was likewise terminated. At the end of the film, the monster's face melted back into the "civilized" physiognomy of the dead doctor, and the desire for normality was finally achieved at the cost of his life. The Hyde half of the American population was thus shown to be a scientifically invented abnormality that functioned to sustain the image of a cultured, educated normality—and the death of the doctor undid the falsely configured dichotomy to show that such apparent opposites were, in truth, one and the same. Directed by an expatriate Russian Jew during the overt rise of totalitarian fascism in Europe, the film highlighted a popular engagement with eugenic rhetoric that exhibited a double, or two-headed, fear: first, the fear of entropy and decay, and second, the fear that one would be judged and found wanting in a culture that threatened to remove all such examples of parasitic drag.

Although such popular cultural products often reflected an overarching conformity to a culturally produced image of normality based on eugenic thought, things were never so simple. Underlying the assertive confidence that the middle-aged man could regain ascendancy, *Life Begins at Forty* barely concealed an underlying fear of aging and degeneration in a culture that fetishized youthful vitality and physical strength. In many ways, the central aim of the book was to assuage the anxiety that those who had passed the prime of life (and perhaps their procreative or childbearing years) would no longer have a role in a dynamic, youthful, and energetic nation. To counteract this fear, Pitkin wrote in his chapter "Fools Die Young" that to have reached forty itself was an indication of eugenic success, as "the silliest, the stupidest, the most vicious, and the most reckless of your generation" tended to expire before that age. "One of the richest rewards of life after forty is the infrequency of fools" in one's life, he wrote.[64]

The photo of Roosevelt and Macfadden also exhibits an ambivalent rhetoric (fig. 2.1). The mirrored pose between the president-to-be and the self-improvement guru appears to indicate both the possibilities and the limits of self-help. For one thing, Roosevelt's success relies on concealing his disability; he remains sitting in the car, the ultimate symbol of mass production, not standing like the "natural" strongman Macfadden.

Unlike Roosevelt, Macfadden had been born a self-confessed weakling of poor Irish origin, the son of an alcoholic father and a mother with tuberculosis, and he was anything but well born—to many eugenicists, he should not have been born at all. Only a few months after the picture was taken, Americans elected Roosevelt despite his paralysis, not so much because he had eliminated it but because he had managed to fight it so well. Harnessing the strength and vitality of the American people was no simple process, whether of breeding, exercise, or environmental or economic reform. Yet at the time of the photograph, there were high hopes among many Americans that these reforms would work together to produce a fitter nation and a more secure future for all.

Notes

1. Walter B. Pitkin, *Life Begins at Forty* (New York: McGraw-Hill, 1932), 3.

2. Walter B. Pitkin, *A Short Introduction to the History of Human Stupidity* (New York: Simon and Schuster, 1932), 322–23.

3. This fact is illustrated by the common use of natural disasters, such as floods or earthquakes, as metaphors for the economic Depression; for examples, see Michael Denning, *The Cultural Front: The Laboring of American Culture in the Twentieth Century* (New York: Verso, 1997), 265. Michael Szalay discussed this in his *New Deal Modernism: American Literature and the Invention of the Welfare State* (Durham, NC: Duke University Press, 2000), 148.

4. The imagery of the forgotten man is discussed in chap. 2 of Susan Currell's *The March of Spare Time: The Problem and Promise of Leisure in the Great Depression* (Philadelphia: University of Pennsylvania Press, 2005).

5. Franklin D. Roosevelt, "The Forgotten Man," radio address, Albany, NY, April 7, 1932. Available at the Franklin and Eleanor Roosevelt Institute at http://www.feri.org/. Accessed January 18, 2006.

6. Earle Looker, "Franklin Roosevelt's Come-Back from Invalidism," *Physical Culture* 47, no. 4 (April 1932): 17–19, 55–57.

7. Roosevelt, "The Forgotten Man."

8. "Man of the Year 1932," *Time*, January 2, 1933. Available at http://www.time.com/time/special/moy/1932.html. Accessed August 7, 2005.

9. Edgar Sydenstricker, "The Vitality of the American People," in *Recent Social Trends in the United States: Report of the President's Research Committee on Social Trends*, ed. President's Research Committee on Social Trends (New York: McGraw-Hill, 1933), 632.

10. Quoted in Donald J. Mrozek, "Sport in American Life: From National Health to Personal Fulfillment, 1890–1940," in *Fitness in American Culture: Images of Health, Sport and the Body, 1830–1940*, ed. Kathryn Grover (Amherst: University of Massachusetts Press, 1989), 34. For further discussion of health and fitness movements in the United States, see Michael Anton Budd, *The Sculpture Machine: Physical Culture and Body Politics in the Age of Empire* (New York: New York University Press, 1997), and Harvey Green, *Fit for America: Health, Fitness, Sport and American Society* (New York: Pantheon Books, 1986).

11. Bernarr Macfadden, *The Encyclopedia of Health and Physical Culture*, vol. 4 (New York: Bernarr Macfadden Foundation, 1931, rev. ed. 1950), 1526, 1528.

12. Pitkin, *Life Begins at Forty*, 89.

13. The film *Dr. Jekyll and Mr. Hyde* (directed by Rouben Mamoulian) was released on December 31, 1931, thereby making it a popular film of 1932. See also *Freaks* (1932) (directed by Tod Browning).

14. Franklin D. Roosevelt, "The First Inaugural Address," March 4, 1933. Available at the Franklin and Eleanor Roosevelt Institute Web site, http://www.feri.org/. Accessed January 18, 2006. The full quotation is: "This great Nation will endure as it has endured, will revive and will prosper. So, first of all, let me assert my firm belief that the only thing we have to fear is fear itself—nameless, unreasoning, unjustified terror which paralyzes needed efforts to convert retreat into advance."

15. The influence of eugenics on the social sciences was discussed by Robert Proctor in "Eugenics among the Social Sciences: Hereditarian Thought in Germany and the United States," in *The Estate of Social Knowledge*, ed. JoAnne Brown and David K. Van Keuren (Baltimore, MD: Johns Hopkins University Press, 1991), 175–208.

16. Warren S. Thompson and Pascal Whelpton, "The Population of the Nation," in *Recent Social Trends in the United States: Report of the President's Research Committee on Social Trends*, ed. President's Research Committee on Social Trends (New York: McGraw-Hill, 1933), 56.

17. Stefan Kühl, *The Nazi Connection: Eugenics, American Racism and German National Socialism* (New York: Oxford University Press, 1994), 83. This transformation was intended, in part, to distance the movement from growing anti-Semitism in Germany. Wendy Kline also discussed this issue in her chapter on family health reform and marriage guidance from 1930 to 1960, in *Building a Better Race: Gender, Sexuality, and Eugenics from the Turn of the Century to the Baby Boom* (Berkeley: University of California Press, 2001), 124–56. On the history of the debate over the influence of environment within the eugenics movement, see Hamilton Cravens, *The Triumph of Evolution: The Heredity-Environment Controversy, 1900–1941* (Baltimore, MD: Johns Hopkins University Press, 1988).

18. "A Eugenics Programme for the United States," *Eugenics Review* 27, no. 4 (January 1936): 322.

19. This trend was also apparent in Scandinavian countries and Germany, as eugenically oriented governments sought policies to encourage a higher birthrate and a fitter population.

20. This essay is not intended to be a criticism of New Deal public health programs, which undoubtedly provided much-needed assistance to the economically disadvantaged at the time. I do, however, aim to show that popular eugenic rhetoric was grounded in ideas of cultural decline or improvement that appeared in parallel with recovery policy. Although welfare was designed for the betterment of society as a whole, eugenicists found the policy in keeping with their ideas about eugenic improvements via reform. I do not attempt to establish here how much official government sanction there was of eugenic policies, although more eugenic sterilizations took place in individual states during the Depression than ever before. For more on eugenics and politics of the Left, see Diane Paul, "Eugenics and the Left," *Journal of the History of Ideas* 45, no. 4 (Fall 1984): 567–90. A cultural parallel is the relationship between eugenics and modernist literature, discussed by David Bradshaw in his "Eugenics: 'They should certainly be killed,'" in *Concise Companion to Modernism*, ed. David Bradshaw (London: Blackwell, 2003), 35–55. For contemporary comments about eugenics and modernizing the state in the early thirties, see Frances Oswald, "Eugenical Sterilization in the United States," *American Journal of Sociology* 36, no. 1 (1930): 65–73.

21. For an examination of the shifting rhetoric of eugenics and the way eugenicists adapted it to a variety of political stances including feminism and socialism, see Marouf Arif Hasian, *The Rhetoric of Eugenics in Anglo-American Thought* (Athens: University of Georgia Press, 1996).

22. Frederick Osborn, "Development of a Eugenic Philosophy," *American Sociological Review* 2, no. 3 (June 1937): 395.

23. Frederick Osborn, "The Comprehensive Program of Eugenics and Its Social Implications," *Living* 1, nos. 2–3 (May-August 1939): 38.

24. Ibid.

25. Letter from Martha Gellhorn to Harry Hopkins, November 11, 1934, in Box 66, Harry Hopkins Papers, Franklin D. Roosevelt Library; available at http://newdeal.feri.org/hopkins/hop08.htm. Accessed January 18, 2006.

26. Ernest Groves, "Adaptations of Family Life," *American Journal of Sociology* 40, no. 6 (1935): 774.

27. Reported by Norman Himes in "Memorandum," *Eugenics Review* 27, no. 1 (1935): 22.

28. H. L. Mencken, "Utopia by Sterilization," *American Mercury* 41 (1937): 399, 408.

29. Sydenstricker, "The Vitality of the American People," 622. Sydenstricker used this as an example of the arguments that were current at the time, not necessarily as his own viewpoint.

30. Thompson and Whelpton, "The Population of the Nation," 56.

31. For discussions of success and self-help formulas, see Lawrence Chenoweth, *The American Dream of Success: The Search for the Self in the Twentieth Century* (North Scituate, MA: Duxbury, 1974); John Cawelti, *Apostles of the Self-Made Man* (Chicago: University of Chicago Press, 1965); Moses Rischin, ed., *The American Gospel of Success* (Chicago: Quadrangle Books, 1965); Richard Weiss, *The American Myth of Success* (New York: Basic Books, 1969); Richard Huber, *The American Idea of Success* (New York: McGraw-Hill, 1971); Stephen Recken, "Fitting In: The Redefinition of Success in the '30s," *Journal of Popular Culture* 27, no. 3 (Winter 1993): 205–22; Arthur Schlesinger, *Learning How to Behave* (New York: Macmillan, 1947); Sarah Newton, *Learning to Behave: A Guide to American Conduct Books before 1900* (Westport, CT: Greenwood Press, 1994).

32. See, for example, Mark Pittenger, *American Socialists and Evolutionary Thought, 1870–1920* (Madison: University of Wisconsin Press, 1993), and Richard Hofstadter, *Social Darwinism in American Thought* (Philadelphia: University of Pennsylvania Press, 1944).

33. Walter B. Pitkin, *Take It Easy: The Art of Relaxation* (New York: Simon and Schuster, 1935), 225.

34. Osborn, "The Comprehensive Program of Eugenics," 38.

35. Paul Popenoe, "Mate Selection," *American Sociological Review* 2, no. 5 (October 1937): 735, 742.

36. Walter B. Pitkin, *On My Own* (New York: Charles Scribner's Sons, 1944), 410.

37. Pitkin, *Life Begins at Forty*, 143.

38. Ibid., 106.

39. This relationship had been highlighted by a pioneer of euthenics, Ellen H. Richards, who wrote that human vitality relied fundamentally on two equally complementary conditions: heredity and hygiene. In *Euthenics*, she stated that "euthenics precedes eugenics, developing better men now, and thus inevitably creating a better race of men in the future. Euthenics is the term proposed for the preliminary science on which Eugenics must be based." See Richards, *Euthenics: The Science of a Controllable Environment: A Plea for Better Living Conditions as a First Step towards Higher Human Efficiency* (Boston: Whitcomb and Barrows, 1910), viii.

40. Walter B. Pitkin, *Capitalism Carries On* (New York: McGraw-Hill, 1935), 81, 82. Lewis Mumford also made this argument in *Technics and Civilization* (New York: Harcourt Brace, 1934), 256, 262–63, 303.

41. Walter B. Pitkin, *The Psychology of Achievement* (New York: Simon and Schuster, 1930), 3–4. This ratio fits exactly with the American Eugenics Society's billboard "Born to Be a Burden," which was shown at state fairs (Figure 9.2 in this volume). The flashing light panel on the bottom right claimed, "Every seven and a half minutes a high grade person is born in the United States [who] will have the ability to do creative work and be fit for leadership. About 4% of all Americans come within this class."

42. Ibid., 21.

43. Ibid., 473.

44. Pitkin, *Life Begins at Forty*, 124.

45. The following titles by Pitkin give some idea of this body of work: *The Twilight of the American Mind* (1928); *The Art of Rapid Reading: A Book for People Who Want to Read Faster and More Accurately* (1929); *The Psychology of Achievement* (1930); *How We Learn: A Book for Young People with Emphasis upon the Art of Efficient Reading* (1931); *The Consumer: His Nature and His Changing Habits* (1932); *A Short Introduction to the History of Human Stupidity* (1932); *More Power to You: A Working Technique for Making the Most of Human Energy* (1933); *Take It Easy: The Art of Relaxation* (1935); *The Chance of a Lifetime: Marching Orders for the Lost Generation* (1934); *Let's Get What We Want: A Primer in a Sadly Neglected Art* (1935); *Learning How to Learn* (1935); *Capitalism Carries On* (1935); *Escape from Fear* (1935).

46. For examples, see Jeffrey M. Blum, *Pseudoscience and Mental Ability: The Origins and Fallacies of the IQ Controversy* (New York: Monthly Review Press, 1978); Michael M. Sokal, ed., *Psychological Testing and American Society, 1890–1930* (New Brunswick, NJ: Rutgers University Press, 1990); Stephen Jay Gould, *The Mismeasure of Man* (New York: Norton, 1981).

47. Pitkin, *Life Begins at Forty*, 49.

48. Ethel Cotton, *Keeping Mentally Alive* (New York: Grosset and Dunlap, 1931), 202–3. Throughout the rest of the decade, the nonfiction best-seller list contained numerous other self-improvement books, such as Edmund Jacobson's *You Must Relax* (1934); Dorothea Brandt's *Wake Up and Live!* (1936); Marjorie Hillis's *Live Alone and Like It* (1937) and *Orchids on Your Budget* (1937); and Lin Yutang's *The Importance of Living* (1937). Each provided success formulas that offered a similar mix of consolation, inspiration, and despair.

49. Dorothy Canfield Fisher, *Learn or Perish* (New York: Horace Liveright, 1930), 13, 42.

50. Cotton, *Keeping Mentally Alive*; Dale Carnegie, *How to Win Friends and Influence People* (1936; repr., London: Vermillion, 2000).

51. Pitkin, *A Short Introduction*, 471.

52. Ibid., 5.

53. Ibid., 8.

54. Ibid., 524.

55. On the relationship of the mental health movement to eugenics, see Robert Dowbiggin, *Keeping America Sane: Psychiatry and Eugenics in the United States and Canada, 1880–1940* (Ithaca, NY: Cornell University Press, 1997).

56. James L. Mursell, *Streamline Your Mind* (Philadelphia: J. B. Lippincott, 1936), 10.

57. Ibid., 140–41.

58. Pitkin, *A Short Introduction*, 512.

59. Ibid., 519.

60. Hasian, *The Rhetoric of Eugenics*, 141–42. Hasian's book clearly illustrates how eugenic rhetoric displays numerous ambivalencies and inconsistencies that are linked to its widespread permutation in mass culture.

61. Pitkin, *Life Begins at Forty*, 57.

62. Pitkin, *On My Own*, 419.

63. Despite this, many such as Pitkin continued to see overpopulation of the "wrong" types as a cause of social decay. Even after World War II and the full revelation of Nazi atrocities, Pitkin held steadfastly to his eugenic beliefs. In a postscript to *Human Breeding and Survival* (1947), he wrote that "reckless breeding has become strangely like social cancer. Surplus of humans eats away all of us. Is there still time to diagnose this social evil and save us patients? Or have we done too little too late?" See postscript by Pitkin in *Human Breeding and Survival: Population Roads to Peace or War*, ed. Guy Irving Burch and Elmer Pendell (New York: Penguin Books, 1947), 130.

64. Pitkin, *Life Begins at Forty*, 43.

THREE

"Drilling Eugenics into People's Minds"

Expertise, Public Opinion, and Biopolitics in Alexis Carrel's *Man, the Unknown*

Andrés H. Reggiani

ABSTRACT

Andrés Reggiani's insights into the enigmatic Alexis Carrel—Nobel Prize–winning scientist, promoter of holistic medicine and mysticism, social visionary, and best-selling author of *Man, the Unknown* (1935)— focus on his eugenic beliefs as no historian yet has done. Reggiani covers the major biographical developments in Carrel's career, explaining en route how his eugenic beliefs took hold and became instrumental to his progressive project of establishing a "science of man" (in line with the Rockefeller Foundation's goal) *and* to his highly conservative political and social visions. In *Man, the Unknown*, Carrel critiqued democracy as a doomed political system, for he believed the common man was not "fit" for political decision making and leadership. Rather, he advocated the creation of a utopia autocratically ruled by an "enlightened elite" in which the "unfit" would be euthanistically disposed of in gas chambers. The key to this paradox—of progressive science allied to a highly conservative (anti)politics—lies in the authority Carrel extended to biology and medicine as responsible agents for the cultural and medical degeneration he perceived in modern society. Reggiani's essay explores Carrel's strange mixture of science, religion, and right-wing politics, paying special attention to the process by which scientists become experts—as producers and bearers of socially relevant data— obtain peer recognition, achieve high public status, and commit themselves to political agendas to recast society along "scientific" and technocratic lines. Reggiani argues for the necessity of reconsidering Carrel's conservative racist political views both for historical accuracy and because of the ongoing influence of his writings in the Middle East today.

On September 16, 1935, *Time* featured on its cover the Nobel laureate and best-selling author Alexis Carrel (1873–1944). The week before, Carrel had published *Man, the Unknown,* a book in which he endorsed an unorthodox brand of scientific holism, mysticism, and eugenics to overcome the decline of Western civilization. Released simultaneously in the United States and Europe, the book became a huge hit, eventually appearing in twenty translations in over fourteen countries. Carrel's worldwide reputation as a gifted scientist and his friendship with aviation hero Charles Lindbergh brought him wide public attention. The book's commercial success paved his way to becoming a popular cultural commentator. *Man, the Unknown* expressed a worldview that was modern with regard to experimental science yet profoundly reactionary in its social and political implications. On the one hand, it sought to convince ordinary readers that the ills of modern civilization could be cured only by substituting biological values for the hitherto predominant categories of political economy and civil society. On the other, it envisioned a politicized science to assist the "enlightened" powerful elite in the task of remaking humankind. Conceived as an authoritarian form of technocratic antipolitics, Carrel's eugenics offered both the state and the professional expert unlimited powers to "improve" the health of future generations. Put another way, he saw eugenics as politics by other means, that is, as a way of moving beyond the divisiveness and sectarianism of politics and making science the key to solving the crisis of civilization.

It may be a paradox that Carrel's status as a proselytizer of eugenics rose at a time when American scientific racism was on the wane. Yet as the other essays in this book show, despite growing scientific criticism of mainstream eugenicists as fanatical rabble-rousers, racial biological metaphors remained a continuing presence in the American psyche. This fact was reflected in the rising number of states that legalized compulsory eugenic sterilization after 1927, as well as in the subtext of many cultural artifacts produced before and after the New Deal. From this perspective, we may see Carrel's eugenics less as a clear set of scientific concepts than as "a modern way of talking about social problems in biologizing terms."[1]

Until very recently, scholars of U.S. history have neglected Carrel's role as a eugenics propagandist.[2] To begin with, his French roots and enduring attachment to France led many historians to underestimate his impact on the U.S. cultural scene. The same can be said about his aloofness from traditional politics, which made him an unlikely topic for those interested in the history of racism. Moreover, his habit of talking about public issues using spiritualistic metaphors and moralistic clichés placed him closer to the tradition of pseudoreligious thinkers than that of eugenics. What was to become the dominating image of Carrel until the 1990s was, to a large extent, the result of a conscious process of historical rewriting by Catholic authors who, after his death, purged him of his fascist eugenics and reinvented him as a "humanist." Carrel's rallying to the fascist camp and decision to return to France, together with the U.S. entry into World War II, may also have contributed to his erasure from public visibility.

Laboratory Work as Theater

Carrel was born into a Catholic family of the Lyon region in France in 1873. He attended a Jesuit school and in 1900 obtained his medical degree. In 1904, he emigrated to French-speaking Canada, after failing the competitive examinations to obtain a hospital position and being discredited by his confusing participation in a "miraculous" healing in Lourdes, the popular Catholic shrine in the French Pyrenees. At Montreal, the interest aroused by his new surgical technique known as "triangulation"—which consisted of sewing blood vessels along straight, triangle-shaped lines instead of around a circle, thus minimizing surgical manipulation and tissue damage—brought him to the attention of U.S. medical scientists. In 1906, Simon Flexner brought him into the newly created Rockefeller Institute for Medical Research in New York, where Carrel remained until his retirement in 1939. In 1912, the Swedish Academy of Sciences acknowledged his contribution to vascular surgery and organ transplantation by awarding him the Nobel Prize for Medicine. He became the youngest scientist to receive the award; he was also the one who brought the first Nobel Prize to U.S. medicine. In the 1910s, his interests shifted to cell research, and by the following decade, his Division of Experimental Surgery became the leading international center on tissue culture research. This line of inquiry led him to explore the possibility of cultivating whole organs. In the 1930s, he and Lindbergh conducted various experiments and built the first perfusion pump that permitted the culture of complete organs outside the body. By the middle of the decade, his scientific work had been accomplished.[3]

Carrel stands out as one of the most visible scientists of the first half of the twentieth century, a reputation he shared with his Rockefeller Institute colleague Jacques Loeb, a biologist who is best known for his theory of parthenogenesis (reproduction without fertilization). Carrel combined unsurpassable surgical skills with a flair for publicity. And from the outset, his scientific accomplishments were shrouded in an aura of myth. Consider, for example, the amazing blood transfusion that he performed on a two-day-old baby in 1908. No other scientist had tried such a risky operation before. Moreover, he had conducted all his experiments on cats and dogs and had no license to perform surgery on human beings in the United States. Yet despite the risks involved, he operated on the baby on a dinner table and without anesthesia. The surgical feat proved that such operations, although hard to perform for people without Carrel's remarkable manual dexterity, could be also practiced on small children. More important, by showing that laboratory animals were indispensable for improving human surgery, he helped undermine the antivivisectionists' campaign to ban experimentation with live animals.[4]

The award of the Nobel Prize in October 1912 further buttressed his prestige and visibility. He grew increasingly sensitive to public opinion and the media and staged his experiments deliberately in a theatrical fashion, as Bruno Latour described it.[5] His pathbreaking research on tissue and organ culture offers another case in point. Year after year, he claimed (incorrectly, as it turned out) that he was able to keep "alive" a culture of chick embryo cells started in January 1912. Few, however, cared to listen to those biologists who criticized his claims as an "abuse of language"; decades later, others disproved his assertions by showing that cells had a finite existence. Yet overnight, media coverage of Carrel's experiments fed all sorts of wild fantasies. He neither disavowed popular expectations about a soon-to-be-discovered "fountain of perpetual youth" nor objected to his culture of chicken cells being portrayed as an "immortal chicken heart" that laboratory technicians had to "snip off" from time to time in order to "hold it in bounds."[6]

It was not only the nature of the experiments but also their esoteric mise-en-scène that turned them into objects of public fascination. This was most evident in Carrel's elaborate aseptic procedures and picturesque operating room, which was built out of lead and painted darkly; moreover, he made it a requirement for all operating staff to use black surgical gowns and linen in order to reduce glare and maximize vision. This eccentric setting was well captured by a *Time* magazine article titled "Men in Black." On June 13, 1938, the magazine featured Carrel on its cover once again, this time accompanied by Lindbergh and their glass-built perfusion pump. The piece portrayed the French scientist as the "master of purified, black-clad servants" who ruled over a "pure and dark domain" of "black, dustless, germless laboratories."[7] Carrel and Lindbergh's joint work on organ culture furthered people's curiosity and encouraged rumors about mysterious endeavors undertaken at the Rockefeller Institute. A story circulated by the penny press stated that Lindbergh was going to have his heart removed and replaced "by an indestructible one from grateful Dr. Carrel's stock." Another account claimed that the scientist was working in a "closely guarded" laboratory with the purpose of creating a "robot" that would carry the heart, brain, and lungs of different persons "but no soul."[8]

The Crisis of Civilization—What Is to Be Done?

By the mid-1930s, Carrel was at the peak of his fame. He had achieved all his scientific goals, and his interests began to shift to broader issues outside his domain of expertise. This was not an uncommon path for a respected physician like him, who had been trained before the age of biomedical specialization. He was still rooted in the old tradition by which physicians perceived themselves not only as experts in the relief of human suffering but also as professionals with public responsibilities. The decision to express publicly his views on the crisis of civilization and "human problems"—a typically French concept—came rather late in his life. These new concerns coincided with the overall cultural atmosphere of the interwar years. They reflected, in part, the increasingly pessimistic mood with which the elites perceived the social and cultural transformations that shaped Western societies before and after World War I, a trend well illustrated by the success of authors preoccupied with the various manifestations of decline—national, cultural, racial—such as Oswald Spengler, Madison Grant, and T. Lothrop Stoddard, among others.[9] Partly, too, the new concerns were an expression of the cultural redefinition of biomedical practice known as holism, which became very popular in the 1920s and 1930s. Like many other physicians, Carrel felt that scientific medicine had not lived up to the expectations raised by its past victories over humanity's scourges. Increasing overspecialization and the substitution of laboratory-based research for the patient-oriented study of diseases generated an enormous amount of empirical data; yet, so the argument went, this progress was achieved at the cost of breaking down the sick person to a number of smaller units, each of them the territory of a medical subdiscipline. Medical holists, such as Carrel, shared the conviction that physicians should adopt an integral and comprehensive approach to healing that regarded the human person as a unity.[10]

Carrel's political concerns were also a response to the things he had always disliked about the United States, now magnified by the Depression. His views on the country were shaped by his experience as a European expatriate living in New York City, which was becoming the global capital. The megalopolis's eclectic and multiethnic landscape and the social and cultural pathologies associated with modern industrial cities were alien to his provincial sensibilities and struck him as a menace to his sense of order. It is no surprise, then, that he framed his reflections on the United States of the Depression era by collapsing biology and politics into the familiar notion of degeneration, through what Robert Nye, in a different context, has termed the "medical model of cultural decline."[11] Carrel's relationship with the eugenics movement dated back to 1911, when he became the surgical expert of an advisory committee on sterilization set up by the American Breeders Association (ABA) to study the "means for eliminating the defective strains from the population."[12] However, his initial approach to eugenics seems to have been determined by a preoccupation with the "degenerative diseases," a term commonly used for anomalies about which little was known and that were seen as connected to the nineteenth-century notion of degeneration—for example, cancer and cardiovascular and rheumatic diseases.

Carrel addressed these issues in a conference given at Johns Hopkins University in 1925. Before an audience of respected scientists, he sketched out a gloomy picture: modern medicine was able to protect people against infections that killed rapidly but left them exposed to slower and crueler diseases and to brain damage. The average person of his day, he said, was more likely to be "tortured by some form of cancer; afflicted with slow diseases of the kidneys, the circulatory apparatus, the endocrine glands; of becoming insane, suffering from nervous diseases; or of making himself miserable by his lack of judgment and his vices."[13]

For him, the solution lay in discovering the "fundamental principles" of physics and chemistry that ruled the functions of the body. This goal could only be accomplished by a pure physiological science devoted not to discovering useful medical applications but to seeking an "accurate conception of the universe." Physiology should be studied as a pure science far from hospitals and medical schools, by "men possessing the creative imagination and the spirit of the discoverers." Brought together in an "institute of pure science," physiologists, physicists, and chemists would create the "proper conditions for the building up of the science which will occupy the summit of the hierarchy of human knowledge, the science of thinking matter and energy." Only a pure science that sought knowledge in a disinterested way would make it possible to understand and master nature.[14]

A decade later, economic depression, social unrest, and the threat of another war gave these concerns a distinctively cultural and political turn. Degeneration lost its more or less specific medical meaning to become a loose concept that accommodated a broad spectrum of social and cultural phenomena, from cultural standardization to physical unfitness and asocial behavior. Out of these reflections came *Man, the Unknown,* an odd, three-hundred-page synthesis of disparate and loosely articulated topics. The book's opening and closing chapters offered a diagnosis of the crisis and a set of solutions to overcome it. There, the author laid out his holistic and illiberal weltanschauung. The middle chapters combined empirical descriptions of the body's physiological and adaptive functions with claims about spiritual phenomena.

Man, the Unknown's main thesis was simple and even unoriginal, for it argued that a profound crisis was destroying the very structure of Western civilization. The crisis was "neither due to the presence of M. Roosevelt in the White House, nor to that of Hitler in Germany nor of Mussolini in Rome."[15] It was a "crisis of man" caused by the "gap" between material and spiritual progress; this was an old argument first phrased in its modern form by German zoologist Ernst Häeckel and popularized in Carrel's time by sociologist William Ogburn's "cultural lag" theory. The Renaissance, the Enlightenment, and the Industrial Revolution enabled humans to master nature and expand the material bases of society, but they had failed to improve the knowledge of the person as a whole. As a result of this ignorance, society was built following ideological fancies instead of the "laws of nature, body, and soul."[16] The negative consequences of such a capricious civilization-building process expressed themselves in the political, social, and economic turmoil that swept much of the Western world. All this, however, was only the superficial manifestation of the deeper physical and psychological dislocations caused by biological degeneration.

Carrel shared his fellow American eugenicists' obsession with "feeble-mindedness" and other mental pathologies as both symptoms of degeneration and seeds of criminality. Echoing Eleanor Wembridge's *Life among the Lowbrows* (1931), he brought in statistics—so-called hard evidence—to raise awareness about the alarming increase of the "unfit":

> In the State of New York, according to C. W. Beers, one person out of every twenty-two has to be placed in an asylum at some time or other. In the whole of the United States the hospitals care for almost eight times more feeble-minded or lunatics than consumptives. Each year about sixty-eight thousand new cases are admitted to the insane asylums and similar institutions. If the admissions continue at such rate, about one million of the children and young people who are today attending schools and colleges will, sooner or later, be confined in asylums. In the state hospitals there were, in 1932, 340,000 insane. There were also in special institutions 81,580 feeble-minded and epileptics, and 10,930 on parole. These statistics do not include the mental cases treated in private hospitals. In the whole country, besides the insane, there are 500,000 feeble-minded. And in addition, surveys made under the auspices of the National Committee for Mental Hygiene have revealed that at least 400,000 children are so unintelligent that they cannot profitably follow the courses of the public schools. In fact, the individuals who are mentally deranged are far more numerous. It is estimated that several hundred thousand persons, not mentioned in any statistics, are affected with psychoneuroses. . . . The diseases of the mind are a serious menace. . . . They are to be feared, not only because they increase the number of criminals, but chiefly because they profoundly weaken the dominant white races.[17]

His definition of mental "weakness" was not constrained by any clinical criteria, however fuzzy and biased they might be; instead, it reflected an elitist view that likened popular tastes, such as "cheap literature" and "silly public entertainment," to a weak morality. Thus, he saw the panic triggered by Orson Welles's 1938 broadcast enacting an invasion from Mars as proof of a corrupted social fabric.[18]

This gloomy picture was compounded by class and ethnic birthrate differentials between the upper and lower strata of the society, a favorite topic among contemporary eugenicists. At stake was the survival of the white race, as Carrel made clear. "Europe and the United States are undergoing a qualitative as well as quantitative deterioration," he declared. "On the contrary, the Asiatics and the Africans, such as the Russians, the Arabs, the Hindus, are increasing with marked rapidity. Never have the European races been in such great peril as today. Even if a suicidal war is avoided, we will be faced with degeneration because of the sterility of the strongest and most intelligent stock."[19] The declining fertility of the white upper classes would result in the "extinction of the best elements of the race" because the offspring of the more prolific and poor immigrants from "primitive" European countries seemingly lacked "the value of those begotten by the first settlers of North America." He blamed the falling birthrate and the yielding of "inferior offspring" on an "ill conceived education, feminism, and a short-sighted selfishness" that turned women away from their reproductive and childrearing roles.[20] This situation existed because politics interfered in the otherwise healthy struggle for survival. Modern ideologies were doomed to fail because they were incapable of comprehending the human person as a unified whole. Political democracy was particularly pernicious because it hindered the development of the elite by making the struggle for survival no longer necessary. The feebleminded and the intellectually gifted should not be equal before the law, Carrel asserted. Electoral rights and access to higher education should be reserved to "fully developed" individuals. A certain elitist disdain notwithstanding, he praised the Fascist and Nazi regimes for unmasking the democratic "fallacy" and for giving passions and instincts their rightful place in politics. Unlike the liberal democracies, both fascism and Nazism succeeded in creating a "faith that drove the youth to sacrifice itself for an ideal." Fascism, he wrote, was superior because it "infuses with life the products of our mind."[21]

Carrel called for creating a comprehensive "science of man." This new, totalizing field of knowledge would study the human being as a totality. It would reject all conventions and apply the same rigorous criteria to physical, physiological, and psychological processes as well as to extrasensory phenomena.[22] To this end, he devised the Institute of Man, in which savants from all disciplines—or "Aristotle's composites"—would weld their individual thought into a synthetic whole through collective thinking. He borrowed these ideas from the Rockefeller Foundation's president, Raymond Fosdick, who, in *The Old Savage in the New Civilization* (1928), had argued that the complexity of the problems faced by modern society could only be addressed by the collective effort of multidisciplinary experts.[23] Carrel likened them to the medieval monks, warriors, and savants who rose out of the ashes of the Roman Empire. Like their ancient forebears, the universal scientists of the future would organize themselves in secret groups. Isolated from society and free from the burdens of ordinary life, this "higher council of learning" would become an "immortal brain" devoted to engineering a new civilization. The knowledge thus generated would enable "democratic rulers as well as dictators" to impose on the "degraded majority," either "by persuasion or by force," a civilization suitable to humankind.[24]

He urged "drilling" eugenics into people's minds as a social necessity that required "the sacrifice of many individuals." Eugenics was, for him, the only means left to develop a healthy elite at a time when, due to progress in medicine and public health, natural selection was no longer at work. Convinced that social status and biological quality were intimately connected, he proposed several alternatives to check the "predominance of the weak." On the one hand, he called for the substitution of new biological classes for traditional social categories. In the future, individuals should be allowed to rise or sink to the social level that was appropriate to their biological fitness. Trying to improve the weak "artificially" would be useless, for social divisions were not the result of chance, conventions, or uneven distribution of power but a reflection of people's biological worth. Poor peasants and industrial workers owed their inferior status not to social injustice but to their "hereditary organic and psychological weakness." On the other hand, he proposed creating a nonhereditary "biological aristocracy" with the offspring of men of exceptional qualities—"imaginative criminals, great revolutionaries and high-handed businessmen." It was in these families that some of the "ancestral qualities" of the founders of civilization lay hidden, not in those who "muddled along their lives in inferior positions."

Carrel also endorsed various forms of "voluntary" eugenics to discourage the unfit from marrying. Education, he argued, should teach prospective husbands and wives to ponder a partner's biological worth as seriously as they consider material wealth. Thus, he hoped that everyone would come to realize that marrying into a family contaminated by syphilis, cancer, tuberculosis, insanity, or feeblemindedness would be as wretched a decision as marrying into the poor class. Because marriage should serve the goal of eugenics, gender roles had to be "clearly defined." Therefore, individuals should never be allowed to manifest sexual tendencies, mental characteristics, and ambitions of the opposite gender. Likewise, any conduct that prevented the fulfillment of an individual's biological duties should be discouraged. Carrel's peculiar understanding of eugenics excluded any consideration of a person's right to decide on matters concerning his or her life and body. Instead, the concept of "voluntary" eugenics betrayed his ambivalence with regard to the current state of medical knowledge, which did not provide conclusive evidence about the heritability of many degenerative diseases. With the exception of the insane and the criminal, the groups earmarked for negative eugenics, he remained pessimistic about the results that could be expected from medical examinations. Therefore, he considered it "unadvisable to kill sickly or defective children as we kill the weaklings in a litter of puppies."[25]

The final chapter of *Man, the Unknown* closed with a straightforward justification of negative eugenics. How, Carrel asked, should society deal with the "immense number of defectives and criminals"? To answer this question, he followed the arguments favored by most eugenicists in times of economic hardship and collapsed biological worth into financial constraints. He warned that "normal individuals" could no longer be burdened with the "heavy and unacceptable" costs of preserving "the useless and harmful beings" living in prisons and mental asylums. Society should deal with them in a more "economic" manner. He proposed that

> those who have murdered, robbed while armed with automatic pistol or machine gun, kidnapped children, despoiled the poor from their savings [and] misled the public in important matters, *should be humanely and economically disposed of in small euthanasia*

institutions supplied with proper gases. A similar treatment could be advantageously applied to the insane, guilty of criminal acts. Modern society should not hesitate to organize itself with reference to the normal individual. Philosophical systems and sentimental prejudices must give way before such necessity.[26]

These extreme proposals were neither exceptional nor a mere rhetorical device to shock the reader. Two examples illustrate this point. In December 1935, two months after the release of the book, Carrel was invited to give a talk at the New York Academy of Medicine. Before a tightly packed audience, he criticized the medically assisted prolongation of life as a "far greater calamity than death itself" that burdened civilized countries "with those who should be dead." He hailed premature death as a "builder of civilization" because it eliminated "the weak, the diseased, and fools."[27] Around that time, he also received a letter from the German publisher Deutsche Verlags-Anstalt, asking him to make certain changes for the German edition of his book. The publisher wanted Carrel to insert an explicit reference to the racial laws recently adopted by the Nazis.[28] It may be recalled that by the end of 1935, Hitler's regime had enforced several major pieces of racial-biological legislation. In July 1933, the Law for the Prevention of Progeny with Hereditary Diseases substituted compulsory for voluntary sterilization and extended the range of sicknesses regarded as "hereditarily determined." In November 1933, the Law against Dangerous Habitual Criminals allowed criminal-biological experts to confine and castrate persons with two or more convictions for sexual crimes. Finally, in June 1935, the Hereditary Health Courts were empowered to sanction abortions for women who had been categorized as "hereditarily ill." As a result, between January 1934 and the outbreak of World War II in September 1939, some 320,000 people were compulsorily sterilized for allegedly having "recessive" genes that might endanger their offspring. Carrel agreed to the publisher's request and submitted without delay the following text: "The German government has taken energetic measures against the propagation of the defective, the mentally diseased, and the criminal. The ideal solution would be the suppression of each of these individuals as soon as he has proven himself to be dangerous."[29]

We may never know whether his idea of "suppressing" people paralleled Hitler's. In any case, the Nazis did not need Carrel's ideas, but they could use his name to lend scientific respectability to their racial utopia or, worse, present him as their source of inspiration. The evidence bears out this reading of Carrel's relationship with Nazi racism. At the Nuremberg Doctors' Trial of 1946, the head of the program for killing the mentally handicapped, Karl Brand, claimed that the sterilization and elimination of "life not worth of living" (*lebensunwerten Lebens*) was based on American ideas and experiments, and he cited Madison Grant's *Passing of the Great Race* and Carrel's *Man, the Unknown*.[30]

The Best-Selling Eugenicist

After some initial hesitation, Harper and Brothers agreed to publish Carrel's manuscript, based on the author's very visible collaboration with Lindbergh and the public's ongoing fascination with the aviator after the tragic death of his child. In fact, the book was released shortly after the trial and conviction of Bruno Hauptmann, the alleged kidnapper and murderer of Lindbergh's baby. To maximize sales, Harper and Brothers sold rights to publish the book's chapters in condensed format to *Reader's Digest*, for by the mid-1930s, the magazine had a circulation of 1.8 million copies. This smart marketing move brought Carrel to the attention of thousands of American households. After *Reader's Digest* published the first abridged version in December 1935, the book's sales jumped phenomenally, exceeding the most optimistic expectations; some libraries had to set up waiting lists for the coveted copies. The thirty-five hundred copies sold before *Reader's Digest* began publishing condensed versions increased to around two hundred thousand by 1940. In France, the book sold a quarter of a million copies by 1940, when many French came to interpret the crushing defeat by Germany as a confirmation of Carrel's apocalyptic forecasts. What was even more remarkable was the book's amazing success outside the United States and France.[31]

Although the 1920s and 1930s were a period of pseudobibliophilia, with many people buying books but not necessarily reading them, certain clues allow us to speculate about the possible reasons for the book's success. Bernt Hansen has argued that the favorable depiction of physicians in comics and other popular genres in the 1940s illustrated the rising reputation of medical doctors in American mass culture.[32] The letters sent to Carrel by hundreds of readers give us another perspective on the responses to the book and the ways it was being read. Most readers acknowledged the author's ability to convey, in accessible language, ideas that the nonexpert public would otherwise have found too intricate and obscure. They thanked him for making the book a fascinating read from which "an ignorant house-wife" and "the man on the street" could profit.[33] By and large, conservative readers shared Carrel's commonsensical ideas about the crisis, and his attack on materialism and his vindication of spiritual values appealed to religious audiences. Catholic, Protestant, and Jewish community leaders welcomed the book as "an oasis of beauty in a wilderness" and a precious source of inspiration for their existential quest.[34] Stephen Wise, rabbi of the New York City Free Synagogue, said to his congregation that *"Man, the Unknown* 'is not merely a great book, it is epochal.' It deals with the destiny of the human genius as significantly as Darwin dealt with the origins of species. I said to the congregation, 'it is not a book to be talked about from the pulpit, but to be discussed in seminar fashion for many hours with a class.'"[35] Few, if any, of Carrel's religious contemporaries protested his eugenics. In fact, one of the most striking things about Carrel, who was raised and remained a Catholic (albeit an unorthodox one), was the way in which his nonscientific work was selectively appropriated, both in the 1930s and afterward. In his own lifetime, religious authors either agreed explicitly with his racist views or took them for granted, as part of a conservative consensus about the corrupt nature of modern civilization.[36]

Understandably, most criticism, especially from liberal-minded thinkers, was directed against his utopian and illiberal elitism. The mid-September issue of *Time* featured, along with a cover portrait of Carrel, a long article mocking some of his ideas as a "colossal joke" and "wild rant."[37] The writer Anne Morrow, Lindbergh's wife and a close friend of Carrel's, ridiculed the scientist's biological elite as a breed of "tall soft-headed athletes."[38] A student from Barnard College labeled *Man, the Unknown* a book "written to and for men" and reminded the Frenchman that many of his ideas were being carried out in the fascist countries, "where women are secluded entirely and are made to produce as many children as possible."[39] An enraged New Yorker attacked him for using his scientific reputation and the terminology of science to make "vain and incoherent speculations" based on prejudices.[40]

In one lengthy review, published by the Sunday edition of the *New York Times,* a Johns Hopkins University professor of biometrics and vital statistics, Raymond Pearl, praised *Man, the Unknown* as the first book that gave "the history of the soul" its rightful place and celebrated the author for his "bold frontal attack upon the smug and narrow orthodoxy" of traditional biology and medicine.[41] Yet Pearl skirted the implications of Carrel's eugenics altogether. This omission is revealing if we consider Pearl's troubled relationship with eugenics. He had played a fundamental role in the eugenics movement and had served with Carrel as an expert on the ABA advisory committee on sterilization. In the 1920s, Pearl distanced himself from the fanaticism and propaganda of mainstream eugenics but avoided aligning himself publicly with its detractors. He refused, for example, to support the campaign led by the anthropologist Franz Boas to unmask Nazi pseudoscientific racism.[42]

Because of the unusual topical mix in *Man, the Unknown*, it is difficult to determine the precise role of each of Carrel's arguments in the reception of the book. To be sure, it was about eugenics. Yet it was more than just an endorsement of scientific racism, for Carrel's biopolitics worked as the underlying subtext of a much broader discussion about decline. For instance, his criticism of urban civilization and people's diminishing capacity to endure hardships due to excessive comfort, inadequate eating habits, and a sedentary lifestyle all had a special appeal to advocates of physical fitness and environmental reform. Uttered by such a respected scientist, these clichés acquired the status of a revealed truth. It was only at the end of the book that Carrel laid out his eugenics openly and in a forceful manner, after the reader had become convinced that something radical had to be done to save civilization. However, accepting his arguments depended on the extent to which eugenics discourse had already shaped the social and cultural imagination and concerns of ordinary people. In other words, the popular reception of his ideas must be understood within the context of a society that had been exposed to a racial-biological discourse for more than three decades.

Man, the Unknown opened new career possibilities for Carrel as a popular "thinker" and intellectual of sorts. In late December 1935, he made one of his rare appearances in public at the New York Academy of Medicine. According to *Time* and *Newsweek*, five thousand people fought their way into the academy's Hoosack Hall (which had only seven hundred seats) to hear the Nobel laureate talk about "the mystery of death"; two thousand of them had to be driven away by the police. The following morning, the *Her-*

ald Tribune, the *New York Times,* and other local papers ran lengthy articles on the event. However, Carrel's controversial statements aroused bitter criticism. Some accused him of endorsing "mercy killing"; others, including his new boss at the Rockefeller Institute, Herbert Gasser, and the University of Chicago physiologist Julius A. Carson, accused him of "misleading the public and injuring science for the shallow fame of personal publicity."[43] Annoyed, Carrel dismissed these attacks as personally motivated and continued speaking in public at the University of Chicago, Darmouth College, and other places.[44] More important, in 1939, as *Man, the Unknown* went through a paperback edition for which he wrote a new and more political preface, Carrel signed up with *Reader's Digest* to write a set of articles on popular health and self-improvement; by and large, they would provide tips for living a healthy, happy, and wholesome life.[45]

Carrel also made plans for setting up the Institute of Man. Influential individuals and prestigious institutions pledged their support to the project. Lindbergh gave a piece of land in Hopewell, New Jersey; Henry Ford offered the facilities of the Ford Hospital in Detroit; and *Reader's Digest* president Dewitt Wallace and the food entrepreneur W. K. Kellogg pledged generous financial contributions. Former Firestone Company executive and religious activist James Newton, a close friend of Carrel's and Lindbergh's, lobbied to bring them into his Christian fundamentalist organization, the Oxford Group for Moral Rearmament, an anti-Communist group set up in the 1920s by James Buchman. Likewise, Yale and the University of Michigan invited him to continue his work on their campuses after retirement from the Rockefeller Institute.[46]

By late 1939, however, the apparent enthusiasm for the Institute of Man showed signs of subsiding. Most of the fault for this seems to have been Carrel's, as he remained unable to decide whether to set up a small center for biological research or a eugenics think tank. Moreover, as war in Europe drew closer, his fascist views left him increasingly isolated within the scientific community. He favored making unlimited concessions to Hitler and lashed out at the antifascist campaign in the American liberal press—and its criticism of Lindbergh's pro-Nazi neutralism—as Jewish and Bolshevik propaganda.[47] After his homeland was defeated militarily in 1940, he returned to France, and in 1941, he went into the service of Marshal Philippe Pétain's pro-Nazi Vichy regime, from which he obtained full support to set up an "institute for the regeneration of the race." Between

1941 and 1944, he headed a government institution that carried out population research with mild eugenic goals, the French Foundation for the Study of Human Problems. He died in Paris in late 1944, amid accusations of treason.[48]

Today, Carrel has vanished almost completely from American popular memory, except, perhaps, among biologists, physicians, and religious leaders. Abroad, however, he lives on in public, educational, and scientific organizations in many countries. Streets, schools, universities, and international conferences are named after him. In early 2000, for example, British biologists acknowledged his scientific contributions by naming two of the first cloned piglets Alexis and Carrel—a decision not well received in France, where he is now mostly remembered as a fascist and racist.[49] Moreover, Carrel has recently been appropriated by radical Islamists in the Arab world to attack Western civilization. The use of his ideas by the very people whose rise in world politics he saw as an example of Western decline reveals the topicality and paradoxical plasticity of his antimodernism.[50] Today, *Man, the Unknown* is still in print, but its current readership is no longer limited to the traditional bourgeois conservative and Catholic audiences of the 1930s through the 1950s. Instead, its literary mix of reactionary spiritualism and radical biopolitics has proven remarkably adaptable to changing circumstances and audiences, offering food for thought—and action—to late-twentieth-century Occidentalists.[51] The key to this adaptability lies in the author's ability to exploit the enduring image of the United States as a metaphor of a socially and culturally disruptive modernity. Carrel's eugenics can be best understood within this multilayered discourse of decline and loss of authenticity.

Notes

1. Frank Dikotter, "Race Culture: Recent Perspectives on the History of Eugenics," *American Historical Review* 103 (1998): 467–78.

2. For a historiographical update on eugenics, see Dikotter, "Race Culture"; Robert A. Nye, "The Rise and Fall of the Eugenics Empire: Recent Perspectives on the Impact of Biomedical Thought in Modern Society," *Historical Journal* 36 (1993): 687–700; and Philip J. Pauly, "The Eugenics Industry—Growth or Restructuring?" *Journal of the History of Biology* 26 (1993): 131–45. Recent research on American eugenics, in addition to those works listed in the notes of the preceding essays in this volume, include Edwin Black, *The*

War against the Weak: Eugenics and America's Campaign to Create a Master Race (New York: Four Walls, Eight Windows, 2003); Christina Rosen, *Preaching Eugenics: Religious Leaders and the American Eugenics Movement* (Oxford: Oxford University Press, 2004); Nancy Ordover, *American Eugenics: Race, Gender, Queer Anatomy and the Science of Nationalism* (Minneapolis: University of Minnesota Press, 2003); Nancy Gallagher, *Breeding Better Vermonters: The Eugenics Project in the Green Mountain State* (Hanover, NH: University Press of New England, 1999); William H. Tucker, *The Science and Politics of Racial Research* (Urbana: University of Illinois Press, 1994); and Philip R. Reilly, *The Surgical Solution: A History of Involuntary Sterilization in the United States* (Baltimore, MD: Johns Hopkins University Press, 1991).

3. For an English-language discussion of Carrel's scientific work, see Andrés Reggiani, *Mystic Eugenics: Alexis Carrel and the Sociobiology of Decline* (New York: Berghahn Books, 2006).

4. On the repercussions of the operation, see John D. Rockefeller, "Some Random Reminiscences of Men and Events," *World's Work* 17 (1908): 10,997–98; Samuel W. Lambert, "Melena Neonatorum with Report of a Case Cured by Transfusion," *Medical Records of New York* 73 (1908): 885; T. Wood Clarke, "The Birth of Transfusion," *Journal of the History of Medicine* (Summer 1949): 337–38; and L. G. Walker, "Carrel's Direct Transfusion of a Five-Day-Old Infant," *Surgery, Gynecology, and Obstetrics* 137 (1973): 494–96. For a critical appraisal of medical experimentation on humans and animals, see Anita Guernini, *Experimentation with Humans and Animals: From Galen to Animal Rights* (Baltimore, MD: Johns Hopkins University Press, 2003), and Susan Lederer, *Subjected to Science: Human Experimentation in America before the Second World War* (Baltimore, MD: Johns Hopkins University Press, 1997).

5. Bruno Latour and Steve Woolgar, *Laboratory Life: The Construction of Scientific Facts* (London: Sage, 1978).

6. See, for example, Geneviève Grandecourt, "The Immortality of Tissues: Its Bearing on the Study of Old Age," *Scientific American*, October 26, 1912, 344; Grandecourt, "What Is Old Age? Carrel's Research on the Mechanism of Physical Growth," *Scientific American*, November 29, 1913, 400; Carl Snyder, "Carrel, the Mender of Men," *Collier's*, November 16, 1914, 12–13; Lewis Freeman, "Healing Wounded Soldiers to Order," *World's Work* 23 (1917): 431–32; "Chicken Dead since 1912, Heart May Beat Forever," *Newsweek*, December 23, 1933, 28; George Kent, "Dr. Alexis Carrel Believes We Can Read Each Other's Thoughts," *American Magazine*, March 1936, 20–21, 142–44; Albert H. Ebeling, "Dr. Carrel's Immortal Chicken Heart," *Scientific American* 166 (1942): 22–24; H. S. Williams, "When Does the Body Die? Experiments in Sustaining Life in Tissues of Dead Animals," *World Today* 21 (1911): 1454-58; "Potential Immortality," *Literary Digest* 44 (1912): 1153–54; "Carrel and the Span of Life," *Survey* 29 (1912): 170–71; Frank P. Stockbridge,

"New Miracles of Health," *Cosmopolitan* 54 (1912): 75–84; B. J. Hendrick, "On the Trail of Immortality," *McClure's Magazine* 40 (1913): 304–17; J. Middleton, "Flesh That Is Immortal," *World's Work* 28 (1914): 590–93; "Immortality of Animal Tissue and Its Significance," *Golden Bank* 7 (1928): 787–89. For an updated appraisal, see Jan Witkowski, "Carrel's Cultures," *Science* 247 (1990): 1385–86; Witkowski, "Carrel's Immortal Cultures," *Medical History*, vol. 24, no. 2 (1980): 129–42; and Witkowski, "Alexis Carrel and the Mysticism of Tissue Culture," *Medical History* 23 (1979): 279–96.

7. "Men in Black: Dr. Carrel's Tissue Culture Research," *Time*, June 13, 1938.

8. "Mechanical Heart-Lung Keeps Life Going in Showcase," *Newsweek*, June 29, 1935; "Glass Heart," *Time*, July 1, 1935; Arthur Train Jr., "More Will Live," *Saturday Evening Post*, July 23, 1938, 5–7; letter from Lou Wedemar to Alexis Carrel, undated, and letter from Carrel to Wedemar, October 1, 1936, in Alexis Carrel Papers, Georgetown University (hereafter cited as ACP).

9. Madison Grant, *The Passing of the Great Race: The Racial Basis of European History* (New York: Charles Scribner's, 1916); T. Lothrop Stoddard, *The Revolt against Civilization: The Menace of the Under-Man* (New York: Charles Scribner's Sons, 1922); Oswald Spengler, *The Decline of the West*, trans. Charles F. Atkinson (New York: Alfred A. Knopf, 1928). For a comparative analysis of the concept of decline, see Arthur Herman, *The Idea of Decline in Western History* (New York: Simon and Schuster, 1997), and Daniel Pick, *Faces of Degeneration: A European Disorder, c. 1848–c. 1918* (New York: Cambridge University Press, 1996).

10. For a comparative discussion of biomedical holism, see Christopher Lawrence and George Weisz, eds., *Greater than the Parts: Holism and Biomedicine, 1920–1950* (New York: Oxford University Press, 1998).

11. Robert A. Nye, "Degeneration and the Medical Model of Cultural Decline in Fin-de-Siècle France," in *Political Symbolism in Modern Europe: Essays in Honor of George L. Mosse*, ed. Seymour Drescher, 19–41 (Ithaca, NY: Cornell University Press, 1982).

12. Bleecker Van Wagenen, "Preliminary Report of the Committee of the Eugenic Section of the American Breeders Association to Study and to Report on the Best Practical Means for Cutting Off the Defective Germ Plasm in the Human Population," in *Problems in Eugenics: Papers Communicated to the First International Congress Held at the University of London, July 24th–30th, 1912*, ed. Eugenics Education Society (Adelphi, England: Eugenics Education Society, 1912), 460–79.

13. Alexis Carrel, "The Future Progress of Medicine," *Scientific Monthly* 21 (1925): 55.

14. Ibid., 56–57.

15. Alexis Carrel, *Man, the Unknown* (New York: Harper and Brothers, 1939), xiii. I have also used the Penguin edition of 1948. Subsequent references to each edition are indicated by the year of publication.

16. Carrel, *Man, the Unknown* (1939), ix–xxv.

17. Carrel, *Man, the Unknown* (1948), 147–48.

18. Carrel, *Man, the Unknown* (1939), xii.

19. Ibid., xi.

20. Carrel, *Man, the Unknown* (1948), 93, 274.

21. Carrel, *Man, the Unknown* (1939), xiv; (1948), 249–50.

22. Carrel, *Man, the Unknown* (1939), 56–57; (1948), 121–22, 278–79.

23. Carrel, *Man, the Unknown* (1939), 278–91; Raymond Fosdick, *The Old Savage in the New Civilization* (Garden City, NY: Doubleday, Doran, 1928), and *Wanted: An Aristotle* (Garden City, NY: Doubleday, Doran, 1924).

24. Carrel, *Man, the Unknown* (1939), 276–77, 291–96.

25. Ibid., 296–302.

26. Ibid., 290–91. Emphasis added.

27. Alexis Carrel, "The Mystery of Death," in *Medicine and Mankind*, ed. Iago Galdston (London: D. Appleton, 1936), 197–217.

28. Letter from Gustav Kilpper to Alexis Carrel, December 16, 1935, ACP.

29. Letter from Alexis Carrel to Gustav Kilpper, January 1, 1936, ACP. The German edition of Carrel's book was published in 1937 as *Der Mensch, das unbekannte Wesen*.

30. Stefan Kühl, *The Nazi Connection: Eugenics, American Racism, and German National Socialism* (New York: Oxford University Press, 1994), 101.

31. Cass Canfield, *Up and Down and Around: A Publisher Recollects the Time of His Life* (New York: Harper's Magazine Press, 1971), 128–31.

32. Bernt Hansen, "Medical History for the Masses: How American Comic Books Celebrated Heroes of Medicine in the 1940s," *Bulletin of the History of Medicine* 78, no. 1 (2004): 148–91.

33. Letter from A. Folliot and R. Ricard to Alexis Carrel, October 28 and December 12, 1935, ACP.

34. Letter from Minister Charles Hardesty (Methodist Episcopal Church of Sheridan, Wyoming) and Dean Dumper (Trinity Cathedral of Newark, New Jersey) to Alexis Carrel, March 16 and 22, 1936, ACP.

35. Letter from Rabbi Stephen Wise to Alexis Carrel, December 31, 1935, ACP.

36. For the American case, see Stanley L. Jaki, "Two Lourdes Miracles and a Nobel Laureate: What Really Happened?" September 13, 1998, available at www.cathmed.org (February 1999); Joseph Durkin, *Hope for Our Time: Alexis Carrel on Man and Society* (New York: Harper and Row, 1965); John O'Brien, *Roads to Rome: The Intimate Personal Stories of Converts to the Catholic Faith* (New York: Macmillan, 1954); and Charles Lindbergh's preface to Carrel's *The Voyage to Lourdes*, trans. Virgilia Peterson (New York: Harper, 1950).

37. "Carrel's Man," *Time*, September 16, 1935.

38. Anne Morrow Lindbergh, *The Flower and the Nettle: Diaries and Letters of Anne Morrow Lindbergh, 1936–1939* (New York: Harcourt Brace Jovanovich, 1976), 78.

39. Letter from Rosamund Gleeson to Alexis Carrel, undated, ACP.

40. Letter from Theodor Spitz to Alexis Carrel, 1940, ACP.

41. Raymond Pearl, "Dr. Carrel Ponders the Nature and Soul of Man," *New York Times Book Review*, September 29, 1935, 3, 23.

42. Kühl, *The Nazi Connection*, 68.

43. "Herald of Immortality Foresees Suspended Animation," *Newsweek*, December 21, 1935; "Points by Prizemen," *Time*, December 23, 1935.

44. See also his speeches delivered at the Association of Life Insurance Presidents and the American Association for Health, Physical Education, and Recreation, on December 3, 1937, and December 26, 1940. Carrel, "The Prolongation of Life," *Vital Speeches of the Day*, January 15, 1938, 200–202; Carrel, "What Type of Physical Fitness for America?" *Vital Speeches of the Day*, February 13, 1941, 187–88.

45. Letter from Walter Price to Alexis Carrel, December 13, 1935; letters from Alexis Carrel to Attale Guigou, December 16, 1938, May 3, June 2, and June 13, 1939, all ACP. Carrel wrote a series of five articles for *Reader's Digest:* "Breast Feeding" (June 1939), "Married Love" (July 1939), "Do You Know How to Live" (August 1939), "Work in the Laboratory of Your Private Life" (September 1940), and "Prayer Is Power" (March 1941).

46. Letter from Edward Moore to Alexis Carrel, March 14, 1939, ACP; Emily Newell Blair, "What I Found Out about the Oxford Movement," *Liberty* (January 1, 1938); James Newton, *Uncommon Friends: Life with Thomas Edison, Henry Ford, Harvey Firestone, Alexis Carrel and Charles Lindbergh* (San Diego, CA: Harcourt Brace Jovanovich, 1987).

47. Letter from Alexis Carrel to Attale Guigou, November 16, 1938, and October 29, 1940, ACP. See also Max Wallace, *American Axis: Henry Ford, Charles Lindbergh, and the Rise of the Third Reich* (New York: St. Martin's Press, 2003).

48. On Carrel's activities during the German occupation of France, see Andrés Reggiani, "Alexis Carrel, the Unknown: Eugenics and Population Research under Vichy," *French Historical Studies* 25 (2002): 331–56.

49. Nigel Hawkes, "Clones Raises Transplant Hopes," *Times* (London), March 15, 2000.

50. On the discovery of Carrel by Islamic thought, see Reggiani, *Mystic Eugenics*.

51. Ian Buruma and Avishai Margalit, *Occidentalism: The West in the Eyes of Its Enemies* (New York: Penguin Press, 2004).

FOUR

"Explaining Sexual Life to Your Daughter"

Gender and Eugenic Education in
the United States during the 1930s

Michael A. Rembis

ABSTRACT

In this essay, Michael Rembis discusses the use of eugenics education manuals as one strategy to make contemporary eugenic theory relevant and accessible to a broader American public, particularly to well-educated, white, middle-class girls and women prior to marriage. The enforcement of sterilization statutes was accomplishing the goals of negative eugenics, but in the United States, unlike in some European countries, laws were not widely passed to enforce the goals of positive eugenics. Instead, education in the home and classroom paved the way to informed personal choice, a choice that conservative mainline eugenicists hoped would lead more women to forgo a college education in favor of early, responsible motherhood (or at least to take a course on "mothercraft" while in college). Rembis examines the American Eugenics Society's goals for eugenic education, as well as those of other organizations such as Paul Popenoe's Institute of Family Relations, and the manuals created for home, high school, and college use. In doing so, he broadens our understanding of the reach of eugenics to a younger audience, an influence that perhaps bore fruit in the postwar baby boom. Like Kline, Coffey, and others in this volume, Rembis concurs that during the social and economic upheavals of the 1930s, women were the primary target for eugenicists' efforts to stabilize and enlarge the eugenic family.

Parents look to it that your children are taught
to recognize the difference between a rose or a
thistle. It may save them a lifetime of heartache
and misery.

HERMAN H. RUBIN, *Eugenics and Sex Harmony*[1]

The education of our youth should include the
knowledge which would prepare them to
make the proper choice in marriage, not
merely on account of the happiness of the
contracting parties, but for the sake of the
children which may result from the union.

SAMUEL J. HOLMES, *The Eugenic Predicament*[2]

"Explaining Sexual Life to Your Daughter" is the title of one of the chapters in Herman H. Rubin's *Eugenics and Sex Harmony*, which was first published in 1933. Rubin, who was a medical doctor and a member of the American Eugenics Society (AES) and the Eugenics Research Association (ERA), intended his 550-page illustrated volume to appeal primarily to a white, middle-class reading public eager for the latest medical and scientific information regarding eugenics, sex, marriage, and family life. In the book's foreword, Winfield Scott Pugh characterized *Eugenics and Sex Harmony* as "encyclopedic" in scope and explained that Rubin wrote the book "in a language easily understood." Pugh assured readers that it was a "valuable guide book for every household."[3] Rubin, moreover, promised readers "recent fascinating medical discoveries" and the latest information on the prevention of disease, as well as advice for "common disorders" such as "intestinal stagnation."[4] He also sought to foster a deeper understanding of eugenics and the importance of being eugenically "fit" among an American reading public that, in general, remained skeptical and unsupportive of the relatively new science.[5]

Rubin was not alone in his mission to bring eugenics to the masses. Throughout the 1930s, experts in a number of fields "bombarded" Americans with an avalanche of literature devoted to the promotion of eugenics and what they considered eugenic ideals, most notably "the feeling of genuine obligation towards the coming generation."[6] Proponents of eugenic education used a burgeoning interest in genetics and sex education, as well as anxieties brought on by the sweeping transformations of the early twentieth century and the specific social and economic unrest of the

1930s, to argue for the inclusion of eugenics in the popular discourse on human heredity and reproduction. Ultimately, they sought to make instruction in eugenics a critical component of modern childrearing within the home and the ever-expanding public school and college curricula, thereby solidifying its position as an acceptable and legitimate science.

Although eugenic education found its way into countless homes and classrooms during the 1930s, surprisingly little has been written about it. Scholars such as Steven Selden, Nancy Gallagher, Wendy Kline, and Gregory Dorr have made important initial forays into the history of eugenic education, but much work remains to be done.[7] Eugenics had become so broad and so diffuse and its advocates so diverse by the 1930s that no single study can claim to present a comprehensive analysis. Dorr, for example, has analyzed the importance of eugenics in the teaching career of Ivey Foreman Lewis at the University of Virginia, while Gallagher has explored the critical role that education played in the efforts to breed better Vermonters. Kline has analyzed the connection between eugenics and the movement toward marriage and family planning during the interwar period, and Selden has chronicled the increasing presence of eugenics in the college classroom during the first half of the twentieth century. The type of eugenic education investigated in this chapter is but one strand of a much larger discourse that centered on the rationalization of human reproduction and the reinforcement of race, class, and gender hierarchies. The essay presents a study of the efforts of the predominantly white, male, middle- and upper-class members of the AES and the ERA to devise and implement a highly gendered system of eugenic education during the 1930s, one that focused almost exclusively on influencing the reproduction of the nation's most eugenically fit young women. It is an important strand, and one that continues to influence popular perceptions of love, courtship, marriage, and childrearing.[8]

Defining Eugenic Education

Before the members of the AES and the ERA could implement a practical eugenics education program, they had to address several fundamental questions: What exactly was eugenic education? How would it be implemented? What purpose would it ultimately serve? And what were its goals and objectives? Prominent eugenicists answered these very important questions in similar ways.

According to eugenicists, education had always been a vital component of their science. Samuel J. Holmes, professor of zoology at the University of California, argued in 1933 that eugenic education had its roots in the work of the British founder of eugenic theory, Sir Francis Galton.[9] By the early twentieth century, eugenicists in the United States openly recognized the need for eugenic education and worked diligently to make it an important part of the nascent social hygiene and sex education movements.[10] After World War I, many eugenicists increasingly argued that eugenic education in the home, school, and college was vital to both racial and social improvement. They argued that state intervention alone would ultimately accomplish very little and that experts and politicians needed to place greater emphasis on education. As Major Leonard Darwin, a prominent member of the Second International Congress of Eugenics and author of *The Need for Eugenic Reform* (1926), argued, experts and the state did not need to "lay down rigid rules of conduct." They merely needed to "teach those not living up to standard to regulate their conduct with due regard to the welfare of any children who may or may not be born in the future"; in that way, many of the "harmful innate defects would appear less frequently in future generations."[11] Throughout the 1920s, proponents of eugenics formed local, state, national, and international societies in part to promote eugenic education.[12]

By the early 1930s, members of the AES had outlined a very detailed eugenic curriculum that they hoped would someday be implemented in college, high school, and, to a certain extent, grammar school classrooms. The curriculum ultimately became part of *Tomorrow's Children* (1935), written by Ellsworth Huntington, a Yale professor and president of the AES. As Huntington argued in the book's preface, *Tomorrow's Children* represented an attempt by the AES to state in "simple but accurate language the main principles of eugenics and their application to social problems." The book, he noted, was a "composite" that drew freely from several studies conducted by AES members. It was written in question-and-answer format and was intended for "intelligent people who make no claim to scientific knowledge."[13] Huntington argued that although social and industrial leaders, professionals, and legislators were certainly in need of eugenic education, the individuals most in need were the "intelligent young people, especially those in universities, colleges, and high schools."[14] The AES members who shared in the preparation of *Tomorrow's Children* expressed divergent perspectives on many of the book's minor points, but they agreed on the "main outlines of the program" set forth by Huntington.[15]

According to Huntington, a eugenic education emphasized seven main points. Students would first learn the elements of *biology*, with special attention being given to reproduction and the reproductive organs in both plants and animals. Second was *genetics*, which, Huntington stated, included "heredity, mutations, natural selection, Mendelian laws, relations between heredity in plants, animals, and man." Third was *eugenics*, which addressed the "relative roles of heredity and environment, genius, defectives, pedigrees, innate qualities as influenced by economic and social conditions, density of population, education, industrialism, and so forth." The fourth component of the curriculum was *demography*, which Huntington defined as the "science of population, dealing with the numbers of people in any given area, birthrates, deathrates, survival rates, composition of the population in different social classes, countries, races, etc." Fifth was *the family*; on this point, students would learn "inter-relations of its various members, factors determining its size, mate selection, etc." The sixth component was *eugenics in history*, which included instruction in the effects of "migration, occupations, disease, war, political conditions, etc." This component also involved instruction in "selecting, developing, and segregating different types of people," with special attention given to "race and its significance, racial traits, race mixtures." The seventh and final component of the eugenics curriculum, *eugenics and social problems*, included instruction on "crime, dependency, industry, government, etc."[16] However, although the type of eugenic education advocated by the AES obviously included a broad range of topics, Huntington contended that this did not necessarily pose a problem to busy teachers.

He and Frederick Osborn, who served as secretary and treasurer of the AES during the 1930s, argued that the myriad topics covered under eugenic education could most easily be introduced in connection with established courses in biology, sociology, history, and economics. Courses in eugenics and in the problems of population could also be taught on their own, independent of other courses.[17] Huntington argued that heredity and reproduction were of such "universal interest to boys and girls" that eugenic principles could be incorporated into "any sort of biological or physiological study, especially in the high school." Even grammar school students needed some biology, which Huntington stressed should always be taught in a way that made eugenic principles evident.[18] Osborn agreed; he stated that a "eugenic attitude" could best be taught "not by teaching eugenics as such, but by acquainting the students all along the line with the materials which go into a sound eugenics. If the materials and attitudes are well integrated, the students will have eugenic attitudes as a natural part of their preparation for living." Osborn went on to note that instruction in eugenics as a separate field should be made available only to "some advanced students, especially those in postgraduate work," but that eugenic ideals could be integrated into virtually all curricula.[19] The notion that teachers could use a broad array of coursework to inculcate eugenic ideals and attitudes in their students became the defining characteristic of eugenic education in the 1930s.

Although proponents of eugenic education never established a clearly articulated set of eugenic ideals and attitudes, one needs only to examine the goals that experts hoped to achieve to gain a good sense of the principles and perspectives they sought to instill in American youth. G. P. Prets, a European scholar attending the Third International Congress of Eugenics in New York in 1932, stated that the "eugenically educated citizen" would feel responsibility toward posterity, which would express itself in "entering into marriage and having or not having children."[20] In a similar vein, Huntington argued that once the "principles of eugenics are more widely understood a new set of *mores*, or habits as to marriage will grow up." "Intelligent people," he declared, "will understand more fully than now that the quality of a mate and of the children likely to be born to that mate can be judged by the general quality of a mate's near relatives." Huntington went on to say that as Americans became more proficient in analyzing prospective mates, the nation's young people would create a "taboo against marriage between two people with such defects as unusually hot tempers, hereditary deafness, undue sensitiveness, and the like."[21] In general, advocates of eugenic education hoped to instill in students the ethic expressed by Paul Popenoe: "You are the product of what has gone before; and by your marriage you are taking a share of responsibility for the future evolution of mankind, as well as for your immediate happiness."[22] Experts sought to modernize marriage and family life by teaching the value of heredity and by encouraging the nation's young people to choose a eugenically fit mate.

Although proponents of eugenic education focused on the classroom, they agreed that a sound eugenic education began in the home. In *Tomorrow's Children,* Huntington observed that psychologists and educators were "convinced" that "the most important portion of a child's training" occurred in the home and that children of the 1930s often suffered the ill effects of poor parenting, resulting largely from the "innate incompetence of the parents." In his opinion, children could potentially be "doubly handicapped" by inheriting their parents' "weak traits" and by receiving poor training in the home. Eugenicists held out hope in the 1930s that eugenic education could ameliorate some, if not all, of the deleterious effects of poor parenting by making sure that children would be born in homes where they would have "good training." Eugenic education would also greatly reduce the possibility that future offspring might inherit so-called weak traits because prospective parents would be wise in the ways of selecting a eugenically fit mate.[23]

Those who advocated eugenic education hoped to reach parents through popular media, such as public lectures, radio interviews, newspaper and magazine articles, and, of course, books. Rubin's *Eugenics and Sex Harmony* was one of the more popular eugenic manuals during the 1930s, going through several reprints in that decade alone. The work is truly encyclopedic, and much of what Rubin discussed falls outside the scope of this analysis.[24] It does, however, provide valuable insight into the type of eugenic education that parents and their children could receive in their homes during the 1930s. Like other eugenicists, Rubin believed that eugenic education in the school was imperative but that it had to begin in the home. He made a "plea to parents" to be forthright with inquisitive children and to begin educating them early in their lives.[25] Rubin urged parents to provide a broad understanding for children and to discuss everything from sex, reproduction, and the transmission of venereal disease to the "Danger of Petting," and the "Fascination of Dress."[26] But above all else, it was every parent's "bounden duty" to put his or her children on the "right road to marriage." According to Rubin, parents' obligation to their children was complete only when they had steered them through the "whirlpools and rapids of their early love-life, and finally see them happily married."[27] Although Rubin advocated something he referred to as *"understanding companionship"* in marriage (emphasis in original), the advice he provided in *Eugenics and Sex Harmony* remained highly gendered, which was not uncommon among proponents of eugenic education.[28]

Many eugenicists believed that eugenic education offered an ostensibly humane and socially acceptable means of controlling—or at least greatly influencing—mate selection and human reproduction. They thought it would provide young people eager for insight into the mysteries of human heredity with the knowledge necessary to choose suitable life partners. The eugenically fit couple would then immerse themselves in a lifetime of learning and communication in an effort to foster a positive marriage experience and create a loving, nurturing, and, more important, scientifically sound home in which they could bear and rear a socially acceptable number of eugenically fit offspring. Eugenic education would not, however, be limited solely to enhancing the propagation of fit Americans. It would also be used to minimize the reproduction of individuals whom eugenicists considered unfit.[29] Although institutionalization and sterilization remained very real options for most eugenicists during the 1930s, education was incresingly recognized as a viable long-term method of improving human heredity.[30] Samuel Holmes even went so far as to declare that "eugenic education is the *sine qua non* for the adoption of any kind of measure looking toward race betterment. It is as necessary for the cure of our dysgenic ills as a knowledge of medicine is for curing the ills of the body."[31] He concluded that "all people's choice in marriage depends upon standards which are influenced to a considerable degree by education" and that "if knowledge of the fundamental principles of heredity and eugenics should haply come to be possessed by most inhabitants of a nation, it might do much toward promoting race betterment."[32] For many eugenicists, education provided a practical, relatively inexpensive, and socially acceptable means of controlling human reproduction.

Rationalizing Eugenic Education

Once they had defined eugenic education, members of the AES and the ERA set about legitimizing its existence through a number of complex means. They argued that an increased demand among a more sophisticated student population, which was beginning to understand the importance of both heredity and environment in shaping human beings, had compelled teachers to incorporate more eugenics instruction in the classroom. Although they argued that theirs was a more democratic science, eugenics proponents also remained deeply concerned with the "differential birthrate" and contended that eugenic education was necessary to prevent "race suicide." They ultimately argued that they were making marriage and family life modern by "reorienting" the country's youth, especially young, white, middle-class women, toward the production of eugenically fit offspring.

The nature-versus-nurture debate had been running for decades, but it was not until the 1930s that the AES announced it was "consciously enlarging its interests" to include both heredity and environment in its eugenic program.[33] Scientific advancements, as well as the specific social and economic hardships brought on by the Great Depression, forced the organization to expand its eugenic paradigm to include a greater emphasis on the environment during the 1930s. According to the AES, heredity and environment had become inextricably linked because science at that time offered no better test for the "biological fitness for parenthood" than "the desire for children rather than the satisfaction of other wants" and "the ability to provide home conditions which will give every child a fair chance."[34] This newfound emphasis on environment led many eugenicists to support eugenic education during the 1930s. It also provided them with a potent rationale for their field's existence. For them, eugenics in the 1930s had become "nothing less than an attempt to reorient human desires among a substantial proportion of our people."[35] An AES pamphlet published in 1935 declared that "such a task calls for the highest effort on the part of those responsible for education in the home, the school, and the college."[36]

Proponents noted that increased awareness among young people of the importance of both heredity and environment in determining the quality of future offspring was compelling them to take a more rational and scientific—in short, a more modern—approach to marriage, which in turn was leading to the increased demand for instruction in eugenics. In *The Eugenic Predicament* (1933), Holmes wrote that biology students frequently informed him that their attitude toward marriage and having children had been "radically changed" as a result of what they had learned about heredity. As he saw it, most intelligent young people of the 1930s who were contemplating marriage had at least the intent to "choose wisely," and they usually wanted "a number of healthy and intelligent children, although of course not too many." Holmes and other proponents of eugenic education argued that there were "good reasons for believing that a little knowledge of heredity" made students more discriminating in the choice of their life partners.[37]

Ernest R. Groves of the University of North Carolina, eugenicist, founder and director of the marriage and family conferences, and the first professor in the country to offer a college course for credit on marriage, supported Holmes's assertion wholeheartedly. In *Preparation for Marriage* (1936), Groves argued that young people of the 1930s needed "preparedness for marriage more than ever was true before."[38] He stated that because of their desire for preparedness, young people were "more careful than they used to be in considering before marriage any possible complication due to their inheritance."[39] Groves then explicitly linked preparedness for marriage with an increased need for eugenic education. He noted that although some experts no longer emphasized the heritability of certain traits, the idea of inheritance was "so well established by study and experiment" that it was not open to doubt on the part of "reasonable persons." He went on to say that it was the certainty among reasonable persons regarding human heredity that made eugenic education possible. Eugenics, according to Groves, was *the* science that studied the problems of being "well born," and young people were "beginning to know this and to give thought to it before they marry, and especially before they have children."[40] According to both Holmes and Groves, scientific advancements made primarily during and after World War I were enabling young people of the 1930s to adopt a more modern attitude toward inheritance and preparation for marriage, which in turn was leading to the growing demand for eugenic education.

In an effort to strengthen their appeal to students and the general reading public, proponents of eugenic education explicitly attacked claims that theirs was an undemocratic science. In the midst of the Great Depression and an increasing awareness of German eugenic programs, many eugenicists worked diligently to separate themselves, at least rhetorically, from any measures that might be considered racist, classist, or strictly hereditarian. As one newspaper reporter put it, most eugenicists in the 1930s were keenly aware that eugenically desirable individuals could be found in every social class and that biological inheritance was only one factor among many that determined eugenic fitness.[41] Frederick Osborn argued that the creation of new aspirations, new motivations, a better social environment, and a new eugenic social consciousness were very much "in accord with democratic ideals." He declared that eugenic reforms would actually "supplement all other efforts at social advance."[42] In discussing Osborn's work, a reporter for the *Science News Letter* assured readers that the objectives of the "newer eugenics" were "not particularly racial," nor were they "centered upon sterilization or such techniques." Rather, they were concerned with "making the best of what we have through education. This applies to determining who shall be born into the world as well as what happens to them later." "Most emphatically," the reporter declared, "eugenics today does not desire to make a selection between social, economic, or racial groups."[43] Many eugenicists, especially those who supported eugenic education, were mindful of critics and quick to point out their sensitivity to diversity within the American population. The new emphasis on democratic ideals apparent in the writing of many eugenicists during the 1930s did not, however, preclude them from continuing to make broad generalizations concerning the supposed fitness of certain segments of the population, which ultimately greatly affected their views on education.

Despite their rhetorical convictions regarding democracy and equality, eugenicists remained greatly concerned with older notions of race suicide, or what they referred to during the 1930s as the differential birthrate.[44] Huntington declared in 1935 that the differential birthrate was the "chief evil" that eugenicists sought to "correct."[45] Eugenicists argued that certain segments of the population—namely, those individuals who lacked a high degree of eugenic fitness—were out-reproducing fit members of American society. Although eugenicists claimed that one's fitness was not necessarily dependent on one's ethnicity, race, national origin, class, or social status and that "most Americans" were indeed fit, they continued to highlight certain segments of the population that they believed were polluting the U.S. gene pool with large, dysgenic families.[46] More often than not, eugenicists pointed to unskilled urban workers and rural folk who had more than two children and lived meagerly as the harbingers of racial decline. They also singled out middle- and upper-class, predominantly white, college-educated women who chose to limit the size of their families through the use of birth control as the unfortunate villains in the battle both to save Western civilization from moral ruin and economic bankruptcy and to improve its genetic inheritance.[47] Although they claimed that theirs was a democratic science, eugenicists' own class, race, gender, and ability biases continued to influence their notion of fitness throughout the 1930s.

The declining birthrate among the country's most fit population re-mained a primary concern of those eugenicists who promoted eugenic ed-ucation. Huntington contended that individuals who displayed the most intelligence, foresight, thrift, self-control, and other "high qualities" tended to have much smaller families than individuals who were "most deficient in these qualities."[48] There were exceptions, of course, and Huntington made note of them. He and other eugenicists stated, however, that the differential birthrate most definitely favored less fit citizens. According to their statistics, families receiving public aid, especially the "less competent types," had two or three times as many children as college graduates, who, on average, did not have more than two children per couple.[49] Eugenicists argued that two children per family was not enough to tip the reproductive scales in favor of the nation's fit households. In most cases, two children were not even enough to maintain a stable population: children died be-fore reaching maturity; they failed to marry; and once married, some failed to have children of their own.[50] Conservative eugenicists therefore sought to reverse what they referred to as the "wrong kind" of differential birthrate by promoting a system of eugenic education that would prepare fit youth for marriage and family life and aid them in finding suitable mates.[51]

Despite its appeal to modernity, the eugenic education being offered in the 1930s was, in many ways, a reaction against rapidly changing social and cultural mores. The differential birthrate combined with the rise of the "new woman" and the Jazz Age, as well as an increase in both the di-vorce rate and the age at which most middle- and upper-class women and men married, sparked fears among eugenicists that modern civilization was spiraling rapidly toward its own demise.[52] As other scholars have shown, primarily white, middle-class women had been attending college and gradu-ate or professional schools in increasing numbers for decades; this trend continued, although not unchecked, throughout the 1930s.[53] The marriage rate, which had declined to an all-time low during the early 1930s, re-mained low for the rest of the decade. The birthrate also declined, while the divorce rate increased, to the point where one in six marriages ended in divorce.[54] The 1930s, moreover, were a time when young single women actually experienced a greater opportunity to become self-reliant and when popular culture, especially movies and fan magazines, glamorized single working women.[55] As historian Elaine Tyler May argued, hardships brought on by the Depression caused many Americans to "abandon the constraints of the past and move forward, boldly, into the future," which ultimately led a large number of them to rearrange and in some cases redefine marriage, family, school, and work relations. May pointed out, however, that the Depression also "created nostalgia for a mythic past in which male breadwinners provided a decent living, and homemakers were freed from outside employment."[56] Ironically, proponents of eugenic education sought to use modern science to reconstruct that mythic past, which seemed to be eluding them throughout the 1930s.

As noted, most eugenicists wanted to use education as a means of reestablishing marriage and family as a priority among the nation's most fit women and men. Osborn stated that the type of education he and his colleagues were advocating was inherently conservative. It implied a return to the "old moralities" but with a new and modern emphasis on rational planning and preparedness for marriage and family life, which included scientifically sound mate selection, childbearing, and childrearing.[57] Although they included both sexes, proponents of eugenic education focused their campaign largely on young women, especially those attending college. Most eugenicists agreed with Paul Popenoe's assertion that sex "played a somewhat larger part in the life of woman than of man" and that "if there is to be any difference in emphasis [in education], women should have more thorough preparation for family life than do men."[58] The result, at least in part, was the creation during the 1930s of college-level courses that were aimed primarily at women and specifically dealt with marriage, family, and eugenics, as well as concerted efforts to inculcate eugenic ideals in young women and girls in their homes, grammar schools, and high schools.[59]

Proponents of eugenic education argued that young women who delayed marriage and childrearing to finish high school and attend college and, in some cases, graduate or professional school were jeopardizing their own future, as well as the future of the race. Popenoe held that it was "little less than a crime to advise girls to wait until they are 30 or more to marry, in order to enjoy life more fully, get a better preparation, or what not."[60] He declared that a mother and father did their daughter "a great disservice" when they seized on "some trivial talent" that the girl possessed, such as musical ability, and urged her to prepare herself for a career rather than for marriage. According to Popenoe, there was "probably not one such case in a hundred where the advice is really justified; but the girl, misled by the vanity of her parents, and the praise of incompetent teachers who want a pupil . . . spends great amounts of time and money in training only to find later that there is no career for her, or, if there is, that she would have preferred a family."[61] Eugenicists insisted that parents should help their daughters fulfill their biological destiny and become good wives and mothers; anything less would be a tragic waste of time and effort.

Popenoe and other eugenicists rooted young women's apparent "revolt" against marriage and family life in the "wrong" education they received at home and at school, as well as the "agitation of mismated wives and disappointed spinsters."[62] As evidence of the first claim, Popenoe pointed to the course offerings at various women's colleges. Bryn Mawr, for example, offered young women four courses in Sanskrit in 1926 but none in what Popenoe referred to as "mothercraft," which, put simply, was a course designed specifically to prepare young women for marriage and family life and often included instruction in eugenics. He went on to note the absense of mothercraft classes at Wellesley, though it offered six courses in geology;[63] Mount Holyoke, which offered eight astronomy courses; Smith, which had seventeen courses in mathematics; and Vassar, the last school on Popenoe's list of culprits, which offered eighteen courses in Greek and three more in Greek archaeology. Popenoe condemned what he referred to as the "smug satisfaction of the eastern women's separate colleges" whose "own obsolete point of view" was a particular "stumbling block" to racial progress because "so many young girls look to this group for leadership and inspiration."[64] By the mid-1920s, Popenoe and other eugenicists were arguing that young women needed a new type of education—a eugenic education, which would not only prepare them for marriage and family life but also impress on them the importance of bearing and rearing an adequate number of fit children. After the onset of the Great Depression in 1929, proponents of eugenic education would achieve their goals.

In many ways, the Depression enabled conservative eugenicists to place an increased emphasis on the importance of women's traditional roles as wives and mothers in maintaining the race. The author of an article entitled "Eugenics as the Cure for All the Race's Ills," which appeared in the *Literary Digest* in 1932, claimed that "the raising of a family is still [a woman's] chief and noblest duty, and that mainly upon her depends the future of the race." The author added that women had "a function in the scheme of things which can not be delegated."[65] According to another eugenicist, the "continuance of the race and the quality of the race" rested primarily with women. The same eugenicist went on to argue that in order to avoid life choices that they might "later regret as a major error in their lives," it was "highly desirable" that all intelligent individuals, especially women, understand the eugenic implications of their decisions, as well as "other simple biological facts" as early as the period of adolescence.[66] Jan Sanders, a eugenicist from Rotterdam attending the Third International Congress of Eugenics in New York in 1932, argued that women had "an inescapable obligation" to the race and to society.[67]

During the 1930s, most conservative eugenicists who considered marriage and family life to be the ultimate goal of fit women attempted to use the social and economic chaos caused by the Depression to eradicate gains made by feminists in education and elsewhere. In 1926, Popenoe, who was by no means a liberal, argued that education for the two sexes simply needed to be increasingly "differentiated," which meant that women needed more courses on mothercraft.[68] By the early 1930s, however, many eugenicists had begun making more radically conservative claims. Sanders, for example, declared that society needed to "get rid of the idea of feminism in its old form, according to which women should be men's equal in every respect, professionally, politically, and as regards salary." In his opinion, the theory of the "so-called equality of the sexes" was "absolutely incorrect, not only physiologically and biologically but also socially and politically." Sanders argued that women and men each had their own particular task to perform in the world and that the woman's "main duty always has been and always will be the family." "The university woman must know, understand, and feel," Sanders declared, "that marriage and children represent, after all is said and done, the highest ideal."[69] Proponents of eugenic education used the shifting social and economic climate of the 1930s to reverse gains made by feminists and women in general by instilling eugenic ideals that favored family and marriage in the core curriculum of the nation's grammar and high schools, colleges, and universities.

One place where the new eugenic ideals were manifested repeatedly was in the ongoing discussion of the use of birth control among the country's fit population.[70] As the AES argued in 1935, birth control held "enormous possibilities for good, and also for evil."[71] If it was used to prohibit less fit individuals from reproducing, then it held much potential for good. If, however, the nation's fit couples used birth control to limit the size of their families to less than four children, then the AES considered birth control to be evil. Most conservative advocates of eugenic education highlighted the latter and not the former in their attack on the birth control movement. Henry Fairfield Osborn, one of the most outspoken critics of birth control, lamented its proliferation as "positively dysgenic or against the interests of the race" precisely because it was being used by those individuals whom eugenicists deemed most fit to reproduce.[72] Conservative eugenicists who supported eugenic education hoped that it would be used to counter arguments being made by feminists and other liberals in favor of the unfettered use of birth control by the most fit couples in the United States.

Beginning in the 1920s and continuing through the 1930s, few eugenicists were more critical of the birth control movement than Paul Popenoe. In a scathing critique, he characterized it as "pseudo-biological" and argued that it had become "a quasi-religious cult, its god a modern Moloch whom only the continual sacrifice of little children can prevent from wreaking vengeance on his abject worshippers." Like other new "cults," Popenoe continued, the birth control movement was "marked by zeal, fanaticism, intolerance, and enjoyment of mild martyrdom, together with a lack of a sense of humor." He declared that "the present Birth Control cult should be repudiated by all responsible people." According to Popenoe, the "sob sisters" of the birth control "press bureaus" did contraception a great disservice by not speaking of it in terms of its value in promoting a healthy, eugenically fit family life.[73]

Unlike his fellow AES member, Herman Rubin held a much more liberal, less dogmatic view of birth control. He argued in *Eugenics and Sex Harmony* that it seemed "almost inconceivable" that, in the "enlightened age" of the 1930s, "there should exist men so bigoted, so grossly ignorant, and so lacking in all the fine qualities of decency and justice that they would force maternity upon unwilling women." He also referred to prominent birth control advocates Margaret Sanger and Marie Stopes, as well as scores of others, as "fine, upstanding women."[74] Yet Rubin, like other proponents of eugenic education, was unable to separate the issue of birth control from concerns about marriage and family life. Though he promoted "elective, not enforced motherhood," he also stated that "in all *nor-*

mal women there is a desire for motherhood; an overwhelming desire to mother and rear children."[75] He informed his readers that a eugenically sound marriage included birth control and the rational spacing of children and that the uninhibited distribution of contraceptive information would actually promote healthy, long-lasting marriages with plenty of eugenically fit children.[76]

Men such as Rubin and Popenoe may have approached eugenic education from different perspectives, but they agreed on the need to counter what they considered the negative influences exerted by birth control advocates, college professors, members of the popular media, and feminists; they would do so by instilling in young, white, middle-class, and usually well-educated women a new set of eugenic ideals that emphasized marriage, family, and motherhood. As Frederick Osborn and others argued, young men and women who went to college were all too often subjected to various influences that led them away from marriage and parenthood.[77] According to its proponents, eugenic education would correct the seemingly selfish, materialistic ideals of a fit modern couple by providing them with a new "orientation in life."[78] Eugenic education should begin in the home, they believed, but ultimately, much of the responsibility for reorienting the youth lay with the nation's schoolteachers and college professors. As late as 1940, while Europe was at war with Nazi Germany, Osborn argued for increased eugenic education in all of the nation's schools. Eugenics, he stated, provided "values for living, values which should be made articulate to, and through, students at all levels." Osborn believed that the schools were largely responsible for teaching young people their proper roles in the broader society, and unless schools incorporated a more comprehensive eugenic program, those students most responsive to education would likely fail to reproduce "their kind."[79]

Implementing Eugenic Education

Eugenic education quickly made its way into countless homes and schools across America during the 1930s. Eugenicists attending the Third International Congress of Eugenics in New York in 1932 boasted that their science had "become a highly popular subject for parlor talk and best sellers."[80] In addition to making its way into parlors and onto bookshelves in the 1930s, eugenic education was also being incorporated in the curricula of grammar and secondary schools and colleges and universities throughout the country. It had become an important part of numerous courses, including sex education, biology, general science, hygiene, social science, psychology, home economics, literature, religious education, and specific courses on marriage and the family. Many of the nation's leading colleges and universities had, in fact, begun offering some level of eugenic education as early as 1909.[81] Historian Hamilton Cravens found that "the number of colleges and universities offering courses in eugenics increased from 44 in 1914 to three hundred and seventy-six in 1928, when according to one estimate, some 20,000 students were enrolled."[82] The number of courses at all levels continued to rise during the 1930s. More important, however, the content of the courses shifted to include marriage and family life, which, as noted earlier, was the primary goal of proponents of eugenic education.

Although specific data are difficult to obtain, anecdotal evidence suggests that the advocates of eugenic education were quite successful in implementing their program during the 1930s. In 1937, just ten years after Professor Groves offered the first practical course on marriage and eugenics at the University of North Carolina, over 200 of the country's 672 colleges and universities offered similar courses.[83] In March 1937, the AES held a special conference in New York City to consider eugenic education in universities, colleges, and high schools, and approximately thirty organizations sent representatives to the meeting.[84] Historian Beth Bailey reported that "when *American Magazine* ran an article on college marriage courses and the scientific approach to love in 1937, it prompted thousands of letters from readers and a follow-up article by Professor Groves. The same year, *Good Housekeeping* offered a 'College Course on Marriage Relations' in its pages, with the first 'lecture' given by Groves."[85] Two years later, one of Groves's colleagues, Bayard Carter, a professor at Duke University, taught the first graduate-level course on the medical aspects of marriage and the family, which also included instruction in eugenics.[86] By the end of the decade, 375 colleges and universities had courses on marriage and the family, all of which included instruction in eugenics.[87] Professor Groves's 1938 prediction that almost every college and university would have a complete course in marriage within one generation seemed likely to be realized.[88]

Eugenic education extended well beyond the colleges, however. In Los Angeles, staffers at Paul Popenoe's Institute of Family Relations, which opened as an independent nonprofit organization in 1930, spent much of their time distributing materials to teachers in secondary schools across the country and helping local high schools prepare their students for marriage and family life.[89] In December 1933, the institute sponsored an all-day regional conference on family relations at the Pasadena Presbyterian Church that included panels on heredity and eugenics. The conference also featured two sessions on marriage and choosing a eugenically sound mate.[90] According to Popenoe, the institute's staff always attempted to "find community machinery to further the various aspects of the eugenics program, and in this way provide for a continuing effort to better local conditions."[91] He noted further that the institute served as "a clearing house and educational center for as much as possible of the existing scientific information that will make for success in marriage and parenthood."[92] Couples who sought counseling at the institute received a long list of books to read and also attended lectures and discussions on one or more of the following topics:

> (1.) The personal, social, and eugenic values of marriage and the family; (2.) The biological basis of marriage, difference between the sexes and the importance of understanding this physical, mental, and emotional differentiation, for the promotion of successful mating; (3.) The choice of a mate; (4.) Concerning relations and attitudes within the family in general; and in particular, those relating to division of labor and division of authority; family finances, the use of leisure time, and parent-child relationships; (5.) Supposed substitutes for marriage, as compared with normal family life; and the psychological problems involved in the relationships of the two sexes before marriage; (6.) Causes of family difficulties and how they may be avoided.[93]

Although Popenoe questioned seriously the efficacy of a eugenics program that intervened, in most cases, only after a couple decided to marry and start a family, he remained adamant that "education for marriage and parenthood" was one of the most important eugenic programs.[94]

In 1938, S. Edmund Stoddard, who taught high school in Blackfoot, Idaho, stated that it had become essential to provide students with a course in genetics and eugenics. "By educating our students," he said, "we shall be gradually developing a public opinion which will be conscious of the force of heredity." To those individuals who objected to offering a course on eugenics to high school seniors, Stoddard explained that students all over the country were getting married and becoming parents and that "it would seem a worth-while education for these young people to realize the responsibility of marriage and the vital role of inheritance, and also environment, in the rearing of their children. Certainly young married people should know the facts of marriage."[95] Unfortunately, Stoddard did not leave behind a detailed lesson plan. There were, however, other proponents of eugenic education who did produce clearly articulated, content-related goals.

One such individual was Herbert L. Stahnke, a graduate student in the College of Education at the University of Arizona. In 1934, Stahnke completed a master's thesis entitled "A Suggested Program of Eugenics Education in High School Biology," in which he wrote of the increasing demand for eugenic education and the need to impress on young people the great necessity of "selecting a mate carefully and with a thought as to their obligation toward the next generation."[96] He argued, moreover, that a comprehensive program of eugenic education in the high school needed to incorporate what he referred to as "sex instruction" and "genetic instruction," in addition to specific instruction in eugenics. Stahnke asserted that sex instruction would "tend to develop a normal and sane attitude toward the sex side of life," whereas genetic instruction would "emphasize the importance of an individual's genetic constitution and 'inculcate ideals that will lead to an improvement of the racial stock, and to the adoption of a voluntary resolve by the individual to refuse, where feasible, to transmit or allow the transmission of mental or physical defect.'"[97] He developed the following list of goals for his high school biology class:

a. An opportunity for young people to develop a wholesome and appreciative attitude toward matters relating to sex.

b. A scientific vocabulary for the discussion of eugenics.

c. Answers to the natural questions of young people in such a way as to prevent morbid and to develop healthy attitudes toward sex matters.

d. A means for strengthening the character of boys and girls against common temptations of youth.

e. A way to give young people some conception of the responsibilities of parenthood in the light of modern science.

f. A means of disseminating eugenics information and for correcting the erroneous concepts pertaining to eugenics that laymen possess.

g. A device for inculcating information and ideals needed to guide young people in selecting a mate and to help them in their married life.

h. A field for leisure time activities.[98]

Stahnke clearly sought to modernize marriage and parenthood through the use of modern science. He also hoped, however, to instill "wholesome and appreciative attitudes" in students and "strengthen the character of boys and girls against common temptations of youth." It was precisely this tension and apparent contradiction that motivated the implementation of eugenic education during the 1930s. For its advocates, eugenic education seemed to provide the most effective means not only of rationalizing and modernizing sex, marriage, and reproduction but also of re-creating a mythic past in which traditional gender roles dominated the home and workplace.

Yet another master's thesis, written by Lunah Ward Wallace (who was also in the College of Education at the University of Arizona during the 1930s), provides further insight into class content at the elementary and secondary levels and further illustrates the connections between modern science and so-called traditional values. Wallace contended that any course that sought to develop "correct home ideals" had to instruct young people with regard to marriage in a manner that would enable them to "appreciate its relation to and its influence upon the future of the race."[99] Wallace further stated that instruction on correct home ideals had to include instruction on heredity. For kindergarten children, this teaching would entail the "observation of family relationships." Plant fertilization and crossbreeding would be covered in grades one through six. And a study of the infamous Kallikak family and "race improvement" would be included in grades seven through twelve.[100]

In addition to inculcating eugenic ideals and providing content knowledge, eugenic education would, according to it proponents, also provide an element of socialization that would enable fit students to meet and form meaningful relationships. In Popenoe and Roswell Hill Johnson's *Applied Eugenics*—first published in 1918 and, according to Huntington and the AES, the most widely used eugenics textbook by the 1930s—there was a chapter entitled "The Improvement of Reproductive Selection (1. Sexual)"; in it, the authors urged educators to create a learning environment that encouraged the increased socialization of fit women and men. One scheme highlighted by Popenoe and Johnson consisted of assigning students a "eugenic rating" to rank them according to intelligence, physical health, and "ancestry." "This combined rating," the authors explained, "would be given to each member of the class, but only the names of those who ranked in the upper 25% would be given out. This would call attention to graduates who might be good eugenic material and who perhaps for some other reason might be passed over."[101] Popenoe and Johnson also hoped to create a public record that would allow individuals to acquire eugenic information about a prospective mate.

Not all of the plans for the eugenic socialization of the nation's students were quite so intrusive. Eugenicists did, however, urge all educators and administrators at the high school and college levels to create an atmosphere, both in the classroom and on campus, that would encourage fit students to marry and have families. According to Popenoe and Johnson, only "emotionally abnormal" individuals deliberately chose not to marry and have children, but some students, especially women, found that they became "gradually and unintentionally cut off from opportunities for marriage," a situation they were sure to "bitterly regret" as they grew older.[102] Popenoe and Johnson, as well as other eugenicists, felt that schools needed to meet their "responsibility" to foster eugenic marriages "squarely," not only through curriculum but also through classroom management, extracurricular activities, sports, and (at the college level) housing arrangements.[103] In the opinion of those who championed eugenic education, students attending high school and college during the 1930s needed every possible opportunity to meet and fall in love with a eugenically fit mate.

Conclusion

The 1932 undergraduate conference on marriage at Wesleyan, attended by delegates from "scores" of eastern colleges, was brought to a close with an address entitled "The Modern Approach to Marriage," delivered by Clarence G. Campbell, president of the Eugenics Research Association. The *New York Times* reporter covering the conference summarized the address by stating that "happy marriages are not made in heaven but instead are the result of intelligent idealism, based on a knowledge of the principles of human adaptation."[104] Campbell's speech—indeed, the conference on marriage itself—would not have been possible just a few years earlier. Rubin recognized this point when, in *Eugenics and Sex Harmony,* he suggested that "perhaps our grandparents might turn a double somersault in their graves if they could only realize what our race is coming to—using brains, instead of a thick neck and powerful back muscles in pushing the chariot of progress up the hill of racial evolution."[105] By the early 1930s, it appeared to proponents of eugenic education that society was well on its way to making marriage and family life modern through the use of science.

In many ways, the social and economic upheaval of the Great Depression provided the members of the AES and the ERA with an unprecedented opportunity to make themselves heard by an American public that was reeling socially and economically. The promoters of eugenic education used newspapers, magazines, and books as well as other popular and academic means to step into the national spotlight and attempt to correct what they considered the wrong kind of differential birthrate. In the process, they helped to alter permanently not only grammar school, high school, and college curricula but also the ways in which a whole generation of primarily white, middle-class women and men viewed marriage and family life.

For many eugenicists, education became one of the most important means of improving both society and the race during the 1930s. They viewed eugenic education not as repressive and undemocratic but as liberating and uplifting. Despite their egalitarian rhetoric, however, eugenicists remained wedded to notions of fitness that continued to be intimately linked with dominant ideas about "normative" manifestations of class, race, gender, and ability. According to Professor Holmes, sexual selection, or the process of choosing a mate, was "a means by which ideals of manhood and womanhood [could], in a measure, effect their own realization."[106] For most eugenicists, the ideals on which popular notions of manhood and womanhood were based tended to be reminiscent of earlier, more traditional gender roles. Proponents of eugenic education, moreover, tended to view stable, white, middle- and upper-class families with four or more children as the paragons of eugenic fitness. Although it would be extremely difficult to measure precisely the extent to which eugenic education influenced young people who came of age after 1930, it is interesting to note that following World War II, most young women surveyed said that they would like to have four children—the exact number that eugenicists had been urging them to have for nearly two decades.[107]

Notes

1. Herman H. Rubin, *Eugenics and Sex Harmony* (New York: Pioneer Publications, 1936), 198.

2. Samuel J. Holmes, *The Eugenic Predicament* (New York: Harcourt Brace, 1933), 179.

3. Rubin, *Eugenics and Sex Harmony*, v, vii. Pugh was a urologist who lived and worked primarily in New York City and was also a commander (retired) in the U.S. Navy Medical Corps.

4. Ibid., ix, x.

5. For contemporary criticism of eugenics, see Holmes, *The Eugenic Predicament*, chap. 6.

6. Clarence Darrow, famed defender of John Thomas Scopes and an outspoken critic of eugenics, used the term *bombarded* to describe the onslaught of eugenic literature in the United States during the interwar years; see Darrow, "The Eugenics Cult," *American Mercury* 8 (June 1926): 129. Although Darrow published his critique in 1926, all of the evidence indicates that the onslaught of eugenics literature and the criticism of that literature continued throughout the 1930s. Holmes referred specifically to Darrow in *The Eugenic Predicament*, chap. 6; see also Herbert L. Stahnke, "A Suggested Program of Eugenics Education in High School Biology" (master's thesis, University of Arizona, 1934). The quote is taken from J. Crosby Chapman and George S. Counts, *Principles of Education* (Boston: Houghton Mifflin, 1924), 232. Although the Chapman and Counts book was first published in 1924, it continued to influence educators during the 1930s; see Stahnke, "A Suggested Program."

7. Gregory Michael Dorr, "Assuring America's Place in the Sun: Ivey Foreman Lewis and the Teaching of Eugenics at the University of Virginia, 1915–1953," *Journal of Southern History* 2 (May 2000): 257–96; Nancy L. Gallagher, *Breeding Better Vermonters: The Eugenics Project in the Green Mountain State* (Hanover, NH: University Press of New England, 1999); Wendy Kline, *Building a Better Race: Gender, Sexuality, and Eugenics from the*

Turn of the Century to the Baby Boom (Berkeley: University of California Press, 2001); Steven Selden, *Inheriting Shame: The Story of Eugenics and Racism in America* (New York: Teachers College Press, 1999); Selden, "Resistance in School and Society: Public and Pedagogical Debates about Eugenics, 1900–1947," *Teachers College Record* 90 (March 1988): 61–84; Selden, "Educational Policy and Biological Science: Genetics, Eugenics, and the College Textbook, c. 1908–1931," *Teachers College Record* 87 (Fall 1985): 35–51.

8. See also Kline, *Building a Better Race,* chap. 5.

9. Holmes argued that Galton also referred to persuasion and enlistment of private charity as means to achieve eugenic ends; see Holmes, *The Eugenic Predicament,* 166, 176.

10. Charles B. Davenport, director of the Department of Experimental Evolution at Cold Spring Harbor, New York, and secretary of the Eugenics Section of the American Breeders' Association, recognized the need for eugenic education in his *Heredity in Relation to Eugenics* (New York: Henry Holt, 1911), 4, 5. See also Winfield Scott Hall, "The Relation of Education in Sex to Race Betterment," *Journal of Social Hygiene* 1 (December 1914): 68–69.

11. Leonard Darwin, "The Aims and Methods of Eugenical Societies," *Science* 54 (7 October 1921): 313–23, and *The Need for Eugenic Reform* (New York: D. Appleton, 1926).

12. Obviously, eugenic societies were very active in scientific research and politics, as well as education.

13. Ellsworth Huntington, *Tomorrow's Children: The Goal of Eugenics* (New York: John Wiley and Sons, 1935), vii.

14. Ibid., 69.

15. Ibid., viii.

16. Ibid., 69. See also Stahnke, "A Suggested Program"; Paul Popenoe and Roswell Hill Johnson, *Applied Eugenics,* 3rd ed. (New York: Macmillan, 1933), 228–79; S. Edmund Stoddard, "Genetics and Eugenics in Secondary Schools," *School and Society* 48 (August 20, 1938): 245–49.

17. Frederick Osborn, *Preface to Eugenics,* rev. ed. (New York: Harper and Brothers, 1951), 275–82; this work was originally published in 1940.

18. Huntington, *Tomorrow's Children,* 70.

19. Osborn, *Preface to Eugenics,* 273–77. For more on eugenic education in schools and colleges and eugenic ideals and attitudes, see Otis W. Caldwell, "Some Aspects of Instruction in Eugenics," in *A Decade of Progress in Eugenics: Scientific Papers of the Third International Congress of Eugenics* (Baltimore, MD: Williams and Wilkins, 1934), 167–70; Lemo Dennis Rockwood, "Eugenics Education in Secondary Schools and Colleges," *Journal of Home Economics* 29 (June 1937): 387–88; Stahnke, "A Suggested Program"; Stoddard,

"Genetics and Eugenics in Secondary Schools"; Lunah Ward Wallace, "Responsibility of the Home and the School for Developing Correct Home Ideals" (master's thesis, University of Arizona, 1931).

20. G. P. Prets, "Eugenics and Education," in *A Decade of Progress in Eugenics*, 137.

21. Huntington, *Tomorrow's Children*, 87–89.

22. Paul Popenoe, *Modern Marriage: A Handbook for Men* (New York: Macmillan, 1940), 90.

23. Huntington, *Tomorrow's Children*, 5–8.

24. Rubin discussed everything from tuberculosis, malaria, diabetes, and psycho-analysis to "What Causes Sleep-Walking," "The Mystery of Twins," and "The Real Reason Men Prefer Blondes"; see Rubin, *Eugenics and Sex Harmony*, ix, x.

25. Ibid., 92–97, 158–62.

26. Ibid., pt. 1, pt. 3, and pt. 7.

27. Ibid., 95.

28. For an explanation of understanding companionship, see ibid., 180–86.

29. Holmes argued that "the more frequently dysgenic marriages meet with general disapproval, the less likely they are to be contracted; and the more widely a knowledge of heredity becomes diffused, the more frequently will people with hereditary defects re-frain of their own free will from passing them on to their children"; see Holmes, *The Eu-genic Predicament*, 178, and 166, 176–80 for positive eugenics.

30. For more on sterilization and eugenics during the 1930s, see Kline, *Building a Better Race*.

31. Holmes, *The Eugenic Predicament*, 179–80.

32. Ibid., 166, 176.

33. American Eugenics Society, *A Eugenics Program for the United States* (New Haven, CT: American Eugenics Society, 1935), 5. See also Kline, *Building a Better Race*.

34. American Eugenics Society, *A Eugenics Program for the United States*, 16.

35. Ibid., 7.

36. Ibid.

37. Holmes, *The Eugenic Predicament*, 178.

38. Ernest R. Groves, *Preparation for Marriage* (New York: Greenberg, 1936), 11.

39. Ibid., 33.

40. Ibid., 35, 36.

41. "Topics of the Times: Eugenics Grows Human," *New York Times*, May 7, 1938, 14; see also Stahnke, "A Suggested Program"; Paul Popenoe, *The Conservation of the Fam-ily* (Baltimore, MD: Williams and Wilkins, 1926).

42. "Rearing of Children Held Society's Duty," *New York Times*, December 1, 1938, 3.

43. "Man's Control over Life Is Prime Science Contact: Both Births and Deaths Are More Subject to Human Decisions and Man-Made Environment Than Ever Before," *Science News Letter* 34 (October 15, 1938): 247.

44. Although Daniel Kevles argued that the new "reformist outlook" that came to dominate much of the eugenic thinking during the interwar years "diffused the long-standing eugenic concern with the differential birthrate," popular sources indicated quite the opposite. Many of the eugenicists who wrote and published in popular books, magazines, and journals during the 1920s and 1930s expressed a deep-seated concern with what they labeled the differential birthrate. See Kevles, *In the Name of Eugenics: Genetics and the Uses of Human Heredity* (Cambridge, MA: Harvard University Press, 1995), 174, and chap. 11.

45. Huntington, *Tomorrow's Children*, 10.

46. Popenoe, *Modern Marriage*, 90.

47. Huntington referred to the "wrong kind of differential birthrate" in *Tomorrow's Children*, 10. The American Eugenics Society also made reference to the differential birthrate in the 1930s, in *A Eugenics Program for the United States*, 3. Major Leonard Darwin referred to the differential birthrate as well, in *What Is Eugenics?* (London: Watts, 1928), 13–15, as did F. C. S. Schiller in *Social Decay and Eugenical Reform* (London: Constable, 1932), 13–16. In their chapter entitled "How May Education Promote the Family Life?" in which they discussed eugenic education, J. Crosby Chapman and George S. Counts also mentioned the differential birthrate; see Chapman and Counts, *Principles of Education*, 225. See also Popenoe, *The Conservation of the Family*, 125–53.

48. Huntington, *Tomorrow's Children*, 10.

49. Ibid.

50. Ibid., 11.

51. Ibid., and Kline, *Building a Better Race*.

52. For a concise articulation of eugenicists' claims regarding the late marriage and low fertility of well-educated individuals, see Osborn, *Preface to Eugenics*, 280–82. Virtually all proponents of eugenic education discussed this point. See also Popenoe, *The Conservation of the Family*; Popenoe and Johnson, *Applied Eugenics*; Huntington, *Tomorrow's Children*.

53. Charles L. Vigue, "Eugenics and the Education of Women in the United States," *Journal of Education Administration and History* 19 (July 1987): 51–55.

54. Elaine Tyler May, *Homeward Bound: American Families in the Cold War Era* (New York: Basic Books, 1988), 39, 40; Kline, *Building a Better Race*, 124. Beth Bailey found that "between 1930 and 1932, the marriage rate fell 13.5 percent, and average age at marriage rose significantly during the decade"; see Bailey, *From Front Porch to Back Seat:*

Courtship in Twentieth-Century America (Baltimore, MD: Johns Hopkins University Press, 1988), 120.

55. May, *Homeward Bound*, 40, 41.

56. Ibid., 38.

57. Osborn, *Preface to Eugenics*, 292.

58. Popenoe, *The Conservation of the Family*, 180.

59. For more on marriage and family courses in the 1930s, see Bailey, *From Front Porch to Back Seat*, chap. 6.

60. Popenoe, *The Conservation of the Family*, 25.

61. Ibid., 26.

62. Ibid., 40.

63. Popenoe noted that Wellesley was, at the time of his investigation, making efforts to create courses on marriage and family; see ibid., 181.

64. Ibid.

65. "Eugenics as the Cure for All the Race's Ills," *Literary Digest* 114 (September 10, 1932): 22.

66. Clarence Campbell quoted in ibid., 22–23.

67. Sanders quoted in ibid., 23.

68. Popenoe, *The Conservation of the Family*, 181.

69. Sanders quoted in "Eugenics as the Cure," 23.

70. For more on eugenics and birth control during the Depression, see Linda Gordon, *Woman's Body, Woman's Right: Birth Control in America* (New York: Penguin Books, 1990).

71. American Eugenics Society, *A Eugenics Program for the United States*, 4.

72. Osborn quoted in "Eugenics as the Cure," 22.

73. Popenoe, *The Conservation of the Family*, 139–53, quotes on 139, 145, 148.

74. Rubin, *Eugenics and Sex Harmony*, 255.

75. Ibid., 258, 259; emphasis added.

76. Ibid., 255–80.

77. Osborn, *Preface to Eugenics*, 269. See also Huntington, *Tomorrow's Children*; Popenoe and Johnson, *Applied Eugenics*.

78. Osborn, *Preface to Eugenics*, 273. All proponents of eugenic education spoke of instilling new values and ideals in the nation's young people. See also Huntington, *Tomorrow's Children*; Popenoe and Johnson, *Applied Eugenics*.

79. Osborn, *Preface to Eugenics*, 273–74.

80. H. J. Muller, "The Dominance of Economics over Eugenics," in *A Decade of Progress in Eugenics*, 138.

81. Selden, *Inheriting Shame*, 48.

82. Cravens quoted in ibid., 49.

83. Bailey, *From Front Porch to Back Seat*, 125–27.

84. Rockwood, "Eugenics Education in Secondary Schools and Colleges," 387–88.

85. Bailey, *From Front Porch to Back Seat*, 125–27.

86. Winifred Mallon, "Colleges Heed Pleas for Study of the Family," *New York Times*, April 16, 1939, D5; Mallon, "Pioneer Attacks 'Educational Lag' in College Training for Marriage," *New York Times*, April 15, 1939, 21.

87. Mallon, "Colleges Heed Pleas"; Mallon, "Pioneer Attacks 'Educational Lag.'"

88. Bailey, *From Front Porch to Back Seat*, 125.

89. Popenoe, "Marriage Counseling," in *A Decade of Progress in Eugenics*, 210–21; see also Kline, *Building a Better Race*.

90. Kline, *Building a Better Race*, 144, 145.

91. Popenoe, "Marriage Counseling," 219.

92. Ibid., 221.

93. Ibid., 219.

94. Ibid., 210–21; Kline, *Building a Better Race*.

95. Stoddard, "Genetics and Eugenics in Secondary Schools," 245–49.

96. Stahnke, "A Suggested Program," 5–8, quote on 6.

97. Ibid., 6, 7; Stahnke was quoting from Chapman and Counts, *Principles of Education*.

98. Stahnke, "A Suggested Program," 8.

99. Wallace, "Responsibility of the Home and the School," 12.

100. Ibid., 81; see also Henry H. Goddard, *The Kallikak Family: A Study in the Heredity of Feeble-Mindedness* (New York: Macmillan, 1912).

101. Popenoe and Johnson, *Applied Eugenics*, 233.

102. Ibid., 235–36.

103. Ibid., chap. 14; Osborn, *Preface to Eugenics*.

104. "Decide Marriages Not Heaven Made," *New York Times*, December 11, 1932, 35.

105. Rubin, *Eugenics and Sex Harmony*, 275.

106. Holmes, *The Eugenic Predicament*, 179.

107. Bailey, *From Front Porch to Backseat*, chap. 6.

FIVE

Defending Jeeter

Conservative Arguments against Eugenics in the Depression Era South

Betsy L. Nies

ABSTRACT

As Betsy Nies's title implies, eugenics was a highly contested issue in the American South. Northerners and Southerners alike—progressive in outlook—often promoted a stereotype of the South, with its sizable population of "poor white trash," as the "degenerate" child of the nation, rife with disease, illiteracy, and poverty. Southern intellectuals, in particular the Southern Agrarians, resented this stereotype, reacting to it and the eugenics movement overall as an ill-informed Northern intrusion into Southern cultural practices. Nies encapsulates this debate through a study of Erskine Caldwell's 1932 novel *Tobacco Road* and the Broadway production of the work a year later, by playwright Jack Kirkland; Nies also analyzes the critical commentary on each work that appeared in the press as well as in public arguments between conservative Donald Davidson and his opponent, H. L. Mencken.

Progressives and conservatives alike sought to locate the source of Southern degeneracy. Was it the low-quality genetic stock of early immigrants—supposedly criminals and lazy, lower-class English—or was it harsh environmental circumstances that had driven a fine, well-bred folk into steep decline? Jeeter Lester, the main character of *Tobacco Road*, fit the dysgenic stereotype of a poor white tenant farmer—or so some critics said. The Southern Agrarians defended Jeeter's type, arguing that the stock of poor whites was sound but that their plight was the result of punishing environmental conditions caused by the economic intrusion of northern capitalism. The nature-versus-nurture debate thus was recast in light of the long-standing regional vendetta between

the North and South; eugenic control, like Northern control, threatened Southern autonomy and therefore was resisted by regional de-
fenders. Nies shows as well that the nature-versus-nurture dilemma
was definitely in flux, with some foregrounding hereditarian
influences and others favoring environmental factors as the cause for
an individual's success or failure.

> The term "poor white" has been . . . and still is
> . . . responsible for much poorly directed
> thinking about the South.
>
> A. N. J. DEN HOLLANDER[1]
>
> Sterilize the males of the present generation
> [of sharecroppers], and so cut off the flow of
> their congenital and incurable inferiority.
>
> H. L. MENCKEN[2]

In 1937, when H. L. Mencken recommended that a benevolent patron do-
nate money to pay males of the Southern sharecropping class to "climb
on the table" and voluntarily submit to sterilization, he hit a sore spot for
conservative Southerners. His plan to pay sharecroppers to undergo this
eugenic procedure (cheaper than "supporting an ever-increasing herd of
morons") spoke to larger regional tensions, namely, the Southern fear of
denigration in the national press and the desire among Southern tradition-
alists to maintain a positive, separatist identity in a region sinking deeper
and deeper into poverty.[3] The Agrarians, a group of twelve men who shared
a philosophical belief that the South should avoid modernization and return to an agricultural lifestyle, published *I'll Take My Stand: The South
and the Agrarian Tradition* (1930), and the battle intensified on a rhetorical
level over whether strengthening an agrarian economy would return the
South to prosperity or whether Southerners needed to adopt a more progressive mentality. One subject in this discursive struggle was eugenics, a
science that conflicted sharply with white conservative beliefs about family, religion, and race. As a class-based movement, eugenics challenged the
control of the family over its members' reproductive rights, the importance
of religion over science, and the South's long history of white supremacy.[4]
Conservatives sought to rescue the poor white as a site of eugenic horror
from the national spotlight as a part of their ongoing efforts to return to a
past with clear ideological boundaries between the demonized North and
the idealized South.

Traditional visions of the Southerner as a productive, autonomous farmer tending fertile lands were sorely disrupted by the 1930s when the South's predominantly agricultural economy faltered, pushing many farmers into tenancy and sharecropping. Indeed, by 1930, 1.5 million of the South's inhabitants were tenant farmers (according to one estimate, 60 percent or more of the farmers in eight Southern states).[5] By 1935, two-thirds of such farmers were white, with large numbers of African Americans migrating to the North during the century's first decades. In 1937, a government survey revealed that two-thirds of the nation's tenants and sharecroppers lived in the South.[6] Their plight intensified with the onset of the Depression. The economy of the region worsened with drops in cotton prices, the region's leading money crop (from 35 cents per pound in 1919 to 5.7 cents per pound in 1932).[7] Falling prices, poor management of farming land, erosion, and drought, among other factors, forced many farmers into tenancy and sharecropping. Inadequate nutrition, lack of education, and limited access to medical care contributed to the widespread presence of pellagra and hookworm, which affected their physical and mental welfare.

Efforts to help this population came from the federal and state governments, challenging the conservative image of the farmer as a self-sufficient individual. President Franklin Roosevelt passed the Agricultural Adjustment Act of May 1933, which paid Southern farmers, between 1934 and 1939, to raise other crops besides cotton. The Farm Security Administration, headed by Mississippian Will Alexander, offered loans to tenant farmers to buy land.[8] In 1937, the Resettlement Agency was developed to move farmers from unproductive land to fertile tracts. Such national efforts to assist Southern farmers failed in many respects, but they created a visibility for the Southern poor in the national press. Images of tenant farmers and sharecroppers dotted the pages of *Life, Look, Time,* and *Fortune,* and tales of degeneracy, incest, pellagra, hookworm, illiteracy, physical deformity, and low intelligence peppered the accounts of both the Resettlement Agency and the Works Progress Administration.[9] Such representations countered traditional images of wholesome countrified living. Conservatives—including such well-known Agrarians as Andrew Nelson Lytle, John Crowe Ransom, and Donald Davidson—fought back. They battled a range of negative images that emerged from both Northern and Southern quarters, raising a question about the nature of the poor white's demise. Was he or she a certifiable eugenic disaster or a victim of changing social and economic structures?

Two prominent progressive Southerners of the 1930s, Erskine Caldwell and H. L. Mencken, provided answers, obtusely and directly, to this question. Caldwell, a Georgian writer, offered an ambivalent response, yet his work reinforced the worst stereotypes of poor whites that the decade had to offer. In 1932, he published *Tobacco Road,* his novel about the Lesters, a farming family from the sand hills of Georgia. Lazy, lustful, starving, diseased, and illiterate, the family, with its patriarchal head Jeeter, signified a typical representation of "poor white trash." Playwright Jack Kirkland underscored the lascivious and humorous nature of the characters in his 1933 play, which ran on Broadway and across the nation for the next seven years. The book itself was quite textured—including both Agrarian and progressive lines of argument, based on a eugenic study that was itself ambivalent about the hereditary background of this crowd—but the play reduced the Lester family antics to highly sexualized comedy. Conservatives were rightly horrified as commentators across the nation affirmed the truthfulness of the presentation. Although Caldwell never made it clear if the Lesters were inherently inferior, his partner in criticism of poor white Southerners, H. L. Mencken, showed no such hesitation. Poor white Southerners were, he asserted, genetically inferior. His essays and commentary sparked the ire of the outspoken Agrarian Donald Davidson, a longtime regional defender. A review of the ideological tenor of the science and representations of poor whites in the works of such Southern progressives reveals the issues posed to conservatives trying to retain imaginatively a positive image of a region mired in economic uncertainty.

The institution of eugenics in the South created a particular ideological problem for conservatives, in part because of its progressive nature. Progressives emphasized the authority of the state over the family and softened divisions between regions with their focus on modernization. As Agrarian Stark Young wrote in *I'll Take My Stand,* "[O]ur Southern family instinct, the home, the sense of parents, the endless cousins, uncles, and aunts, the nostalgia for one's own blood" was part of a larger "racial instinct" to care for all members of the family "no matter what imperfections may appear."[10] Eugenics shifted care for the "unfit" from the family to the state and instituted what many perceived as an intrusion of northern mores. Southerners had a history of keeping the mentally and physically challenged at home, but eugenics reinforced the authority of the state. Regional tensions arose with its arrival. Edward Larson suggested that those who practiced eugenics in the South "were cast in the role of missionaries preaching a foreign gospel in hostile territory."[11] Indeed, financial assistance to further eugenic research often did come from the North, with its more developed educational institutions and financial resources. For example, members of the National Committee on Mental Hygiene toured the South in between 1916 and 1923, helping Southern social reformers complete surveys to determine the magnitude of the number of "feebleminded."[12] Following such surveys, institutions were opened in Alabama, Florida, Georgia, Louisiana, Mississippi, South Carolina, and Tennessee; similar institutions had already been established in Kentucky, North Carolina, and Virginia.[13] Such institutions offered housing for those deemed unfit and, after 1927, involuntary sterilization as well.

Eugenics also challenged the conservative commitment to white supremacy, based not only on racial hierarchy but also on symbolic alignments between classes. The South was imaginatively one country with one ruling class. This regional identity was split with the integration of eugenics. For example, when Alfred E. Priddy, superintendent of Virginia's Lynchburg State Colony, selected Carrie S. Buck, a poor, white teenage mother whose own mother and sister had been institutionalized, as a candidate for sterilization, he emphasized class division. In the state case against Buck in 1925, Priddy argued, "These people [the Buck women] belong to the shiftless, ignorant and moving class of anti-social poor whites in the South."[14] The Virginia statute served as a model for other sterilization laws in the South after the Supreme Court, in *Buck v. Bell* (1927), declared Virginia's law constitutional. Surveys of eugenic institutions indicate that, as in the North, class was a significant factor in patient selection. For example, as Steven Noll noted, "In South Carolina, a survey of the 1,088 patients admitted to the [all-white] training school [for the feebleminded] in Clinton from its opening in 1920 until 1937 revealed that 70.8 percent of those who entered their institution came from families of tenant farmers or unskilled or semiskilled laborers."[15] This class fell within the category of "white trash," a label that, according to popular lore, came from African Americans. Eugenicists were not afraid to invoke this perspective. An Atlanta pediatrician referred to the "South's 'poor white trash,' so aptly named by the Negro," and argued that this group, composed of "individuals who are not physically, mentally or emotionally capable of reproducing normal offspring," should be sterilized. He concluded, "Let us take stock of this rubbish."[16] His accusations spoke in part to the traditional Southerner's fear of eugenics: could Southern poor whites be inferior to African Americans?

Such ideological questions played themselves out in relation to the health of poor whites whose diseases, specifically hookworm and pellagra, were tracked by the scientists. By the 1930s, it was known that the diseases resulted from environmental problems. Hookworm, contracted by walking around barefoot, could lead to anemia, extreme hunger, and exhaustion. Pellagra, caused by a lack of niacin, one of the B-complex vitamins found in meat, fish, whole grains, and vegetables, resulted in mental impairment, including hallucinations. Between 1909 and 1914, Rockefeller commissions worked with Southern state and county health departments in examining 1.3 million people; they discovered seven hundred thousand with hookworm—a population that included 39 percent of all schoolchildren, most of whom were white.[17] Linked to emaciation and "extreme lassitude, both mental and physical," hookworm was, as one *New York Sun* reporter claimed, responsible for what eugenicists had termed the "Germ of Laziness."[18] Discovering the etiology of pellagra carried implications for institutionalization; one historian reported that early studies—the work of a 1908 effort by the National Association for the Study of Pellagra and the 1909 National Conference on Pellagra held in Columbia, South Carolina, at the State Hospital for the Insane—indicated that a third of all insane asylum inmates suffered from the disease.[19] When Charles Davenport, director of the Eugenics Record Office in Cold Spring Harbor, New York (from 1910 to 1934), assumed leadership of the Pellagra Commission in 1913, he argued in the group's final report that contracting pellagra was, in fact, linked to a hereditary predisposition.[20]

Conservatives responded to such attacks on their own ideology by reevaluating the importance of the poor white within Southern history, softening class divisions, and shifting the focus from hereditary factors to the environment as the cause for economic and social degeneracy. For example, in the anthology *I'll Take My Stand,* Agrarian Andrew Nelson Lytle, in "The Hind Tit," argued that Northern travelers had mistakenly labeled the yeoman farmer as "pore [sic] white trash."[21] Actually, Lytle argued, he was the repository of Southern traditions: folk songs, the hunt, and respect for the land and tradition all resided in this symbolic man. His downfall economically and socially resulted from the growth of capitalism and the movement from sustenance to tenant farming, stripping the farmer of his ability to direct his own future. Such forces, for Lytle, functioned metaphorically like a eugenicist, rendering the yeoman farmer culturally and economically "impotent."[22]

In the same volume, John Crowe Ransom defended the poor white, arguing that in antebellum society, he was not so different from the squire; class boundaries were fluid. Northern capitalists, once again, had turned the farmer's attention from sustenance farming to a greater dependence on cash-crop farming. Like Lytle, Ransom saw the yeoman farmer as a transmitter of cultural and spiritual traditions, with the mighty hand of progress removing him from his natural relationship to the land. Contained within this industrial monster was an emulation of science (replacing a dedication to God). Referring to the "great numbers of these broken-down Southerners . . . still to be seen in patched blue-jeans, sitting on ancestral fences, shotguns across their laps and hound-dogs at their feet, surveying their unkempt acres while they comment shrewdly on the ways of God," he found their "defect" (their laziness) not to be an inherited, undesirable trait but rather a strength. Ransom argued, "[T]here is something heroic, and there may prove to be yet something very valuable to the Union, in their extreme attachment to a certain theory of life. They have kept up a faith which was on the point of perishing from this continent."[23] Both authors pointed to environmental agents in the downfall of poor whites; they had been rendered sterile socially and economically by the phantom eugenicist, the North.

In 1934, in William Terry Couch's progressive volume *Culture in the South*, A. N. J. Den Hollander made the terms of the Agrarian argument explicitly antieugenic. Although Couch was profoundly critical of the Agrarians, he included articles by Donald Davidson and John Donald Wade; Den Hollander's article, "The Tradition of 'Poor Whites,'" translated the Agrarian argument into scientific terms. Like Lytle, he traced repeated accounts of Northern travelers who theorized about the nature of "po' Buckra's" problems—the results of years of degeneracy in Anglo-Saxon lines. One traveler wrote that the poor whites were "the most degraded race of human beings claiming an Anglo-Saxon origin that can be found on the face of the earth—filthy, lazy, ignorant, brutal, proud, penniless savages."[24] Den Hollander argued these Northern visions of Southerners—including those of

Harriet Beecher Stowe, who wrote a chapter on "poor white trash" in her *Key to Uncle Tom's Cabin* (1853)—were ill-informed; most poor whites were yeoman farmers, and their poor economic and physical condition was not based on degenerate heredity (impossible to prove) but rather on "geographic and rural isolation [and] lack of economic and educational opportunities."[25] He challenged eugenicists to define the meaning of "pure Anglo-Saxon" stock, noting the arbitrary relationship between a set of behavioral or physical traits and the qualities of "homo Nordicus," those of Nordic descent (common eugenic parlance).

The conservative desire to defend the poor white took on even greater significance for conservative Southerners after the publication of Erskine Caldwell's *Tobacco Road* in 1932. In the novel, Jeeter Lester, the father of seventeen children (five of whom are dead), lives in a dilapidated shack on land owned by a lenient Captain John, who has allowed Jeeter and his family to stay on the land indefinitely, as long as the shack stood. He previously had supplied Jeeter with the credit to buy fertilizer and cotton seed, but once farming was no longer lucrative, Captain John went off to the city, leaving Jeeter to rely on his own resources. Augustan loan sharks fill the void, charging high interest rates and pushing Jeeter into a situation common to tenant farmers: he cannot get the land to produce enough cotton to pay back the bills and thus sinks deeper and deeper into debt and gradually into starvation.

The family group carries the imprint of the stereotypical poor white— they are physically deformed, lustful, half-starved and disease-ridden, and, as the merchants in town note, without much sense. Jeeter's daughter Ellie has a harelip; Bessie, a preacher's widow who marries sixteen-year-old Dude, son of Jeeter, has no cartilage in her nose. Several children in the neighborhood are Jeeter's progeny; he lusts for his son's wife and struggles with incestuous desires. The family strains to see Bessie and Dude consummate their marriage. All the Lesters consume snuff, a common antidote to hunger among poor whites, and two members suffer from pellagra. Additionally, these "poor white trash" are looked down on by their black neighbors, who watch and laugh at Ellie as she scoots across the ground to mate with her neighbor, Lov. Symbolically, a group of African Americans yell gleefully as they pass Jeeter, Bessie, and Dude on the road when their car breaks down. The Lesters, in all, reflect the Agrarians' greatest nightmare; the family relationships have disintegrated. The son Dude runs over the grandmother with a car, not giving it a second thought, and even though Jeeter's mother is still alive, no one moves to help her. In this book, Caldwell presents religion as a sham: no matter how much Jeeter trusts God, nothing comes of his faith. In the end, he and his wife burn to death in their home.

Despite its anti-Agrarian presentation of this farming family, the book contains an Agrarian critique of modernity, in line with the group's philosophy. Like Andrew Lytle, who pointed to the building of roads, the arrival of industry, and particularly the motorcar as responsible for the white farmer's demise, forcing him to become the runt of the litter, sucking the sow's hind tit, Caldwell suggests that the automobile—and an addiction to quick material rewards—helped further the tenant farmer's downfall. When Dude marries Bessie so he can drive her new car, the family cohesion dissolves quickly. The car itself was bought from scheming car salesmen who duped Dude and his new wife; they failed to educate them about caring for the car, so it loses oil, ruining the engine. Additionally, any engagement in the more settled town seems to hasten this family's moral devolution. Bessie unwittingly is used by a hotel manager as a prostitute when she stays in town with Jeeter and Dude. The children have scattered to the mills, leaving the parents to fend for themselves in their old age.

Notwithstanding the novel's critique of Agrarianism—Jeeter's "inherited love of the land" contributes to his ruin—*Tobacco Road* also contains a certain eulogy to an agricultural way of life. Lov comments at Jeeter's burial, "He was a man who liked to grow things in the ground. The mills ain't no place for a human who's got that in his bones. The mills is sort of like automobiles—they're all right to fool around in and have a good time in, but they don't offer no love like the ground does." He continues, "The ground sort of looks out after the people who keeps their feet on it. When people stand on planks in buildings all the time, and walk around on hard streets, the ground sort of loses interest in the human."[26] The text thus carries a form of Agrarian chant—something valuable will be lost if people leave the land—yet it also carries a progressive thread. An intrusive narrator comments, "Co-operative and corporate farming would have saved them all."[27]

The nuances of Caldwell's text may have been rooted in the eugenic study on which it was based. Caldwell's father, Ira S. Caldwell, was a Presbyterian minister who had long worked with the poor. In a social experiment, he had moved a family of poor farmers from the country to the town of Wrens, Georgia, trying to help them become self-supporting. Despite his efforts (enrolling the children in school, securing a job for the father, recommending that they attend his church), the family returned to their old home and their former impoverished existence. This family formed the basis for the Lesters.[28]

Ira Caldwell's study of the extended family of four hundred members, published in 1930 in *Eugenics* (the journal of the American Eugenics Society), served as a coda to his experiment. Even though he recommended sterilization of the Bunglers, as he called them, to keep them from overrunning the countryside, he actually portrayed eugenics as a class-based science, throwing his own romantic, conservative light on the family. He remembered it was a substitute teacher, a "healthy, well developed young lady of the much lauded Nordic type," who introduced him to the term *white trash*.[29] In his own characterization, he debunked the import of her characterization by stating that the Bunglers had "an excellent biological inheritance," given their "large physical stature," "their great strength and physical fitness," their low infant mortality rate, and their longevity. Though he described the intelligence of several members as low, he pointed out there was an "absence of insanity" or physical deformity in the group. He lamented that "a man can be so poor that it is difficult for him to be healthy in body or mind."[30] He indicted geographic and social isolation, along with hookworm, as the causes of their demise. His report contained an inherent class criticism of those who would critique the Bunglers, who would, as one Bungler woman commented, "cheat honest, hard-working people out of all they make." It was snobbishness in the schools—like Ira's teacher's—that kept them from attending. Ira reinforced the strength of their family ties in contrast to stereotypical representations of poor whites. He found "comparatively little illegitimacy" and strong "marriage bonds." Unlike the Lesters of his son Erskine's novel, these poor whites lacked incestuous urges; they were "remarkably free from intermarriage."[31] He described them as victims of "economic and social tragedy," an ironic statement given his representation of the Bunglers as worthy of eugenic sterilization.[32]

The ambivalence that is woven through both the father's and the son's work made little difference in terms of regional responses to Jeeter: he became the symbol of all that was wrong in the South, a representative who sparked eugenic commentary from both Northern and Southern locations. After Erskine Caldwell published a series of articles for the *New York Post* on the dire living conditions among poor white tenant farmers, which included images of babies sucking from a dog's teat along with dung eating, investigators for the *Augusta Chronicle* went into the Wrens-Keysville region, where the Bunglers had lived, to see if the conditions described in the articles and in Caldwell's book and play really existed.

One anonymous reviewer for the *Augusta Chronicle,* reflective of other writers as well, argued that Caldwell had misrepresented the South; even if he had had good motives for exposing the poverty and squalor of the white Southern poor, he should have stated that he had used "poetic license" when writing *Tobacco Road.* He should have told Northerners that the novel represented not a "typical picture" but rather an exaggeration: there were actually were very few of Jeeter's type living in the region (less than I percent of the population).[33] Other local writers in Augusta argued that people of Jeeter's type, who should be considered for eugenic measures, were actually "derelicts" (individuals who did not earn any money) and in a class below tenant farmers; very few, they noted, lived in their area.[34] Other writers responded by invoking their own blood heritage, striking a eugenic argument in favor of the South. In an article in the *New York Post,* one Southerner declared that the poor whites of Georgia were "almost pure-blooded people of Anglo-Saxon strain." In response to Caldwell's criticism of Georgia's Governor Eugene Talmadge, whom Caldwell claimed had not distributed relief to the poor whites, the writer in the *Post* charged it was the Northern "carpet baggers" who were rigging the economy, once again favoring one race over another.[35] The implicit defense of Jeeter—harkening back to Civil War terminology—carried the suggestion that an attack on Southern poor whites was an attack on white supremacy. The desire to separate Jeeter from their region as a point of identification was profoundly undercut by the very conditions the *Chronicle* writers reported: starvation, disease, lack of sanitation, and poor medical care. The failure of federal or state aid to reach these recipients was also made clear.

The local response to the play, the book, and the articles by Caldwell created more extensive debates beyond the pages of the *Augusta Chronicle.* One reviewer in the *New York Times* described the play as "another of those familiar plays about Southern imbeciles, who never bathe, rarely eat and are generally disagreeable."[36] Brooks Atkinson, also of the *Times,* stated,

"[T]he theatre has never sheltered a fouler or more degenerate parcel of folks than the hardscrabble family of Lester"; he found truth in the play, which he felt "chronicled the complete degeneracy of the Georgia cracker." Atkinson said the play had "moments of merciless power when the truth is flung into your face with all the slime that truth contains." This truth included the lascivious nature of Jeeter, his "animal sensuality," and the degradation of his family, "ragged, foul, starving and lazy."[37] The slippage from entertainment to truth dogged reactions to the play, which emphasized the Lesters' rampant sexuality. The play was repeatedly challenged in court on charges of indecency, and it was banned in several cities, attracting even more national attention. One critic claimed that at least seven million people saw the play between 1934 and 1940 in its national run across the country.[38] The confusion over whether it represented the real truth of Southern sharecroppers was compounded by Caldwell's defense of it. In his published notes on the play, he described the Georgian scenes that served as his inspiration.[39] Theodore Dreiser, in recommending *Tobacco Road* for a Pulitzer Prize in drama, wrote that it represented an "honest and forceful reality."[40] Although Caldwell had intended his novel to be an experiment in realism, it was the humor and sexuality of the play that captured audience interest.

Showing their regional investment in defending Jeeter, conservative Southerners responded with annoyance. Referring to the "thousands" of tenant farmers in his district, Georgia Democratic Representative Braswell Deen tried to get the play banned in Washington, DC, based on its "untruthful . . . sketch" of Southern life.[41] Agrarian John Donald Wade entered the discussion in 1936, stating, "Mr. Caldwell has apparently persuaded himself and many others, among them the editors of the intellectual weeklies in New York, that Jeeter Lester and his kind are fairly typical of twenty million Southern countrymen."[42] Although he felt the book carried an "implicit accusal [sic] of New York itself as largely responsible for the conditions the book tells about," he argued that that critique was lost on play audiences. He noted that New Yorkers would see the play as a vindication of the Civil War; he theorized sarcastically, "They [the New Yorkers] have learned a great deal about an alien and *primitive* people. And they have had their vanity flattered (never was a New Yorker so depraved) and their consciences set easy (if the people whom the Civil War disrupted were of *this* stamp, then disruption was what was the best for them)"[43] (emphasis added). The framing of Caldwell's text as an indictment of Northern attitudes was echoed in later years by Agrarian Donald Davidson. Referring to Caldwell's publication about poor Southerners, *You Have Seen Their Faces* (1937), completed with photographer Margaret Bourke-White, Davidson quipped that it was actually all Southerners who were the tenants of the North.[44] Conservatives sought to polarize debates even though Caldwell never stated that the South was itself an imbecile, but as Wade noted, the Lesters were represented as "morons," and many believed they represented the Southern population at large. For his part, Caldwell argued that the play and the book were not intended as an exaggeration but were part of a progressive effort to draw attention to the horrid living and economic conditions in the region.[45]

Arguments over Jeeter's type intensified as the decade progressed, and more prominent voices joined in the debate. The essayist and journalist H. L. Mencken proved to be the conservatives' greatest nemesis. His desire to sterilize poor white farmers of Jeeter's ilk awakened the ire of Davidson, who was quick to enter the fray; he remained a prominent defender of traditional regional identity throughout his life. Mencken's challenge to the white supremacist ideology of the South found voice much earlier in the century yet came into full bloom in the 1930s in his piece about the sterilization of sharecroppers. His essay "The Sahara of the Bozart" (beaux arts), published in a shortened form in the *New York Evening Mail* in 1917 and then in 1920 in his essay collection *Prejudices: Second Series*, started his eugenic diatribe and functioned as a launching point for an extended exchange with Davidson.[46] He insisted that class lines between whites were very strong, fueling—based on eugenic grounds—the intellectual demise of the region. Mencken's refusal to credit any Southerners, except one, with literary, philosophical, or artistic accomplishments caused profound rage among many Southern readers. He wrote, "Once you have counted James Branch Cabell . . . you will not find a single Southern prose writer who can actually write. . . . [W]hen you come to critics, musical composers, painters, sculptors, architects and the like, you will have to give it up, for there is not even a bad one between the Potomac mud-flats and the Gulf. Nor an historian. Nor a sociologist. Nor a philosopher. Nor a theologian. Nor a scientist. In all these fields the South is an awe-inspiring blank."[47] Mencken argued that the lack of "beaux arts" resulted from the diminishing streams of aristocratic blood. Though an aristocratic Old South did exist at one time, he suggested, it had been replaced by the New South, composed of poor whites. "There remains, at the top, a ghost of the old aristocracy. . . . But it has lost all of its old leadership to fabulous monsters from the lower depths," he wrote.[48] He painted an image of this literary, scientific, and philosophic wasteland as a product of "blood"—eugenic waste.

In Mencken's opinion, resolving this dire situation required eugenic measures. He recommended treating poor whites like the new immigrants of the North, the objects of eugenic censure:

> The immigrants of the North have been studied at great length, and [there is] . . . elaborate data as to their racial strains, their stature and cranial indices, their relative capacity for education. . . . But the older stocks of the South, and particularly the emancipated and dominant poor white trash, have never been investigated scientifically, and most generalizations about them are probably wrong. For example, the generalization that they are purely Anglo-Saxon in blood. . . . The chief strain down there, I believe is Celtic. . . . It is highly probable that some of the worst blood of western Europe flows in the veins of the Southern poor whites. . . . The original strains, according to every honest historian, were extremely corrupt.[49]

Mencken located poor whites as descendants of indentured servants, with lines between upper and lower classes clearly drawn, precluding intermarriage: "Poor whites went unfertilized from above, and so missed the improvement that so constantly shows itself in the peasant stocks of other counties"; class differences in the Old South were "congenital."[50] Mencken described "Negroes" who mixed bloodlines with upper-class whites as producing strong art, literature, and music, turning their noses up at unions with poor whites. He claimed Southerners had called him a "Bolshevik Jew," an indication perhaps of the Southern tendency to fight fire with fire, eugenic attacks with eugenic rebuttals.[51] From there, the argument intensified.

In the 1930s, Mencken was openly critical of the Agrarians, calling them, in his review of *I'll Take My Stand* in 1931, "sufferers from nostalgic vapors."[52] Founder and editor of the *American Mercury* since 1925, Mencken used the journal to publish statistical studies that proved the backwardness of the South in terms of education, culture, economy, and law and order. In a piece that was published in three parts and titled "The Worst American State," Mencken concluded Mississippi was the worst state in the United States (followed by a host of other Southern states). He wrote, "In the midst of its hordes of barbaric peasants there is some native stock of excellent blood. But the young men of this stock, finding few opportunities at home, have to go elsewhere."[53] In 1937, Mencken sharpened his attack, pushing the satirical envelope with his suggestion that someone should offer a $50 reimbursement for every sharecropper willing to step forward and have himself sterilized. His invective struck at the heart of Southern fears about identity—namely, that the region itself had become a moron. Mencken wrote, "If all the lunatics in all the asylums of the country were sterilized hereafter, or even electrocuted, the sharecroppers of Mississippi alone would produce enough more in twenty-five years to fill every asylum to bursting. The one and only remedy is to strike at the source of all incompetence, whether social or economic, mental or physical."[54] He encouraged a man who found "God and Wall Street . . . implacably against him . . . to climb on the [operating] table under his own steam." Since environmental assistance—giving farmers houses, appliances, and instructions for farming—had failed to bring sharecroppers out of financial despair, he recommended that male sharecroppers volunteer for sterilization to "cut off the flow of their congenital and incurable inferiority" in order to "decrease . . . the production of subnormal children."[55]

Davidson countered Mencken's attacks on the South by quieting any discussion of class differences between whites and reasserting implicitly a racial hierarchy between whites and blacks. Like the other Agrarians of *I'll Take My Stand,* he painted the Northeast as the real culprit in destroying the Southern white family. He took Mencken's argument and, point by point, reversed the fantasy it contained. Whereas Mencken argued that the emerging poor whites were primarily of "Celtic" background—the "worst blood of Western Europe"—Davidson proposed that Southerners comprised the "largest proportion of the old colonial stock, relative to 'foreign strains'" (referring to the new immigrant strains that were flooding the Northeast), thus erasing Mencken's emphasis on any relationship between bloodlines and class. Mencken had commented on the mixing of strains in the South—black and white, with poor whites comprising their own separate category—but Davidson overlooked any racial mixing, stating that "Scotch-

Irish and English stock" lived "side by side with the Afro-Americans." He countered Mencken with his own eugenic attack: "In the Northeast have concentrated the recent waves of immigration, chiefly from Mediterranean and Central-Europeans stocks: the Italians, Greeks, Portuguese, the Jews from many countries"; he lamented that only in "upper New England and New York does the old colonial stock maintain its hold, and even there is it somewhat invaded by French-Canadian *habitants*."[56] The Northeast, he said, had encouraged a "gross over-emphasis on industrialism and speculative finance, with a corresponding injury and neglect of agriculture and small business."[57] Like a bad eugenicist, it had rendered the South and other regions "impotent" through the "manipulation of their resources and population by a paternal and 'foreign' agency."[58]

Davidson illustrated his point by portraying an ideal eugenic family (complete with a "hundred and fifty Negroes") that presumably existed before the onset of industrialism; his image combined an emphasis on ancestry with a certain homespun quality that silenced any references to class divisions, even as it reinforced the traditional racial divisions that had characterized Southern history. This white family subsisted on the land and gazed on the "portraits of . . . ancestors, looking down from their frames above great-grandfather's sideboard." With their neighbors, they enjoyed "simple family dinner[s]"; they swapped jokes, hunted possum, and listened to "the voices of Negroes, sifting through the dusk."[59] This family defied class definition in its combination of ancestral portraits, extensive property holdings (African American slaves), and family hunting practices (hunting possum, an activity often associated with poor whites). There was fecundity, growth, and fruitful reproduction, both human and otherwise, before the northern father intervened with his industries and monopolization of the commercial market.

Interestingly, in his counterattack on Mencken, whom he named explicitly, Davidson created a fantasy of the South as wielder of the eugenicist's knife. He imagined that some people in the South might like to see the North rendered "impotent," lacking in contributions to the nation; he similarly argued that the North was already "sterile" for a number of reasons. Referring to Mencken and other critics of the South, he commented, "If they had any strong positive belief, it was in the power of science to determine the conditions of human life. . . . They did not believe very firmly in anything; but they disbelieved stoutly in a very great deal. . . . They had cast off loyalties to place or kin." Davidson linked the lack of emphasis on family to the background of these critics. They consisted, he said, "of two sorts: migrants to New York from some region of the hinterland, from which they had escaped in search of a career; or scions of the newer immigrant stock."[60] He nodded here to Mencken, who had moved from Baltimore to New York, "a foreign city, with an amazing preponderance of heterogeneous new racial stocks." Davidson considered New York "cosmopolitan," influenced by foreign ideas, and "decadent," with "the rationalized despair of European groups" that bred literary sexual dysfunction. The literature thus produced was one of perversion: "[U]nder the guise of literary classics, the works of voluptuaries and perverts, the teeming pages of *Psychopathia Sexualis,* and all the choicest remains of the literary bordellos of the ancient and modern world" were created.[61] Davidson used sexual metaphors to indicate a nonnormative sexuality, exactly the type of sexuality eugenicists feared—one that was nonproductive and beyond the bounds of family. He concluded that "the metropolitan promise of New York is sterile."[62]

Defending the South, then, meant defending its history. Eugenics threatened what conservative Southerners held dear: the myth of the happy cotton plantation, where "Negroes" were in their places and whites honored their ancestral lines. Their descendants were a motley crew, but they still represented the past with their imagined homespun goodness, hunting parties, and jokes told on porches on late Sunday afternoons. Eugenics meant giving up this fantasy and acknowledging the deep impoverishment of the Southern farmer—black or white. Eugenics suggested that poor whites were as degenerate as blacks, an ironic challenge to a system of racial supremacy by a deeply racist and class-based science. Eugenics struck at the core of white conservative Southern identity and the ongoing struggle to resist becoming a part of the nation. As William Faulkner noted in his 1933 introduction to *The Sound and the Fury,* "[T]he South . . . is dead, killed by the Civil War. There is a thing known whimsically as the New South to be sure, but it is not the [S]outh."[63] Evoking a romanticized past and ascribing to the poor white yeoman status, writers found a range of ways to rescue Jeeter metaphorically from the eugenicist's scalpel, indicating that the resistance to eugenics as a measure to stem reproduction among lower-class whites was heavily inflected by concerns about regional identity during the economically troubled 1930s.

Notes

1. A. N. J. Den Hollander, "The Tradition of 'Poor Whites,'" in *Culture in the South*, ed. William Terry Couch (Chapel Hill: University of North Carolina Press, 1935), 414.

2. H. L. Mencken, "Utopia by Sterilization," *American Mercury* 41 (1937): 403.

3. Ibid., 408.

4. See Edward Larson's argument on this point in *Sex, Race, and Science: Eugenics in the Deep South* (Baltimore, MD: Johns Hopkins University Press, 1995), 7–14.

5. Rupert Vance, *Human Geography of the South* (Chapel Hill: University of North Carolina Press, 1932), 191.

6. J. Wayne Flynt, *Dixie's Forgotten People: The South's Poor Whites* (Bloomington: Indiana University Press, 1979), 67; see also Herman Clarence Nixon, "Farm Tenancy to the Forefront," *Southwest Review* 22 (1936): 11–15.

7. Flynt, *Dixie's Forgotten People*, 65–66.

8. Ibid., 84. See also Pete Daniel, "The Legal System and Sharecropping: The South since 1933," in *Race and Class in the American South since 1890*, ed. Melvyn Stokes and Rick Halpern (Oxford: Berg, 1994), 79–102.

9. See Stephen Fender's essay within this volume and Stuart Kidd's review of the Resettlement Agency's studies on the Hollow Folk in "The Reinvention of the Southern Poor White," in *Rewriting the South: History and Fiction*, ed. Lothar Hönnighausen and Valeria Gennaro Lerda (Tübingen, Germany: Francke, 1993), 219–30.

10. Stark Young, "Not in Memoriam, but in Defense," in *I'll Take My Stand: The South and the Agrarian Tradition* (Baton Rouge: Louisiana State University Press, 1977), 336, 347.

11. Larson, *Sex, Race, and Science*, 17.

12. For a history of surveys and the opening of institutions, see Steven Noll, *Feeble-Minded in Our Midst: Institutions for the Mentally Retarded in the South, 1900–1940* (Chapel Hill: University of North Carolina Press, 1995), 11–26.

13. Ibid., 12.

14. A. S. Priddy quoted in Deposition of Harry Laughlin in Virginia Circuit Court of Amherst County, *Buck v. Priddy*, April 13, 1925, in Harry H. Laughlin, "Analysis of the Hereditary Nature of Carrie Buck," in *The Legal Status of Eugenical Sterilization* (Chicago: Fred J. Ringley Co., 1930), 17.

15. Ibid., 195.

16. W. L. Funkhouser, M.D., "Human Rubbish," *Journal of the Medical Association of Georgia* 26 (1937): 197.

17. C. W. Stiles, "Early History, in Part Esoteric, of the Hookworm (Uncinariasis) Campaign in Our Southern States," *Journal of Parasitology* 33 (1947): 1–18. Cited in Allen Chase, "False Correlations = Real Deaths: The Great Pellagra Cover-Up, 1914–1933," in

Genetic Destiny: Race as a Scientific and Social Controversy, ed. Ethel Tobach and Harold M. Proshansky (New York: AMS Press, 1976), 101.

18. "A Newly Recognized Factor in American Anemias—'The Germ of Laziness,'" *Popular Science Monthly* (February 1903): 381–83.

19. Chase, "False Correlations," 101.

20. Charles Davenport, "The Hereditary Factor in Pellagra," *Archives of Internal Medicine,* 18, no. 1 (July 1916): 15.

21. Andrew Nelson Lytle, "The Hind Tit," in *I'll Take My Stand,* 211.

22. Ibid., 245.

23. John Crowe Ransom, "Reconstructed but Unregenerate," in *I'll Take My Stand,* 16.

24. Den Hollander, "The Tradition of 'Poor Whites,'" 416.

25. Ibid., 429.

26. Erskine Caldwell, *Tobacco Road* (New York: Signet, 1932), 158. Karen Keely, in her study of eugenics within the text, found Caldwell wavering between condemning the "morally bankrupt people in Augusta" and the Lester family members for their own depravity. See Keely, "Poverty, Sterilization, and Eugenics in Erskine Caldwell's *Tobacco Road,*" *Journal of American Studies* 36, no. 1 (2002): 42.

27. Caldwell, *Tobacco Road,* 60.

28. Dan B. Miller, *Erskine Caldwell: The Journey from Tobacco Road* (New York: Alfred A. Knopf, 1995), 124–25.

29. I. S. Caldwell, "The Bunglers: A Narrative Study in Five Parts," *Eugenics* 3, no. 6 (June 1930): 203.

30. Ibid., 3, no. 7 (July 1930): 249–51.

31. Ibid., 3, no. 9 (September 1930): 335.

32. In her review of Caldwell's study, Keely describes the senior Caldwell as "never tak[ing] the eugenics hard line," blaming the social and economic conditions, instead of heredity, for the Bunglers' destitute condition (35). I agree with her conclusion yet also see a critique of eugenics present in his narration.

33. Editorial, "The Caldwell Issue and Long Range Rehabilitation," *Augusta Chronicle,* March 24, 1935, 4.

34. "Investigation Is Made to Determine Basis Caldwell Had for All His Writings," *Augusta Chronicle,* March 10, 1935, 1, 19.

35. James Barlow Jr., "Letter to the Editor of the *New York Post*: 'Share Cropper Conditions Denied,'" *New York Post,* March 6, 1935, 10.

36. Walter Winchell, *New York Times,* December 5, 1933, quoted in Miller, *Erskine Caldwell,* 195.

37. Brooks Atkinson, "Henry Hull in *Tobacco Road,* Based on the Novel by Erskine Caldwell," *New York Times,* December 5, 1933, 31.

38. Miller, *Erskine Caldwell,* 198–202.

39. Erskine Caldwell, "Mr. Caldwell Jots Down a Few Notes on Georgia and 'Tobacco Road,'" *New York Times,* December 1, 1935, X7.

40. Theodore Dreiser, Dartmouth Scrapbooks, vol. 2, 22, quoted in Miller, *Erskine Caldwell,* 198.

41. "'Tobacco Road' Winds Its Way into Congress," *New York Herald Tribune,* 7 April 1936, 14.

42. John Donald Wade, "Sweet Are the Uses of Degeneracy," *Southern Review* 1 (Winter 1936): 455.

43. Ibid., 454.

44. Donald Davidson, "Erskine Caldwell's Picture Book," *Southern Review* 4 (Summer 1938): 18.

45. Erskine Caldwell, "Tobacco Roads in the South," *New Leader,* June 13, 1936, 4, reprinted in *Critical Essays on Erskine Caldwell,* ed. Scott MacDonald (Boston: G. K. Hall, 1981), 48–50.

46. Reprinted in *A Mencken Chrestomathy,* ed. H. L. Mencken (New York: Alfred A. Knopf, 1967), 184–95.

47. Ibid., 186.

48. Ibid., 186–87.

49. Ibid., 189–90.

50. Ibid., 192, 191.

51. Ibid., 194.

52. H. L. Mencken, "Uprising in the Confederacy," *American Mercury* 22, no. 87 (March 1931): 380.

53. Charles Angoff and H. L. Mencken, "The Worst American State," *American Mercury* 24, no. 95 (November 1931): 371.

54. Mencken, "Utopia by Sterilization," 405.

55. Ibid., 406, 403.

56. Donald Davidson, *Regionalism and Nationalism in the United States: The Attack on Leviathan* (New Brunswick, NJ: Transaction Publishers, 1991), 103; italics in original.

57. Ibid., 113.

58. Ibid., 119.

59. Ibid., 152–54.

60. Ibid., 161.

61. Ibid., 163.

62. Ibid., 166.

63. William Faulkner, "An Introduction to *The Sound and the Fury*" (1933 edition), reprinted in *Mississippi Quarterly* 26 (1973): 411.

SIX

Poor Whites and the
Federal Writers' Project

The Rhetoric of Eugenics in the
Southern Life Histories

Stephen Fender

ABSTRACT

Stephen Fender's chapter, more than others in this collection, clarifies how difficult a struggle it was, even for progressive thinkers in the 1930s, to separate a belief in the preponderant influence of environment from claims about the influence of heredity and the hereditary studies made by so prominent by eugenics activists in the 1910s and 1920s. Fender examines the Federal Writers' Project (FWP) in the South, particularly the influences informing the project as initiated by William Terry Couch and the writings that were published as part of the FWP. He finds that Couch chose as his models for the "life histories" two works—*Human Factors in Cotton Culture* by Rupert Vance (1929) and *Hollow Folk* by Mandel Sherman and Thomas Henry (1933)—which, despite their authors' stated disavowal of the causal effects of eugenics, still heavily reflected the methods and assumptions of earlier family studies made or used by the Eugenics Record Office.

The first half of Fender's essay establishes the connections in style and content between his two chosen models and earlier studies, including the infamous Jukes and Kallikak family studies. Fender then moves to the texts of the Southern FWP, arguing that the essays also carried eugenic biases in style and content. Specifically, he contends they linked environmental conditions to the character of the families being written about; they expressed unconscious biases about appropriate family size for families of different classes; and they gave little voice to poor tenant farmers but let landowners speak in their own words. By starting the life histories (or, as Fender puts it, the case studies) of tenant-farming families with disparaging descriptions of the local environment, authors wittingly or unwittingly resurrected lingering Lamarckian equations of bad environments with bad heredity (so clear in the late-nineteenth-century Jukes and Kallikak studies). This murkiness—was the tenant farmer's poor state caused by environmental influences or by heredity?—caused the life histories to seem more eugenically motivated than Couch actually intended.

Life histories are often considered the most democratic form of literary production. From Henry Mayhew's *London Labour and the London Poor* (1851) to Studs Terkel's *Division Street, America* (1966), *Hard Times* (1970), and *The Good War* (1984), these miniautobiographies set out to give ordinary people the chance to speak for themselves. Certainly, an egalitarian motive lay behind the greatest American effort to collect vernacular personal narratives from around the nation, the life histories program undertaken by the Federal Writers' Project (FWP) of the Works Progress Administration (WPA) during the Great Depression of the 1930s. Yet William Terry Couch, who first suggested the idea of the life histories to the FWP, originally conceived the project to serve a very different purpose.

For Couch, who ran the University of North Carolina (UNC) Press and directed the whole of the southeastern region of the FWP, the life histories were to be a way of investigating the intractable problems of the Southern economy. In particular, Couch was concerned by the physically, morally, and culturally debilitating effects of tenant farming, sharecropping, and low-paid work in the cotton mills of the Southern states—the notorious ambience, in other words, of Erskine Caldwell's fiction. Thus, constructed from the outset as a "problem," renters and employees without real property were largely denied the expression of their independent voices when interviewed by the Southern life history writers, whereas their counterparts among landowners and professionals were treated as though they had stories of genuine interest to tell. This division, based on class, between hopeless sociological specimens and energetic sources of individual enterprise was anything but egalitarian. Further complicating the matter, the terminology employed by these Southern writers borrowed the rhetoric of the notorious Eugenics Record Office of a generation earlier when characterizing the problems of the landless poor. The southern life histories therefore deserve particular analysis for the ways in which they reflected eugenic ideology, despite a general shift on the part of authors toward a belief favoring environment over heredity as a causal instrument in the cultural condition of populations.

———•◦•◦•———

In the middle of the Great Depression, Franklin Roosevelt's WPA gained momentum as a means to increase American purchasing power by putting the unemployed back to work. For the most part, the relief workers planted forests, graded roads, and developed outdoor vacation spots, but the New Deal was sufficiently enlightened to extend the idea of public works beyond the material infrastructure, recruiting a total of forty thousand artists to serve four Federal Arts Projects. One of these was for writers, the others for theatrical workers, musicians, and people involved in the visual arts. At its height, the FWP hired approximately sixty-seven hundred writers, clerks, typists, and personnel directors for projects ranging from collecting the life histories of ordinary people to the production of the state guidebooks, which, alongside conventional tourist information, covered the history, culture, and social and physical geography of each of the forty-eight states.

The writers so employed were not just those who had already established reputations as novelists or journalists; almost anyone who could put together a coherent paragraph was considered eligible. "We must get over the idea that every writer must be an artist of the first class," said the director of the project, Henry G. Alsberg: "I think we have invested art with this sort of sacrosanct, ivory-tower atmosphere too much. The craftsmen who worked on the cathedrals were anonymous. . . . I think cheap books, less fuss about our sacred personalities, and more service to the common cause in the fight against fascism . . . would bring us very much closer to the masses."[1] Such enthusiasm for cooperative expressions of the vernacular also suffused the prose of the FWP's National Folklore Section, edited by Benjamin Botkin. Looking back from a thirty-year distance to recall the work of the FWP, he remembered, "[T]he project had to utilize all degrees of writing talent and all varieties of literary skills in a cooperative undertaking which . . . would be a collective and composite portrait of America."[2] So both the means of acquiring the stories and the stories themselves were meant to be expressions of the collective.

Botkin's concept of folklore—or what he had already begun to call folksay—was both enlightened and democratic, if a trifle romantic. He understood culture to mean social custom and practice, however humble, as well as *Kunst*, or high art. The way into the living, contemporary creativity of American regional culture, he thought, was through its folklore, a far more reliable window into local creativity than the increasingly strident and accessible media of mechanical reproduction. He expressed this view in his instructions to field-workers: "Folklore is a body of traditional belief, custom, and expression, handed down by word of mouth and circulating chiefly outside of commercial and academic means of communication." All material was to be taken from oral sources, exactly as heard. "Take down everything you hear," he instructed, "just as you hear it, without adding, taking away, or altering a word or syllable. *Your business is to record, not to correct or improve*" (emphasis in original).[3] Above all, as Botkin described later, the idea was to catch the essence of "oral literature," "the forthrightness, tang, and tone of people talking; the immediacy and concreteness of the participant and the eyewitness, and the salty irony and mother wit which, like the gift of memory, are kept alive by the bookless world."[4]

Recent theorists of autobiography would dismiss as naive Botkin's assumption that the voice of the people could somehow be transmitted in its pristine subjectivity to the reading public. Potential problems included the ideology implicit in the narrative structure of the interview; the tendency of subjects to collaborate with their audience in constructing what was supposed to be their own version of the past; and above all, the social or racial gap between the interrogators and their subjects—a barrier so insurmountable as to prompt theorist Pierre Bourdieu's pessimistic assessment that in the gathering of peasant or working-class autobiographies, "the controlled classes do not speak, they are spoken."[5]

Additionally, the basic assumptions lying behind the project differed from state to state and between whole regions and the central office. Botkin recalled the divergence between his own objectives and those of Couch, who "was primarily interested in the life history as a sociological document . . . recalling the life of a people . . . through different types." Botkin primarily had been "interested in a kind of folkloristic life history, in which the emphasis was on fantasy and idiom, the two being inseparable in folk-say."[6]

Since it was Couch who first came up with the idea of the life histories, it is worth examining the reasons for and the exact nature of his "sociological" orientation. Alarmed at the extent to which the South had become a byword for social and economic backwardness and almost a symbol of the nation's economic problems, Couch had begun to use his position at the UNC Press to encourage and promote books dealing with problems specific to the region. His massive compendium, *Culture in the South* (1934), collected essays on various aspects of Southern life—its occupations, social and physical geographies, politics, labor relations, education, and literature.

Couch was concerned with (and for) the lives of ordinary Southerners—black and white, female and male—not with the romantic perceptions or mythic representations that dominated literary fashion of the 1920s and 1930s. He demanded an analysis of Southern problems based on a study of the past and an observation of the present that integrated knowledge of economics, employment rights, and forms of social control, illustrating their impact on the lives of ordinary people. Above all, he believed, no human quality was innate and no institution so rooted in tradition that it could not be reformed. In short, his analysis of the problems and his hints at their solutions comprised a truly progressive agenda. Yet the resulting Southern life histories were anything but progressive. In the case of sharecroppers and tenant farmers, these supposedly autobiographical accounts, gathered explicitly to throw a clear light on their "problems," presented a hapless, rootless, shiftless, and degenerate population—victims of a seemingly intractable economic system, incapable of planning for the future, improvidently producing numbers of children beyond their means to support them, and generally turning their backs on modern life.

How and why did such an enlightened ambition turn so pessimistic and reactionary, portraying a desolate landscape in which neither the system nor its human victims could be improved? The answers lie in the particular mixture of literature and sociology in which Couch's concerns were embedded and the ways in which his program for inquiry and reform had already absorbed—whether consciously or not—the rhetoric of the mainline eugenics. Only by tracing the Southern life histories back to their discursive origins do the reasons for this strange transmission become apparent.

By the middle of 1937, the state guidebooks, which had preoccupied the FWP until then, began to be completed and published. Casting about for new projects to take their place, Alsberg memoed the regional and state directors asking for ideas. Couch suggested using the writers in the Southern states to investigate specifically Southern problems, under headings such as "Cases of Landlord-Tenant Relations," "Poor Whites in the South," "Rural and Urban Slums," and so forth. But above all, as he wrote to Alsberg, he wanted to see "Life Histories of Tenant Farmers and Their Families. Very little information on this subject is available. The kind of material I have in mind is best illustrated by the case histories . . . of *Human Factors in Cotton Culture* by Rupert B. Vance. I left a copy of this work with you when I was in Washington. Material of this kind seems to be of the greatest importance. It ought to be collected from every Southern state, from all types of tenants, sharecroppers, share renters and renters."[7] This memo makes the important point that however we may remember the FWP life histories—whether through the gritty vernacular of a Chicago window cleaner interviewed by Studs Terkel, through Ralph Ellison's reported comments of a hip black musician in Harlem, or through the thousands of personal narratives from other American regions and occupations, from cowboys in Texas to fishermen in Maine—the life histories were first conceived within two paradigms, that of the South and that of its problems.

Rupert B. Vance's book and others recommended by Couch in this same message to Alsberg provide a clue to why the Southern life histories were to diverge so markedly from Botkin's more folkloristic investigations. Any study of poor whites in the South, Couch wrote, should start with Vance's article on that topic in *Culture in the South*. But he noted that the best book yet on the problem, the "techniques" of which "it would be highly desirable to apply," was a study of isolated Appalachian mountain communities called *Hollow Folk*, published in 1933. What sort of essays and books were these? And why did Couch consider their techniques to be so appropriate to the investigation of tenant farmers and poor whites in general?

Hollow Folk records a systematic study of five communities in the Blue Ridge Mountains, each one graded on its accommodation to modernity. From the outset, the authors of the work were anxious to establish their scientific credentials. "Two psychologists and their assistants, a nutritionist, a psychiatrist and sociologists took part in the investigation," they wrote in their preface. "In addition a field worker intimately acquainted with the mountain people lived amongst them continuously for two years gathering social and economic data."[8] What seems to have motivated the study was the scandalous realization that these "unlettered folk"—who had

"no community government, no organized religion, little social organization" and whose "children never had seen the flag nor heard of the Lord's
Prayer"—were descended from that "almost pure Anglo-Saxon stock" that
elsewhere had settled the New World and helped to build the country.[9]
What had gone wrong here? How had they degenerated to this?

"Colvin Hollow" (all the names of people and places in the work are
fictitious) lay at the lowest cultural level of the five communities. There,
babies were born onto beds of rags without medical supervision and grew
up in an environment in which "during the warm days of spring hosts of
flies, fresh from their feasts on human excrement deposited in the woods,
pour[ed] into the cabin and settle[d] on the infant."[10] In such surroundings, conventional hygiene was impossible. There were no baths, not even
an "ole' swimming hole" for the kids, and no toilets, not even outhouses—
just the woods. Residents' diet consisted of corn and cabbage taken from
fields "almost choked with weeds," supplemented with salt pork, dried apples, and occasional rabbits and squirrels garnered from the dwindling
range of wildlife in the woods around them.[11]

Housing was equally primitive. The people lived in log cabins, of
which only a very few had front porches and one glass window nailed in
place.[12] The interiors of the cabins were typically decorated with pictures
torn from mail-order catalogs (an image that Walker Evans, the legendary
iconographer of poor white squalor, would revisit)—pictures of "silk un-
derwear, farming implements, dishes and poultry" that would never be ordered.[13] The home, as a center of community life, was usually as deficient
as the house: "Children do not frolic. . . . [E]lders do not talk freely. There
is little visiting from one cabin to another. There are no family reunions or
holidays."[14]

Under the heading "Love and Morality," the writers offered the following example to justify that significant pairing of topics. "Mazie, living
in a small cabin in the midst of Colvin Hollow, is the mother of four illegitimate children. . . . There were [sic] no duplication of paternity. The fa-
thers of these children were married men, according to Mazie. One was a
close relative of hers."[15] As this implied, "'love' in the hollow calls for little
more than physical gratification," the authors opined.[16] Thus, they established an equation—or, rather, insinuated it—between unlicensed breeding
unchecked by the poverty and disease that would normally slow childbearing
and further physical, economic, and moral decline. The authors presented

a cybernetic system out of control, lacking the feedback to keep it within bounds, as the mechanism for the degeneration of that "almost pure Anglo-Saxon stock"; the poorer they were, the more they bred, and the more they bred, the poorer they got.

The authors' much-vaunted scientific credentials did not result in a sound scientific study, and their work failed to serve the community with detachment, especially when the topics under examination grew less tangible, as in the chapters titled "Desire and Worry" and "Education, and Mentality." As for desires, the Colvin Hollow children were content when handed a piece of candy—or, even better, a chew of tobacco. Some wanted money but had no idea of its value: "A penny was received as gratefully as a half dollar; two pennies please a child more than one quarter."[17] Among the adults, few had any anxieties. "No man worries about losing a job. He has none to lose. Nobody worries about paying bills. There are none to pay. Nobody is tortured with a gnawing conscience."[18] In this impertinent bit of mind reading, the unacknowledged cultural bias of the authors suddenly surfaces. Not only could they quickly detect a bad conscience, they could also imagine no cause for it other than a broken commercial contract.

Yet it is important to keep in mind that these authors were discussing not the genetic disabilities of these mountain people but the low level of their cultural accommodation. This work was a study of environment, not heredity—of the nurture rather than the nature of these isolated mountain people. The communities were graded, after all, according to how cut off they were from the main currents of modern life: the institutions of county, state, or country; markets; education; supplies of electricity and piped water; medical care; and, in general, the myriad social and commercial transactions that the authors of the study associated with the modern world.

In its explicit orientation toward these marginal country people, *Hollow Folk* did not participate in the rage for eugenics so fashionable during the 1920s, when the Eugenics Record Office (ERO) sent field-workers out to gather data to demonstrate that the economic fecklessness, sexual promiscuity, and general cultural backwardness of the rural poor were all "cacogenic" traits, the cause as well as the result of many decades of degeneration through inbreeding.[19] Instead, *Hollow Folk* made clear the authors' preference for environment over heredity as an explanation for the backwardness of these mountain communities. Pointing out that many of the younger mountain people had been out-migrating in order to better their condition, the authors added, "If the geneticists are correct about the effect of the deterioration of germ plasm with time it would appear that the newer generation would be *less* apt to seek a change than the older."[20]

Other experts within Couch's ambit were equally explicit in their refusal of the genetic explanation for the backwardness of the rural South. Rupert Vance's "Profile of Southern Culture," which appeared in Couch's *Culture in the South,* came down heavily in favor of the determining effects of the physical environment, blaming hookworm and pellagra for "much of the South's retardation." "The handicaps of the South are not inherent in the geographic and biological scheme of things," Vance said, just in case readers missed the point of his progressive analysis. "They partake in the nature of historical accidents and economic blunderings; they are amenable to science and social engineering; and they may be overcome."[21]

Despite some authors' rejection of the so-called germ plasm as an operative variable, the fact that these people had been left "unprotected" was seen by others as leading to hereditary decay, since impoverishment and ignorance put them at risk of exposure to "racial" poisons such as moonshine and syphilis. For all the distance they tried to put between themselves and the eugenicists, the authors of *Hollow Folk* and the various contributors to Couch's *Culture in the South* still hit the theme of degeneration very hard. According to them, the existing state of affairs showed degeneration in everything from timber, wildlife, and mineral resources to the human "stock," so much so that, for all their explicit distancing from eugenics, these progressive authors generated an atmosphere of general decline strikingly reminiscent of those field investigations published under the auspices of the ERO.

For example, one ERO description of an extended family, "the Pineys," set this scene for their existence: "Between the coastal plain and the fertile land east of the Delaware River lies 2,000 square miles of almost pure sand. . . . It was originally covered with a splendid growth of pines, interspersed with iron-producing bog lands. This primeval wealth of New Jersey was long ago exploited, and there was left only a scrubby growth that but slowly replaces the timber of the past."[22] As in *Hollow Folk,* the setting was described as a region (though, in this case, not the South) whose physical geography had come down in the world, fallen from its "primeval" wealth into near sterility, an all-but-hopeless habitat. The social geography reflected this decline; the inhabitants were cast out and "recognized as a distinct people by the normal communities." Not that they had always been so degenerate: "Not a few of our 'Pine Rat' friends . . . can be traced back directly to where they branch from excellent families, often of sturdy English stock."[23] From this condition, the downward trajectory had been as steep as it was inevitable, until finally, whole families were implicated in the "cacogenic" regress; one family had "eleven children" and lived "in a ramshackle house for which they pay no rent and the father and mother gain a living by gathering moss in winter and berries in summer." The authors asserted the hereditary corollary: "The oldest boy is in the reformatory at Jamesburg, and the oldest daughter, having been committed to the State Home for Girls, had been put out on probation in a good family."[24]

In contrast to the fundamental premises of eugenic control, Couch's Southern writers were described as social Darwinists in a field of environmental determinism. That is, they treated societies as Darwin had treated species, arguing that individuals and societies either progressed or degenerated according to how successfully they competed with one another within a given environment. Both the degree of competition and the suitability of the environment were variables. In other words, not all geographic settings were equally favorable for economic and cultural development, but the fiercer the competition, the better the chance of overcoming the environmental disadvantages. This stance is a long way, philosophically speaking, from some eugenicists' teachings that the germ plasm was deteriorating due to inbreeding between degenerates. But on the scale of a human lifetime, constrained by a system in which laws, politics, and economics left the sharecropper and others who did not own land more or less unprotected, these grand forces behind degeneration must have looked and felt much the same, whether they resulted from hereditary decay or from insufficient competitiion within an adverse environment.

Historians have attempted to explain this large area of overlap between two philosophies so apparently opposed to each other during the 1930s by using the separate but related concepts of eugenics and environmentalism. They have suggested that what the two systems had in common was a belief in biological engineering to produce a population fit enough to improve the existing order. Where these two systems differed was in their stances on segregation and socialization. That is, eugenicists wanted to cut off the reproductive influence of marginal groups from normal society, whereas environmentalists worked to integrate marginal groups back into

the mainstream. As science historian Donald A. McKenzie states, "I[I]t appears that mainstream environmentalism has not challenged the fundamental eugenic model of society as an actual or potential individualist
meritocracy. . . . Both involve similar meritocratic social theories, . . . but
they involve different strategies of control."[25]

Above all, the opposing systems of social control shared a common
rhetoric, based on a grammar of "data" and "psychiatric investigation." The
instrument on which the *Hollow Folk*'s authors relied for such measurements, the Stanford-Binet test, was a method of assessing intelligence quotient (IQ) introduced from Switzerland by the eugenicist H. H. Goddard to
"scientifically" grade mental ability. Later, it became widely used for individual testing in public schools and institutions throughout the United
States, before being thrown out as too culture-specific to serve as an objective test of intelligence. Indeed, the Stanford-Binet test landed the authors
of *Hollow Folk* in some fairly embarrassing contradictions of social observation, such as when they asked the children of Colvin Hollow to define a
"post office." "The majority of those who tried to define this word said that
a post-office was a place with baskets of apples in front of it. Some added
further details, such as, 'and some men sitting at the door.' They had seen
the post-office in Oakton Hollow which is also the general store," the authors stated, but "no one directly associated mail with the definition of
post-office, probably because mail rarely comes into Colvin Hollow. . . . So
far as these children were concerned," they added, "much of this test was
in what amounted to a foreign language."[26] Clearly, a community with no
ties to the outside world—where property was unowned and uninsured,
where the people paid no taxes and subscribed to no political party, where
residents could not afford to order from Sears Roebuck for work shirts and
overalls let alone a milking machine or a new tractor, and where people
could neither read nor write—was indeed unlikely to "associate mail with
the definition of post-office."

In the spirit of a supposedly detached "scientific" sociological inquiry,
the subjects of these studies were presented not so much as individual people, families, and communities but instead as anonymous representative
types. Hence, the collective pseudonyms employed for various clans in the
ERO studies—"the Kallikaks," "the Dack Family," "the Happy Hickories"—
were reflected in the pseudonymous "Hollows" in *Hollow Folk* and in the
Southern life histories as well. Finally, these anonymous people had to be

150

treated as "cases," a much-repeated word; they were not allowed to speak for themselves but were described from a distance, sometimes in the passive voice, by the impersonal scientific investigator. What all this rhetorical apparatus produced was the impression of an unstoppable process—a force quite beyond the control of the individuals on whom it was bearing. Thus dehumanized and robbed of their free will, the subjects were presented as hapless victims for whom there was, ultimately, little hope. Whether their plight was due to genetic or social decline did not really matter; either way, the situation was irresistible and irreversible. These features are all combined in those "case histories . . . of *Human Factors in Cotton Culture* by Rupert B. Vance," of which Couch wrote so approvingly to Alsberg and later excerpted and distributed as a model for the kind of life histories he wanted his team to produce.

Take, for example, Vance's "Case History of a Share Renter" (one among many cases in his book), about a man given the pseudonym "John Smith" whose "story is set down just as he told it not three afternoons ago." It begins with John's father, "Jim Smith," who "married a wife" who could not read or write but could work. "Children were born," but they "were not healthy," for "fat meat and corn bread, with an occasional ration of biscuit" were not "conducive to health." As a result, eight of the couple's children died, with only John surviving. At age twenty-three, he married, and neither he nor his young wife had ever "been to school a day in their lives." Instead, they went to work, first as wage earners and then as sharecroppers. "The next spring his wife had a baby. She had been working hard in the field all spring, and the baby died. She hadn't a doctor." They had to buy their food and other supplies from the landlord's commissary. At the year-end reckoning, John had made $206 from his cotton, of which he owed the commissary "just a little less than $200." And that was a good year. Lacking education, John "didn't know how to figure it out." He thought he could do better, so he moved to another landowner. But his debt moved with him. This happened again and again. Every year, his wife had another baby. And so "history repeated its grim cycle, more children, more debt, more moving from place to place." John's cumulative worldly wealth at the time of the interview consisted of "three mules, two pigs, 11 chickens, a wagon, four plows, harness, an old buggy, a few squalid pieces of furniture, a wife, seven children, two cur dogs," and a debt of $1,400.[27]

Despite Vance's presentation of this material as a life history, the narrative offered is not, in fact, a life story, despite being told by the subject "just three afternoons ago." Rather, the narrative more closely is what its title claims: a case history mediated through the point of view of a supposedly detached observer. As such, the narrative unfolds in a deadpan tone of "scientific" objectivity. The subjects are anonymous, and the women and children are not even given fictional names. The passive grammatical mode reflects their lack of agency: instead of the couple having children, children are born. The statistics are exact and inescapable, and the inventories of gain and loss are accurately documented down to the last "cur dog." Yet for all its apparent detachment, Vance's narrative voice is anything but neutral. On the contrary, it is packed with judgments and values: that having children every year is the height of irresponsibility when one cannot provide them a healthy diet or medical care; that lack of education renders one vulnerable to the figures deployed at the year-end reckoning; that lighting out from a landlord will result not in freedom but in further enslavement to a financial system one does not understand; and finally, that everything, from the return on labor to the health of children, gets worse each time that "history repeat[s] its grim cycle."

Receiving an enthusiastic go-ahead from the central FWP office, Couch began work on his project for the southern life histories, based on *Hollow Folk* and Vance's case histories. He already knew what sort of people he wanted to investigate; what he needed to determine was how his fieldworkers should set about the task and what kinds of questions they should ask the millworkers, tenant farmers, and sharecroppers. Ida L. Moore, an unemployed schoolteacher and Couch's first recruit to the project, came up with the answers. The outline of questions she set out for future interviews were a long way from Botkin's interest in the "forthrightness, tang, and tone of people talking." Rather than a program for the retrieval of traditional folk culture, her list reads as a series of questions to be posed by a health visitor or someone inquiring into the suitability of a home for an adoption, much like the ERO questionnaires. The questions move through increasingly value-loaded categories such as "size of family," "effect of family size upon financial status of family," "attitudes toward large families," "number of years of school attendance," and "causes of limited education." Religion is mainly significant for its "influence . . . on morals." Inquiries into "cleanliness and order of house" are important, as is "pride in possessions."[28]

It may be nothing more than a coincidence that so many of the Southern life histories emerged and were classified under collective pseudonyms such as those so favored by the ERO reporters, but the effect was to invoke a scientist's arms-length distancing from a specimen and an erasure of the subject's individuality. Hence, "the Farlows" and "the Belks" identify two impoverished millworkers' families, one in North Carolina and the other in South Carolina. In her own reporting, Moore was especially prone to collective family pseudonyms. "The Wilsons," "the Hollifields," "the Haithcocks," "the Dunnes," and "the Renns" all figure among her titles for interviews with millworkers and tenant farmers.

This approach, however, may have stemmed directly from prior eugenic studies, whose influence on education by the time Moore was in school was significant. High school and college textbooks, such as Ernest Steel and Ella White's *Hygiene of School, Community and Home* (1932), "cited mental defectiveness as hereditary and classified as mentally defective 80 per cent of all truants, 50 per cent of paupers, . . . 50 percent of prostitutes." Maude Lee Etheredge's *Health Facts for College Students* (1934) actually cited "the Kallikaks," perhaps the best-known collective-pseudonym family in the ERO literature, as proof that pauperism, prostitution, and petty criminality were all hereditary.[29] Moore's own education, therefore, may have been peppered with such eugenicist thinking on health and welfare issues, influencing her choice of questions for the subjects of the life histories and the narratives she produced from her interviews.

For example, Ida Moore's interview of "the Haithcocks," done in West Durham, North Carolina, in July 1938, begins:

> Down in Monkey Bottoms in a small four-room house there lives a family of four women, two men, and four children. . . . In the particular house already mentioned Haithcocks, Ways, Fosters, and Piners live in dreary confusion. . . . Freida Haithcock and Hulda Foster sit in this room hours at a time, both fortified by a generous quantity of snuff, tagging the tiny sacks and dreaming of the day when they will again have a job in the mill. Together they share a tin can spittoon which is obligingly shifted from one to the other as the need arises. Flies swarm thickly about the poorly

screened house and hunt out the bread crumbs scattered by the three oldest children.[30]

The women's avid snuff taking may have been a detail lifted directly from Erskine Caldwell's writings, but the tone of voice and the insinuated connection between physical setting and moral disposition, though probably inspired by Vance and the authors of *Hollow Folk*, also shared the rhetoric of the ERO reports. In this panoramic moral view of the Haithcocks' case, the decrepit landscape of Monkey Bottoms slid imperceptibly into the physical and social disorder within the house. While Freida and Hulda dreamed idly of steady jobs, the flies were already exploiting the poorly maintained household defenses and the children's slovenliness, moving in to undermine the family's health.

In some Southern life histories, this specter of degeneration was invoked so deliberately as to bespeak a serious literary ambition. Anne Winn Stevens set the scene of her "interview" with Lester Garren and his wife, tenant farmers to whom she gave the pseudonym "Riddle," in Fletcher, North Carolina, in March 1939 as follows:

> At the top of a ragged hill grown over with scrubby oaks stands a dingy, four-room cabin. The two rooms of which it consisted originally had been painted green, but except for a few streaks here and there the paint has long since rubbed off. A lean-to of rough boards has been added. . . . Although pleasant, green fields rimmed by distant mountains partially encircle the hill, this house near the railroad tracks is as unprepossessing as the shacks in the meanest mill village. . . . At the back of the house is an irregular clearing, muddy in wet weather, dusty in dry, and cluttered with small stones. Here stand the barn, stables, and corncrib, patched loosely with rough boards. They have never been painted. . . . "My husband patched 'em up loose on purpose," said Mrs. Riddle "so if we move he can pull down his boards and take 'em with him."[31]

The writer went to great lengths to derive a sense of deterioration from— or impose it on—the surrounding landscape. Had another person passed by, he or she might have seen an agreeable, if not beautiful, country scene, but according to Stevens, the hill was decidedly "ragged" and the cabin "dingy" and neglected. Even her syntax mimicked this downward trajectory: "*Although* [set amid] pleasant, green fields," the house remained "unprepossessing." Repeatedly, good news was immediately swallowed up by bad.

Interestingly, in Stevens's life history of the Garrens, the subject's voice made one of its rare appearances, lightly inflected with just enough accent to add local color to the country setting. Yet the quote chosen also expressed the rootless world of the tenant farmers, in which permanent constituents of the landscape, such as barns and stables, were kept "patched . . . up loose" so they could be moved along with their owners. What could more perfectly symbolize the provisional status of the tenant farmer? What does not seem to have occurred to Stevens is that keeping buildings portable when materials are costly and cash short is an entirely rational response to the precarious condition of people who might be evicted at the year's end. Instead, for Stevens, the picture was one in which tenancy, uprootedness, and decrepitude were seamlessly interstitched to form a moral tableau.

One common feature of the dismal scenes presented in the Southern life histories was the existence of too many children. This situation was shown to be both the cause of the families' poverty, as when sudden illnesses confronted them with unexpected medical bills, and also the effect of their backwardness and improvidence. Ida Moore emphasized this in her study of "the Dunnes," an impoverished millworking family descended from tenant farmers. "Sally Dunne was the mother of thirteen children," Moore wrote, "three of whom are dead and three married. Seven of the children ranging from two and a half to eighteen lived with their mother and father." Moore met Sally and some of her offspring sitting on the porch tagging tobacco sacks. She noted that Sally's "unwieldy body bulges over the sides of her chair and an enormous tumor gives her the appearance of permanent pregnancy." Both the mention and the placing of this last detail are truly grotesque in their hidden judgment. Related as it is by Moore to her pregnancies, the tumor serves as an Old Testament–style, biter-bit punishment for the woman's progenetive excess, and by converse association, her pregnancies become an illness, something to be excised by a surgeon could she afford one. Meanwhile, Sally's daughter Stella, who lived with her mother, had a child of her own, not much younger than her uncles and aunts. Moore wrote, "Stella looks out into the yard where her baby is playing with her young sisters and brothers. 'I hope I don't never have another one,' she says. 'I had a miscarriage from lifting a heavy tub of water when he wasn't more than a year old. I went to the doctor and asked him what a woman could do to keep from havin' babies. I'm tryin' to do what he told me.'"[32]

Poor schooling was another common index of hapless improvidence in these life histories. "'If you ain't got learnin' you can't get the kinda work that helps you,'" Mary Cox, of Tryon, North Carolina, told Adyleen G. Merrick in November 1938: "'I never got no education. I always had somebody to look after and no time for nothin' else.'"[33] In other instances, people who had the opportunity to become educated were depicted as lacking the will to do so. For instance, another sharecropper, John Autrey of Clinton, North Carolina, also lamented his lack of education. In one of the few passages in which he was allowed to speak for himself, he confessed, "'I didn't get no place [in school]. I can write my name, but I hated school so much that I did not learn to read.'" What he did like to do was to "loaf . . . at the poor farmers' club, the filling station."[34]

The Southern FWP writers did not lack sympathy for millworkers, tenants, and sharecroppers—far from it. Instead, they saw all these people as part of the Southern "problem"—victims of an exploitative system. As such, they had to be reported on, rather than listened to, and so their lives were treated in the pseudoscientific tone so prevalent in the ERO reports and *Hollow Folk*—as the subjects of a survey rather than individuals whose lives told in their own words might be of interest. Consequently, when the interviewers' voices took precedence over those of the respondents (which was often), their rhetoric sometimes assumed an oddly generalizing frame of reference, as though about a specimen under observation. "You walk uneasily through the confusion which is their home," wrote Ida L. Moore of the Dunnes: "You look at the dirty floor and your mind is brought back to the fact that the woman who keeps this house is 'settin' out on the back porch.'"[35] But just who was this "you"? Moore's interrogative style disguised the fact that it was she herself, speaking in the generalizing second-person plural, so as to implicate the reader and the right-thinking world at large in her judgment—the standard from which the Dunnes, whose eccentricity was marked out by that condescending quotation "'settin,'" had fallen away.

And sometimes the discourse did not just ape the rhetoric of the ERO but led through it right back to its founding premises. The life history of "Sallie Brown," of Lowndes County, Alabama, dated September 27, 1938, was presented almost entirely in the words of the anonymous writer. Sallie's tenant-farmer family inhabited an antebellum mansion, but the "beautiful architectural attractiveness, the memories of its former grandeur and cultural atmosphere" were now decayed and forgotten. Sallie's state was similarly fallen. Her "weak-hearted father still spent his times at the crossroads stores and continued to discuss the crops, weather, etc., etc., stimulated by an occasional 'done.' Thus it is seen that the ranks of Sallie's force are thinned out, which at best were too feeble."[36] If the writer felt any embarrassment here about embracing the theory of genetic decline, she hid that eccentric philosophy under the revealing phrase *thus it is seen*. This use of the characteristic passive mode of a scientific report on an experiment—"a test-tube was taken"—was another promiscuously generalizing device, used conventionally to express disinterested findings but employed here to naturalize the hidden determinism of an observer who was anything but neutral and disinterested.

The tone adopted by these same field-workers when they interviewed people of middle-class status—whether farm owners, businesspeople, or professionals—was entirely different, for these more independent people were not considered part of the Southern "problem." Consequently, in their stories, the same topics covered in the lives of the Southern country poor got a very different spin. Loafing, shifting relationships, and imbibing too little education or too much alcohol were usually deprecated in reference to a tenant, an employee, or a customer, but when the landowners or businesspeople admitted to these practices, such behaviors were typically taken as signs of independence, initiative, and strong constitution. Similarly, an above-average number of children in middle-class families was considered an index not of sexual excess but of a robust patrimony. Where the owners and professionals were frequently pulling up stakes and drifting, their actions were usually seens as a sign not of their fecklessness but of their enterprise and their willingness to accept temporary discomfort to better their position. Above all, the owners, businesspeople, and professionals got to speak for themselves, in the sense that what seemed to be their own words formed a predominant proportion of the discourse, if not the whole of it.

Additionally, their comparative rootedness seemed to bestow on the landowners another advantage not perceived in the lives of tenants, sharecroppers, and millworkers: the dimension of historical perspective. They could, in other words, claim membership in a tradition. Anne Winn Stevens—for whom the lives of tenant farmers Lester Garren and his wife could be characterized in terms of "barn, stables, and corncrib, patched loosely with rough boards" that could be knocked down and taken with them if they decided to move—was altogether more impressed with a family of dairy farmers whom she interviewed in February 1939. "'My father,'" she quotes "Brad Suttles" (David M. Snelson) as saying, "'was with Lee's Army, and was wounded in the Seven Days' Battle around Richmond. After Lee's surrender, my father came back to the mountains, married, and settled down to farming his own land.'" And as it happened, the geography of both the house and its setting rooted that family in the local landscape as firmly as in history:

> The 72-acre Suttles farm, which has belonged to direct descendants of the pioneer settler . . . ever since he cleared and developed the tract, is almost all bottom land, and very fertile. . . . On the North and east is a sheltering range of low, wooded hills, which protects the valley like a huge arm, curved defensively. Some of the spur ridges have treeless, grassy slopes, where the farm's herd of Guernsey cattle may often be seen grazing. . . . The . . . farmhouse . . . is a two-story structure of the Colonial type seen often in New England, . . . framed and protected by a hill on the north. There is one immense boxwood near the small front porch.[37]

The contrast to the Riddles' "dingy, four-room cabin" on top of the "ragged hill grown over with scrubby oaks" could not be more marked. Here, all was orderly, decent, and protected. Like that "immense boxwood" next to the farmhouse redolent of the nation's most traditional domestic architecture in New England, the Suttles seemed to have been there almost forever. Though it was only a 72-acre hill farm, the point was that they owned it.

The relatively favorable treatment of these other white Southerners appears to have been directly related to their relationship to the land and the fact that they owned real property. Because the agency granted by ownership seems to have defended them from the status of "problem," they were insulated from the imputations of sociologists and eugenicists alike that they were the victims of an irreversible, degenerative decline. In other words, a much older set of values was unconsciously being brought into play—a doctrine, going back through Thomas Jefferson to John Locke, that all private and public virtue flowed from the yeoman farmer because identity was established and defined by the ownership and the improvement of property.

Conversely, a recurrent critique that surfaced in so many of the share-croppers' and tenant farmers' life histories was their persistence in a pre-capitalist or even, in some cases, precommercial environment. "'We have never owned a horse or a mule or a cow or any tools or anything to ride in,'" the wife of sharecropper "Jim Jeffcoat" told W. O. Forster in Durham County, North Carolina, in 1939. The family had never owned a house and never would, she thought. In terms of their economic progress, she told Forster, "'We seem to move around in circles like the mule that pulls the syrup mill.'"[38] Not to have a permanent house or job was one thing; not to have bought tools and animals to work the land was more serious. Without money or the habit of managing it, the shiftless were condemned to endless unpleasant surprises, such as doctors' bills and the annual settlement with the landlord that always left them worse off than the year before.

"I came away from this home," wrote W. O. Forster, of Mary and John Allen in Clinton, North Carolina, "feeling that these people are living in an obscure corner away from the main current of life stirring in the nation." Part of the Allens' backwardness was that they did not know "how to estimate an adequate income."[39] They and others like them were also doomed to foolish spending and to be prey for sharp merchants, as encountered by Stella, daughter of the Dunnes:

> When she and Bill were first married, they selected a bedroom suite, a cedar chest, an upholstered chair, two linoleums, and a big fine oil stove. When she first saw the bedroom suite marked at $39.50, she thought it must really be the greatest bargain in town. When, after the sale was made, the proprietor began adding carrying charges which brought the price up to $61 she was a little baffled, but he explained to her just how easily the payments could be made. The bill for the furniture came to $200 and she and Bill had paid all of it but $80 at the time they lost their jobs. She doesn't yet see why they couldn't let her keep at least the bedroom suite.[40]

Thus estranged from the world of competent commercial exchange, these tenants and employees often resorted to more marginal activities. Mary Cox explained that when the mill shut down, she "'took a bucket and went out blackberryin'. I made me a dollar in two days and more than that the next week.'" When things really got desperate, she bought illicit corn liquor and resold it at night for up to five times what she paid for it.[41] Similarly, in November 1938, "Clem Finley," a tenant farmer in County Richland, South Carolina, told John L. Dove that he would go "'over to Columby t'morrow with a load of kindlin' for the market. And then I've got a little snake bite to deliver to a certain fellah or two over thar.'"[42]

Dispassionately viewed, these activities would seem to be at least as commercial—indeed, enterprising—as any business stratagem. But the writers of Southern life histories were seldom dispassionate. It was not so much the illegality of bootlegging that was judged but the marginality of the trade. It was as though these people were not just excluded from routine getting and spending—which would be sad—but that they were willfully excluding themselves—which made them seem stubbornly resistant to modernity. Beyond that, they also seemed to be getting away with something: they had somehow escaped from the pressures that weighed on those who made up normative, middle-class society.

This feeling of skepticism or even hostility on the part of authors toward people who had escaped the grind of modern commercial life can be detected in the life histories, in *Hollow Folk,* and in ERO field studies. A detail much insisted on in the ERO report on "the Pineys" was the marginal status of their economy. To "gain a living," they gathered moss in winter and berries in the summer. An earlier generation of Pineys used to go hunting for cranberries: "It was the Yankee agent of one of the owners of the furnace at Hanover who in 1850, as tradition has it, first conceived the idea of improving the wild cranberry through cultivation. Up to this time, the fruit had been gathered and sold much as the huckleberry is at present. As an old woodchopper of the district put it, 'Used to be, cranberries was everybody's—*you* could go or *I* could go or anybody.'"[43]

Similarly, what marked the children of Colvin Hollow off from the rest of the world was not just that they "had never seen the flag or heard the Lord's Prayer" but that they valued a chaw of tobacco over a bag of candy and could not tell a penny from a half dollar. Here, only ten miles from "the summer camp of the President of the United States," lived people who traded without cash, made a living from their garden patches, and supplemented their diet with fish and small game gathered from the surrounding woods. At least, they did so until the mountainsides took on a new value due to demand from the tan-bark industry and were closed off to the people.[44]

Henry Alsberg, director of the FWP, had wanted the project to recruit a new vernacular style into the "common cause in the fight against fascism." His was the language of the Popular Front, reflecting that moment when the Communist Party—USA decided to join the noncommunist progressives of the New Deal against fascism, racism, and union bashing. As historian Michael Denning has shown, many liberal New Dealers in general and the writers, actors, managers, and bureaucrats of the Federal Arts Projects in particular felt they were furthering the political and cultural ambitions of the Popular Front by giving voice to disadvantaged farmworkers, factory hands, and ethnic and racial minorities.[45] Since Mayhew's *London Labour and the London Poor* in 1851, life sketches of ordinary people have been one constituent of democratic—or at least nonelitist—cultural programs.

And so it generally proved in the work of the FWP. From cities and towns all over the United States and from industries, shops, farms, and fisheries came something (notwithstanding Pierre Bourdieu's pessimism) passably resembling the voice of the people. But the Southern branch of the project turned out very differently. Though W. T. Couch also wanted to pay new attention to a forgotten people, his fixation with what he took to be a set of problems particular to the American South involved him in the literature and sociology of environmental determinism, a field of study that paradoxically fashioned its modes of analysis and expression after its exact philosophical antithesis, the biological determinism of the ERO. As a result, the rhetoric he and his writers adopted infected his progressive program and ultimately suppressed the very voices he wanted to amplify.

Notes

1. Henry G. Alsberg, "Extemporaneous Remarks at the Second American Writers Congress, June, 1937," in *The Writer in a Changing World*, ed. Henry Hart (New York: Equinox Cooperative Press, 1937), 245.

2. B. A. Botkin, "We Called It 'Living Lore,'" *New York Folklore Quarterly* 14 (1958): 196; reprinted in *Voices: The Journal of New York Folklore* 27 (2001), available at http://www.nyfolklore.org/pubs/voic27-3-4lliving.html.

3. B. A. Botkin, "Supplementary Instructions to the American Guide Manual: Manual for Folklore Studies," 1938, in Box A4, Folder 5, Federal Writers' Project: American Guide, File 1524–1942, Library of Congress Manuscript Division, Washington, DC.

4. Botkin, "We Called It 'Living Lore,'" 197.

5. Pierre Bourdieu, "La paysannerie, une classe object," *Actes de la Recherche en Sciences Sociales* 17-18 (November 1977): 4, cited in Pierre Lejeune, "The Autobiography of Those Who Do Not Write," in his *On Autobiography*, ed. Paul John Eakin, trans. Katherine Leary (Minneapolis: University of Minnesota Press, 1989), 199.

6. Botkin, "We Called It 'Living Lore,'" 198.

7. W. T. Couch, Chapel Hill, N.C., to Henry Alsberg, April 22, 1938, Box 2, Folder 26, Southern Historical Collection no. 3709, Federal Writers' Project Papers, Manuscript Department, University of North Carolina Library, Chapel Hill (hereafter cited as UNC-FWP). He specifically referred to p. 260 of *Human Factors in Cotton Culture*.

8. Mandel Sherman and Thomas R. Henry, *Hollow Folk* (New York: Thomas V. Crowell, 1933), vii.

9. Ibid., 1.

10. Ibid., 27.

11. Ibid., 42, 44.

12. Ibid., 49.

13. Ibid., 50.

14. Ibid., 43.

15. Ibid., 159.

16. Ibid., 161.

17. Ibid., 102.

18. Ibid., 106.

19. See the invaluable selection of ERO reports, with an extended introduction, edited by Nicole Hahn Rafter, *White Trash: The Eugenic Family Studies, 1877–1919* (Boston: Northeastern University Press, 1988).

20. Sherman and Henry, *Hollow Folk*, 195–96; emphasis added.

21. Rupert B. Vance, "Profile of Southern Culture," in *Culture in the South*, ed. W. T. Couch (Chapel Hill: University of North Carolina Press, 1934), 35.

22. Rafter, *White Trash*, 165.

23. Ibid.

24. Ibid., 173.

25. Donald A. McKenzie, *Statistics in Britain, 1865–1930* (Edinburgh: Edinburgh University Press, 1981), 49–50; this work also offers a summary of the literature on the overlap between environmentalism and eugenics in the 1930s.

26. Sherman and Henry, *Hollow Folk,* 124.

27. Rupert B. Vance, "'The Case History of a Share Ranter.' Taken from Human Factors in Cotton Culture by Rupert B. Vance. Adapted from the Raleigh News and Observer. Sept. 25, 1921." Typescript, Box 8, Folder 109, UNC-FWP.

28. W. T. Couch and Ida L. Moore, "Notes on the Collection of Life Histories in the South" and "Outline for Life Histories," Box 8, Folder 109, UNC-FWP.

29. Christina Cogdell, "The Futurama Recontextualized: Norman Bel Geddes's Eugenic 'World of Tomorrow,'" *American Quarterly* 52, no. 2 (2000): 193–245, 202; see also Gregory Michael Dorr's work on the place of eugenics in Southern education, "Assuring America's Place in the Sun: Ivey Foreman Lewis and the Teaching of Eugenics at the University of Virginia, 1915–1953," *Journal of Southern History* 46 (2000): 257–96, and his *Segregation's Science: The American Eugenics Movement and Virginia, 1900–1980,* forthcoming from the University of North Carolina Press.

30. Ida Moore, "The Haithcocks," American Life Histories: Manuscripts from the Federal Writers' Project, 1936–1940, Library of Congress; database searchable under titles as noted at http://memory.loc.gov/ammem/wpaintro/wpahome.html (hereafter cited as ALHM).

31. Ida Moore, "'All Our Folks Was Farmers,'" ALHM.

32. Moore, "The Dunnes," ALHM.

33. Adyleen G. Merrick, "Mary Cox," ALHM.

34. W. O. Forster, "John and Sarah Autrey," ALHM.

35. Moore, "The Dunnes," AHLM.

36. Anon., "Sallie Brown," AHLM.

37. Anne Winn Stevens, "Mountain Farming at Its Best," AHLM.

38. W. O. Forster, "Jim Jeffcoat," in *Such as Us: Southern Voices of the Thirties,* ed. Tom E. Terrill and Jerrold Hirsch (Chapel Hill: University of North Carolina Press, 1978), 58–59.

39. W. O. Forster, "Mary Allen," AHLM.

40. Moore, "The Dunnes," AHLM.

41. Merrick, "Mary Cox," AHLM.

42. John L. Dove, "A Pile of Sawdust," AHLM.

43. Rafter, *White Trash,* 170.

44. Sherman and Henry, *Hollow Folk,* 1, 11, 13, 121.

45. Michael Denning, *The Cultural Front: The Laboring of American Culture in the Twentieth Century* (New York: Verso, 1996).

SEVEN

The Descent of

Yoknapatawpha

Eugenics and the Origins of Faulkner's World

Barbara E. Ladner

ABSTRACT

Like Betsy Nies's chapter on Erskine Caldwell's *Tobacco Road* (1932), Barbara Ladner's essay examines eugenics as a trope in Southern fiction, specifically as a cultural force shaping the familial struggles that activate William Faulkner's fictional world. Faulkner's use of eugenic ideas is complex—and intentionally so. Throughout his novels set in Yoknapatawpha County, an aristocratic Southern family (the Sartorises) competes against a lower-class, highly reproductive clan that recently immigrated to the region (the Snopeses). In keeping with this eugenically based struggle for dominance, Faulkner at times expresses other conservative eugenic views in his novels, such as privileging nature over nurture and giving many of his criminal characters some physical deformity. The genetic correlation between inner moral character and exterior physiognomy was commonly asserted by eugenicists in the late 1920s and into the following decade. Albert E. Wiggam, for example, after judging a Miss Universe beauty pageant in Galveston, Texas, in 1929, stated, "'Beauty is woven into the protoplasmic fabric of the race with all that is admirable and excellent,'" and Ellsworth Huntington, in *Tomorrow's Children* (1935), asserted that "physical and mental superiority tend to go together, . . . therefore improvement of the population in any important trait will bring improvement in other traits," including moral ones.[1]

Yet Faulkner established these eugenic assumptions only to tear them down, as Ladner clearly shows, in a number of ways. For example, he added a few defective traits to the wealthy Sartoris line, thereby upsetting (as did the Ann Cooper Hewitt sterilization case) the standard class assumptions that conservative eugenicists were promoting. In doing so, he may have been voicing decided support for Clarence Darrow's stance critiquing H. L. Mencken's strong anti-Southern eugenic views as hashed out in the *American Mercury* in 1925. Even more telling than the existence of a few defective traits among the aristocracy in Faulkner's works, however, is the fact that the overall narrative of his novels presents the decline, not the triumph, of the Sartoris line. Ladner concludes that despite clear knowledge and literary use of the principles of eugenics and the realization of their potential applicability to Southern society, Faulkner, like the Southern Agrarians, rejected eugenics as a solution to the South's problems.

According to the mid-twentieth-century literary critic Malcolm Cowley, William Faulkner's unequaled "labor of imagination" was not simply "to invent a Mississippi county that was like a mythical kingdom" but also to make it "complete and living in all its details."[2] Most important to the development of those living details, however, was the seed of family history, which gave Southern history depth and resonance for the American struggle with heritage versus progress. In this essay, I argue that eugenics was the prism through which Faulkner first saw the families that peopled his world. The role of eugenics in his oeuvre not only added Gothic colors to his pastoral setting but also provided the structuring principles of his family sagas.[3] In the images he used to characterize this family—closely paralleling the language of "race improvement"—and in the role competing families played in his Yoknapatawpha novels, Faulkner's multiple rhetorics of history, family, and the transformation (decline, modernization) of the South most clearly critiqued the logic of "race purity."[4]

After a sojourn with author Sherwood Anderson's New Orleans artistic circle in 1925, Faulkner made early attempts at fiction that yielded a never-published love story entitled "Elmer" and the novel *Mosquitoes*, which satirized the New Orleans art world. But by February 1927, he had returned to Mississippi and begun work on two manuscripts that explored the Mississippi material toward which Anderson pushed him.[5] One of them, *Flags in the Dust*, published in 1929 as *Sartoris*, portrays an aristocratic family noted for the Civil War heroism of its patriarch. The other, *Father Abraham*, recounts the adventures of the Sartoris family's nemesis, the Snopes clan, and develops a partial outline of the Snopes trilogy chronicling the insinuation of Flem Snopes and his many relatives into Yoknapatawpha County—*The Hamlet* (1940), *The Town* (1957), and *The Mansion* (1958).[6]

Although Faulkner's pre-1927 works reflect his experiences outside Mississippi, *Flags/Sartoris* serves as a "foundation stone for the construction of the Yoknapatawpha saga," not only introducing the town of Jefferson but also tracing themes of family decline.[7] The sons of two important Jefferson families, Bayard Sartoris and Horace Benbow, return from World War I with no clear sense of their function in the New South. Bayard, great-grandson of a Civil War hero, pauses in his drunken drive to self-destruction only long enough to father a son before dying in an ill-advised test flight. Horace, son of a prominent local attorney, gives up dreams of a literary life for the legal practice that supports a beautiful but shallow wife, his only child being the daughter from his wife's first marriage. The plight of a wisteria vine, slowly dying as a rose chokes it, mirrors these faltering lineages: "Bayard stood for a while before his house. The white simplicity of it dreamed unbroken among ancient sunshot trees. Wisteria mounting one end of the veranda had bloomed and fallen, and a faint drift of shattered petals lay palely about the dark roots of it and about the roots of a rose trained onto the same frame. The rose was slowly but steadily choking the other vine. It bloomed now thickly with buds no bigger than a thumbnail and blown flowers no larger than silver dollars, myriad, odorless and unpickable."[8] If the Sartorises and Benbows risk the fate of the wisteria vine, the novel suggests that a group of newcomers, the Snopeses, are fast becoming the odorless, unpickable, stunted rosebushes of Faulkner's world.

Peppered throughout the *Flags* manuscript (published under its original title in 1973) is imagery—largely excised from *Sartoris*—that heightens the suggestion of a biological and genealogical, not simply a cultural or economic, contest between the Snopeses and the "better" families of Jefferson. A passage that survived the editing for *Sartoris* vividly raises the issue of reproduction: "[Montgomery Ward] Snopes was a young man, member of a seemingly inexhaustible family which for the last ten or twelve years had been moving to town in driblets from a small settlement known as Frenchman's Bend . . . where they multiplied and flourished. The older residents, from their Jeffersonian houses and genteel stores and offices, looked on with amusement at first. But this was long since become something like consternation."[9] Here, as well, we get a thumbnail sketch of the rise of Flem Snopes, the central figure in Faulkner's other 1927 work, *Father Abraham*.

The eugenic issues raised by this Snopes migration become clearer when Faulkner describes Byron Snopes, a bookkeeper in the Sartoris bank, in the language of phrenology and criminal typology—"a thin, youngish man with hairy hands and covert close eyes that looked always as though he were just blinking them, though you never saw them closed."[10] Italian criminal anthropologist Cesare Lombroso had claimed that "born criminals are essentially apes living in our midst," and by the 1920s, many diverse publications supported the idea that certain physical characteristics went hand in hand with the "chain of criminal heredity."[11] In 1917, one writer for *Illustrated World* magazine had stated: "It is truly surprising how 'true to form' criminals run. . . . His jaw protrudes. . . . His ears are long. . . . His eyes are keen and piercing, while his brows are slightly low and farther apart than is usual with other men. He has rather prominent cheek bones and a nose that is long, pointed, wide and in alignment with the sloping forehead. . . . It is certain that the criminal often can be recognized by the simple expedient of drawing an imaginary line from the eye to the ear, so that it will touch the highest edge of the latter feature."[12] Later in the novel, it develops that Byron Snopes *is* a criminal—a fetishist who writes obscene letters to Narcissa Benbow and robs the Sartoris bank before disappearing from town. As Snopes's actions become bolder and more desperate, Faulkner's language seems to move from describing the hairy hands of an ape to detailing characteristics even more atavistic. Snopes wipes "his drooling mouth," and we see him "crouching," "scuttling," "darting his eyes . . . as a cornered animal," and "writhing and making smothered, animal-like moanings."[13]

Even as Faulkner uses the language and imagery of eugenics, however, he also complicates the seeming message of heredity, pointing to nonadaptive or primitive traits among the "better" families, as well as among members of the Snopes clan. The *Flags* manuscript opens with a tale about Civil War hero Colonel John Sartoris, and though his great-grandsons seem to have inherited his derring-do, the trait has made them into doomed fools rather than legends. Narcissa Benbow, though offended by Byron's disgusting missives, nevertheless saves them in a drawer. Horace throws over his own literary dreams to marry Belle, a shallow divorcée with "prehensile" hands and a wealthy first husband (Harry), with "his squat legs and his bald bullet head and his undershot jaw of rotting teeth" and a "heavy prognathous jaw."[14]

But it remained for later books—the "flowering" of that early Faulkner manuscript *Father Abraham* into the Snopes trilogy—to develop more fully this imagery of competing family lines. The Snopeses themselves, as well as the novels in which they are central, represent a phase separate from Faulkner's aristocratic family sagas.[15] The Snopeses are a very different sort of family from those of the Civil War heroes treated in so many of Faulkner's other novels. Though clearly dependent on family connections, the Snopeses seem largely immune to most of the values—loyalty, honor, duty, respect, tradition—that make the other family sagas so darkly compelling. This particular family is, instead, focused on the acquisition of money, a taboo subject for Faulkner's genteel aristocrats. Flem and his relatives, therefore, have been often rightly seen as agents and tokens of a dehumanized New South.[16] But it is a mistake to conclude from the Snopeses' lack of a particular set of "family values" that Faulkner conceived of them as outside of his Yoknapatawpha cosmos or as atomistic specimens of modernity, completely divorced from the impact of family background.

Certainly, the opening description in *The Hamlet* of the inhabitants of Frenchman's Bend, a community named for a long-dead, supposedly French plantation owner, does seem calculated to emphasize their lack of background and their abandonment of the past:

> All that remained of [the Frenchman] was the river bed which his slaves had straightened out to keep his land from overflowing in the spring and the skeleton of a huge colonial house which his *heirs-at-large had* been pulling down and *chopping up—walnut newel posts and stair spindles, oak floors which fifty years later would have been almost priceless, the very clapboards themselves—for thirty years now* for firewood. *Even his name was* forgotten, his pride but a legend. . . . The inhabitants of Frenchman's Bend are of Scottish and Irish and English blood. There are Turpins here, and Haleys and Whittingtons, and McCallums and Murrays and Leonards and Littlejohns; and other family names which only the good God himself could have invented.[17]

With the degeneration of the dead Frenchman's antebellum world, the Turpins and McCallums and Littlejohns seem to lack the sense of history, of looking back to a generation of Titans and heroes that the Compsons, McCaslins, and Sartorises so clearly have. The characters that people *Father Abraham/The Hamlet* do not live in a world haunted by ghosts, heroic ancestors to which they must constantly compare themselves. By the time *The Hamlet* (1940) was published, Faulkner tells us that many of the names represented in Frenchman's Bend, "like Riddup and Armstid and Doshey," not just the equally ersatz-sounding name Snopes, "could have come from nowhere since no man would deliberately select one of them for his own."[18]

But as suggestive as this supposed "pastlessness" might be for such agents of modern transformation, the manuscript's extensive expansion into *The Hamlet* (the first of the *Father Abraham* novels) asserts a very concrete and influential past for the Snopes clan.[19] Ratliff (an outgrowth of Suratt in *Father Abraham*) as well as episodes in Faulkner's Civil War tale *The Unvanquished* (1938) give the Snopes clan a history that stretches, like that of the Compsons and McCaslins, back to a heroic age. Indeed, Ratliff's focus on how events "soured" Ab Snopes, though not completely explaining why Ab burns barns, does more, in some ways, to clarify the effects of the past on the present than do the stories of the landholding families that barely survive in the present. Ratliff's homespun account of nature versus nurture—his assertion that "Old man Ab aint naturally mean. He's just soured"—counters mainline eugenic assumptions on the role of inborn traits, suggesting a sort of class analysis and prompting a hypothesis that the wealthy members of the community are now paying for the class insults that Ab had to endure under the burden of being a poor white farmer and mule-trader in a world made by landholders.[20]

However, much of *The Hamlet*'s biological imagery often seems to play with privileging nature over nurture. The Snopes women are compared to "the two last survivors of a lost species"; I. O. Snopes has a "weasel-like quality," and Flem is a "frog-like creature" who barely reaches Eula Varner's shoulder.[21] Gail Mortimer described in some detail Faulkner's biological and evolutionary language, arguing that the Snopeses' encroachment on Frenchman's Bend and Jefferson represents a Darwinian struggle for survival of the fittest. Linking the 1927 *Father Abraham* manuscript as well as that of *Flags* to the 1925 Scopes monkey trial, Mortimer concluded that "Darwinian thought appears to have suggested to Faulkner a horrifying image of mankind existing without precisely the human qualities that comprised so much of his own identity as a Southern gentleman."[22]

A metaphor of mindless competition is not completely satisfactory as a framework for interpreting Faulkner's work, powerful and frightening as the Darwinian model of gradual usurpation of niches by better-adapted individuals might have been. Though not always the Christian moralist some critics have made him out to be, Faulkner demonstrated an enduring concern with the *human* motivations of his characters. Darwinism certainly dominated headlines in 1925, but it faced an uphill battle for influence. By contrast, eugenic theories of race improvement influenced policy, ranging from the Immigration Restriction Act of 1924 to the decisions of local child welfare officials.[23] At a time when school districts were still fighting over whether evolution might be included in biology curricula, high school students and magazine readers across the country were being taught that humanity could be improved if only we wisely manipulated our collective "germ plasm." The old notion that "blood tells" now seemed confirmed by Gregor Mendel's experiments with dominant and recessive heritable traits. Supporters claimed for eugenics a precision "exact as botany."[24] By the 1920s, a host of materials touted the value of making the choice of a mate according to wise, eugenic principles and warned of the dangers of allowing "degenerate family stocks" to reproduce.[25] So widespread was the influence of eugenics that it altered William Jennings Bryan's views from acceptance of a mild, "creationist" version of evolution to opposition to all forms of Darwinism.[26]

Two families made infamous by a host of writers in promoting eugenic ideas and policies mirror the Snopes clan in their more troubling traits. Popularly known as the Jukes and the Kallikaks, they emerged as compelling symbols of the dangers of allowing "degenerate" stocks to reproduce. While both family names were fictional—they sound like the Frenchman's Bend names that came from nowhere—the families themselves were real. Their members supposedly exhibited criminality, prostitution, pauperism, and feeblemindedness at sufficiently high rates to thus "prove" the heritability of such traits. The Jukeses had been "discovered" in 1874 by New York City merchant Richard L. Dugdale, whose amateur interest in social problems led him to survey the inmates of New York's rural Ulster County jail. Finding six members of the same family all in jail at once, he began to trace that family's history "in the hope that he might lay bare the causes of crime and pauperism."[27] He learned that they lived in "one of the crime cradles of New York" in conditions he clearly found repellent.[28] "Most of the ancestors were squatters upon the soil, and in some instances have become owners by tax-title or by occupancy," he described: "They lived in log or stone houses similar to slave-hovels, all ages, sexes, relations and strangers 'bunking' indiscriminately."²⁹ He traced them back to one "Max Jukes" (born ca. 1720–40), reputed to be "'averse to steady toil,' working hard by spurts and idling by turns," as well as "a hard drinker, jolly and companionable."³⁰ So pervasive were criminality and pauperism in the family descended from Max that Dugdale found "their family name *had come to be used generically as a term of reproach*," and he labeled the female head of the line "the Mother of Criminals."³¹ But predating eugenics per se and innocent of the rediscovery of Mendel, Dugdale raised concern about hereditary traits while emphasizing the power of environment, as Lamarckian theory proposed, to reinforce or counter negative characteristics. Later, many eugenicists seized on this early "family study" in support of hereditarian explanations for crime, poverty, and feeblemindedness.³²

Like Dugdale, Henry Goddard, head of the Training School for Feeble-Minded Girls and Boys in Vineland, New Jersey, was concerned with how such hereditary traits determined human conduct. With his 1912 book *The Kallikak Family: A Study in the Heredity of Feeble-Mindedness,* he did much to codify the eugenic theories that would so influence laws and policies in the United States for several decades.³³ Using a three-part classification system for intelligence that labeled feebleminded mental "defectives" as "idiots," "imbeciles," or "morons," he diagnosed a young girl at the training school as feebleminded, specifically a moron; morons were considered the most dangerous variety because they might appear normal.³⁴ Identifying her with the pseudonym "Deborah Kallikak," Goddard traced local recollections, records, and family trees back six generations to a pre-Revolutionary progenitor. Dubbed "Martin Kallikak Sr.," this patriarch had an illegitimate liaison with a tavern girl that supposedly produced offspring in which, "no matter where [Goddard] traced them, . . . an appalling amount of defectiveness was found," whereas his marriage "to a woman of good stock produced human excellence in an undisturbed progression."³⁵ Though focusing his studies on intelligence, which he contended his researchers could gauge "by sight," Goddard included in his report photographs of some members of the "defective" branch of the family.³⁶ Showing their debased living conditions, gaping mouths, and heavy brows above dark, slitted eyes, these pictures seemed to be graphic proof of the degenerate depravity of this flawed line.³⁷ Goddard concluded even more certainly than had Dugdale that criminality and immorality were, via intelligence, inherited. "The intelligence controls the emotions and the emotions are controlled in proportion to the degree of intelligence. . . . It follows that if there is little intelligence the emotions will be uncontrolled and whether they be strong or weak will result in actions that are unregulated, uncontrolled and, as experience proves, usually undesirable," he stated.[38]

With such dire issues at stake, he advocated institutionalization of these defectives so that they might be properly cared for and prevented from reproducing.[39] By the 1930s, the American public had responded to reports of this type not only with immigration restrictions but also with eugenic sterilization laws in thirty-five states, including Mississippi.

Faulkner's focus in the Snopes trilogy on "peasants" and "poor whites," particularly in The Hamlet, determines some of the Snopeses' traits, such as their tenuous hold on any kind of economic security and Flem's handmade shirts. But in other respects, the Snopeses exhibit traits that place them beyond the general profile for poor, white southerners and thus suggest a kind of degeneracy reminiscent of the Jukeses and the Kallikaks. The Snopeses seem used to living in houses that "'aint fitten for hawgs,'" such as Mink Snopes's "dozen different sorry and ill-made rented cabins." Major De Spain seems both nonplussed and surprised by his new tenant's laziness when Ab says, "'I figure I'll start tomorrow. I dont never move and start to work the same day.'" Physically, as well, the Snopes men seem less than healthy, robust specimens. Ab has "a pair of eyes of a cold opaque gray between shaggy graying irascible brows and a short scrabble of iron-gray beard as tight and knotted as a sheep's coat," and Flem has eyes "the color of stagnant water." Eck Snopes has an extremely low forehead and a "face which seemed to have been a mere afterthought to the thatching of the skull," whereas I. O. Snopes is "a frail man . . . with a talkative weasel's face." In Goddard's eyes, the strongest proof of defect in the Snopes line would have been Ike Snopes, the hulking idiot whose face "had been blasted empty and clean forever of any thought." For Dugdale, the many negative uses for the word Snopes itself (such as Ratliff's comment that "Will Varner looks like he is fixing to snopes forever") would have been very telling.[40]

Although Faulkner's language points to a very strong Jukes-Kallikak-Snopes connection, the impact of the eugenics debate on his regional vision seems to have gone beyond these simple Snopes familial traits. An even stronger parallel to the familial structure of Faulkner's vision, competing family lines, may be drawn with one of the most notable contributions to the popular debate on eugenics. Shortly after the Scopes trial, Clarence Darrow turned his attention to one of the paradigms of eugenic proof in the October 1925 issue of the *American Mercury*. In an article entitled "The Edwardses and the Jukeses," he traced a comparison of the family trees of Jonathan Edwards and Max Jukes—six hundred notables in the Edwards line compared to nearly five hundred paupers, prostitutes, and other criminals in the Jukes line.

The intriguing juxtaposition of the Edwardses, exemplars of the nation's best colonial families, with the Jukeses, synonyms with ill fame, was not new.[41] But Darrow examined the analysis of these neighboring families, one from western Connecticut and the other from eastern New York, complicating and criticizing the stereotypes they seemed to embody.[42] Beyond noting "that Jonathan Edwards had ancestors" and that "with every marriage . . . new blood has been brought into the Edwards stream of inheritance," he suggested that in an estimated forty thousand Edwards descendants, "possibly some of them have received outdoor or indoor relief [public assistance]. There is even room for a few inmates of jails. Who knows? Perhaps if one looked closely enough and had the facts, one might find here and there in the 40,000 a few morons and an imbecile or two."[43] Finally, by detailing the cruelty of Jonathan Edwards's theology, he even questioned the nobility of the line's titular head.[44] And as for the Jukeses, Darrow argued (echoing Dugdale, though informed by cultural anthropology) that their criminal, lazy, and licentious behaviors "were due more to environmental conditions than to any hereditary determiner." As a result, he was not surprised "that the stock of the Jukeses showed marked improvement in those members who migrated to other parts of the country and brought up their children outside of what Dugdale called 'the crime cradle of the State of New York.'"[45]

Faulkner was in Europe at the time Darrow's article appeared, but intriguing parallels arise between Darrow's analysis and Faulkner's family sagas. As one of the Southerners impressed and probably influenced by H. L. Mencken's "Sahara of the Bozart," Faulkner had met Mencken in New Orleans in 1925; the previous year, Mencken had founded the *American Mercury*.[46] In all probability, Faulkner took up even back issues of that fount of cultural commentary—and later outlet for his own stories—on his return to the South in December 1925.[47] As he began to untangle the strands of history and family peculiar to his "little patch" of Mississippi, the notion of two family lines, one high-born, the other low, was clearly seminal and even essential in shaping his Yoknapatawpha cosmos. Early in 1927, Faulkner's friend Phil Stone prepared a press release about the writer's latest projects: the first was a comic story of a large clan "of typical 'poor white trash,'" the second "a tale of the aristocratic, chivalrous and ill-fated Sartoris family."[48] The eugenic scenario of dueling genealogies—of good germ plasm and bad germ plasm battling for supremacy and even for the national soul—yields profound resonances in Faulkner's regional family dramas and is plainly evident in his *Father Abraham* and *Flags in the Dust* manuscripts. Judging by the reviews that appeared after *The Hamlet* came out, such parallels were not lost on readers. Cowley noted the conflict between "the caste of Sartoris" and "the miserable clan of Snopes."[49] Another reviewer saw a connection between "the Snopeses as a tribe" and "a dozen Kallikaks."[50]

Yet Faulkner's sense of genealogical degeneracy and failing family lines seems strongest among his aristocrats. Indeed, the project he completed after *Flags in the Dust* was *The Sound and the Fury* (1929), the tale of a high family brought low, complete with its own idiot. The Compson family history appears to demonstrate the sort of speculation that Darrow indulged in about the Edwardses.[51] Published in the same year as *Sartoris*, *The Sound and the Fury* foregrounds biological aspects of family decline in its extended opening section, which is told from the point of view of Benjy Compson, the idiot descendant of the prominent family. Depicting the declining fortunes of this once-great, landowning family, the novel engages one of the prime concerns of many eugenicists: the protection of good genetic lines from corruption. Descended from one of the first settlers of Jefferson and a former governor, the family now progresses toward dissolution.[52] In addition to gradually losing their landholdings, family members also suffer from promiscuity, illegitimacy, idiocy, emotional instability, alcoholism, and suicide.[53] Though they have the fine lineage eugenicists would endorse, the later generations exhibit problems that might have gotten a poorer family rounded up for institutionalization and sterilization.[54] Indeed, in Faulkner's appendix to *The Sound and the Fury*, written in 1945, he reports not only that Benjy Compson had finally gone to the asylum in 1933—as brother Jason suggests after Benjy allegedly molests a young girl in 1910—but also that he had been castrated (Faulkner uses the horse-breeding term *gelded*) in 1913.[55] This graphic sterilization theme finds parallels in less overtly eugenic incidents in two of Faulkner's most sensational novels, *Light in August* (1932), in which Percy Grimm castrates and murders Joe Christmas, and *Sanctuary* (1931), with its lynching of Lee Goodwin for allegedly raping Temple Drake.[56] The awful "logic" of forcibly protecting eugenic, racial, and sexual purity pervades Faulkner's world in ways that reveal its horror.

By graphically illustrating practices associated with eugenic theory and attributing degenerate traits to his ascendant agents of the New South, particularly many of the Snopeses, Faulkner did much more than add color to a dark underbelly of Southern life. To an audience familiar with the Jukes-Kallikak mythology, such traits would tap a large reservoir of repulsion and anxiety at the possibility that this formerly isolated family would pollute the mainstream population and influence the future of the race/region/nation. Since Faulkner himself found Flem Snopes and what he represented morally terrifying, he would naturally have characterized the family so as to underscore such negative reactions.[57]

Even more central to the importance of eugenics in the Snopes legacy, however, was the movement's inextricable link to the modernizing forces Faulkner feared would dehumanize the American people. And in a modernizing world in which science sought to rationalize knowledge, industrialization sought to rationalize production, and market finance sought to rationalize exchange, eugenics sought to rationalize the ineffably irrational: romance, sex, and reproduction.[58] From the moment Faulkner describes Jody Varner's "quality of invincible and inviolable bachelordom," he announces the persistent issues of sex, marriage, reproduction, and inheritance that will be played out in highly charged stories of Labove and Eula, Houston and Lucy Pate, and Ike Snopes and the cow, which rage around Flem.[59] But these dramas never engage or interest the leader of the Snopes clan until he sees a way to profit by marrying Eula because Flem, the impotent bringer of accurate books and cash exchange to Varner's store, is the prime rationalizer.

In many ways, the prevailing order in *The Hamlet* is, as the title of its last section, "The Peasants," suggests, a closed, peasant world but one threatened by destabilizing, cosmopolitan forces. Flem is the locus of many of these forces, most notably in his movement out of farming and into the Varner store. Flem tells Jody, "Aint no benefit in farming. I figure on getting out of it soon as I can."[60] He wants a job in the store, and we can read this change in Flem's fortunes as a movement away from the nature that had traditionally supported his people. This one change by itself creates some instability in the community simply because it is new.

> They were gathered even before the sun was completely gone, looking now and then toward the dark front of Varner's store as people will gather to look quietly at the cold embers of a lynching or at the propped ladder and open window of an elopement, since the presence of a hired white clerk in the store of a man still able to walk and with intellect still sound enough to make money mistakes at least in his own favor, was as unheard of as the presence of a hired white woman in one of their own kitchens.[61]

Flem's career change also belongs to important changes taking place in the Southern economy. The plantation pattern of agriculture remained, but its share of Southern prosperity was declining as industrialization and "merchandizing" supplanted it.[62]

In the Snopes trilogy, especially through Flem, Faulkner took on most clearly the implications of modernization for the South, and there, the eugenic method, message, and madness found their strongest, though most distorted, reflection. This family was from the very sort of background against which the eugenicists warned, and depicting it as financially successful may have been Faulkner's joke; despite eugenicists' efforts, perhaps the Jukeses and the Kallikaks of the world were winning. More important, Faulkner suggested that the attempt to "preserve the race" was destroying the only thing in it worth saving—its emotional and sometimes irrational soul. The Yoknapatawpha family dramas portrayed families derived not only from Faulkner's personal stories but also from the eugenic discourse of the interwar period, with enough problematic traits to go around. Faulkner's treatment of the families that peopled and configured his world—and struggled for control and inheritance of it—did not reflect an embrace of eugenic "wisdom" but a rejection of its horrors and misguided logic. Indeed, the imagery and rhetoric of eugenics gave Faulkner a nexus for his themes—decline, family, race, inheritance, incest (inbreeding), sex, and the irrational impulses that surrounded them all—structuring his fictional world in a metaphor and cause for the radical dehumanization against which he hoped to endure.

Notes

1. "Beauty on Parade," *Glen Falls (New York) Post*, June 15, 1929, in the Leon Whitney Scrapbook, American Eugenics Society Papers, American Philosophical Society, Philadelphia; and Ellsworth Huntington, *Tomorrow's Children: The Goal of Eugenics* (New York: John Wiley and Sons, 1935), 16.

2. Malcolm Cowley, "Introduction," in *The Portable Faulkner*, ed. Malcolm Cowley (New York: Viking Press, 1951), 2. In addition, Cowley asserted that Faulkner's "double labor" was also "to make his story of Yoknapatawpha County stand as a parable or legend of all the Deep South." Though not denying readings that cast characters as allegorical representatives of events and trends in Southern history, I will attempt to place aspects of Faulkner's vision within a broader, national cultural context that explores American attitudes toward and policies about progress and its relationship to historical and biological antecedents.

3. Other critics have noted eugenic or evolutionary imagery in Faulkner's fiction. Examples include Tomiyama Takao, "Who Is Popeye? Faulkner and Eugenics," in *Literature, America and Capitalism*, ed. Orishima Masashi, Hiraishi Takaki, and Watanabe Shinji (Tokyo: Nan'undo Press, 1993), 135–60, and Gail Mortimer, "Evolutionary Theory in Faulkner's Snopes Trilogy," *Rocky Mountain Review of Language and Literature* 40, no. 4 (1986): 187–202. Works on Faulkner's treatment of "white trash," with similar imagery, include Julia Leyda, "Reading White Trash: Class, Race, and Mobility in Faulkner and Le Sueur," *Arizona Quarterly: A Journal of American Literature, Culture, and Theory* 56, no. 2 (2000): 37–64.

4. Though the Snopes novels seem almost to ignore the existence of black-white race issues in the South, the rejection of eugenics implied by these novels also calls into question the logic of racist ideologies. Like the Clarence Darrow essay that will be discussed later in this chapter, the novels question any determining role for biological inheritance in individual or family success.

5. "You're a country boy," Anderson told Faulkner; "all you know is that little patch up there in Mississippi where you started from. But that's all right too. It's America too." That little piece of advice stands out among Faulkner's influences, which the author himself so often obscured, because it is so readily linked to his homely description of Yoknapatawpha County as his own "little postage stamp of native soil." Anderson quoted in Joseph Blotner, *Faulkner: A Biography* (New York: Random House, 1974), 415. Faulkner quoted in David Minter, *William Faulkner: His Life and Work* (Baltimore, MD: Johns Hopkins University Press, 1980), 80.

6. Although the later two novels complete the path set in *The Hamlet* for Flem's ascendancy and ultimate defeat, the first is the volume most often grouped with Faulkner's

major works as rounding out the white cast of aristocrats, "trash," and upstarts in the richly historical novels of the thirties. Malcolm Cowley's April 1940 review called it "Faulkner by Daylight," "a new sort of novel for William Faulkner, less somber, more easygoing and discursive"; see Cowley, "Faulkner by Daylight," *New Republic* 102, no. 16 (April 15, 1940): 510.

7. Lawrence Thompson, *William Faulkner: An Introduction and Interpretation* (New York: Barnes and Noble, 1963), 8.

8. William Faulkner, *Sartoris* (New York: New American Library, 1964), 23; this work was originally published in 1929.

9. Ibid., 147, and William Faulkner, *Flags in the Dust* (New York: Vintage Books, 1974), 181.

10. Faulkner, *Flags,* 84.

11. Stephen J. Gould, "Criminal Man Revisited," *Natural History* 85, no. 3 (March 1976): 16; Albert Marple, "How to Recognize a Criminal," *Illustrated World* 26 (February 1917): 844.

12. Marple, "How to Recognize a Criminal," 842–44.

13. Faulkner, *Flags,* 293, 299–300.

14. Ibid., 211, 204, 205.

15. Flem brings the upstart themes explored in Popeye (a central character in the sensational rape-and-lynching novel *Sanctuary* [1931]) and Thomas Sutpen (the dynasty-building protagonist of *Absalom, Absalom!* [1931]) squarely into the family arena. Sutpen wants a family, but Flem already has one. Sutpen's desire to found a dynasty looks toward his family's future, whereas Flem, whose impotence prevents any dynastic ambitions on his part, uses his family's past (his father's barn burning) to create his own opportunities in the business world of Frenchman's Bend. The one family member who seems concerned with loyalty and honor, Sarty of "Barn Burning," flees his association with the Snopes aspirations.

16. This reading has been standard since Malcolm Cowley's review of the novel: "But in Faulkner's novels the war had never ended. It has merely been transformed into another struggle between the heirs of the slaveholders, who try rather feebly to live by the old code, and the new bankers and demagogues who have absolutely no standards but pecuniary success." See Cowley, "Faulkner by Daylight," 510.

17. William Faulkner, *Father Abraham,* ed. James B. Meriwether (New York: Random House, 1983), 15. Italicized phrases are as they appear in Faulkner, *The Hamlet* (New York: Random House, 1940), 3–4. The 1927 *Father Abraham* manuscript was twenty-four typewritten pages, of which p. 23 is missing.

18. Faulkner, *Hamlet,* 4.

19. The Snopeses are commonly read as agents of modernization (and an alienation/atomization that accompanies it). See especially Warren Beck, *Man in Motion: Faulkner's Trilogy* (Madison: University of Wisconsin Press, 1976).

20. Faulkner, *Hamlet*, 29.

21. Ibid., 47, 64, 147.

22. Mortimer, "Evolutionary Theory in Faulkner's Snopes Trilogy," 198.

23. In 1924, researchers' claims to objective studies proving the hereditary inferiority of many European immigrants had led to the Immigration Restriction Act; see Stephen J. Gould, *The Mismeasure of Man* (New York: W. W. Norton, 1981), 157.

24. French Strother, "What Eugenics Is—and Isn't," *World's Work* 49 (February 1925): 446. I use the term *eugenics* to refer to notions that emphasize encouragement of "good" traits and discouragement of "bad" traits within a species; I use *evolution* to refer to competition between species or at least between largely distinct gene pools. However, both ideas include reference to fitness and suggest a struggle for survival. One key way in which Faulkner's works represent a rejection of eugenics is that whereas most eugenicists expressed concern that allowing so-called degenerates to reproduce would weaken the race or species, Faulkner's portrayal of the Snopeses implies that many supposedly bad traits either lead to greater success or at least do not prevent it.

25. Ibid., 444.

26. "[William Jennings] Bryan decried the entire [eugenic] program as 'brutal' and at Dayton [site of the 1925 Scopes trial] offered it as a reason for not teaching evolution"; see Edward J. Larson, *Summer for the Gods: The Scopes Trial and America's Continuing Debate over Science and Religion* (Cambridge, MA: Harvard University Press, 1997), 28.

27. Mark H. Haller, *Eugenics: Hereditarian Attitudes in American Thought* (New Brunswick, NJ: Rutgers University Press, 1963), 21.

28. Robert L. Dugdale, *The Jukes: A Study in Crime, Pauperism, Disease, and Heredity* (New York: G. P. Putnam's Sons, 1877), 13.

29. Ibid.

30. Ibid., 14.

31. Ibid., 8, emphasis in original; Haller, *Eugenics*, 22.

32. See especially Albert Wiggam, *The Fruit of the Family Tree* (Indianapolis, IN: Bobbs-Merrill, 1924).

33. Henry Herbert Goddard, *The Kallikak Family: A Study in the Heredity of Feeble-Mindedness* (New York: Macmillan, 1912).

34. "Two categories of a tripartite arrangement [of mental deficiency] won general acceptance: idiots could not develop full speech and had mental ages below three; imbeciles could not master written language and ranged from three to seven in mental age.

(Both terms are now so entrenched in the vernacular of invectives that few people recognize their technical status in an older psychology). . . . [T]he more threatening realm of 'high-grade defectives'—the people who could be trained to function in society, the ones who established a bridge between pathology and normality. . . . with mental ages of eight to twelve" needed identification to provide limits, segregation, and curtailed breeding. H. H. Goddard "christened these people 'morons,' from a Greek word meaning foolish"; see Gould, *Mismeasure*, 158–59.

35. Goddard, *The Kallikak Family*, 16. J. David Smith concluded that Deborah Kallikak was probably not "feeble-minded" but instead dyslexic or subject to some other learning disability; see Smith, *Minds Made Feeble: The Myth and Legacy of the Kallikaks* (Rockville, MD: Aspen Systems, 1985), 17, 23–26. That possible error in Goddard's analysis, however, does not alter the effect of Goddard's "proof" of hereditary feeblemindedness on public perceptions of the day. Goddard's data on immigrant feeblemindedness, along with data collected by Robert M. Yerkes in World War I, were among the most influential in promoting immigration restriction; see Gould, *Mismeasure*, 157.

36. Gould, *Mismeasure*, 165.

37. Ibid., 171. In revisiting the Kallikaks, Stephen Jay Gould found that, with the book's faded ink, "it is now clear that all [these] photos . . . were phonied by inserting heavy dark lines to give eyes and mouths their diabolical appearance." R. E. Fancher, in "Henry Goddard and the Kallikak Family Photographs: 'Conscious Skullduggery' or 'Whig History'?" *American Psychologist* 42 (1987): 585–90, and Leila Zenderland, *Measuring Minds: Henry Herbert Goddard and the Origins of American Intelligence Testing* (Cambridge: Cambridge University Press, 1998), however, contended that darkening features was a common publishing practice to make photos reproduce better.

38. Quoted in Gould, *Mismeasure*, 161.

39. Ibid., 163–64.

40. Faulkner, *Hamlet*, 51, 13, 235, 15, 8, 22, 62, 65, 63, 85, 162 (in order of mention).

41. Clarence Darrow, "The Edwardses and the Jukeses," *American Mercury* 6 (October 1925): 147–57. Darrow's article was a direct response to Wiggam in *The Fruit of the Family*, who had discussed the Edwards-Jukes comparison in his call for "opportunities which encourage those of good blood to mate with their own kind" and, going beyond Dugdale's recommendations, "stern measures which will insure that those of positively bad blood produce no children at all"; quoted in Darrow, "The Edwards and the Jukes," 147. Goddard had discussed the comparison (*Kallikak*, 51–68), and an earlier scientific account appeared in *Heredity in Relation to Eugenics* (New York: Henry Holt, 1911), by Charles Davenport of the Carnegie Institute of Washington.

42. Darrow, "The Edwardses and the Jukeses," 157, stated, "These two historical sires are first discovered living less than two hundred miles from each other. I, for one,

am willing to contend that it is a safe bet that Max came from the East, and a not unreasonable guess that the ancestors of the Edwardses and the Jukeses were mixed."

43. Ibid., 148, 151, 153.

44. Darrow commented that "the amazing thing to me is why anybody of this generation or any other should *want* to be traced to Jonathan Edwards. . . . Except for his weird and horrible theology, he would have filled no place in American life"; ibid., 153.

45. Dugdale, *The Jukes*, 156, 157.

46. Blotner, *Faulkner*, 443–83, 329, 394; H. L. Mencken, "Sahara of the Bozart," in *Prejudices: Second Series* (New York: Alfred A. Knopf, 1920), reprinted in *A Mencken Chrestomathy*, ed. H. L. Mencken (New York: Alfred A. Knopf, 1949), wherein Mencken took credit for sparking the Southern Renaissance. Mencken may even have prepared Faulkner's imagination for the influence of Darrow's essay by the eugenic language in "Sahara of the Bozart." Just one brief example is illustrative: "The immigrants of the North have been studied at great length . . . for elaborate data as to their racial strains, their stature and cranial indices, their relative capacity for education, and the changes that they undergo under American *Kultur*. But the older stocks of the South, and particularly the emancipated and dominant poor white trash, have never been investigated scientifically. . . . It is highly probable that some of the worst blood of western Europe flows in the veins of the Southern poor whites"; see Mencken in *The American Scene: A Reader*, ed. Huntington Cairns (New York: Alfred A. Knopf, 1965), 162–63.

47. Faulkner later sent many stories to Mencken, some of which were published in the *American Mercury*, and his friend Sherwood Anderson also published there frequently, with five stories appearing in the magazine between 1924 and 1927.

48. Minter, *William Faulkner*, 77.

49. Cowley, "Faulkner by Daylight," 510.

50. Louis Kronenberger, "The World of William Faulkner," *Nation* 150 (April 13, 1940): 481.

51. As they appear in *Flags in the Dust/Sartoris* and *The Unvanquished*, the Sartorises also seem to justify some of Darrow's skepticism toward the high-born. The violence and "wild foolishness" of the Sartoris men in the name of honor and chivalry, though more benign, is reminiscent of Jonathan Edwards's violent, extreme theology in the name of a loving God; see Minter, *William Faulkner*, 84.

52. This is according to the appendix Faulkner wrote to *The Sound and the Fury* in 1945; see Faulkner, *The Sound and the Fury & As I Lay Dying: Two Novels by William Faulkner*, Modern Library Edition (New York: Random House, 1946), 7.

53. The Compsons sell their last plot to send the eldest son, Quentin, to Harvard for one year, after which he commits suicide, and to pay for the wedding of their only

daughter, Candace (Caddy), only to have the marriage end in divorce a year later when she becomes pregnant by a lover.

54. In fact, members of poor families deemed unfit were often taken into custody and offered a "choice" between continued incarceration in an asylum and submitting to a vaguely explained operation that turned out to be sterilization. Six brothers, their sister, and two cousins from Brush Mountain, Virginia, were rounded up over a few days and "systematically sterilized under a Virginia law compelling such operations for those ruled unfit"; see Edwin Black, *War against the Weak: Eugenics and America's Campaign to Create a Master Race* (New York: Four Walls, Eight Windows, 2003), 3–4.

55. Faulkner, *Sound and the Fury*, 19.

56. William Faulkner, *Light in August*, Modern Library Edition (New York: Random House, 1959), 439–40: "Now you'll let white women alone, even in hell," Grimm shouts as "from out the slashed garments about [Joe's] hips and loins the pent black blood seemed to rush like a released breath."

57. Minter, *William Faulkner*, 179.

58. As in the eugenics movement throughout the United States, eugenics in the South relied heavily on the support of professionals, who were involved with progressive "improvements" in many areas of society. "Indeed, southern eugenicists were cast in the role of missionaries preaching a foreign gospel in hostile territory, because even eugenicists who hailed from the South typically stood apart both as members of the region's small professional class or its beleaguered progressive minority and as zealots of a new, scientific doctrine that had originally developed elsewhere and that still most flourished outside the region"; see Edward J. Larson, *Sex, Race, and Science: Eugenics in the Deep South* (Baltimore, MD: Johns Hopkins University Press, 1995), 17.

59. Faulkner, *Hamlet*, 6. Each of these stories represents a kind of sexual obsession.

60. Ibid., 23.

61. Ibid., 28.

62. "Available evidence seems to indicate, however, that the chief profits of these were no longer derived directly from agriculture but from merchandising (their own tenants forming an important nucleus of customers) and from other forms of business enterprise"; see Benjamin Burks Kendrick and Alex Mathews Arnett, eds., *The South Looks at Its Past* (Chapel Hill: University of North Carolina Press, 1935), 112.

PART TWO

VISUAL CULTURE
AND EUGENICS

EIGHT

The American Adonis

A Natural History of the "Average
American" (Man), 1921–32

Mary K. Coffey

ABSTRACT

In this essay, Mary Coffey closely analyzes a sculpture—*The Average American Male*—that was on display at the American Museum of Natural History in New York City during the Second and Third International Congresses of Eugenics, in 1921 and 1932, respectively. Created by Jane Davenport Harris, the figure embodied, in plaster, the compiled anthropometric measurements taken from U.S. Army recruits during World War I. Such anthropometric studies had been used by eugenicists since the late nineteenth century to analyze various criminal, professional, and racial "types," and at times, they were visually codified through the use of composite photography. Sculpture took this process one step further, putting "average types" into three-dimensional form for examination.

Based on the exhibitionary contexts, contemporary reviews, and speeches made at each of the congresses, Coffey reads the varied interpretations of *The Average American Male* in 1921 and 1932. When first on display, the sculpture was paired with a composite sculpture of a "Harvard athlete," and the contrast showed the degeneration to the Nordic type caused by race mixing with less evolved, white racial strains. In 1932, however, eight years after the passage of the Immigration Restriction Act, the sculpture read more as a sign of the degeneracy of the average American male resulting from the differential birthrate. Coffey proposes that as eugenicists shifted their focus to white, middle-class, educated women who were having few children as the primary cause for a national genetic decline, interpretations of the sculpture also shifted.

MARY K. COFFEY

Her essay thus offers a very interesting art historical perspective on the ways in which changing historical contexts affect the meaning of works of art (or, in this case, a "work of science").

The "Masterpiece" versus the "Modeled Chart"

In 1932, writing for the *New York Times*, art critic Edward Alden Jewell asked rhetorically, "What is a work of art and what is a work of science?" He was responding in particular to a 22-inch plaster sculpture of the "average man" then on display at the American Museum of Natural History (AMNH) in an exhibition organized in conjunction with the Third International Congress of Eugenics, held from August 21–23, 1932 (fig. 8.1). The broader concern animating his remarks pertained to the growing authority of science to quantify and represent man over and against aesthetic canons of ideal beauty, in short, the preference for naturalism and the statistical "type" over the "perfection of form" found in sculpture or, as Jewell put it, the "Masterpiece" versus the "Modeled Chart." He wrote, "There he stands. . . . All about him are solemn two-dimensional charts; he, this startling amalgam of 100,000 doughboys, no doubt authentic to the most picayune degree, boasts three dimensions. He is in the round. He is a piece of sculpture. Is he a work of art? *No*, he is not. . . . What one here encounters is, fundamentally, the difference between a scientific and an aesthetic composite. The difference is enormous."[1]

In what followed, Jewell compared this "condensed doughboy" to the *Idolino*, a Greek sculpture from the fifth century BCE, and a Twelfth Dynasty statue King Horus from ancient Egypt, each of which, he asserted, eschewed naturalism or "truth to nature" in favor of a stylized "synthesis of ideal attributes fused into a unity."[2] Arguing on behalf of such aesthetically derived syntheses, Jewell bristled at the reduction of humanity to the base sum of statistical measurements. Man, he continued,

> may . . . be looked upon as that "quintessence of dust;" but unlike that luckless objectified eugenic figment of the brain at the museum, he must also, despite his manifold fallings [*sic*] be considered potential heir to Hamlet's generalized panegyric: "What a work is man! how noble in reason! how infinite in faculty! in form and

186

Fig. 8.1. The Average American Male by Jane Davenport, 1921. Reproduced in Harry H. Laughlin, *The Second International Exhibition of Eugenics* (Baltimore, MD: Williams and Wilkins, 1923), 69.

moving how express and admirable! in action how like an angel! in apprehension how like a god! the beauty of the world! the paragon of animals!" No, this does not fit the natural history boy in the least.[3]

Given the resoundingly positive response to the congress and exhibition chronicled in the press and suggested by the over fifteen thousand registered visitors to the exhibit, contemporary readers might be relieved to find such a fervent objection to eugenic methods and their implications for "Mr. Average Citizen."[4] However, the representational alternatives that Jewell espoused—Shakespeare, classical antiquity, ancient Egypt—were not merely highlights from the Western canon, they were also period signifiers of the racial inheritance of white Anglo-Saxons, what Henry Fairfield Osborn, director of the AMNH, referred to as those ancestors of the "best strains of Old American stock."[5] Jewell's essay, although a defense of humanism against scientific positivism, was also an anxious response to the apparent degeneracy of white manhood on display at the AMNH and its implications for the representative status of the white male body as the bearer of civilization.

Jewell's reaction to the "average man" on display at the museum provides a point of entry into an examination of how visual culture (sculpture, scientific illustration, and museum exhibition) helped to communicate, legitimize, and naturalize the claims of eugenicists to broad popular audiences. His opposition to a regnant regime of scientific and popular representation—the statistical composite—registered anxieties about the national body that emerged in the 1930s, in part as a consequence of a "Decade of Progress in Eugenics."[6] Jewell's objection pointed to a shift in eugenic discourse between the Second International Congress of Eugenics, convened in 1921, and the Third International Congress of 1932, for *The Average American Male* was exhibited at both. However, when the sculpture debuted, it prompted no public opposition and went unnoted in the press. Why was this small plaster composite at all disturbing in 1932 but seemingly unremarkable in 1921?

What follows tracks the historical links between aesthetics, race, and citizenship communicated visually through public statuary and scientific displays in order to illuminate how the "average man" both partook of and ruptured the visual logic of whiteness. However, resurrecting the differences in the stated aims of the two congresses demonstrates that the reception of the sculpture depended less on its formal properties than on the situated meaning derived from the rhetoric of its display. Between 1921 and 1932, eugenicists shifted their attention from the problem of immigration to the problem of white, middle-class reproduction. Within the former discursive framework, the composite sculpture provided evidence of the dysgenic body of the immigrant; within the latter, it became a normative representation of the national body—the "average American." As will become clear, this recoding of the sculpture not only provoked Jewell's ire but also was part of an intensified attempt on the part of eugenicists to discipline white womanhood in the wake of the liberalized morality of the 1920s and in the midst of the progressive social reforms of the New Deal. Thus, although the racial integrity of the nation, epitomized by the bodies of white men, was the purported problem, the real fault, according to eugenicists, lay with white, middle-class women who had forfeited their proper role as the breeders of good stock in favor of economic independence, controlled reproduction, and the fulfillment of careers. Within this context, the display of degraded national manhood at the AMNH was offered as proof of the nation's "eugenic predicament" and deployed to convince the bearers of the race to become the "mothers of tomorrow."[7]

Standing Soldiers, Degenerate Doughboys

This dubious Adonis was a plaster composite of one hundred thousand World War I veterans, representing the physique of the "average American male of the present generation."[8] Jane Davenport, daughter of Charles B. Davenport, the founder of the Station for Experimental Evolution at Cold Spring Harbor and a leading promoter of eugenics in the United States, sculpted the figure based on data her father collected while conducting research on army recruits for the Surgeon General's Office of the War Department during World War I.[9] Charles Davenport's research concerned one million recruits, but his daughter's sculpture was derived from the measurements of only those who qualified as "white," although, as will become clear later in this essay, that designation was simultaneously understood as a "mixed-race" category in the 1920s.[10]

Jane Davenport was certainly not an artist; however, her sculpture did partake of the classical tradition that Jewell praised. Standing in contrapposto and molded in white plaster, Davenport's man invoked—if only to disappoint—the numerous plaster casts of Greek and Roman statuary still prevalent in the nation's municipal art museums. As an icon of not only civilization but also self-consciousness (signaled in the purposive stance and arrested movement of the figure), classical sculpture—in particular the Apollo Belvedere—was the dominant representational form of whiteness in scientific illustration. In *Standing Soldiers, Kneeling Slaves,* art historian Kirk Savage asserts that classical sculpture was essential to the visual taxonomies of racial science and theory from the naturalists of the Enlightenment through the mid-twentieth century. Describing the notorious illustration from Josiah Clark Nott and George Robbins Gliddon's *Types of Mankind* (1854), he notes that the hierarchy asserted between white man, the "Negro," and animals is communicated visually through a vertical progression that moves upward from the head of a chimpanzee to a caricature of a black man to a profile bust of the Apollo Belvedere. Next to each carefully identified figure, the illustrator has rendered the representative crania in such a way that the skull of the "Creole Negro" resembles that of a "Young Chimpanzee" more closely than that of the "Greek."[11] As a sign of physical beauty, intelligence, and civilization, the Apollo Belvedere, deployed in this manner, secured an automatic identification between whiteness, culture, and human transcendence. Thus, Savage concluded, "the importance of the aesthetic dimension of racial theory cannot be overemphasized, and sculpture served as the aesthetic standard."[12]

Savage's characterization of the racial politics of scientific illustration is indeed consistent with the exhibitionary practices at the AMNH. The anthropological displays prepared by William K. Gregory for the museum's Hall of the Natural History of Man repeated this strategy several times. Gregory's hall was a permanent museum exhibit timed to open with the Third International Congress of Eugenics. "Inspired by the same purpose which inspired the temporary exhibits of the Eugenics Congress," it endeavored to give an introduction to comparative human anatomy, explaining human evolution through displays that paralleled the human skeletal structure, organs, musculature, and nervous system with that of other vertebrates.[13] In a case tracing the evolution of the human face, entitled "Our Face from Fish to Man," a series of casts depicted sharks, reptiles, mammals, and apes and culminating in a faux marble bust of the Apollo Belvedere (fig. 8.2). The penultimate cast presented the "Australian bushman," described as "a survivor of a relatively early human stage."[14] Compared to the smooth, alabaster pallor of "Our Face," the atavistic bushman

Fig. 8.2. "Our Face from Fish to Man," 1932, display in permanent exhibition at the American Museum of Natural History. Reproduced in William Gregory and Marcelle Roigneau, *Introduction to Human Anatomy: Guide to Section I of the Hall of Natural History of Man* (New York: American Museum of Natural History, 1934), 46.

was dark and hairy, displaying a "prominent" brow, "wide" nose, and "retreating" chin. As in the Nott and Gliddon illustration, this figure was positioned between a "young gorilla" and the "civilized European."[15] Employing the anthropometric truisms of eugenic science, the label explained not only who "we" are but also how "our" physical appearance demonstrates "our" superiority to the anachronous Aborigine: "The classic Greek head emphasizes the characteristics of the civilized European. Thus the forehead and braincase are very large, the nose narrow, prominent and delicate, the mouth small and the chin prominent."[16]

This example corroborates Savage's claim that the sculpture of antiquity "became an authenticating document of a normative white body," enabling an automatic conflation between the "white race" and man and relegating "inferior racial types" to a "liminal status, wavering between the

realm of man and the realm of animals."[17] This example was not an anoma-
lous instance within the museum's displays but rather was typical of the
comparative exhibits throughout Gregory's hall. In a subsequent chart,
the classical body of antiquity once again stood in for the "White" race
(fig. 8.3).

Entitled "Man among the Primates," the chart reiterated this hierarchy
by presenting a tree of life with man's branch next to that of the "Anthro-
poid Apes."[18] In this display, the category of man was subdivided by race,
with the "Australian race" (again) placed at the same level as Cro-Magnon
man and the "African," "Red," "Yellow," and "White" races lined up along
a slightly inclining plane at the uppermost left of the chart.[19] The relative
stage of development attributed to each race was indicated through dress
and disposition, with the African and Red races wearing loincloths and
holding spears (signs of primitive culture and embodiment); the Yellow
race dressed in a flowing robe, holding a book, and posed in a gesture of
public address (signifying the more advanced but purportedly "stagnated"
civilization of Asian cultures); and the White race depicted through the
flexed and fit body of the classic Greek athlete. The idealized nudity of the
White figure, as opposed to that of the Red and African figures, demonstrated how whiteness implies the ability to master the body and thus
overcome the animal nature of the physical embodiment. Unmarked, an
aesthetic icon, but bearing none of the visible trappings of anthropological
culture, he and only he represents civilization fully achieved.

Given the tendency in Euramerican scientific discourse to represent
whiteness as the pinnacle of evolutionary progress through the ideal beauty
of the Apollo Belvedere and the contemporary visual context of the exhibits
in Gregory's hall, the outrage Jewell expressed when confronted with such
a degraded reflection becomes more understandable. Although so-called
inferior races had long been rendered as natural "types," whiteness had always been identified with high culture, lifted out of space and time as an
ideal rather than a scientific specimen. As an image of the national body,
the American Adonis cast the nation in decidedly white and masculine
form—but in a degraded state of nature rather than an exalted state of culture. Located at the start of the exhibit, this statue invoked the authority of
scientific realism and the aesthetic canons of classical antiquity. However,
far from presenting a heroic ideal, this "average American" gave material
evidence of the dysgenic effects of industrialization and social decadence

Fig. 8.3. "Man among the Primates," 1932, display in permanent exhibition at the American Museum of Natural History. Reproduced in William Gregory and Marcelle Roigneau, *Introduction to Human Anatomy: Guide to Section I of the Hall of Natural History of Man* (New York: American Museum of Natural History, 1934), 61.

on the social body. As a 1932 article in the *New York Times* put it, "The Average American, to be presented . . . to the public with the authenticity of statistics, suffers by comparison with the sculptural heroes on current public monuments. He is of slight build, more suggestive of life behind a desk than anything calesthenic [sic]."[20]

Savage's work traces the conversion of the "classical body" into an icon of Anglo-American heroism to the monument boom after the Civil War. The proliferation of sculptures of heroic leaders and the "standing soldier" typology inscribed the racial hierarchy of scientific illustration onto the emergent national public sphere, as blacks were either absent from national memorials or depicted as supplicants to a benevolent white paternalism (fig. 8.4). Whiteness was thus produced and standardized through a visual contrast between classical and grotesque bodies in the public statuary of a newly unified nation. Further, the pervasive assertion of the classical body as the normative image of whiteness strengthened the conceptual link between whiteness, the national body, and physical fitness.

White Races and the "Rising Tide of Color"

Historian Mathew Frye Jacobson argues that U.S. republicanism associated physical fitness with the capacity for self-government and therefore the rights of citizenship.[21] Democratic *self*-government entailed the ability to choose reason above passion, and it placed a premium on "reflection, restraint, and self-sacrifice," virtues necessary if a polity of individuals were to act as a "homogenous body" for the "public good."[22] From the 1790 Naturalization Act in which "free white persons" were granted citizenship through the twentieth-century debates over immigration, the association between whiteness and fitness for citizenship remained. However, the definition of whiteness would be subtly modified in response to changes in immigration patterns, demographics, and popular ideas about racial degeneracy. Scientific and popular eugenics would only solidify the conceptual links between racial stock, physical vigor, and intelligence. If the standing soldier typology helped to naturalize the whiteness "tacitly but irretrievably written into republican ideology" by providing a generic image of the standard citizen (read white, male, and fit), the degenerate doughboy called into question the "average American's" fitness for self-rule and thereby the very future of American democracy.[23] The peril that a racially mixed citizenry posed for a democratic nation was, in fact, the immediate concern of the Second International Congress of Eugenics. As stated at the outset, Davenport originally sculpted her American for the eugenics exhibition

Fig. 8.4. Monument to the Civil War Soldier, Lebanon, New Hampshire, an example of the "standing soldier" genre of public statuary. Photo by Mary K. Coffey.

mounted at the AMNH in 1921, where it was exhibited to no apparent alarm. Just as in the 1932 exhibit, the statuette was situated within displays dedicated to promoting eugenic science as a means for race betterment but in a way that "the man of ordinary intelligence and education . . . without special scientific training, could readily comprehend and appreciate."[24] However, in the 1921 exhibit, unlike the 1932 display, Davenport's sculpture was paired with a statue of a composite athlete sculpted from the measurements of the "50 strongest men of Harvard."[25] Displayed at opposite ends of Darwin Hall, a long, rectangular gallery with eighteen information booths along each side, these two small statues embodied the Alpha and Omega of whiteness as it was understood in the 1920s.

Jacobson asserts that the period between 1840 and 1924 witnessed a shift "from the unquestioned hegemony of a unified race of 'white persons' to a contest over political 'fitness' among a now fragmented, hierarchically arranged series of distinct 'white races.'"[26] Prior to the 1840s, whiteness was defined within a political struggle over slavery, and consequently, blacks provided the foil to whites of European descent. However, afterward, due in part to the overly expansive category enshrined in the 1790 Naturalization Act (which categorized all Europeans as white so as to enable immigration and maintain the demographic advantage of whites over blacks), as well as the demands of industrialization, mass immigration provided the backdrop for the redefinition of whiteness as a plural and internally differentiated category. Nativists, who identified predominantly with "Anglo-Saxon" or "Nordic" stock, reacted to the influx of German, Irish, Italian, and Jewish immigrants and placed themselves at the top of a hierarchy of white races in which "Teutons," "Semites," "Celts" and "Mediterraneans" (among others) were deemed inferior in mental character and physical ability. The political crisis generated by immigration was exacerbated by the "race suicide" of World War I, which in turn spawned a xenophobic discourse about the "Rising Tide of Color against White World Supremacy," to quote Harvard professor Lothrop Stoddard's notorious screed.[27]

Henry Fairfield Osborn, president of the Second International Congress, revealed the political stakes of the 1921 congress and its exhibits in his "Address of Welcome" when he began by declaring:

> I doubt if there has ever been a moment in the world's history when an international conference on race character and betterment has been more important than the present. Europe, in patriotic self-sacrifice on both sides of the World War, has lost much of the heritage of centuries of civilization which never can be regained. ... In the United States ... [w]e are engaged in a serious struggle to maintain our historic republican institutions through barring the entrance of those who are unfit to share the duties and respon-

sibilities of our well-founded government. The true sprit of American democracy that *all men are born with equal rights and duties* has
been confused with the political sophistry that *all men are born
with equal character and ability to govern themselves and others,* and
with the education sophistry that education and environment will
offset the handicap of heredity.[28]

Osborn's comments betray the assumed link between republican citizenship and white racial privilege while also drawing a distinction between
native-born whites and the unfit European races who threatened "our his-
toric republican institutions." Further, Osborn noted the difficulty eugenic
reformers faced in a democracy based on white equality, a problem
Leonard Darwin also lamented in his own address to the congress, when
he stated that "governments which depend on the suffrages of the people
are of necessity always somewhat timid in regard to unpopular reforms;
and until eugenics becomes popular—when will that be, I wonder!—there
is not the slightest chance of eugenic reform moving forward with too
rapid strides."[29] The palpable sense of the urgency eugenicists felt in 1921
to both influence immigration policy and legitimate eugenics itself ran
throughout the papers presented and was encapsulated in Darwin's re-
mark that "eugenics has been called a dismal science, but it should rather
be described as an untried policy."[30]

The exhibition, in particular, was charged with both popularizing eugenics and convincing legislators that eugenic policies were necessary to
ensure the future racial stock of the United States. Thus, special invitations
were issued to members of Congress and "persons particularly interested
in the inborn nature and fortunes of races and families."[31] Additionally, the
general public was given free admission and encouraged to sign a registry
noting their interest in eugenic research and a "desire to promote the purpose of the Congress and the exhibit."[32] Nativist concerns over the effects
of unchecked immigration were evident in charts entitled "Approaching Extinction of 'Mayflower' Descendents," "Growth of United States Population
by Immigration and by Increase in Native Stock," and "Marriage and Birth
Rate in Relation to Immigration."[33] Exhibits explaining how physical and
mental measurements were taken or how the principles of heredity could
be determined through pedigree charts helped to familiarize the audience
with the implements and methods of eugenic science. Foremost among
these were statistics and their visual equivalent, the composite photograph.

Sir Francis Galton, the "father of eugenics," had pioneered the use of composite photography in his studies of criminals, but he also applied it to "fit" populations through the compilation of photographic records of families for the purposes of deducing "family likeness" and thereby proving, through physiognomic evidence, the role of heredity in the transmission of inborn traits. Photography, which Galton referred to as "pictorial statistics," helped eugenicists legitimate their science because of its claims to empirical truth and unimpeachable fact.[34] The 1921 exhibition was thus replete with data communicated through visual techniques that both performed an irrefutable and empirical truth and sought to put that truth in the service of governmental policy recommendations. In addition to pedigree charts tracing the inherited genius and talent in the "Agassiz Family of Scientists," "Hopkins Family of Educators," and "Morgan Family of Capitalists," there were composite portraits of college students from Wellesley, Harvard, Amherst, Vassar, Cornell, Smith, and Williams, as well as "Horse-car conductors," "Portland Physicians," and the "Members of the National Academy of Science."[35] These composites, based on Galton's method, were submitted by Davenport's Eugenics Record Office at Cold Spring Harbor and claimed to show a "striking resemblance" among people of the same class and profession.[36] These examples show how the evidentiary properties of photography worked in conjunction with eugenic presumptions about the relationship between physiognomy and the supposedly inborn traits of genius and intellect.

With these displays as a backdrop, Davenport's *Average American Male* functioned as irrefutable, visual proof of the eugenicists' warnings about the dysgenic effects of immigration on the nation's racial stock. Contrasted with the vigorous and idealized body of the composite Harvard athlete, the average male's slight shoulders, distended belly, and lack of firm musculature implied that the national (white) body was degenerating as a result of an improvident mixing with inferior European stocks. For visitors to the 1921 exhibit, the composite athlete offered the "Aristogenic" Anglo-Saxon as an emblem of the "Native Stock" eugenicists hoped to protect from the "Rising Tide of Color" through immigration reform.[37] Those "particularly interested in the inborn nature and fortunes of races and families" could aspire to the Harvard ideal while measuring themselves against the "average American" without destabilizing their assumptions about white racial superiority. By 1932, this comparison was no longer possible, as the "average American" was displayed without the "Harvard athlete" to balance him out, thereby presenting visitors with visual evidence of white degeneracy without differentiating between a native racial aristocracy and the dysgenic racial groups of recent immigrants.

"The American Now in the Making"

If *The Average American Male* was displayed in 1921 as an icon of an inferior, internally differentiated form of whiteness to convince audiences, popular and professional alike, that immigration reform was necessary, what purpose did the statuette serve in 1932, almost a decade after immigration had been restricted to such a degree that even Lothrop Stoddard was no longer concerned about the so-called rising tide of color?[38] The answer to this question is revealed, in part, by the fact that *The Average American* was exhibited without the "Harvard athlete" in 1932, an exhibitionary circumstance that definitively changed its meaning. Dysgenic immigration might have been stemmed, but without the specter of inferior white bodies flooding the nation, newer concerns emerged. In particular, eugenicists began to highlight the threats of a racially mixed, polyglot population in which undesirable groups purportedly reproduced much faster than their more desirable brethren. The supposed dangers of this situation were made even more urgent in the 1930s by the Depression, which some eugenicists viewed as a result of the overproduction of inferior people rather than poor economic policy or the isolationist mentality that they themselves had helped to foster.

To understand why a degenerate image of the "average American" was maintained over a eugenic one despite the successful outcome of one of the eugenicist's main political agendas at the Second International Congress, one can return to Jacobson's discussion of the shifting paradigms of racial classification between 1924 and the end of World War II. Over this period, he argues, the idea of race as color slowly displaced biological notions of racial difference, as "Caucasian" came to replace the less "scientific" and pluralized categories of whiteness. Jacobson attributes this shift to a combination of factors, foremost among them the passing of the Johnson Act in 1924, which drastically restricted immigration and thus lowered the political stakes of delineating racial distinctions among whites. Along with immigration restriction, he argues, the great northward migrations of Southern blacks helped to reconsolidate whiteness as a "monolith of privilege" in urban centers and the Western states.[39]

The 1932 exhibition took place within this period of transformation, and in retrospect, it marked a high point for the eugenics movement, for the crimes of the Nazi regime would soon discredit eugenics as a pseudo-science and force its practitioners to change their rhetoric and regroup in the name of genetics.[40] However, in 1932, eugenics had not yet been fully discredited, and the Third International Congress of Eugenics was actually convened to celebrate that "decade of progress in eugenics" championed in its title. Despite the economic crisis of a worldwide Depression, dele-gates at the congress were actually more optimistic about the future of their endeavors than they had been in 1921, when they felt they still needed to convince a disbelieving public of the rectitude of their cause. Having per-suaded the U.S. Congress of the necessity for immigration restriction, American eugenicists argued that the Third International Congress and the exhibition ought to "emphasize the fact that eugenics is concerned pri-marily with racial and family-stock quality in the turn-over of population from generation to generation."[41] Within this context, *The Average American Male* functioned not as a representation of the dysgenic immigrant body but rather as a figure of the normative national body.

Positioned in the 1930s as a visual picture of the "average American," Davenport's sculpture tapped into a popular discourse that emerged after Columbia psychologist Harry Hollingworth published his "composite por-trait" of the average man derived, in part, from the physical examination and mental tests of World War I recruits undertaken by Charles Davenport and Robert Yerkes, respectively, and popularized by Carl Brigham in 1923.[42] The title of a *New York Times* article announcing Hollingworth's rather dismal conclusions stated, "The Average Man Found by Science, He Is Shown to Be Superstitious, Ill Educated, Conventional and Possessing the Mind of a Boy of 14 Years." Commenting on the novelty of this kind of scientific inquiry, the reporter wrote:

> Science now turns its attention to the average man. Not so long ago it was the mentally defective, the diseased or the criminal whose characteristics were most industriously studied. Then the attention of science turned to the person with very high intelli-gence and unusual abilities. Now science gives us a picture of the man who does most of the work of the world, fights most of the battles, likes the movies, believes in stories with a happy ending and becomes the father of the generations of the future.[43]

Warren Susman has noted that the science of statistics propelled a burgeoning interest in the "average American" over the course of the 1920s and 1930s.[44] In addition to the establishment of information-gathering organizations such as the Bureau of Labor Statistics and the Carnegie Institute (the latter a funder of Davenport's research at Cold Spring Harbor), local communities sponsored competitions to find the "average American," and best-selling authors such as Jack London and John Steinbeck turned their literary talents to depictions of the common—at times tragic, at times heroic—men of the United States.[45]

Similarly, anthropologists, sociologists, and eugenic scientists also set about limning a normative image of the American, and in 1932, the *New York Times* ran a series of articles under the banner "The American Now in the Making," in which eight "students of our national traits" were asked to answer a question: "What is an American?" With the exception of the sociologist William Fielding Ogburn, the respondents forwarded racial arguments about the "American physiognomy."[46] However, all presumed the representative American to be white, male, and—regardless of region and whether of "old" or "new" stock—a member of a single race.[47] Similarly, while praising many of his features, each viewed the "American Now in the Making" to be, like the young nation, an unfinished product. The implicit conflation between nation and race was most evident in British anthropologist Sir Arthur Keith's contribution, in which he stated outright that "nations are incipient races" and argued that the United States was only beginning to come into its own now that the tide of immigration had been stemmed. "The Americans, Old and New, have resolved to be a single nation, a single race," he proclaimed: "They are cutting themselves off from all the other peoples of the world by high tariff walls and immigration barriers. . . . Patriotism is the force behind nation-building and race-building. Patriotism today calls upon the citizens of the United States to be 100 per cent American."[48]

"Not More but Better Americans"

Keith's remarks demonstrate the extent to which eugenics informed ideas about both race and nation. Moreover, his comments make clear that even as the plural racial categories of Old and New Americans were becoming unified into a single race/nation, the country was not yet 100 percent American. This odd condition of being at once "white" and "mongrel" American—but not yet 100 percent so—was captured perfectly in Davenport's

American. This discursive context helps explain the didactic function of her sculpture within the exhibit at the Third International Congress of Eugenics. As both a representative and degenerate American, *The Average American Male* could no longer be easily dismissed by white viewers as a representation of the dysgenic body of the racially mongrel immigrant. Within the context of the 1932 exhibition, the popular discourse on the average American, and the rhetorical thrust of the papers delivered at the Third International Congress, the sculpture was exhibited and consistently interpreted within the press as an alarming mirror image of average (read white) Americans (recall Jewell's analysis). The purpose of this alarm within the context of the congress and exhibition seems to have been to convince visitors of the importance of controlled reproduction so that they might join in the eugenic project of race betterment, an agenda heavily promoted by delegates in the numerous papers presented during the proceedings and avidly chronicled in the press.

In his opening address to the 1932 congress, Henry Fairfield Osborn invoked his contribution to the *New York Times* debate over national character, reiterating his contention that Americans possessed the strong and weak points of their ancestral "Nordic" as well as more recent "Alpine and Mediterranean" stocks. "Far inferior to men of other races," the American, argued Osborn, should "freely admit" his inferiority and, "as far as possible, rectify" it through education.[49] What is significant here is that Osborn used the terms *race* and *American* interchangeably, acknowledging the presence of different "stocks" but nonetheless claiming that they formed a collective national character rather than insisting on discriminating between true natives and foreign interlopers, as was the tendency in the 1920s. Rather, by 1932, "the American race" was a singular term and seemed to refer automatically to a composite of what would soon be called ethnicities rather than hierarchically arranged white races. Given this subtle but significant shift in how supporters of eugenics understood race and national character, the meaning of race betterment that Osborn argued for in his opening address becomes clearer. If participants in the congress focused on the external threat of immigration to American racial purity in 1921, they spent more energy in 1932 on the internal threat of unequal birthrates among Americans and the issue of race improvement. Asserting that the Third International Congress of Eugenics had "peculiar significance" for Americans, Osborn concluded his address by stressing the importance of birth selection and controlled reproduction with his slogan "Not more but better Americans."[50]

In 1921, eugenics had been defined for the public in the exhibition as simply "the science of the improvement of the human race by better breeding . . . [or] the conscious (as opposed to instinctive) self-direction of human evolution." But in 1932, a large introductory text elaborated this definition in ways that made the concern for national reproduction explicit (fig. 8.5).[51]

Titled "What Eugenics Is All About," the text read, in part:

> Eugenics is that science which studies the inborn qualities—physical, mental, and spiritual—in man, with a view to their improvement. Nothing is more evident in the history of families, communities and nations than that, in the change of individuals from generation to generation, some families, some races, and the people of some nations, improve greatly in physical soundness, in intelligence and in character, industry, leadership, and other qualities which make for

WHAT EUGENICS IS ALL ABOUT

Eugenics is that science which studies the inborn qualities – physical, mental and spiritual – in man, with a view to their improvement.

Nothing is more evident in the history of families, communities and nations than that, in the change of individuals from generation to generation, some families, some races, and the people of some nations, improve greatly in physical soundness, in intelligence and in character, industry, leadership, and other qualities which make for human breed improvement; while other racial, national and family stocks die out – they decline in physical stamina, in intellectual capacity and in moral force.

Both good and bad qualities are hereditary. It follows that every family and every race, as well as every nation, has its own eugenic problems. When the new generation is produced by sound and capable families The breed of man tends to improve." If, however, the more degenerate members of the community produce the greater number of children, then "the breed of man degenerates."

The eugenical future of your community – and in parallel fashion of your family and your nation – depends upon (a) who moves into your community to become the ancestors of a portion of its future citizens, (b) how the present members of the community – both native and adopted – marry, and (c) how many children the different families have in relation to the "excellence of the hereditary stuff out of which they are made."

Eugenics, then, concerns improvement in the breed of man. Obviously it is closely parallel, in essential nature, to the improvement in domestic plants and animals; but it is clear that in man the methods of mate-selection, and of reproducing from the best and forbidding reproduction by the most inferior, must be different from the methods employed in plant and animal breeding. Applied eugenics works essentially through long-time education, in which young people build up an appreciation of the importance of "blood" and "breed" – that is of the hereditary foundations of individual and family success. In the long run, the appreciation of good blood is counted on to influence mate-selection and "family-size ideals" – unconsciously perhaps, but just as really and as powerfully as wealth, social position and charming personal qualities.

LIKE A TREE EUGENICS DRAWS ITS MATERIALS FROM MANY SOURCES AND GIVES THEM ORGANIC UNITY AND PURPOSE

EUGENICS IS THE SELF DIRECTION OF HUMAN EVOLUTION

A FOUR-PANEL SURVEY OF EUGENICS.

EXHIBITED BY THE EUGENICS RECORD OFFICE, CARNEGIE INSTITUTION OF WASHINGTON. COLD SPRING HARBOR, LONG ISLAND, N.Y.

Fig. 8.5. "What Eugenics Is All About," on display at the 1932 Third International Congress of Eugenics, American Museum of Natural History. At some point, this piece became panel one of a four-panel display made by the Eugenics Record Office, all of which hung in the Hall of Science Building at the Century-of-Progress Exhibition, Chicago World's Fair, 1933, next to the "Genetics" display. Courtesy of the Buffalo Museum of Science, Buffalo, New York.

human breed improvement; while other racial, national, and family stocks die out—they decline in physical stamina, in intellectual capacity and in moral force. . . . The eugenical future of your community—and in parallel fashion of your family and your nation—depends upon (a) who moves into your community to become the ancestors of a portion of its future citizens, (b) how the present members of the community—both native and adopted—marry, and (c) how many children the different families have in relation to the excellence of the hereditary stuff out of which they are made.[52]

As points (a), (b), and (c) reveal, immigration, though still appearing first in the list of dangers to community, family, and nation, was augmented by the related and clearly more emphasized issues of marriage and reproduction in this definition. Further, the direct address employed in the rhetorical style of this panel demonstrated that the congress and exhibit, although they appealed to a general audience, were particularly targeting the sentiments of women. As the members of family and community most responsible for the maintenance of "blood" and "breed," women were the implicit subjects of this entreaty. The other three panels of the racist display, perhaps added the following year for exhibit at the Chicago World's Fair, honed in even more closely on what types of women should be having children—those of the Roosevelt, rather than the "Ishmael," variety—and the number of children needed—namely, four per family (figs. 8.6, 8.7, and 8.8).

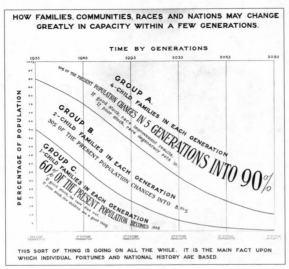

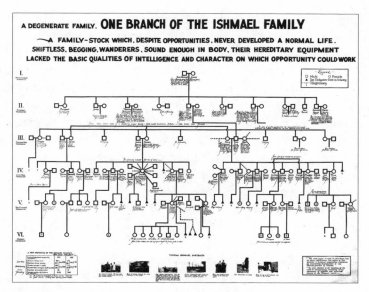

Figs. 8.6, 8.7, and 8.8. "How Families, Communities, Races, and Nations May Change Greatly in Capacity within a Few Generations," "One Branch of the Ishmael Family," and "The Roosevelt Family-Stock," panels two, three, and four of the four-panel display made by the Eugenics Record Office. These panels may have been displayed at the 1932 Third International Congress of Eugenics, American Museum of Natural History, and certainly were hung in the Hall of Science Building at the Century-of-Progress Exhibition, Chicago World's Fair, 1933, next to the "Genetics" display. Panels two and three courtesy of the Buffalo Museum of Science, Buffalo, New York; panel four reproduced in Harry H. Laughlin, "A Description of the Wall-Panel Survey of Eugenics Exhibited in the Hall of Science, Century of Progress Exposition, Chicago, 1933–34," *Journal of Heredity* 26, vol. 4 (April 1935): 159.

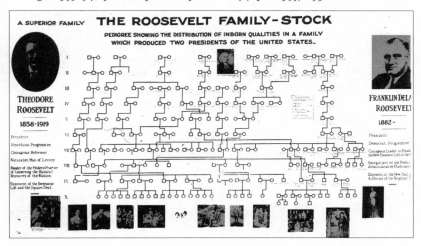

This rather extensive explanation suggests that the organizers of the exhibition were looking ahead to the long-term racial improvement of the national community and that they saw the exhibit as an important means for incorporating average Americans (that is, middle-class whites) into the project of improving the "hereditary stuff" of not only the "breed of man" but, more important, the (white) nation. Stressing the importance of education and, more significantly, marriage and family counseling, the text disclosed that immigration restriction was no longer the primary concern. Having dammed the tide of color, mainline conservative eugenicists now turned their gaze inward to focus on the national population and concerned themselves instead with domestic reproduction. Thus, the less than impressive physique of Davenport's American seems to have been employed to convince this public of the need for increased reproduction among so-called Aristogenic families.

To this end, the rhetorical appeals of the wall text and displays were augmented by interactive exhibits and activities that encouraged visitors to subject themselves and their families to eugenic analysis. For example, the Eugenics Record Office staffed its exhibits at the AMNH with attendants who gave blank pedigree charts to visitors so that they could trace their family's heredity. In another exhibit on physical anthropometry that argued "finger tip patterns are controlled by heredity," visitors could have themselves fingerprinted.[53] And in a booth promoting the establishment of eugenics libraries in high schools and colleges, visitors encountered cases with pamphlets containing instructions on "how to prepare a family pedigree" along with "field data on economic value of lives," sample questionnaires and other do-it-yourself materials, in addition to a mock-up organized in accordance with "modern library practice."[54]

Given that eugenics had always been concerned with the relative reproduction rates of fit and unfit populations, why did the organizers of the exhibition and congress in 1932 feel the need make such an extensive case for the importance of the "change of individuals from generation to generation"? What were the perceived threats to Aristogenic mate selection and reproduction that persuaded eugenicists to elaborate their mission in pursuit of a program of "long-time education, in which young people build up an appreciation of the importance of 'blood' and 'breed'"?

Average Men, Better Women

If immigration and the dysgenic effects of war framed the Second International Congress of Eugenics, the dangers of what organizers called propaganda accounted for the urgency underpinning the Third International Congress. In his presidential address, Charles Davenport enumerated the "crusading" enemies of eugenics, namely, "prohibition propaganda, the laborless-child propaganda, the birth control propaganda and the rest."[55] After commending the progress of sterilization legislation in Denmark, England, and the Netherlands and the restriction of immigration in the United States, Davenport suggested that "mate selection" was increasingly recognized as an important place for eugenic instruction. "The necessity of emphasizing [eugenic] ideals now," he intoned, "is partly the spread of non-biological theories of equality of breeding stocks, . . . the undue emphasis on economic, rather than biological considerations in mate selection and in reproduction."[56] Henry Fairfield Osborn, serving as vice president of the congress, echoed Davenport's call in his keynote address, entitled "Birth Selection vs. Birth Control." Invoking the current "cataclysmic crisis" of overpopulation, overproduction, and overcapitalization, Osborn chastised "prisons, reformatories, asylums, great public financial offerings, great national and local appropriations, [and] great tides of human kindness and generosity," arguing that these reformist efforts were "merely palliatives and temporary expedients."[57] Dispensing with progressive social movements (that is, socialism, state welfare, and women's liberation), he instead advocated "positive eugenics" as the foremost remedy for the restoration of "progressive civilization" and the eventual reduction of the "millions of people who are acting as dragnets or sheet-anchors on the progress of the ship of state."[58]

Galton had made a similar argument when he inaugurated eugenics with the publication of his book *Hereditary Genius* in 1869. Following his lead, nineteenth-century eugenicists centered their efforts on "negative" remedies such as compulsory sterilization for the "deviant" and "feeble-minded." However, by the 1930s, as the proceedings of the Third International Congress suggest, eugenicists were more concerned with "positive" reforms signaled by their promotion of better mate selection. This shift in rhetorical emphasis and policy recommendations has led many historians to argue that by the 1930s, eugenic science was on the wane. But Wendy Kline has contended that this reorientation from what Osborn called "birth control" to "birth selection" marked not the disappearance of eugenics but rather its transformation into family planning.[59] Significantly, this transformation displaced the locus of racial anxiety from the bodies of so-called degenerate men and women onto those of the white middle class.

Despite the problems posed by a host of "non-biological theories of equality," the primary enemies for Osborn and Davenport were the proponents of birth control and women's independence. For Osborn, the declining birthrate of "American stock" could be directly attributed to women's advocates who sought to relieve women of their share in the "hard struggle for the existence of the race."[60] Chiding birth control propagandists, he endorsed the assertion of a fellow delegate, Clarence G. Campbell, that "the continuance of the race and the quality of the race rests primarily with women. In short, women are more essential to racial survival than men. . . . In any woman who possesses valuable traits which she has inherited and which she can pass on to offspring, the disposition to evade this obligation is a manifest racial delinquency."[61] Osborn promoted instead the positive eugenics of "birth selection," which sought legal measures to curtail the procreation of unfit women while simultaneously encouraging increases in the birthrate among desirable populations. To rectify what Davenport characterized as the "slow and tardy" breeding habits of the "most intellectually successful strains," Osborn estimated, via "unimpeachable statistics," that "an average of four-children families is essential to secure the perpetuation of a desirable family strain."[62] His remarks were in line with the majority of delegates, who delivered papers entitled "Measures to Encourage the Fertility of the Gifted," "The Reduction of the Fecundity of the Socially Inadequate," "Aristogenics," and "Evidence of the Rapidly Decreasing Birth Rate in Families in Which Highly Intelligent Children Occur."[63] Osborn's remarks reveal that the "woman question" was at the heart of the congress's agenda—which was, in the words of Jan Sanders, a Dutch delegate, to "[win] women over to the idea of the large family."[64]

In light of the "woman problem," *The Average American Male*, as a national body, could also have invoked period anxieties about the racial repercussions of women's liberation. The growing power of antibiological accounts of social inequality, in particular with regard to race, nation, and gender, helps to explain the pointed and defensive critique of "propaganda" on the part of the congress's organizers. Constructing their claims as unbiased truth was essential because eugenicists distinguished their science from the mere "opinions" of propaganda on this basis. Davenport defined propaganda as "the organized effort to get accepted some principle the truth and value of which have not been, or can not be, demonstrated but of whose importance the propagandists hold a strong opinion. They are, if not morally surely *emotionally,* certain of its truth and undertake a crusade, or indeed, a warfare to lure or force others to accept their way of thinking."[65] His definition could easily hold for the activities of eugenicists! This desire to combat the truth claims of their opposition is what animated their own endeavors to reinforce the scientific truth of eugenics through the empirical claims of statistics, photography, and composite sculpture. The empirical claims of these technologies were also vital in 1921 (and, indeed, had been throughout the history of eugenics). However, at the Second International Congress, the goal was still to legitimate eugenics as a science. By 1932, the struggle had moved away from legitimation and toward substantiation. The battle over truth was now with progressive groups that shared many of the presumptions of eugenics but contested its biological reductionism. The birth control advocates comprised one such group. Like eugenicists, they sought to lower the birthrate among poor women; however, in arguing for reproductive rights en masse, they disrupted the implicit and highly conservative gender politics of eugenics.

The composite sculpture of a hundred thousand World War I doughboys, although a remnant of an earlier set of concerns, was recontextualized in 1932 to serve the new needs of the congress. Within this changed discursive context, this would-be Adonis performed a remarkably delicate balancing act. On the one hand, it maintained the superiority of the white middle class as well the homology between this group and the nation as a whole. On the other hand, it presented proof of the physical (and therefore racial) degeneracy of this privileged group. As a grotesque body, *The Average American Male* gave visible testimony to the decadence of the national body and the need for eugenic reform, but it did so by providing an image of the nation that was presented in the congress's speeches as a problem of racially delinquent white womanhood. Thus, one might argue that the original project of eugenics, invented to legitimate white social hegemony and preserve the privileges of the professional middle class, had come home to roost.

"The average American male" maintained masculine authority for whiteness by concentrating the blame for physical degeneracy on the bodies and behavior of white women of the "best stock." The contextual positioning of this male body therefore helped to substantiate eugenicists' claims about the perils of birth control and perversely enabled their attempts to maintain control over women's reproductive work. As feminists have argued, the political legislation of sexuality and reproduction is the mechanism through which citizenship and rights are determined and therefore the means through which the unequal power relations of race, class, and nation are maintained.[66] In 1932, the visual polemics of the "average American" were employed in the battle to "win women over to the idea of the big family" by promoting the biological management of the social body so as to discipline white womanhood, "improve the race," and cure the crisis of "over-production" in all senses of the word. The shifting meaning of Davenport's sculpture between the 1921 and 1932 congresses demonstrates how the *privileges* of whiteness, rather than the *status* of whiteness, are constantly being negotiated and reallocated to maintain and manage gender, race, and class inequality. Perhaps this explains why Edward Alden Jewell's defense of humanity was the only public objection to the exhibitionary argument mobilized and authorized by the plaster composite.

Despite the somewhat degraded appearance of *The Average American Male* at the AMNH, Ales Hrdlicka, curator at the National Museum of Anthropology and an ardent eugenicist, was more sanguine in his contribution to the *New York Times* series on the "Average American Now in the Making" in 1932. Indeed, he proclaimed that the average American man "[is a] virile, enterprising, cheerful, bright-eyed, modern human! His faults are those common to the human lot, and less than in most. On the whole, where unspoiled, he is a very desirable representative of present humanity." In regard to the American woman, however, his assessment was more tempered: "She is not yet, perhaps, all that she could be. Conditions have not as yet been fully propitious to her. She is still searching for her true place."[67] If the eugenicists of 1932 would have their way (and several of the essays in this volume suggest that they did), the American woman would soon find her "true place" not in the working world, the social sector, or the political arena but rather as a "mother of tomorrow" ensuring the survival of the race.

Notes

1. Edward Alden Jewell, "The Masterpiece and the Modeled Chart," *New York Times,* September 18, 1932, 9; emphasis in original.

2. Ibid.

3. Ibid.

4. Statistics provided in "Part 2: The Exhibit," in *A Decade of Progress in Eugenics: Scientific Papers of the Third International Congress of Eugenics, Held at American Museum of Natural History, New York, August 21–23, 1932* (Baltimore, MD: Williams and Wilkins, 1934), 486. The *New York Times* covered the congress and exhibit throughout the week, providing summaries of papers delivered and discussing aspects of the exhibition. Though some writers, such as Jewell, balked at the average man, the journalists covering the event did not criticize eugenics or the arguments presented by the delegates they covered. Their response seems to indicate a general acceptance of the premise of the congress. See "Birth Control Peril to Race, Says Osborn; 'Birth Selection' the Remedy in Crisis of Over-Population, He Tells Eugenics Congress," *New York Times,* August 23, 1932, 1, 2; "Eugenicists Analyze Traits of Heredity behind Presidents," *Washington Post,* August 21, 1932, 9; "Eugenics Congress Opens Here Today, Scientists of Many Nations to Attend Sessions at the American Museum," *New York Times,* August 21, 1932, 15; "Holds Capitalism Bars Eugenic Goal; Prof. Muller of Texas Asserts Profit Motive Is Inimical to Welfare of Race," *New York Times,* August 24, 1932, 8; "Major Darwin Predicts Civilization's Doom Unless Century Brings Wide Eugenic Reforms," *New York Times,* August 23, 1932, 16; "Urges Open Door to Healthy Aliens, Dr. D. F. Ramos of Cuba Would Subject All Immigrants to a 'Biological Investigation,'" *New York Times,* August 23, 1932, 16.

5. Henry Fairfield Osborn, "Birth Selection vs. Birth Control," in *A Decade of Progress,* 41. For a discussion of the significance of Greek antiquity to racial science, see Kirk Savage, *Standing Soldiers, Kneeling Slaves: Race, War, and Monument in Nineteenth-Century America* (Princeton, NJ: Princeton University Press, 1997). For a discussion of the crafting of Egypt as the foundation of a white, European civilization, see Martin Bernal, *Black Athena: The Afroasiatic Roots of Classical Civilization,* vol. 1 (London: Free Association Books, 1987). For a period argument, see Henry Fairfield Osborn's contribution to a debate on "The American Now in the Making," run in the *New York Times,* in which he writes, "Even as you scratch the Russian to discover the Tartar, you scratch the American to discover the man of the Elizabethan age." Throughout his remarks, he contended that the original Anglo-Saxon stock of the "first comers" derived their essential character from the "English Bible, Shakespeare and Milton"; see Henry Fairfield Osborn, "An Elizabethan," *New York Times,* January 17, 1932, 14.

6. This was the title of the Third International Congress of Eugenics.

7. See Wendy Kline, *Building a Better Race: Gender, Sexuality, and Eugenics from the Turn of the Century to the Baby Boom* (Berkeley: University of California Press, 2001), 16–19.

8. See "Average American No Adonis to Science; Plaster Composite of 100,000 Males Is of Slight Build, Except Abdominally," *New York Times,* August 22, 1932, 19.

9. The results of this research were published in Albert G. Love and Charles B. Davenport, "Physical Examination of the First Million Draft Recruits: Methods and Results," in War Department: Office of the Surgeon General, *Bulletin,* no. 11 (Washington, DC: Government Printing Office, 1919). The author of the sculpture was variously referred to as Jane Davenport and Mrs. R. G. Harris, her married name. That Jane Davenport and Mrs. R. G. Harris were one and the same was confirmed in a letter sent by Charles Davenport to C. E. Boyer, in which he wrote, "The data on which the plaster model composite of 100,000 veterans of the World War was made are to be found in the 'Army Anthropology,' being volume XV of the 'Medical Department of the U.S. Army in the World War,' 1921. This model was made by my daughter on data which she had in part worked over during the war." Letter is in the folder C.E. Boyer, Charles Davenport Papers, American Philosophical Society, Philadelphia, PA. Citation provided by Christina Cogdell.

10. As the many displays put together by Charles Davenport's Eugenics Record Office demonstrate, the statistical and demographic data he derived from his study of recruits at demobilization pertained to whites only; however, this category was delineated into eight races, which he listed as Polish, German, French, Italian, English, Hebrew, Scotch, and Irish. See "Description of Exhibits," in Harry H. Laughlin, *The Second International Exhibition of Eugenics* (Baltimore, MD: Williams and Wilkins, 1923), 36–37.

11. Josiah Clark Nott and George Robbins Gliddon, *Types of Mankind* (Philadelphia: J. B. Lippincott, 1854), 458.

12. Savage, *Standing Soldiers, Kneeling Slaves,* 11.

13. "The Exhibit," in *A Decade of Progress,* 507.

14. William Gregory and Marcelle Roigneau, *Introduction to Human Anatomy: Guide to Section I of the Hall of Natural History of Man* (New York: American Museum of Natural History, 1934), 46.

15. His neighbors were identified as such in the explanatory text; see Gregory and Roigneau, *Introduction to Human Anatomy,* 46.

16. Ibid.

17. Savage, *Standing Soldiers, Kneeling Slaves,* 9–11.

18. Gregory and Roigneau, *Introduction to Human Anatomy,* 61.

19. This hierarchical division of the races of mankind was typical of the day. The Field Museum of Natural History in Chicago inaugurated a similar exhibition in 1933, filled with Malvina Hoffman's racial sculptures, that also charted the progression of human development through a racial hierarchy that began with the "Australian" race and then moved through the "African," "Mongoloid," and "White" races. See Henry Field, *The Races of Mankind: An Introduction to Chauncey Keep Memorial Hall* (Chicago: Field Museum, 1933).

20. "Average American No Adonis to Science," 19.

21. Matthew Frye Jacobson, *Whiteness of a Different Color: European Immigrants and the Alchemy of Race* (Cambridge, MA: Harvard University Press, 1998), 26.

22. Ibid.

23. Ibid.

24. This mandate was stipulated by Harry H. Laughlin when soliciting exhibitors. See "Suggestions Relative to Eugenics Exhibits," in Laughlin, *The Second International Exhibition of Eugenics*, 16.

25. The sculpture was described as such in the "Floor Plan of the Exhibition," reproduced in Laughlin, *The Second International Exhibition of Eugenics*, 12.

26. Jacobson, *Whiteness of a Different Color*, 42.

27. Lothrop Stoddard, *The Rising Tide of Color against White World Supremacy* (New York: Charles Scribner's Sons, 1921). Stoddard was an exhibitor at the Second International Congress, where he showcased his book and reproduced enlarged maps from the book's illustrations demonstrating the distribution of the "primary races" throughout the world, the "Categories of White World-Supremacy," and the distribution of the "white races." See Laughlin, *The Second International Exhibition of Eugenics*, 35.

28. Henry Fairfield Osborn, "Address of Welcome," in *Scientific Papers of the Second International Congress of Eugenics: Eugenics, Genetics and the Family*, vol. 1 (Baltimore, MD: Williams and Wilkins, 1923), 1–2. Emphasis in original.

29. Leonard Darwin, "The Aims and Methods of Eugenical Societies," in *Scientific Papers to the Second International Congress of Eugenics: Eugenics, Genetics and the Family*, vol. 1 (Baltimore, MD: Williams and Wilkins, 1923), 15.

30. Ibid., 7.

31. Laughlin, *The Second International Exhibition of Eugenics*, 20.

32. Ibid. Laughlin stated that although no official records were kept, the museum estimated that between 5,000 and 10,000 persons attended the exhibit during its one-month run, out of which 821 signed the registry.

33. These charts are reproduced in Laughlin, *The Second International Exhibition of Eugenics*, 74–75, 98–101, and 144–45.

34. David Greene, "Veins of Resemblance: Photography and Eugenics," *Oxford Art Journal* 7, no. 2 (1984): 14.

35. Laughlin, *The Second International Exhibition of Eugenics*, 130–31.

36. Ibid., 36.

37. The term *Aristogenic*, as defined in the exhibition, referred to "families most highly talented in body, mind and temperament." *Practical eugenics*, or what Darwin meant by "untried policy," was characterized as both "cacogenic control" and "constructive activities" through which eugenicists sought to "raise the level of inborn human values." Cacogenic control proceeded by "cutting off the descent lines of those individuals who are so meagerly or defectively endowed by nature that their offspring are unable to care for themselves and consequently entail a drag upon the more effective members of society," whereas "aristogenic or constructive activities" worked "by securing fit matings [sic] and higher fertility" among fit families. See Laughlin, *The Second International Exhibition of Eugenics*, 21.

38. Jacobson, *Whiteness of a Different Color*, 98.

39. Ibid., 95. In this respect, it is important to note how much more attention was paid to the migration patterns of "Negroes" in the 1932 exhibit.

40. Troy Duster, *Backdoor to Eugenics* (London: Routledge, 1990), and Daniel J. Kevles, *In the Name of Eugenics: Genetics and the Uses of Human Heredity* (New York: Alfred A. Knopf, 1985).

41. Harry Laughlin, "Historical Background of the Third International Congress of Eugenics," in *A Decade of Progress in Eugenics*, 8.

42. Carl C. Brigham, *A Study of American Intelligence* (Princeton, NJ: Princeton University Press, 1923). In addition to the Surgeon General's Office of the U.S. Army and Navy, statistics were also provided by life insurance companies, police departments, and high schools and colleges where intelligence testing and physical measurements had been implemented as a product of Robert Yerkes's army mental tests and the popularization of eugenic science through local fairs and the "fitter family" contests.

43. Lorine Pruette, "The Average Man Found by Science, He Is Shown to Be Superstitious, Ill Educated, Conventional and Possessing the Mind of a Boy of 14 Years," *New York Times*, May 1, 1927, 4.

44. Warren Susman, ed., *Culture and Commitment, 1929–1945* (New York: George Braziller, 1973), 187–88. The excerpt Susman reproduces as exemplary of this period phenomenon is Walter B. Pitkin's "The American: How He Lives," which was originally published in 1932 in a volume of essays edited by F. J. Ringel and entitled *America as Americans See It*. For a discussion of Pitkin's relationship to eugenics, see Susan Currell's essay in this volume.

45. A casual survey of newspaper headlines from the period between 1927 and 1933 reveals the myriad ways the figure of the average man was invoked. See, for example, "Average Man of America on Average Chicago Visit, Roy L. Gray, Selected in National Survey, Sees Board of Trade, Pit, Stockyards, the Mayor and the Municipal Pier. Usual 'Wish You Were Here' Post Card Sent to Wife. Happy to Be Average, but Ambitious of Her Children's Future," *Washington Post,* October 22, 1927, 1; "Average Man Seen Studying Politics," *Washington Post,* May 1, 1932, 7; "How Man's Life Is Spent, on the Average—Nearly One-Third in Sleep," *Washington Post,* March 1, 1930, 6; "Increase in Savings; Average Man Has $322," *New York Times,* April 17, 1927, Real Estate section, 1; "Yale Dean Says Hope Lies in Average Man; Tells Undergraduates That Christ Did Not Believe All Men Were Created Free and Equal," *New York Times,* March 5, 1928, 23.

46. See, for example, "The American Now in the Making," *New York Times,* January 17, 1932, 1. Ogburn was the only contributor to refute the biological argument for race character. He proffered, instead, the cultural argument developed by Franz Boas and his followers that would soon become the dominant way of talking about race. See William F. Ogburn, "Dynamic, Less Poetic," *New York Times,* January 17, 1932, 14.

47. See James Treslow Adams, "Abounding Zest," Ales Hrdlicka, "Live and Let Live," Sir Arthur Keith "Ideals at Work," William J. Mayo, "He Is Courageous," Henry Farifield Osborn, "An Elizabethan," Simeon Strunsky, "Life, Liberty, a Job," and William Allen White, "Rugged Individualism," all in the *New York Times,* January 17, 1932, 1, 2, 14, 15.

48. Keith, "Ideals at Work," 2.

49. Osborn, "Birth Selection vs. Birth Control," 40–41.

50. Ibid., 40.

51. Laughlin, *The Second International Exhibition of Eugenics,* 21.

52. Descriptive wall panel exhibited by Harry Laughlin, reproduced in "The Exhibit," *A Decade of Progress,* pl.3. Photos of panels one through three of what became, at some point, a four-panel display are also in the archives of the Buffalo Museum of Science, Buffalo, NY. On the display of the panels at the Chicago World's Fair, see Christina Cogdell, *Eugenic Design: Streamlining America in the 1930s* (Philadelphia: University of Pennsylvania Press, 2004), 85–91.

53. "The Exhibit," in *A Decade of Progress,* 491.

54. Ibid., 495–96.

55. Charles B. Davenport, "Presidential Address: The Development of Eugenics," in *A Decade of Progress in Eugenics,* 19. As this string of "propagandists" suggests, Davenport identified a number of interest groups associated with progressive social reform. Although Davenport remained somewhat oblique about the enemies of eugenics, H. F.

Osborn was much more forthcoming. In his address to the congress, Osborn highlighted the problem of overpopulation and proceeded to debunk both "individualists" and the "sentimentalists" who advocated birth control as its solution. Thus, even though he identified the six "overs" menacing contemporary society—"over-destruction of natural resources," "over-mechanization," "over-construction," "over-production," "over-confidence in future demand and supply," and "over-population"—he characterized the first five as symptoms of the last. As a consequence, the bulk of his remarks concerned the unnatural and harmful effects of birth control. See Osborn, "Birth Selection vs. Birth Control," 29–41.

56. Davenport, "Presidential Address," 18.

57. Osborn, "Birth Selection vs. Birth Control," 29.

58. Ibid.

59. Kline, "Positive Eugenics: The 'Mother of Tomorrow,'" *Building a Better Race*, 16–19.

60. Osborn, "Birth Selection vs. Birth Control," 37.

61. Ibid. Clarence G. Campbell made this argument in his address to the congress, "The Physical Factors in Race Survival," in *A Decade of Progress in Eugenics*, 283–94.

62. Osborn, "Birth Control vs. Birth Selection," 38.

63. Each paper is reproduced in *A Decade of Progress in Eugenics*, 353–63, 364–68, 380–86, and 403–9.

64. Jan Sanders, "Measures to Encourage the Fertility of the Gifted," in *A Decade of Progress in Eugenics*, 353.

65. Davenport, "Presidential Address," 19; emphasis in original.

66. See Gayle Rubin, "The Traffic in Women: Notes on the Political Economy of Sex," in *Toward an Anthropology of Women*, ed. Rayna Rapp Reiter (New York: Monthly Review Press, 1975), 157–210; Jacqueline Stevens, *Reproducing the State* (Princeton, NJ: Princeton University Press, 1999).

67. Ales Hrdlicka, "Live and Let Live," 2.

NINE

Smooth Flow

Biological Efficiency and Streamline Design

Christina Cogdell

ABSTRACT

In this chapter, adapted from her book *Eugenic Design: Streamlining America in the 1930s* and reprinted here by permission of the University of Pennsylvania Press, Christina Cogdell examines the eugenic implications of contemporary discourses about biological efficiency in three areas: eugenicists' concerns for national efficiency (signified by a national, positive, eugenic differential birthrate); health reformers' and the general public's consternation over bodily constipation; and industrial designers' insistence on tapered, streamlined product designs. At first glance, these three areas appear unrelated, but in fact, all made manifest a similar rhetoric and group of ideas about national racial progress and the blockades that seemingly threatened it, which originated in the terminology and ideology of the eugenics movement.

For example, otherwise known as "civilized colon" because of its almost exclusive appearance in middle- and upper-class whites, constipation was seemingly threatening the demise of national productivity and intelligence. It was believed at the time that once feces stagnated in the colon, parasitic bacteria rapidly reproduced and released poisonous toxins into the bloodstream, causing symptoms ranging from lethargy to sexual disinterest to outright mental degeneracy. Eugenicists, too, feared "poison in the blood," although their concerns focused much more on the blood of the "national body." For just as waste that failed to progress through the colon supposedly released toxins into the blood, so, too, according to the eugenicists, was the national body being poisoned and national intelligence lowered by the introduction of the blood of the "less evolved," who seemingly reproduced as quickly as parasites in a "civilized" colon. As Henry Fairfield Osborn phrased it in a 1932 *Forum* article, the rapid reproduction of these "unfit" individuals served as "dragnets . . . on the progress of the ship of state" by slowing down the national economy through the cost of their care and dysgenically contributing to the national birthrate.

In the 1930s, industrial designers were not immune to this national concern for biological efficiency. Not only did they personally suffer from occasional internal blockage, they also metaphorically applied the concept to their designs. For example, in 1935, Egmont Arens promoted a national highway system as the cure for the country's "communications constipation." More revealing than this example of one designer's concern, however, was the rise of streamlining itself as the style of the decade, for the primary theoretical goal of its promoters was the promotion of unhindered, efficient, forward evolutionary progress accomplished through the removal of "parasite drag." By bringing all protrusions in their designs into line with a streamline curve, designers minimized the kinks and eddies that would physically or psychologically retard the efficient forward thrust of their designs. This chapter thus examines the goal of smooth flow as it permeated U.S. culture on a variety of levels, showing how the streamline style resonated with and reinforced contemporary concerns, many of which were overlaid with eugenic implications regarding enhanced fertility, intelligence, and power.

> This age needs streamlined thinking to keep
> pace with our streamlined machines.[1]
>
> DESIGNER EGMONT ARENS, in notes for
> his speeches on streamlining in the
> mid-1930s

In 1937, in an advertisement for a laxative, Petrolagar Laboratories, Inc., of Chicago, attempted to capitalize on the popularity of streamliner trains by invoking their promptness and regularity as the model for the ideal intestinal functioning of a modern urbanite (fig. 9.1).[2]

Caught up in "high speed living" that encouraged "unfavorable eating and working conditions" and contributed to "neglected habits," commuting businessmen frequently suffered from "faulty elimination" and "chronic constipation." Unlike the on-track, on-time regularity of the modern streamliner train, the contents of modern man's intestinal tract typically ran late, if they arrived within the day at all. The educational advertisement therefore suggested seeing a physician who could prescribe the necessary changes to one's schedule, diet, and exercise program, as well as the laxative Petrolagar, to restore regularity to one's system.

218

GENTLE AIDS
To Regular Elimination

MAINTAINING A REGULAR SCHEDULE

IN THIS era of high speed living, our practice of daily hygiene is often forsaken to accommodate modern modes of transportation and communication. Especially in the metropolitan areas is this true, where unfavorable eating and working conditions are contributing factors to neglected habits. It is this inclination to place the value of time and convenience above the importance of good health that is largely responsible for faulty elimination and resultant chronic constipation.

THE bowel, like a modern railway train, must have a regular schedule of operation. There should be no delay. A fixed time, preferably soon after breakfast, should be allocated each day for bowel movement.

EQUALLY important to regular elimination are diet and exercise. You should have a particular time for eating and exercising to avoid indigestion and subsequent constipation.

CONSULT your physician for a proper diet and exercise to assist in establishing a regular habit time of bowel movement. Your

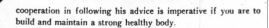

cooperation in following his advice is imperative if you are to build and maintain a strong healthy body.

THIS is the second of a series of educational advertisements on "Gentle Aids to Regular Elimination" by the makers of Petrolagar (an emulsion of pure mineral oil—65%—with agar-agar). Petrolagar, because it performs only a lubricating and softening function, is also a "gentle aid" to regular elimination. However, like diet or any other measure, Petrolagar should not be self prescribed. It is harmless, but certainly not a "cure-all." Best results in dealing with difficulties of the intestinal tract will invariably be obtained when a physician is given the opportunity to make a careful diagnosis and prescribe whatever measures fit the individual case. Another advertisement in this series will appear next month.

PETROLAGAR LABORATORIES, INC.
8134 McCormick Boulevard ◆ Chicago, Ill.

Fig. 9.1. Laxative advertisement for Petrolagar Laboratories, Inc., Chicago, 1937.

In its use of the streamliner as a symbol for intestinal efficiency, the advertisement built on a metaphor popularized by health enthusiast John Harvey Kellogg throughout numerous publications, including his three-hundred-page book *The Itinerary of a Breakfast: A Popular Account of the Travels of a Breakfast through the Food Tube and of the Ten Gates and Several Stations through Which It Passes, Also of the Obstacles Which It Sometimes Meets* (1918, 1926). In this work, he described the "normal itinerary of a meal" passing through the "food tube," otherwise referred to as the "alimentary subway." "Train Late: Held at Stomach Station for 2 hours. Bowel Gate (No. 5) refused to open. Losing Time: Wreck at Colon Gate (No. 7). Ileocecal valve refuses to close, track obstructed with rubbish. 8 hours late. Losing Time: Collision with heavy train backing up. . . . Losing Time. . . . 35 hours late." Finally, "train arrives at last, after clearing track with dynamite (castor oil), forty hours late."[3] Besides the visual imagery, the pun of track/tract, and the popularity of streamliner trains, what drew health-conscious individuals of the interwar period to such analogies? One answer surfaces when considering the broader cultural and ideological pursuit of "smooth flow," a pursuit that conjoined notions of the efficiency of bodies and products with the eugenic idea known as "national efficiency." Consider, for example, the conceptual similarities between these different loci—eugenics, constipation, and streamline design—of the concern for smooth flow.

Efficient living was a primary pursuit of eugenicists and progressives alike, many of whom based their life's work and even their daily habits on its principles. Efficiency could be physical, concerned with minimizing the use of time or space in a daily routine, or economic, aimed at maximizing profits through reducing waste or adjusting work practices to increase worker health and productivity. It could be moral, tied to values of living simply so as to charitably share with others, or biological, measured in terms of bodily energy, function, and output and enhancing the chances of evolutionary success. Because of this wide range of potential applications, efficiency as pursued by eugenics supporters took several forms, shaping both the overall direction of the movement and the arguments used to win support for its causes.

The term *national efficiency* specifically referred to strategies of human management intended to maximize the nation's resources in terms of labor productivity, economic expenditure, and its biological bequests to the future. The term *unfit* reflected this fundamental concern, as it was applied to those deemed unable to positively contribute to the nation's economy as well as to its genetic inheritance. During the Depression, when funds were scarce, eugenic propaganda played on public concerns about national economic waste in order to strengthen acceptance for policies that would eliminate those who were "born to be a burden on the rest" (fig. 9.2).

One display used at state fairs featured red lights that flashed periodically to mark the intervals explained by the sign's text: how often a person was born in the United States, how frequently large amounts of tax dollars were wasted on the care of "defectives," and the comparatively slow rate at which "high grade" people who were "fit for leadership" arrived on the scene. Lectures at museums and local fairs in the 1930s, like the sermons delivered for the American Eugenics Society (AES) sermon contests of the late 1920s, described how the nation's blood "stream" was being "blocked" and "polluted" by an influx of undesirable genes from so-called degenerates, whose high rate of reproduction was supposedly flooding the nation with poisonous blood. This poison imposed a "drag" on the forward progress of the nation by threatening to halt the rise of national intelligence and by

Fig. 9.2. "Some People Are Born to Be a Burden on the Rest," exhibition panel from a "fitter families" exhibit. Photo in the scrapbook of the American Eugenics Society, AES Papers. Courtesy of the American Philosophical Society.

draining state coffers of financial reserves—hence Henry Fairfield Osborn's reference, in his address to the Third International Congress of Eugenics, to these "parasitic" individuals as "dragnets . . . on the progress of the ship of state."[4] Smooth flow could be restored to the nation's evolutionary stream and political economy only by shifting the balance of the national birthrate from the dysgenic to the eugenic in the interest of national efficiency.

The outward concern for smooth flow on a national level extended inward as well, manifesting in the broad-based, early-twentieth-century revolt against constipation. Otherwise referred to as "civilized colon," since the condition seemingly occurred only in "civilized" individuals due to their heightened rationality, weak physical condition, and business occupations, constipation was causing the American people to almost universally suffer "from a food blockade in the colon." Instead of being merely an "inconvenience," according to health reformers and eugenicists, these blockades posed "a menace to life and health" and were "one of the most prolific of all causes of disease."[5] Issue after issue of the *Saturday Evening Post* in the late 1920s and early 1930s contained advertisements for remedies for constipation and its accompanying symptoms, and the mundane prevalence of the malady was captured by Edward Hopper in his painting *Drug Store* (1927).[6] From the 1910s onward, Americans consumed massive amounts of Kellogg's breakfast cereals, Quaker Oats, laxatives, agar and paraffin, olive oil, and yeast in their pursuit of personal colonic efficiency. Some of the wealthier attended Kellogg's Battle Creek Sanitarium for diagnosis; after they ingested a meal tinctured with bismuth, X-rays of their intestines revealed problem areas where the colon was prolapsed or kinked and thus blocked the flow (fig. 9.3). These "crippled" or "delinquent" colons were thought to cause "autointoxication," a disease whereby "putrefactive poisons" and toxic ptomaines released by rapidly reproducing bacteria in slow-moving feces were absorbed into the bloodstream, causing "poison in the blood."

Autointoxication was said to produce a plethora of negative symptoms, ranging from "chronic disease" to "premature senility." One frequently experienced "headache, depression, skin problems, chronic fatigue, damage to the liver, kidneys and blood vessels." More specifically, it was thought to cause "colitis, . . . gall stones, . . . neurasthenia, . . . paralysis, insomnia, . . . and even insanity."[7] Of these ills, those in the mental realm were some of the most feared, though others also offered significant cause for alarm. Ac-

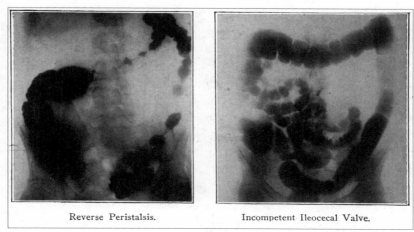

Reverse Peristalsis.   Incompetent Ileocecal Valve.

Fig. 9.3. Colon X-rays, in John Harvey Kellogg, *Itinerary of a Breakfast* (New York: Funk and Wagnalls, 1918, 1926), 125.

cording to medical texts, these maladies arose, in large part, from the "inefficiency" of a blocked digestive tract. If one's digestion were slow, the poisons constantly being produced unnecessarily and excessively over-worked the other "poison-destroying" organs in the body, such as the kidneys and liver, causing their eventual collapse in addition to an overall generally "lowered bodily efficiency" that increased sickness and lessened productivity.[8]

Even more seriously, constipation was seen as stunting national evolutionary advancement by slowing the mental, moral, and racial progress of the nation. "Poison in the blood" not only increased mental lethargy and degeneracy, it also seemingly blurred the moral conscience of those under its influence. For example, the editor of *Health Culture* magazine, W. R. C. Latson, envisioned how the "food intoxication" caused by a feast including meat (he was a vegetarian) might "lead to acts of violence or immorality, at the memory of which the perpetrator looks in horror and amazement. The diner leaves the table intoxicated with a dozen poisons. A heated argument, a word too much, a moment of frenzy, a sudden blow; and the next morning he awakens to find himself a criminal." Alternately, a hand could be "laid on his arm, a voice whispers in his ear; and he turns aside to follow the scarlet woman—the scarlet woman whose steps lead down to hell."[9] Ministers also emphasized the ungodliness that came from polluting one's body, the "Temple of the Holy Spirit," by eating indigestible food or incompletely masticating it: "A man who through irregular or gluttenous eating ruins his health, is not offering to God such a sacrifice."[10]

Furthermore, in 1932, British doctor Ettie Hornibrook, in her book *Restoration Exercises for Women,* revealed that constipation was hindering "civilized" woman's sexual desire, thus lessening the eugenic birthrate. In her opinion, prolonged constipation was the root cause of women's frigidity, due to the position of the bowels in relation to the vaginal canal. Because the lack of sexual fulfillment was the primary cause of divorce and because divorce posed a chief reason for the declining "civilized" birthrate, she perceived the prevention of constipation in modern women to be one of the chief medical issues of the decade.[11] Because constipation was considered a damper on the productivity, sexual interest, mental clarity, and morality of the "fit," no wonder it was claimed in a eugenics sermon that "the greatest problem, whether we think in terms of the physical, moral, or spiritual life, is the food problem. The decadence of the modern home, the tragedy of disease are great problems, but food is fundamental. All social progress is dependent upon this. Diet and evolution are inseparable."[12]

Perhaps diet and evolution seemed so interrelated in part because of the multiple ideological parallels between concepts of national and bodily efficiency. Kellogg spoke of the "civilized colon" as a "poor cripple, maimed, misshapen, . . . infected, paralyzed, inefficient, incompetent," descriptors that were commonly applied to the "unfit," who, like the colon, were the site of waste in the national body.[13] Through his word choice—in which he described the gustatory nerves at the entrance to the digestive system as regulators at "the inspector's gate" that afforded "important and intelligent protection against injury from foreign substances not intended by nature to be taken into the body"—Kellogg compared the regulatory digestive function of the individual body to immigration officers at U.S. consulates and Ellis Island who probed the backgrounds of prospective immigrants to reject those whose blood they thought would pollute the bloodstream of the national body.[14]

The parallels between immigrants and waste continued inside each respective "body." Internal bodily flow should only progress forward; once it backed up due to blockage, autointoxication began. Likewise, the nation's genetic heritage and evolutionary progress were seemingly being blocked and poisoned by the inclusion of those of lesser evolutionary standing,

whose development had been obstructed or arrested or had even degenerated backward to its current "defective" state.[15] Utilizing the principles of
"colon hygiene," however, one could purify the intake through dietary reform, sterilize bacteria-infested intestinal walls through the regular use of
soapy enemas, and even resort to surgery to cut away obstructions to internal efficiency.[16] Similarly, proponents of "race hygiene" closed the nation's
doors to immigration and turned to surgical sterilization to halt the rapid
reproduction of those who were thought to be a hindrance to national
efficiency. Thus, the causes, consequences, and cures of constipation became a site where the broader goals of smooth flow and national efficiency
were telescoped downward and turned inward.

It was during this period of national obsession over bodily and national
efficiency that streamline industrial design began. Designer Norman Bel
Geddes's illustration of the progress of various shapes in a flowing stream
(fig. 9.4) can be interpreted as diagramming the concerns of all three.

The streamline form could roughly model: a graphic distribution of
the "eugenical classification of the human stock" (consisting of a negligi-
ble percentage of persons of "genius" and "special skill" and 90 percent of
persons of the "normal middle class," with the goal of phasing out the remaining "socially inadequate" 10 percent); the shaping process that occurs
in the intestines as a result of peristalsis; or the motion of a vehicle through
a flowing stream, replete with eddies that Geddes said caused "parasite
drag."[17] Design historians Ellen Lupton and J. Abbott Miller have gone so
far as to interpret streamlining as an "excretory aesthetic" because the
ideal streamlined form so closely resembles the products of bodily elimination and because, as the first major industrial design style, it encouraged
the production of waste through planned obsolescence and the processes

33 DIAGRAM ILLUSTRATING THE PRINCIPLE OF STREAMLINING

Fig. 9.4. Norman Bel Geddes, "Diagram Illustrating the Principle of Streamlining,"
in *Horizons* (Boston: Little, Brown, 1932), 45. Courtesy of the Estate of Edith Lutyens
Bel Geddes.

of consumer purchasing and discarding.[18] Designer Raymond Loewy's evolution charts from 1934, which diagrammed changes in appearance over time
of numerous goods from telephones to railcars, further elaborated the
process of streamlining; as forms became more evolved *and* more streamlined, they became not only less ornamented, per Austrian architect Adolf
Loos's proscription on ornament as "degenerate," but also less fussy and
intricate as, according to Geddes's definition of streamlining, all projec-
tions were eliminated. Streamline designers, like eugenicists and health reformers, thus worked to restore smooth flow by eliminating the poisonous
suction caused by "parasite drag" by bringing into line all disabling, outstanding features that were thought to hinder the forward evolutionary
progress of their respective areas of reform.

Clearly, the pursuit of smooth flow permeated American culture on a
variety of levels, from ideological notions of national efficiency and progress
and eugenic beliefs about racial purity to individual concerns for colonic
efficiency and streamline designers' obsession with the tapering curve. The
style thus resonated with and reinforced these contemporary concerns,
many of which were overlaid with eugenic implications regarding enhanced speed, intelligence, and power. Did streamline designers understand
these implications and this resonance? Let us return to the advertisement
for the laxative Petrolagar targeting the commuting businessman to examine more closely the correlations between streamlining and constipation.

By comparing the "civilized" colon with a streamliner, a highly popular symbol of modernity, the advertisement established an analogy that
highlighted both the strengths and a key weakness of "civilized" man supposedly brought about through evolution. Although his highly evolved rationality had permitted the rapid developments in technology and cultural
advance symbolized by the train, these developments seemingly had come
at a cost to the modern body. His ever-increasing distance from nature,
seemingly dictated by an evolutionary paradigm built on a philosophical
split between mind and body, was exacerbated even further by a regimented
business schedule that was not conducive to answering nature's call. He
therefore had had to learn to apply his great rationality and self-control to
restraining his own bodily urges, and in the process, he acquired the "crippled state of the colon" that was "an almost universal condition among
civilized men and women."[19] After breakfast, for example, instead of automatically going to the toilet and waiting, the businessman hurried to catch

a commuter train that carried him off to his day's work. Similarly, "the ideal of the college girl or the secretary is to go to bed late and then get up as near as possible to the time when she must check in at school or office. . . . Such girls might cure themselves of constipation if they would only get up a little earlier."[20]

The sedentary urban lifestyle, "concentrated foodstuffs," lack of abdominal exercise and strength, and high amount of mental preoccupation all contributed to this "disease of civilization," which the "lesser evolved" seemingly never suffered from due to their presumed lack of rationality, self-consciousness, and inhibition.[21] Offering a classic application of recapitulation theory and the evolutionary paradigm, Kellogg equated the "bowel habits" of "wild animals, wild men, healthy infants and idiots," all of whom, in their "natural" state, supposedly "lack the intelligence necessary to disturb their normal functions" and "have better sense than to interfere with the normal promptings of nature." The Japanese, however, according to many Westerners, including Kellogg, occupied a middle position on the evolutionary ladder, and accordingly, they still exhibited healthy "colon customs." Although they were "rapidly becoming sophisticated," they were "not yet so far away from the influence of their primitive life as to have become obtuse to their physical needs as are the people of the older civilizations."[22]

As Kellogg's comments partially show, "lesser evolved" peoples did possess two bodily qualities desired by the "civilized": fertility and smooth internal flow (and, according to Nicole Rafter in this anthology, a third quality—sound dentition). Popular health writers and doctors, including Kellogg, Hornibrook, and others, thus thought that by emulating certain primitive practices, civilized humans could regain these lost qualities that were so crucial to maintaining their evolutionary edge. After visiting with the superintendent of the Bronx Zoo about the daily habits of the "higher apes" and inquiring about the "regularity" of the "feeble-minded" charges at Randall's Island, Kellogg determined that "three bowel movements a day, indeed, is the prevailing habit among primitive people and the higher apes," with chimpanzees and orangutans going as often as four to six times daily. Recommending that "we must choose our bills of fare from the coarse [vegetarian] products on which our primitive ancestors subsisted and on which our forest cousins still live," he warned that "one bowel movement a day is very marked constipation."[23]

In another application of the idea of recapitulation, because "savages," "semi-civilized people, and the peasantry of civilized nations" evacuated in a "crouching or squatting position," Kellogg strongly suggested that "toilet seats should be low and should have a backward slope." However, given the absence of these qualities in the "ordinary closet seat" of the 1920s, a "stool about eight inches high" could be placed in front of the seat in order to support the feet, so that one's thighs on the abdomen could "compress the bowel."[24] Hornibrook, in *Restoration Exercises for Women*, concurred, favoring the use of a stool to produce stool; in a humorous note in the text, Geddes, who gave this copy to his second wife, Frances Resor Waite, was unclear precisely which stool should be between eight and sixteen inches in size (fig. 9.5).

Additionally, the author promoted abdominal exercises that mimicked the primal swivel of the hips and rejected the jerky, machinelike motions that supposedly came so easily to civilized, white people. By restoring themselves to primitive regularity, modern man and woman would be assured not only of increased vitality and fertility (given Hornibrook's belief in the link between constipation and sexual desire), but also of less likelihood of disease. A "speedy passage" through the bowels ensured that "any putrefactive bacteria chancing to enter the body would be swept through the colon before they had time to establish a footing."[25]

The lore on constipation surfaced in a multitude of popular venues. In addition to learning its woes from lectures and sermons on eugenics, a businessman such as designer Egmont Arens, who was aware of the line of "Harper Books for Business Men, Spring 1932," could have chosen to read *Functional Disorders of the Large Intestine* by Jacob Buckstein or *Peptic Ulcer* by I. W. Held and A. A. Goldbloom.[26] If he happened to work for a large corporation such as U.S. Steel, the Sherwin-Williams Company, or others trying to promote the good health and productivity of their employees, he might have been given *How to Live: The Nation's Foremost Health Book*. The book (prepared by Yale eugenicist Irving Fisher and Eugene Fisk under the Hygiene Reference Board of eugenicist Paul Popenoe's Life Extension Institute) contained chapters with titles such as "The Danger of Hasty Eating" and "How To Relieve Constipation without Drugs," in addition to "Heredity and Mate Choosing" and "Eugenics and Birth Control."[27] In 1939 and 1940, a visitor to the New York World's Fair could have studied the model of the human digestive process presented by the Deutsche

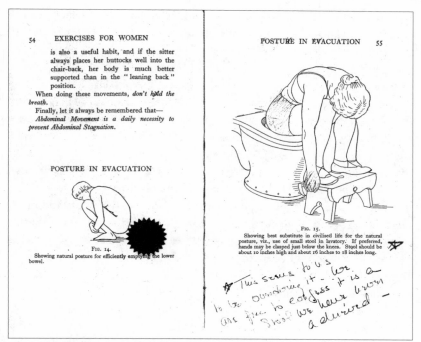

54 EXERCISES FOR WOMEN

is also a useful habit, and if the sitter always places her buttocks well into the chair-back, her body is much better supported than in the "leaning back" position.

When doing these movements, *don't hold the breath.*

Finally, let it always be remembered that—

Abdominal Movement is a daily necessity to prevent Abdominal Stagnation.

POSTURE IN EVACUATION

FIG. 14.
Showing natural posture for efficiently emptying the lower bowel.

POSTURE IN EVACUATION 55

FIG. 15.
Showing best substitute in civilised life for the natural posture, viz., use of small stool in lavatory. If preferred, hands may be clasped just below the knees. Stool should be about 10 inches high and about 16 inches to 18 inches long.

Fig. 9.5. Norman Bel Geddes's copy of Ettie A. Hornibrook's *Restoration Exercises for Women* (London: William Heinemann, 1932), 54–55. In Norman Bel Geddes Papers. Courtesy of the Harry Ransom Humanities Research Center and the Estate of Edith Lutyens Bel Geddes.

Hygiene Museum or toured the Saraka laxative exhibit at the Hall of Pharmacy. The latter contained a "new mechanical device," created by designer Donald Deskey, "consisting of turning disks and flashing lights" that showed "how peristalsis induces rhythmic flow of waste through the colon."[28]

Furthermore, the metaphor of bodily efficiency was applied to one role that the profession of industrial design played during the Depression. Streamlining in product design was considered to be a lubricant to the national economy that restored regular economic flow. Articles and advertisements in trade magazines in the plastics industry, for example, claimed that companies that shifted from handmade ornamental molds to streamlined, machine-cut ones not only would save money through having less costly molds that took less material to fill but also would increase sales through the resultant lower pricing, as well as through the use of innovative colored materials and modern styling. As company after company made this transition and saw sales increase, competitors were forced to follow suit, creating an abundance of commissions for industrial designers as well as a constantly increasing number of streamlined products. Furthermore, designers actively promoted the economic benefits of planned obsolescence, to the extent that having a new model each year became standard company procedure as a way to increase consumer desire and spark sales. Whether the rise of industrial design actually boosted the gross national product is debatable and difficult to prove historically, as historian Jeffrey Meikle has shown. Yet in the mid-1930s, some corporations undoubtedly did claim that redesign had, in fact, increased their sales, due in part to the elimination of waste in materials and production processes.[29]

The familiarity of streamline designers with bodily process and metaphor, as suggested by the previous examples, is confirmed in their archives, almost all of which reveal that health, fitness, diet, and constipation were among their common concerns.[30] Although Raymond Loewy and Walter Dorwin Teague did not leave records of any of their digestive problems, both took pride in keeping fit and eating lightly; Loewy regularly had "an apple and saccharin-sweetened coffee" for lunch and indulged frequently in Turkish baths, ultraviolet rays, calisthenics, massages, and rubdowns at the elite New York Athletic Club.[31] In 1926, Deskey's wife wrote to his mother from Europe that "Donnie" was "sick at his stomach. . . . [T]he dear boy has suffered from one of those refined and discussable maladies this winter called chronic constipation and then he's awfully careless about looking after himself and won't take exercises in the morning as I've started to do, because we get none except a bit of walking to keep us in trim." She lamented how hard he was working, sighing, "If he'd only follow my advice I think he'd be a lot better off, but this very condition makes him too tired and indolent to do the things he needs."[32]

Arens, however, struggled with his colon far more than the others on record. With his flat feet, "poor heart and 'wind,'" he could not "stand violent exercise" and became overweight. From boyhood on, he had been "exceedingly constipated. . . . Constipation would cause pounding in his ears—lassitude, loss of energy, general malaise." Even after visiting several doctors and trying "all kinds of cures . . . Bran—Japanese Seaweed—various gelitenous [sic] preparations . . . cod liver oil in beer," and mineral oil taken through various orifices, "nothing worked" until he discovered that "Feen-a-mint—double dose—would liquefy" the bowel. In 1946, he received advice from a doctor at the Johns Hopkins Hospital to take laxatives and enemas, made of two quarts of water and a teaspoonful of metaphorically poignant Ivory Soap flakes or oil, three times a week. He proceeded to do so for the next ten years and complained of "headache and nausea" if he only washed his lower colon and failed to go deeper. Sounding like an advertisement for Ivory Soap, he affirmatively declared, "The soapy water seems to get past the bottle neck."[33]

Although rarely ill, designer Henry Dreyfuss lived the life of a typical "civilized" businessman that was so frequently bemoaned by health reformers, with one exception: he abstained from alcohol. Breathing "only the barest minimum of fresh air necessary to sustain life" while constantly working in his office, loving "good food," and getting "about as much exercise as a hibernating tortoise," he resorted to diet fads such as the "Clark Gable" to trim down. This oscillating health pattern continued throughout his life. However, whenever he thought a friend was "thickening too much in the midriff," "with a tactlessness he never display[ed] in business," Dreyfuss would "send him a neatly-typed caloric regimen and a portable bath scale." In his pathbreaking book on ergonomic design, *Designing for People* (1955), he thrice mentioned digestion, noting that one of the designer's responsibilities was to lessen those things that impaired digestion. He set a formidable precedent with his sloping toilet seats, a design that matched Kellogg's recommendations in *Itinerary of a Breakfast* (fig. 9.6).[34]

Clearly realizing the demand for such a product in the sophisticated "modern" home, in the late 1930s with the help of medical doctor Janet Travell, Dreyfuss designed a "cleanlined" saddle-seat toilet classily named the "Criterion." The toilet's design dramatically enforced the "hygienic correct posture" during evacuation; the sloped seat angled backward, achieving the "natural" position every time.[35] Only a few years earlier, another designer had heeded Kellogg's advice on toilet design by creating the "toi-lo-let," which hung from the wall "lower than the normal toilet, thus creating an important aid in the relief of constipation. A new patented toilet seat registers the sitter's weight."[36] Various designs by Arens at that time also reflected his desire for smooth flow. Suggestively, given his personal experience, he designed a postwar bathroom that would break the "Bathroom Bottleneck" that many families experienced right before breakfast when everyone was getting ready for the day. His design facilitated

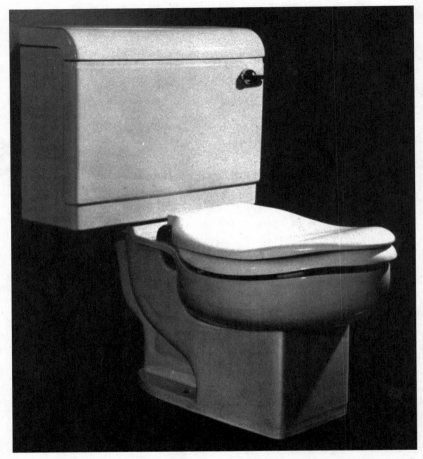

Fig. 9.6. Photograph of the Criterion Closet for Crane Company, ca. 1936, designed by Henry Dreyfuss (American, 1904–72). Henry Dreyfuss Collection, Cooper-Hewitt National Design Museum, Smithsonian Institution, Washington, DC. Gift of Henry Dreyfuss, 1972.

multiple people's use of the room at once by isolating the toilet and the shower in separate enclosures, for privacy.[37] Earlier, in 1935, he had promoted a national highway system as the cure for the nation's "communications constipation." According to Arens, the country was "cramped and paralyzed by an obsolete transportation system. There are no veins through which the blood of National Energy may flow sufficiently strong and fast to keep this great sprawling body nourished."[38] Other designers and clients also expressed their need for smooth flow through streamlined styling. Ex-patriate Austrian architect Frederick Kiesler complained of the "constipated" spatial flow of certain floorplans, and Henry Luce (of *Time* and *Life* maga-zines) solicited Dreyfuss for suggestions on how to streamline the maga-zines' layouts. The designer suggested making *Life* "easy and comfortable to read" in part by having the pictures lead "from one to the next by their arrangement, cropping and selection. Flow is the word."[39]

Dreyfuss's apt statement captures equally well the concerns of eu-genicists, health reformers, and designers. Both "civilized" bodies and the streamline style aimed for speed, regularity, and overall systematic efficiency. A body having these qualities was deemed "fit" and therefore eugenic. It could seemingly forestall disease, increase economic productiv-ity and fertility, prevent mental degeneracy, and serve as a catalyst for na-tional efficiency and racial progress. Like bodies, modern buildings and products were also classified according to their "fitness," the level to which their forms suited their functions. Streamlined products bearing the traits of speed, regularity, and efficiency made the grade. The curved forms in-creased speed in mobile products by lessening drag and in immobile prod-ucts otherwise contributed structural strength, demanded fewer materials, and promoted sales due to their popularity, thereby increasing economic flow to their designers and producers. Flow was, indeed, the word.

These traits of the style are all well known, and one does not need to understand the popular concern with national and bodily efficiency for them to make sense, especially from an economic standpoint and from the standpoint of the physical laws of air and fluid dynamics. Given the style's theoretical roots in biological evolutionary theory, however, and de-signers' familiarity with literal and metaphoric constipation and products intended to alleviate the condition, the possibility that the rhetoric of "speed," "efficiency" and "flow" in streamlining literature intimated eu-genic notions of national and bodily efficiency must be considered.[40] Their archives suggest that some designers did, in fact, correlate speed, intelli-gence, progress, and the reduction of drag with enhanced evolutionary progress.

Arens most clearly spelled out these connections in his speeches, be-ginning with "Creative Evolution of the Printed Word," a speech from 1933 that he also titled "Streamlining the Printed Word" and "Tempo in Ty-pography"; these title changes and the speech's content reflected Arens's belief that evolution was ultimately responsible for the increased tempo of modern times to which streamlining responded. The high level to which speed, streamlining, and evolution were interconnected was borne out through other talks of his, and in some instances, they almost exactly mirrored contemporary eugenicists' concerns. In his lectures on "Streamlining in Nature," delivered around the country between 1934 and 1936, Arens showed his audiences slides of a variety of "high speed conveyances," which he then contrasted with an image of oxen. The oxen exemplified "early transportation" methods such as those used by "the first covered wagons that crossed the continent." His made his point clearly: "To drive a team of oxen does not necessitate fast thinking. A country yokel's slow wit is good enough at [three] miles per hour." Then he flashed a slide of a popular, record-setting race car driver: "Compare that in your mind with Malcolm Campbell going at 300. As soon as he sees an obstruction he has to swerve—or else he hits it. He has to think 100 times as fast."[41] One year later, Ellsworth Huntington, the Yale University professor who was also president of the American Eugenics Society, reiterated this idea in his presidential address in 1937. He stressed that "as life becomes more complicated the need of intelligence and character becomes greater. The drivers and mechanics who operate and care for a fleet of buses need greater intelligence, sobriety, and reliability than did the men of a former generation who drove stage coaches and cared for the horses. . . . Civilization constantly demands higher ability."[42] He had begun this analogy in print in *Tomorrow's Children* (1935), where he argued that, like "driving an automobile at sixty miles an hour . . . the greater the speed, the greater is the need for the utmost perfection" in "good inheritance, good training, and good health." Because "modern civilization has struck a sixty-mile gait," the need for a eugenic society was "greater than ever before."[43]

This idea of the greater rapidity and intelligence brought about by evolution was further elaborated by Arens, who was convinced that certain linguistic developments evidenced racial superiority. In his speech on typography, he described how picture writing was "the most important single step in the history of human evolution," making "civilized society" possible, but that as society had become more complex, writing had shifted from pictures to symbols to words to letters. He attributed "the difference between Western civilization and Eastern" to this latter development. Because the Eastern nations had not made the shift from having separate characters for each word to having letters make up the various words, Arens thought that "a Chinese scholar has to spend all his energy learning the language. There is no energy left for creative thinking. He has to learn hundreds of thousands of symbols."[44] By contrast, Arens stated, "we learn twenty six, which are mastered at the age of ten years. That is the enormous economy of the phonographic system."[45]

Etymologist Paul Hugon agreed that efficient language was a trait of the "civilized." He opened his article "What Makes a Language Easy?"—a copy of which he sent to Arens—with this reasoning: "Because language is the means of interpreting the whole human mind, any language that is adequate to that task in a highly civilized society can never be entirely easy to a savage. "It is only in Teutonic languages, for example, that an electric switch can be simply and conveniently marked 'On' and 'Off.' The Latin languages have no such words. It is only in English that you can say, using the same word 'Go' unchanged in any position: 'Go! You can go! Why don't you go?'"[46] This efficiency, Arens believed, had been produced through the processes of "natural selection" that had weeded out all that was too "slow" and "cumbersome" and increased the tempo at which a text could be read. "This speed increment takes place exactly in proportion as the tempo of life advances," he said.[47]

One such change, ironically, was the shift from text to photographs utilized by magazines such as *Time*. A critic of these photographic magazines explained that "carefully chosen pictures multiply the speed with which words can explain or describe an event. . . . [S]till and motion pictures speed up our learning processes, and tell a story more quickly and effectively than words." But, he warned, "let's be on our guard; for the mental effort required to absorb a story in pictures is slight indeed. . . . Pictures and signs were used by prehistoric man; the ability to use words, or language, is the chief distinction between civilized men and savages." Therefore, "if you are wise, if you wish to gain distinction as a civilized man, *words* will be your tools of thought, you will use *pictures* merely to help you clarify and visualize what you are learning."[48]

Other textual changes to increase reading speed included the rejection of capital letters in graphic design, employed by Bauhaus typographers in their "universal" typeface as well as by an anonymous graphic designer creating the layout on the brochure for the House of Tomorrow at Chicago's Century of Progress Exposition. The designer constructed the text without capital letters at the start of sentences to avoid halting the reader's eye. In his text, he highlighted as well the efficient features of the house's design.[49] Another textual change was the "recognition of the non-sentence" extended by Dr. Janet Aiken, a linguist at Columbia University. Having learned of her accreditation of sentence fragments as proper writing, Arens wrote to her late in 1934 to commend her for making "a very important step in speeding up language to the needs of a fast-moving civilization. . . . We are already consuming too much energy climbing over the mountains and valleys of traditional speech when, as a matter of fact, we should have some straight and graded highway, so that ideas may travel a little faster than they did in the days of the ox-cart." She responded, "While language moves slowly, it does adapt itself to modern needs, does go streamlined to suit the modern tempo."[50]

Presumably, Arens wanted to increase the pace at which ideas moved so that more ideas could be absorbed in ever shorter amounts of time, as was demanded by the rapid evolutionary advance of the age.[51] Many people accepted this latter notion, believing even that evolution itself was accelerating, thanks in part to eugenicists, who were rationally controlling the selection process. Huntington captured this idea with an analogy to a racehorse: "The difference between man as he might be under a sane eugenic regime and man as he actually exists is like the difference between an ordinary old-fashioned carriage horse that can only go a mile in four minutes, and a race horse that goes the same distance in less than two minutes."[52] Geneticists such as H. J. Muller, who discovered the ability of X-rays to cause genetic mutations, were also seemingly speeding up "evolutionary changes over 1000 per cent."[53]

To some, this increased speed demanded increased intelligence, as well as streamlined typographic fonts to further facilitate the increase of intelligence. As Arens asserted so clearly, "This age needs streamlined thinking to keep pace with our streamlined machines."[54] To this end, he praised the typeface used in the body of the *New York Times*. Although the Gothic script of the paper's title emphasized "the long-established *tradition* of the Times," the text was composed of "a very *fast-reading* type. . . . It is vibrationless, quiet, streamlined for speed" (emphasis in original).[55] The civilized person reading it, therefore, could cover many of its articles during a coffee break, acquiring knowledge while at the same time keeping his or her much-needed mental muscles in tone.

Yet at a round-table discussion on "Fashion in Typography" that included Egmont Arens, René Clark, and Joseph Sinel, an anonymous young man in the audience asked a significant question: "Why all the speed? . . . I know when I read a beautiful book, I don't want to rush through it." The panel members all agreed that, for commercial purposes, speed was essential. Clark explained, "We are up against right now a speeding up of our whole civilization—our whole life. The tools we have to control with regard to speed have to be sharpened and have to be made as effective as possible so that we can handle this amazing machine which is tearing along at a great speed. We have to perfect the machinery that holds it in order," and he might have added, lest it fall apart.[56] Arens, in fact, concluded his lecture on "Tempo in Typography" with this very idea: "Our whole civilization may come to a standstill unless we can develop faster tools for thinking." As a style permeating U.S. industrial, graphic, and architectural design, streamlining offered just the tool he desired to maintain the nation's economic and evolutionary edge.

At the same time that the greater intelligence and productivity supposedly brought through evolutionary advance was capturing the public spotlight, corresponding attention was being paid to increases in the area of physical speed based on heredity. A book review of Louis Roule's *Fishes and Their Ways of Life* (1935) caught Arens's eye by stating, "Prof. Roule discourses on the connection between blood and speed (the fastest fishes have the richest blood streams)."[57] Arens was already generally aware of this principle, for in his lectures on "Streamlining in Nature," he included examples of purebred animals, such as the greyhound, whose speed, he said, was "in the blood."[58] Harry Laughlin, superintendent of the Eugenics Record Office, had been making similar determinations as well in his study of the inheritance of racing capacity in the thoroughbred horse. Despite the genetic complexity of the inheritance of traits involved in racing capacity, Laughlin still was certain that "all of the hereditary units which make up racing capacity are inherited in accordance with chromosomal behavior." In the display showing his results at the Third International Congress of Eugenics at the American Museum of Natural History in 1932, he included his discovery that racing speed itself was seemingly accelerating. Based on statistical studies of 150 years of records on racehorses, he determined that "selectively breeding swift horses has progressively produced swifter ones."[59] Whether in horses or humans, swiftness and slowness were derived from one's ancestry, eugenicists believed, *and* were related to how streamlined one's physique was.[60] "In industrial societies, natural selection favored brain power," wrote historian James Whorton: "Heavy musculature work was for 'animals or the lower races.' Greater than usual bulk was thus a burden in the 'race of life'; 'piles of parasitic muscles' required 'an undue amount of nourishment,' lowering bodily efficiency (and thus brain power)."[61] A svelte, streamlined body with an intelligent mind thus represented the evolutionary ideal.

The public thrill for physical speed during the late 1920s and 1930s was apparent in the large amount of news coverage awarded to champions—be they pilots, race car drivers, trains, horses, or dogs—which showed that the breaking of speed records had become a national fascination. The transatlantic flight of eugenics supporter Charles Lindbergh in 1927 evoked national and international hysteria partly because it beautifully symbolized the technological and racial advance of Euro-American civilization. In 1934, multiple newspapers headlined the successes of American planes and trains, which won international races and shattered domestic transcontinental records.[62] More local speed thrills were obtained at the racetrack and show ring, where thoroughbred horses and greyhounds competed to the joy and chagrin of bettors and breeders. The *New York Herald Tribune* and other newspapers offered regular coverage of champion dogs and horses, of which Arens and Teague saved numerous clippings.[63] Illustrations and advertisements in *Vogue* magazine depicted "well-bred" men and women wearing their finest fashions (such as "Whippet" gloves and clothes made from "thoroughbred" fabrics) at the horse and dog races, at times symbolically holding purebred pets at arm's length on a leash.[64]

The greyhound in particular caught the attention of sculptors, designers, advertisers, and businesspeople alike as an apt symbol of evolutionary acceleration, streamline sophistication, and good breeding. Sculptures of the goddess Diana—svelte, classical female nudes alongside striding hounds—graced the gardens and vacation ships of the wealthy, serving less as a reminder of the hunt than as an affirmation of the beauty and fitness of the Euro-American purebred.[65] In 1928, preeminent animal sculptor and feminist Katherine Lane Weems captured the spirit of the race in her sculpture of two racing greyhounds, *Greyhounds Unleashed*, subtly giving a female the edge over her male competitor.[66] Greyhound Bus Company used the racing figure for its name and logo; when Loewy began designing for the

company in the late 1930s, one of his first steps was to make the logo less
bulky and more streamlined by reducing the greyhound's weight and musculature. Throughout the 1930s, hood ornaments of leaping greyhounds,
anchored only by their back legs, graced Ford and Lincoln Zephyr automotive models. Teague streamlined them even further in his 1940 design for
the Lincoln Zephyr Continental and Custom by enclosing the animal's
form within the metal ridge marking the hood's center (fig. 9.7).[67]

Other automobile designers took notice of the greyhound as well,
structurally placing their engines in such a fashion as to mimic the anatomi-
cal arrangement and weight distribution of the dog. For a postwar Stude-
baker design, Loewy wanted the car to "look fast, whether in motion or
stationary. I want it to look as if it were leaping forward. . . . I want one that
looks alive as a leaping greyhound."[68] Visitors to the New York World's
Fair could "Greyhound through the Fair" by riding the buses provided;
some likely even saw a float of "America," symbolized as a mammoth white
racing greyhound setting a fast pace for the world to follow in both technology and racial purity.[69] By the time this float was made in the late 1930s,
European countries (Germany in particular) had already grabbed the torch
of eugenics from the United States and sprinted into the lead. However,

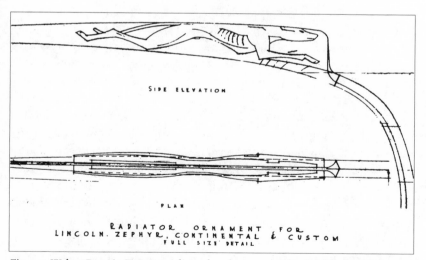

Fig. 9.7. Walter Dorwin Teague, radiator hood ornament for the Lincoln Zephyr
Continental and Custom. On Microfilm roll 35–6, Walter Dorwin Teague Papers.
Courtesy of the Special Collections Research Center, Syracuse University Library.

enough Americans were still absorbed with increases in speed, intelligence, and genetic purity that, from a historical vantage point, the thoroughbred greyhound seemed to have been on its way to becoming a prominent national symbol.[70]

After all, the American Birth Control League founded by Margaret Sanger had been working throughout the 1920s "To Breed a Race of Thoroughbreds," as their slogan declared, and W. E. D. Stokes envisioned his nephew, Anson Phelps Stokes Jr., a potential candidate for the presidency of Yale University in the 1920s, turning the school into a "Stud Farm for boys" that would "graduate men with healthy bodies and healthy minds, trained to realize their duties to their country, themselves and their offspring."[71] "Fitter families" contests across the nation had been promoting this ideal to the middle class by hanging out signs that asked, "Are You a Human Thoroughbred?" (fig. 9.8).

Chesterfield cigarettes took up the theme of the thoroughbred in its advertisements as a way to market its goods to the elite. Church congregations learned not to breed from "'scrubs' but from pure blood . . . and pedigreed stock" and that "whether it be the live stock at the fair, the horses on the track, or a brilliant assemblage of men and women, there is nothing in the world so striking, so inspiring as a thoroughbred. Nature, unaided, . . . produces no thoroughbred class," yet through cooperating with nature, humans could produce the "perfect type, whether it be an American Beauty Rose, . . . a seedless orange, . . . a Morgan or a Clysdale, an Ayrshire or a Jersey, a champion in the Olympic games, or a gentleman and a scholar."[72] Through cooperation with the natural principles of streamlining, designers likewise strove to create the "ultimate type" for each design through "the perfect adaptation of form to function" and the removal of drag-producing impurities.[73] The smooth flow they literally and metaphorically achieved thus had to have resonated, consciously or unconsciously, with the widely popular belief that greater intelligence, speed, and evolutionary progress would come through thoroughbred blood*stream lines.*

Overlaps in the language and ideas of national, bodily, and product efficiency—as embodied in the theories and writings of eugenicists, health reformers, and streamline designers—were multiple and apparent in the interwar period. As Dreyfuss declared, "Flow is the word," and all three utilized the terminology and metaphor of the "stream." Yet in all, the stream was blocked by "massive obstacles" that hindered efficiency and

Fig. 9.8. "Are You a Human Thoroughbred?" Detail of a photo of the Fitter Families for Future Firesides exhibit. Photo in the scrapbook of the American Eugenics Society, AES Papers. Courtesy of the American Philosophical Society.

evolutionary progress. These protrusions, which were socially, genetically, intestinally, or artistically "out of line," caused "parasite drag" (that is, "autointoxication"), a poisonous condition that exponentially decreased productivity by robbing the host of its efficiency, energy, and profits. Affected social groups, colons, and products were described as "delinquent," and their presence evoked fear for the mental stagnation and degeneracy that were thought to accompany them.

To further evolutionary progress, therefore, politicians, health reformers, and designers turned to streamlining as a means of restoring purity to their respective areas of reform. By trimming the waste/waist and reforming the "tail end"—be it an evolutionary "inferior," an obstinate colon, or a nontapering product design—efficiency experts in each case eliminated drag and restored smooth, speedy flow, thereby ensuring continued mental and racial progress. Both designers and eugenicists demanded an overall increase in physical performance, mental speed, and national intelligence as a necessary accompaniment to the seeming increase in the pace of evolution and its increase of the speed of products and production processes. Designers' visions of a speedy, progressive, streamlined technology thus worked hand in hand with the corresponding social amelioration that was proffered tantalizingly through the implementation of eugenics and health reform.

Notes

1. Caption titled "Early Transportation," Box 57, "Writings/Lecture Notes/Slide Captions," Egmont Arens Papers, Special Collections Research Center, Syracuse University Library, Syracuse, NY (hereafter cited as Egmont Arens Papers).

2. Petrolagar advertisement, 1937, reprinted in Ellen Lupton and J. Abbott Miller, *The Bathroom, the Kitchen, and the Aesthetics of Waste: A Process of Elimination*, Ex. Cat. (Cambridge, MA: MIT List Visual Arts Center, 1992), 69. Lupton and Miller offer a psychological interpretation of the fecal metaphor of the streamline style.

3. John Harvey Kellogg, *Itinerary of a Breakfast* (New York: Funk and Wagnalls, 1926), 3.

4. Henry Fairfield Osborn, "Birth Selection vs. Birth Control," *Forum* (August 1932): 79, also quoted in a letter from Charles Davenport to Frederick Osborn dated July 29, 1932, Folder "Henry Fairfield Osborn," Charles B. Davenport Papers, American Philosophical Society, Philadelphia, PA (hereafter cited as CBD Papers). Davenport himself referred to "defectives" as those who put the "brake on social progress"; see letter from Davenport to Chloe Owings dated August 13, 1934, Folder "Chloe Owings," CBD Papers.

5. Kellogg, *Itinerary of a Breakfast*, 96.

6. A useful and accessible collection of laxative advertisements can be found in "Medicine and Madison Avenue," an online collection from Duke University's Rare Book, Manuscript, and Special Collections, available at scriptorium.lib.duke.edu/mma (accessed January 28, 2006).

7. Kellogg, *Itinerary of a Breakfast*, 32, 145–46, and Whorton, *Crusaders for Fitness: The History of American Health Reformers* (Princeton, NJ: Princeton University Press, 1982) 221.

8. Whorton, *Crusaders for Fitness*, 189, and Kellogg, *Itinerary of a Breakfast*, 36, 147.

9. Whorton, *Crusaders for Fitness*, 223.

10. Folders "William E. Griffin, Sermon 16" and "Lewis Kent, Sermon 15," 1926, both in the American Eugenics Society Papers, American Philosophical Society, Philadelphia, PA (hereafter cited as the AES Papers).

11. Ettie A. Hornibrook, *Restoration Exercises for Women* (London: Heinemann, 1932), ix, 11–13, 15–28, 54–55.

12. "Sermon 15," Folder "Lewis Kent, Sermon 15," AES Papers.

13. Kellogg, *Itinerary of a Breakfast*, 71, 107.

14. Ibid., 45–50. On the training of officials at U.S. consulates abroad in immigrant screening techniques, see Folder "Harry H. Laughlin, 1923, #2," CBD Papers.

15. Ellsworth Huntington, *Tomorrow's Children: The Goal of Eugenics* (New York: John Wiley and Sons, 1935), 45; Nancy Tomes, *The Gospel of Germs: Men, Women, and the Microbe in American Life* (Cambridge, MA: Harvard University Press, 1998), 32–60, 127; Kellogg, *Itinerary of a Breakfast*, 63; Whorton, *Crusaders for Fitness*, 168–200.

16. Kellogg, *Itinerary of a Breakfast*, 106–8; on surgery, see Whorton, *Crusaders for Fitness*, 218.

17. A poster, titled "Eugenical Classification of the Human Stock," was on display in the eugenics exhibits at the American Museum of Natural History that accompanied the Second International Congress of Eugenics in 1921; the poster specified these percentages. A photo of the poster is in the archives of the Second International Congress of Eugenics in the American Museum of Natural History Library, New York. On parasite drag, see Norman Bel Geddes, "Streamlining," *Atlantic Monthly* 154 (November 1934): 555–56.

18. Lupton and Miller, *The Bathroom, the Kitchen*, 65, 67.

19. Kellogg, *Itinerary of a Breakfast*, 3.

20. Walter Alvarez et al., *Help Your Doctor to Help You When You Have Constipation* (New York: Harper and Brothers, 1942), 13, 14, 36–37.

21. Ibid.

22. Kellogg, *Itinerary of a Breakfast*, 108–12. By "older civilizations," it seems Kellogg meant civilizations that he considered to be more evolved, that is, more technologically developed, not necessarily those that possessed a longer history.

23. Ibid., 33, 110–11, 82–83, 93.

24. Ibid., 73–76.

25. On the benefits of speedy digestion and circulation, see Kellogg, *Itinerary of a Breakfast*, 224, and Whorton, *Crusaders for Fitness*, 243.

26. See the brochure "Harper Books for Business Men, Spring 1932," in Box 46: "Publicity/Programs," Egmont Arens Papers.

27. Taken from the advertisement for *How to Live: The Nation's Foremost Health Book*, found on the back page of Kellogg, *Itinerary of a Breakfast*, 1926 edition.

28. *Official Guidebook, New York World's Fair, 1939* (New York: Exposition Publications, 1939), 151–52.

29. See Jeffrey Meikle, *Twentieth-Century Limited: Industrial Design in America* (Philadelphia: Temple University Press, 1979), 70–73, 80–82, 96–99, and Lupton and Miller, *The Bathroom, the Kitchen*, 5–8.

30. Charles Davenport attended the Battle Creek Sanatarium; see letter from Davenport to E. L. Eggleston, September 9, 1930, Folder "E. L. Eggleston," CBD Papers.

31. On Teague, see "Walter Dorwin Teague: Dean of Design, a Portrait," *Printer's Ink* (January 30, 1959), Walter Dorwin Teague Papers, Special Collections Research Center, Syracuse University Library, Syracuse, NY (hereafter cited as WDT Papers); on Loewy, see John Kobler, "The Great Packager," *Life*, May 2, 1949: 110–22, located in the Raymond Loewy Papers, Cooper-Hewitt National Design Museum, New York, NY; and "Modern Living," from the Business and Finance section of *Time*, October 31, 1949, Folder "Product Design and Development Division, Speeches and Writings by Staff, 1953–1957," Container 171, Raymond Loewy Papers, Library of Congress, Washington, DC.

32. Letter from Mary Deskey to Donald's mother, Folder "Letters: 1922–26," Donald Deskey Papers, Cooper-Hewitt National Design Museum, New York, NY (hereafter cited as Donald Deskey Papers).

33. See Folder "Medical Records, Misc., 1933–1960," Box 65, Egmont Arens Papers.

34. Folder "Anecdotes, I. D. Book," August 31, 1953, File "Publications: Designing for People (Correspondence, Memos, etc.)," Box 1, Henry Dreyfuss Papers, Cooper-Hewitt National Design Museum, New York, NY (hereafter cited as Henry Dreyfuss Papers); also "Machine Age Artist," *Forbes* (May 1, 1951), and "Management: Art for Profit's Sake," *Investor's Reader* (November 3, 1952), both on Microfiche #13, "Articles about Dreyfuss, Pre-1950," Henry Dreyfuss Papers. See also Henry Dreyfuss, *Designing for People* (New York: Paragraphic Books, 1955), 41.

35. See photos of "Criterion Closet," 1936, 1944, 1953, and the "Neovogue Closet," 1940, Folder "Industrial Design: Cities Service Petroleum Inc.—Crane Co.," Box 2; Microfilm roll #26, "Drawings and Photographs, Crane Co."; Microfilm roll "Crane—1935"; clipping from *House and Garden*, Building Series (August 1950), on Microfiche #13, "Articles about Dreyfuss, Pre-1950"; memo from Henry Dreyfuss to M. Weinstock,

December 24, 1953, Folder "Publications: Designing for People (Correspondence, Memos, etc.)," Box 1; correspondence with Crane Co. in Box "Client Solicitation, Budd Co.—Time, Inc.," all in Henry Dreyfuss Papers.

36. Egmont Arens, "House, Incorporated, New York," December 28, 1934, Folder "Housing—Pre-Fab, Sketches, Notes, Correspondence, Clippings," Box 19, Egmont Arens Papers.

37. "Design for Laving: Postwar Bathroom," *House Furnishing Review* (December 1944), Folder "Clippings about Egmont Arens," Box 46, Egmont Arens Papers.

38. Egmont Arens, "The Road-way Housing Plan," Folder "Roadway Housing Plan Presentation, 1935," Box 27, Egmont Arens Papers.

39. Letter from Henry Dreyfuss to Henry Luce, July 15, 1938, Folder "Time Inc. Client Solicitation," Box "Client Solicitation, Budd Co.—Time, Inc.," Henry Dreyfuss Papers. On Kiesler, see Beatriz Colomina, "The Psyche of Building: Frederick Kiesler's 'Space House,'" *Archis* 11 (November 1996): 70–80.

40. For more information about the connections between streamlining and eugenics, including the biological origins of theories of streamlining, see Christina Cogdell, *Eugenic Design: Streamlining America in the 1930s* (Philadelphia: University of Pennsylvania Press, 2004), chap. 2.

41. Caption for image "Early Transportation," Folder "Writings/Lecture Notes/Slide Captions," Box 57, Egmont Arens Papers.

42. Ellsworth Huntington, "The Future of Eugenics," Folder "Annual Meeting 1937," AES Papers.

43. Huntington, *Tomorrow's Children*, 27–29.

44. Egmont Arens, "Creative Evolution of the Printed Word, or Tempo in Typography" (address to the Eastern Arts Association, April 28, 1933), Folder "Writings," Box 51, Egmont Arens Papers.

45. Ibid.

46. Paul Hugon, "What Makes a Language Easy?" Box 58, Egmont Arens Papers.

47. Arens, "Creative Evolution of the Printed Word."

48. Editorial, "Is It True What They Say about You?" *Scholastic: The American High School Weekly* 29, no. 4 (1936), Folder "Clippings about Egmont Arens," Box 46 "Publicity/ Programs," Egmont Arens Papers.

49. Mike Mills, "Herbert Bayer's Universal Type in Its Historical Context," in *The ABC's of* ▲ ■ ●: *The Bauhaus and Design Theory,* ed. Ellen Lupton and J. Abbott Miller (New York: Herb Lubalin Study Center of Design and Typography, Cooper Union for the Advancement of Science and Art, 1991), 38–49; Brochure for the "House of Tomorrow" in Donald Deskey Papers.

50. Letter from Egmont Arens to Dr. Janet Aiken, November 10, 1934, Folder "Language, Speed In, 1934–50," Box 58, and also letter from Aiken to Arens, 14 November 1934, Box 51, Egmont Arens Papers.

51. See "Scribe," Box 56, "Images and Captions for Lecture Illustrations," Egmont Arens Papers.

52. Huntington, *Tomorrow's Children*, 68.

53. Letter from Charles Davenport to Frederick Osborn, February 10, 1930, Folder "Frederick Osborn," AES Papers, and Folder "Eugenics Record Office—Eugenics Lectures," Charles B. Davenport Papers—Cold Spring Harbor Series, American Philosophical Society, Philadelphia, PA (hereafter cited as CBD-CSH Series). Information about X-rays speeding up mutations taken from a clipping from the *Knoxville (Tennessee) Sentinel*, September 25, 1927, Leon Whitney Scrapbook, AES Papers; the article mistakenly asserted the scientist was Thomas Hunt Morgan, not H. J. Muller.

54. Caption titled "Early Transportation," Box 57, "Writings/Lecture Notes/Slide Captions," Egmont Arens Papers.

55. Arens, "Creative Evolution of the Printed Word."

56. Folder "Fashion in Typography," Box 51, Egmont Arens Papers; also Walter Dorwin Teague, "The Growth and Scope of Industrial Design in the U.S.," *Journal of the Royal Society of Arts* 57 (July 1959): 640–51, Folder "Writings," Box 79, WDT Papers.

57. John Chamberlain, "Books of the Times," *New York Times*, June 21, 1935, Folder "Streamlining 1933–36," Box 59, Egmont Arens Papers.

58. Slide caption for "Champion Greyhound," Box 57, "Writings/Lecture Notes/Slide Captions," and H. Ledyard Towle, "Projecting Your Automobile into the Future," *Automotive Engineering Journal* 29, no. 1 (1931), Folder "Streamlining," Box 59, both in Egmont Arens Papers.

59. See "Sermon 35," Folder "Sermon Contest, 1926, #3," AES Papers; "End of the Year Report," section "Genetics of the Thoroughbred Horse," Folder "H. H. Laughlin, 1929, #22," CBD-CSH Series; Harry Laughlin, "The Value of Certain Measurements in Metabolism in Connection with Researches on the Genetics of the Thoroughbred Horse," Folder "H. H. Laughlin, 1930," CBD-CSH Series; "Science Yields to Luck on Turf," *New York World*, May 30, 1930, Leon Whitney Scrapbook, AES Papers; and earlier, Harvey Ernest Jordan, "Eugenics, Rearing of the Human Thoroughbred" in *Eugenics: Twelve University Lectures*, ed. Morton Aldrich (New York: Dodd, Mead, 1914). See also the exhibits list at the back of *A Decade of Progress in Eugenics: Scientific Papers of the Third International Congress of Eugenics, Held at American Museum of Natural History, New York, August 21–23, 1932* (Baltimore, MD: Williams and Wilkins, 1934), and "Genetics," *Time*, June 10, 1929, Leon Whitney Scrapbook, AES Papers.

60. Charles Davenport, "Lecture: Aims, Work, Results of the Eugenics Record Office," n.d. (but late 1920s to early 1930s), in folder of same title, File "C. B. Davenport," CBD Papers; letter from Laughlin to Albert Blakeslee, October 19, 1936, Folder "H. H. Laughlin, 1936," CBD-CSH Series. See also Folder "Kenneth C. MacArthur, Sermon 32, 1926," AES Papers.

61. Note the parallel of these "parasitic muscles" to the "autointoxication" of the constipated modern body; see James Whorton, "'Athlete's Heart': The Medical Debate over Athleticism, 1870–1920," in *Sport and Exercise Science: Essays in the History of Sports Medicine*, ed. Jack Berryman and Roberta Park (Urbana: University of Illinois Press, 1992), 114, parenthetical comment in original.

62. See "Notable Advances in 1934 in Airplane, Automobile and Railroad Development," *New York Times*, December 31, 1934, Folder "Streamlining—Airplanes"; "Few Weeks Set New Air, Land and Sea Records," *Chicago Daily News*, November 16, 1934, Folder "Streamlining, 1933–36"; "All Records Shattered!" *Aluminum Newsletter* (November 1934), Folder "Streamlining, 1933–36," all in Box 59, Egmont Arens Papers. In same box is a clipping of Malcolm Campbell's record attempt.

63. "King of the Plain, the Winner of the Title Every Time It Has Been Shown," Folder "Streamlining, 1933–36," Box 59, Egmont Arens Papers; clipping, *New York Herald Tribune*, October 9, 1927, Folder "Source Material: Animals, Dogs, Cats, Wild Birds," Box 3, WDT Papers.

64. On the "well-bred" women of *Vogue*, see Folder "Condé Nast, Promotional Materials, Miscellaneous, 1921–22," Box 80, Egmont Arens Papers, as well as numerous advertisements scattered through issues from the 1930s.

65. For example, see Edward McCartan's sculpture *Diana*, bronze, 1922, from *American Masters: Sculpture from Brookgreen Gardens*, Ex. Cat. (Austin, TX: Blanton Museum of Art, 1998), 45, and the photo of the sculptural centerpiece in the Grand Salon of the ship *L'Atlantique*, from "Abord de *l'Atlantique*," *Arts and Industry* (November 1931): 17, Folder "Steamships," Box 17, WDT Papers.

66. On Katherine Lane Weems, see *American Masters: Sculpture from Brookgreen Gardens*, 57.

67. Walter Dorwin Teague, Radiator Ornament for the Lincoln Zephyr Continental and Custom, on Microfilm roll 35–36, WDT Papers.

68. General Motors brochures "Aerodynamics and Streamlining," Box 49, and Charles Kettering, "Research—An Eye to the Future," Folder "Streamlining: Airplanes, 1932, 1935, n.d.," Box 59, Egmont Arens Papers; H. Ledyard Towle, 1931, Folder "Streamlining," Box 59, Egmont Arens Papers. On Loewy, see "Modern Living" in Business and Finance section of *Time*, October 31, 1949, Container 171 "Product Design and

Development Division, Speeches and Writings by Staff, 1953–57," Raymond Loewy Papers, Library of Congress.

69. The slogan "Greyhound through the Fair" was coined by Teague and painted on the buses at the fair; see Microfilm roll 16–30, WDT Papers. The photo of the float of "America" as a greyhound was developed by Charles Dreyer and is found in Box 68, Egmont Arens Papers.

70. The 1933 Nazi compulsory sterilization law was based partly on California's statute and partly on a "model" sterilization law published in 1929 by Harry Laughlin. Prior to Germany's implementation of eugenic policies, the United States had been considered the leader in actualizing eugenic legislation. See Stefan Kühl, *The Nazi Connection: Eugenics, American Racism, and German National Socialism* (Oxford: Oxford University Press, 1994), 39.

71. On Sanger's slogan, see Diane Paul, "Eugenics and the Left," *Journal of the History of Ideas* 45 (1984): 569, n. 5; letter from W. E. D. Stokes to Anson Phelps Stokes Jr., February 7, 1921, and letter from Stokes to Charles Davenport, February 19, 1921, Folder "W. E. D. Stokes, 1920," CBD-CSH Series.

72. Folders "Frederick Adams" and "A. Wakefield Slaten, Sermon 25," AES Papers.

73. Walter Dorwin Teague, "Rightness Sells," reprinted from *Advertising Arts*, n.c., and Teague, "Industrial Design and Its Effects on Sales" (talk to the Advertising Club of Los Angeles, n.d.), both in Folder "Writings," Box 79, WDT Papers.

TEN

Apes, Men, and Teeth

Earnest A. Hooton and Eugenic Decay

Nicole Rafter

ABSTRACT

Earnest A. Hooton, author of *Apes, Men and Morons* (1937) as well as
numerous other academic and popular works, taught in the anthropology department at Harvard University for over forty years, between
1913 and 1954. In this essay, Nicole Hahn Rafter examines Hooton's
fascination with teeth as indicators of racial health, showing that his
concerns on the micro level of the tooth mirrored broader national
concerns voiced by Hooton and other eugenicists. Like Cogdell's discussion of the ways in which eugenic concerns and rhetoric shaped
understandings of the common disease of constipation, Rafter shows
the intricacies and extremes to which eugenic ideas were taken by
Hooton and entertained by his audiences during the 1930s with regard
to the lowly tooth.

   Hooton feared that the current, unhealthy state of the modern
tooth stood as proof of national racial decline. He broadcast this message in a number of ways: in doggerel verse ("I hardly think a brute so
crude / Could blame his teeth on processed food"); through articles
such as his *Scientific Monthly* publication "Apes, Men and Teeth"
(1934); and through academic sermons such as his "Wages of Biological Sin" lecture to Columbia University students, published in the *Atlantic Monthly* (1939). Rafter engages this material with wit. Yet the
details she offers from Hooton's thoughts on teeth—the trope of primitive perfection brought low to civilized decay, the need for mother's
milk (at home, of course)—and the broader points she makes reflect

common concerns and strategies of eugenicists in the 1930s, as they
sought to renew physical vitality and stabilize gender roles in order to
reestablish the traditional family.

Harvard University professor Earnest A. Hooton was famous for his research in physical anthropology and his popular-audience books on evolution and eugenics—but not for his writings on teeth. Obituaries and
memorials written after Hooton's death in 1954 mention his advocacy of
sterilization, his superb skills as a lecturer and public speaker, and his personal warmth and generosity; none mentions his abiding concern with the
nation's dentition. Yet the theme of tooth quality runs throughout Hooton's
work, linking his anthropological studies with his writings on eugenics
and becoming a forceful metaphor for genetic decay. In his essays on eugenics, the deteriorating tooth serves as a warning of disease and the
need for cure, a sign of the softening of American bodies and the erosion
of civilization.

From today's perspective, Hooton's intense interest in teeth borders
on the ludicrous. It amused Hooton himself, and he played with the tooth's
comedic possibilities even while conveying a message of utmost serious-
ness. It is, of course, the message, not the comedy, that merits our interest today because of what it tells us about the history of eugenics in the
United States—a history with growing contemporary relevance. That a
scientist of Hooton's stature could discourse at length on the eugenic
significance of the lowly tooth and that dentists, doctors, orthodontists,
and dental surgeons as well as nonmedical Americans flocked to his addresses indicate that eugenics constituted a topic of normal and legitimate
interest during the 1930s and 1940s. These developments suggest, moreover, that Hooton was contributing to the formation of a eugenics culture
that had specific values, goals, and ways of expressing hope and anxiety—
a culture capable of embracing even a crooked canine as a sign of genetic
peril.

To be sure, tooth decay did not constitute Hooton's primary symbol
for evolutionary regression. For him, as for many eugenicists, intelligence
trumped other indexes of decline, and morons figured more largely than
cavities. Yet Hooton found in the tooth an apt and effective metaphor for
anxieties about disease and insidious rot, together with nostalgia for what
he saw as a stronger, healthier past. Through his discourses on teeth, he became, as it were, dentist to the nation, the white-coated scientist who deliv-

ered distasteful news about silent inner decay and recommended painful eugenic extraction but held out the possibility that proper care might restore the nation's teeth and the nation itself to their former sturdiness and luster.

Hooton's writings on teeth accomplished goals common to many eugenics endeavors: encouraging individuals to monitor their own physical, mental, and genetic hygiene; awakening the public to the possibility of hidden personal and social decay; and promoting self-improvement in the name of race betterment. Teeth linked the *micro* with the *macro*, the individual's incisors and molars with the grand sweep of evolution and the fate of civilization. Moreover, like many eugenics tracts, Hooton's writings on teeth included subtle messages about gender, for they demonstrated the need for incisive male authority—leadership capable of tough decision making on behalf of the human family. He was not the only social theorist to use teeth as an index of social health, but he seems to have been unique among American eugenicists in his emphasis on the mouth and oral hygiene.[1]

This chapter examines Hooton's popular-audience dental discourses of the 1930s and subsequent decades.[2] I ask why Hooton chose teeth to express his eugenic alarms, explore the eugenic arguments in his works on dentition, and analyze what those works indicate more generally about the U.S. eugenics movement. This essay grows out of a larger project on Hooton's attempt in the 1930s to revive criminal anthropology.[3] For that project, I read many of his published works and spent several months in his archives at Harvard University's Peabody Museum—an immersion that alerted me to the frequency of dental motifs in his work.[4] In what follows, I begin with an overview of Hooton's life and career to identify him generally and establish the relationship of his writings about teeth to his work as a whole.[5] Then I describe his work on teeth and its central messages. I conclude with remarks on Hooton's choice of teeth as a eugenics metaphor and his work as a sign of the diversity and vitality of eugenics in the United States during the 1930s.

A Brief Biography

Born in 1887 in Clemansville, Wisconsin, Hooton was the son of a Methodist minister who had recently immigrated from England and a former schoolteacher from Canada. His parents evidently provided powerful examples because education and preaching—in this case, preaching about "the wages of biological sin"—became major preoccupations of Hooton's adulthood.[6] He specialized in classics as a graduate student at the University of Wisconsin, Madison, from which he earned his doctorate in 1911. But soon after entering University College, Oxford, as a Rhodes scholar, Hooton abandoned classics in favor of anthropology and anatomy. At Oxford, he earned two degrees, a diploma (with distinction) in anthropology in 1912 and the B.Litt., a research degree, in 1913.

Thus prepared, Hooton joined Harvard University's Anthropology Department, where he remained until his death forty-one years later. At the time Hooton began teaching, few schools other than Harvard offered a graduate degree in anthropology. Thus, he was able to direct many of the next generation's anthropology doctoral students and to shape the field for decades. An anecdote reported by a former student provides a telling example of Hooton's influence. In the late 1940s and early 1950s, three nearly identical introductory anthropology courses were being taught at Columbia University, the University of Wisconsin, and the University of Michigan, "all by former students at Harvard, and apparently all based on notes taken in Hooton's popular class."[7]

Hooton became an early example of the professorial media star, his activities reported by the *New York Times* and other newspapers and his work profiled by magazines such as *Life, Look, Newsweek,* and *Time.* A witty and stimulating speaker, he participated in radio debates, delivered distinguished lectures series, and addressed Harvard Clubs, eugenics groups, and dental associations. In addition, Hooton wrote for general-interest magazines such as the *Atlantic Monthly* and *Collier's* and for specialized dental journals, developing a pop eugenics form of essay that linked evolution—including the evolution of teeth—to eugenics.

Over the decades, Hooton increasingly devoted himself to "biological preachments"—broadcasting the eugenics message.[8] During the first stage of his academic life, from about 1915 to 1930, he concentrated on pure research, studying skulls and producing scientific monographs. In this early period, according to his résumé, he also published an article in a dental journal and another in a eugenics journal, but in both cases, the aim seems to have been scholarly rather than propagandistic.[9] Gradually, however, Hooton became disillusioned with pure science. "A great deal of the science that is pursued in academic confines is quite dissociated from application and even from aspirations of usefulness," he judged. "It is carried on by self-sequestered individuals who probably have never asked themselves of what use to the world their work is. . . . Theirs is science for science's sake—'pure' in that it is purely useless. Now, rightly or wrongly, I have become 'fed up' with the kind of science that remains theoretical. . . . Science ought to be socially responsible."[10]

During the 1930s—the middle phase of his career—Hooton undertook large-scale surveys of living populations but also made room for eugenic concerns. For example, the massive statistical study entitled *The American Criminal,* on which he labored throughout the 1930s, included a number of "tooth" variables that, had the evidence materialized, would have demonstrated the dental inferiority of criminals; the project as a whole was designed to prove that "the germ plasm which produces [the] criminal is scum."[11] Similarly, *Crime and the Man,* a popular-audience version of *The American Criminal,* was designed to show that criminals are inferior beings who should not be permitted to reproduce. In his middle period, moreover, Hooton started enlivening his writings with cartoons illustrating evolutionary and eugenic points, and the 1930s may also have been when he started producing the humorous verses (most of them undated) on teeth and related matters that were later collected under the title *Subverse.* During the final phase of his career, from 1940 to 1954, Hooton's scholarly interest centered on somatotyping, the effort to correlate various body types with personality traits and abilities. However, he also undertook practical research for businesses and the government, and he spent a great deal of time speaking on and writing about genetic decline.

Why did Hooton increasingly devote himself to eugenics? One factor was a growing sense of urgency. The world seemed to be hurtling toward genetic doom, and Hooton wanted to save it—or at least to provide "evolutionary guidance."[12] This sense of urgency intensified with the advent of World War II because Hooton, who, in any case, tended to interpret social phenomena in biological terms, saw in German and Japanese aggression signs of deteriorating germ plasm.

A second factor prompting Hooton's turn toward popular eugenics was probably disappointment with the reception of his two books on criminal anthropology, which sold poorly and inspired vitriolic reviews. With his efforts to revitalize criminal anthropology grinding to a halt, he started looking for more promising ways to demonstrate the need for eugenics. His turn toward popular eugenics was probably further encouraged by his increasing marginalization within the field of anthropology. Although Hooton towered among the leaders of the discipline, he clung to the notion of racial typologies while younger anthropologists such as Ashley Montagu began questioning the very concept of race and its centrality in anthropology.[13] In other ways, too, Hooton fell behind. At a time when colleagues took increasing interest in cultural and social anthropology, he insisted that biology constituted the primary influence on human development and damned environmentalism as "the universal alibi of human failure."[14] To younger anthropologists, Hooton seemed mired in the "scientific" racism and biological determinism of the past.

Thus, it was probably a combination of factors—Hooton's sense of urgency about the world situation, the failure of his criminals books, and marginalization within his home field—that led him to spend ever more of his energies spreading the eugenics gospel and raising the alarm about tooth decay.

Hooton on Teeth

Nearly twenty years passed between Hooton's initial article on teeth, a 1917 publication titled "Oral Surgery in Egypt during the Old Empire," and his next essay on the topic.[15] The renewal, which reflected the larger shifts in the trajectory of his career, began in 1934 with a *Scientific Monthly* article, "Apes, Men and Teeth."[16] This essay evidently created a buzz, for in 1936 the Harvard Dental School invited Hooton to address a conference, an occasion on which he tried to enlist dental scientists in the eugenics improvement campaign ("Man as Director of Human Evolution").[17] These two pieces appeared between hard covers in 1937, in his collection *Apes, Men, and Morons* (the first one retitled to "Teeth through Time").[18]

Hooton essentially repeated these steps by writing three more pieces that focused partly or mainly on teeth and reprinting them in another pop science collection, *The Twilight of Man. Twilight* included, first, a talk he had given in 1938 at the University of Iowa on "Change and Decay in Americans"; second, another 1938 talk, this one delivered to Chicago-area Harvard Clubs and entitled "The Lantern of Diogenes"; and finally, "The

Wages of Biological Sin," which had begun as a lecture at Columbia University and was published in the *Atlantic Monthly* before finding its final home in *Twilight*.[19]

At least four more works on "masticatory machinery" appeared during the 1940s.[20] The initial article, "An Anthropologist Ruminates on Dentition and Devolution" (1940), was followed by a poem, "Ode to a Dental Hygienist" (1942), by "Anthropometry and Orthodonics" (1946), and by "The Evolution and Devolution of the Human Face" (1946). He wrote what seems to have been his final essay on teeth, "On the Relationship of Physical Anthropology to Dental Science," in 1952.[21] Hooton's ideas about teeth and their significance changed little over the years. He made the same points time and again, often beginning with an account of the tooth's evolution.

The Golden Age of Dentition

Teeth, in Hooton's view, "have had an illustrious past; they have a serviceable present, and with due conservation they will continue to perform an indispensable function in the future of man."[22] The fossil record shows that our distant ancestors had exemplary teeth. Even today, "primitive hunters and food-gatherers the world over almost invariably have excellent teeth, practically immune from decay."[23] Teeth became smaller as the eons passed, but "savage or primitive types" of man that have survived into the present continued to have "broad and capacious" palates. Their incisors still "meet edge-to-edge in most cases; their molars have four good cusps in the upper jaw and five in the lower"; moreover, they are rarely afflicted with malocclusion.[24]

To exemplify the health of the primitive tooth, Hooton turned to the Eskimo, eulogizing his dental prowess in doggerel:

> *The square-jawed, big-toothed Eskimo*
> *Drinks water made from melted snow,*
> *A beverage that must be poor in*
> *The tooth-preserving gas called fluorin.*
> *And yet his teeth are clean and sound*
> *As those of the proverbial hound.*

Later in this poem, the Eskimo gnaws on "frozen fish" while "his female associates . . . chew upon his frozen sandals."[25] Notwithstanding his levity here, Hooton was utterly serious in contending that vigorous exercise of the jaws and teeth was what kept the mouths of primitive men healthy.

In his account of dental evolution, however, there was a "shocking" exception to the rule of robust fossil teeth: Rhodesian man, a prehuman ancestor of man discovered in Africa in 1921 whose remains were "equipped with . . . the worst teeth of antiquity." Hooton described the dental woes of Rhodesian man in detail, emphasizing his caries, abscesses, and a gum line "riddled with pyorrhea—a septic condition . . . which leads to eating away of the bony tooth sockets, loosening of the teeth, [and] the entrance of all sorts of poisons into the system through the absorption of pus."[26] Hooton wrote about Rhodesian man, whom he considered to have been an intermediate type between apes and humans, in several contexts, including doggerel:

> It is the guy, Rhodesiensis
> With whom our tooth decay commences:
> Caries, abscesses, gingivitis,
> Otitis media and arthritis,
> I hardly think a brute so crude
> Could blame his teeth on processed food.
> Perhaps dental degeneration
> Started with germinal mutation.[27]

In Hooton's work, the dental woes of Rhodesian man sound faintly like an origins myth, an explanation for and harbinger of the dental problems endemic in modern civilization. Before Rhodesian man, our ancestors apparently lived in dental paradise, innocent of caries and pain. With Rhodesian man came the fall to dental perdition.

The Whitened Sepulcher of Decaying Dentition

When modern man opens his mouth, Hooton observed, he exposes a "charnel-house . . .—the inadequately whitened sepulcher of a decaying dentition."[28] "Oral pathology," he advised in his final talk on teeth, "whether of teeth or of soft tissues, whether in the nature of caries, gingivitis, mal-occlusions, or general deformations of the dental apparatus—is rampant and increasing."[29] Whereas "most savages show few or no cavities . . . , nine out of ten school children in the United States have decayed teeth, and civilized adults probably show nearly 100 percent of mouths which contain one or more carious teeth."[30] But tooth decay per se worried Hooton less than its consequences. "This decay of the teeth means the introduction into the system of poisons which cause rheumatism and a host of major ailments." Just as dental breakdown seems to have led to an ear infection in the case of Rhodesian man, today "human teeth and the human mouth have become . . . the foci of infections that undermine the entire bodily health of the species."[31]

These poisons form a Hootonian counterpart to the contaminated "blood" and impure "germ plasm" that course through other eugenics writings. They are also analogous to the dangerous but hard-to-recognize morons who show up in so many eugenics tracts, waiting to mate with unsuspecting normal people and thus pollute the gene pool. In the case of rotting teeth, as in these other examples, the contaminating agent works silently and secretly. This is what makes professionals crucial to eugenic protection: only they can detect hidden corruption.

For Hooton, modern tooth decay had a significance far beyond individual suffering or even the total dental misery of the world. It was nothing less than a warning of evolutionary decline and the end of civilization. Infections that started in the teeth undermined the health of the entire species. He pointed out that in "non-human societies, the animal that loses its teeth shortly loses its life,"[32] and he cautioned that unless steps were taken "to discover preventives of tooth infection and correctives of dental deformation, the course of human evolution will lead downward to extinction."[33]

Causes of and Cures for Decay

Hooton explained the fall from dental grace in two ways, starting with evolutionary regression. "There can be no doubt whatsoever," he declared in 1952, that "accelerating dental pathology" stemmed, in part, from "long-continued regressive trends in human evolution."[34] He had been making this same point since 1934, when he attributed dental decline—again, in part—to "degenerative tendencies in evolution."[35] Filling in this argument, Hooton explained that at a very early stage in primate evolution, the hands were relieved of some of their "locomotor duties," thus becoming more useful in eating. But teeth continued "their vigorous function both in chewing and in fighting, until in civilized man the use of tools in the preparation of food [was] carried to such an extent that both mastication and biting [became] superfluous and obsolete." The resultant "atrophy of function" contributed to the teeth we see in modern humans: "blackened and decaying tombstones, set awry in beds of putrescence—a contaminating sieve through which must pass every morsel of food."[36] Hooton did not attempt to illustrate this nasty sieve visually, but he did illustrate his more general point about evolutionary regression by drawing a cartoon of an entire family devolving in front of their television set: "Their Master's Voice" (fig. 10.1).[37] The mental, physical, and political passivity of modern life was causing them all to decay—even the dogs.

Civilized man reinforced this evolutionary regression by manufacturing and consuming "cheap processed food"—the second half of Hooton's explanation for the sorry state of contemporary teeth.[38] Refined and cooked foodstuffs obviated the need for biting and chewing. They rotted teeth and gums. They encouraged devolution of the jaw and its contents. And they failed to nourish, thus weakening the organism's resistance to infection. Time and again, Hooton reported, specialists in dental evolution had demonstrated the "horrible change" that occurred among "primitive peoples" when they switched to "a civilized but stupid diet of processed, manufactured foods too high in energy-producing materials and too low in bone- and tissue-forming constituents." The "well-developed faces, perfect dental arches, and sound teeth of the parents" became the rotten and almost unusable crooked teeth of "the unfortunate offspring."[39] A single glance into the mouth of "the civilized child," Hooton thundered in "Wages of Biological Sin," "reveals the havoc wrought by unbalanced diets of manufactured foods. Dental decay usually sets in before the milk teeth have been shed. Malerupted teeth . . . are the concomitants of defective nutrition and loss of masticatory function. . . . Mother's milk has vanished. The hapless infant is raised on synthetic substitutes for natural foods. His upbringing is not mammalian but chemical."[40] Hooton depicted the results of this foolishness in his cartoon titled "Mother love may survive, but mother's milk has vanished," in which National Mothers' Day is celebrated by a flat-chested Miss Condensed Milk (fig. 10.2).[41]

"Their Master's Voice"

Fig. 10.1. Evolutionary decay in the United States in the mid-twentieth century. Here, Hooton traced American degeneration to physical, mental, and political passivity. Democracy, in his view, could not survive such national deterioration. Earnest A. Hooton, "Their Master's Voice," in his *Twilight of Man* (New York: G. P. Putnam's Sons, 1939), opp. 48.

Fixing Teeth, Fixing Civilization

In his speeches and writings on teeth, Hooton spent more time prophesying "evolutionary death" than suggesting ways to avoid it.[42] He seems to have conceived his role as a eugenicist to be that of an Old Testament prophet or perhaps a Greek seer, a Tiresias of teeth, warning the heedless multitudes of impending doom. Occasionally, he trotted out mild nostrums (in "Teeth through Time," for instance, he called for more and better dentists); and in other contexts, Hooton advocated standard eugenics solutions—

"Mother love may survive, but mother's milk has vanished."

Fig. 10.2. Condensed milk and national deterioration. Hooton associated a decline in breast-feeding with unwomanliness, mental and physical deterioration, and tooth decay, part of a larger trend toward the consumption of artificial and overly refined foodstuffs. Earnest A. Hooton, "Mother Love May Survive, but Mother's Milk Has Vanished," in his *Twilight of Man* (New York: G. P. Putnam's Sons, 1939), opp. 296.

marriage screening, birth control, and sterilization. But when he was addressing after-dinner crowds of dentists or physicians or when he was speaking to Harvard alumni, Hooton merely laid out the evolutionary logic of eugenics, leaving listeners to draw their own conclusions.

In one respect, his eugenic solutions differed from those of most of his contemporaries. Whereas some nineteenth-century followers of Herbert

Spencer had advocated a hands-off policy of noninterference with natural selection—no humanitarian aid whatsoever to the poor and weak—many Americans, including diehard eugenicists, were repelled by the notion of leaving the helpless to starve, evolutionarily beneficial though that might be. As time went on and Progressive reforms took hold, moreover, ever fewer eugenicists demanded total noninterventionism. Hooton, however, continued to look askance at "humanitarianism."[43] In the 1930s, he advised that "relief of the unemployed rots their moral fiber" (much as "eating refined and cooked foods leads to tooth atrophy").[44] Later in life, he grew more strident. "We have monkeyed with natural selection to the extent of permitting men to live beyond their evolutionary and organic quota of years," Hooton explained shortly before he died, "thereby forcing them to eke out their miserable surplus span in the miasma of dental pathology, pain, and corruption. . . . We have stopped the wholesome catharsis of natural selection by preserving the weak and sickly. . . . Those who will not or cannot work are still allowed to eat."[45] Hooton nowhere explicitly advocated denial of food to the dentally debilitated and starving. But he did urge physicians to rethink their "dogma of the sanctity of human life" so that natural selection could return to its job of weeding out the weak.[46] Otherwise, he warned, we will be overrun by rapidly multiplying hordes of biological inferiors.

Hooton's Affinity for Teeth

Why did Hooton write and speak at such length about teeth? Why did he choose the tooth and not some other body part to express his eugenic message?

To discourse on teeth came naturally to Hooton, with his background in physical anthropology. "Teeth tell the tale of human evolution better than any other bodily structure," he wrote in "Teeth through Time."[47] And many anthropologists—not just Hooton—paid close attention to the shape of dental arches and the size of molars in fossil remains. They had to because, as he explained, "teeth are the most nearly imperishable relics of the vertebrate body." Whereas soft tissue decomposes rapidly after death and bones become "a *bonne bouche*" (a tasty tidbit) for "carnivorous animals . . . teeth are singularly unpalatable and indigestible morsels."[48] Thus, to a physical anthropologist casting about for a way to signify evolutionary decline, the tooth would have presented itself quickly.

A second source of the tooth's attraction lay in its inherent interest to professional medical groups—dentists, orthodontists, oral surgeons, and physicians. These were groups with which Hooton was in demand as a speaker; and the individuals in them (civic-minded, middle-class professionals) were most likely to be receptive to eugenics and most capable of implementing it. Hooton began writing popular eugenics pieces on teeth in the early 1930s; dental groups then started inviting him to speak, and so, reciprocal interest developed.

In addition, Hooton turned to the tooth for purely personal reasons—for its association with his vision of a more perfect past. In the golden age or paradise of Hooton's nostalgic longing, men were strong and virile while women breast-fed babies and raised manly sons. Such associations may have had something to do with his own experience as a father of two sons for whom he had had high hopes (he named one of them Newton) but who, to their father's sorrow and disgust, could not get into Harvard College and ended up without professional careers. In any case, Hooton clearly associated healthy teeth with a simpler, more rigorous world. Sometimes, he located it in a distant evolutionary past where men munched on meat bones, women (metaphorically) gnawed on their mates' sandals, and no one disturbed natural selection. At other times, the world of Hooton's nostalgia resembled that of his Wisconsin boyhood at the turn of the twentieth century, as shown in his illustrations for *Twilight of Man*: sparsely populated; free of internal combustion engines; and home to full-figured, simply-dressed, and submissive women and to children who get themselves to school unaided, stomping heroically through the snow (see fig. 10.3).[49] Hooton associated the healthy tooth with not only unblemished enamel but also eugenic paradise—hard, white, and pristine.

Hooton and Eugenics in the 1930s

Historians have emphasized eugenicists' use of weak intelligence as a sign of genetic decay—and rightfully so, since intellectual decline constituted a dominant theme in the eugenics movement internationally. Intellectual decline, moreover, was closely linked to significant historical developments, such as the criminalization of mental retardation and the advent of pen-and-paper intelligence testing. But this focus on eugenicists' morons and

Fig. 10.3. Before and after, health and deterioration. Hooton's eugenicism incorporated nostalgia for his Wisconsin boyhood, when he had stomped to school through the snow, gaining physical and mental vigor en route. In the modern world, clothes-conscious mothers drive children to school—and then kick them out of the car. Earnest A. Hooton, "Going to School, 1900–1939," in his *Twilight of Man* (New York: G. P. Putnam's Sons, 1939), opp. 222.

imbeciles has somewhat obscured their simultaneous elaboration of other tropes—frequent exercise; constrained sexuality; intestinal "regularity" (as in Christina Cogdell's essay in this collection); and, in Hooton's case, sound teeth. We are just starting to recognize the metaphorical range of eugenic rhetoric.

Teeth proved to be a versatile symbol for both genetic decay and genetic health, an ideal signifier of concerns about hidden rot and softening moral fiber, on the one hand, and nostalgia for a tougher, harder, more manly past, on the other. Hooton probed the tooth's humorous potential while at the same time embedding teeth in a quasi-religious discourse of loss and restoration, sin and salvation. Dentition became the point at which his lifelong interests in evolution, anthropology, and eugenics converged, together with a longing for past innocence and purity.

Hooton's example illustrates the diversity in eugenics discourse in the 1930s, a diversity of not only imagery but also substance. Whereas eugenics is frequently associated with racism and nativism, these themes surface only indirectly in Hooton's writings on teeth. He wrote not of African teeth or maloccluded Polish palates but of poor dentition per se. And he carried his message into the heart of the Anglo-Saxon establishment, to medical men and Harvard graduates whom he scolded for their indifference to the decay in their midst. Many eugenicists produced Othering discourses; Hooton indicted members of his own caste.

Hooton's example demonstrates the powerful hold that eugenics could exercise, well into the twentieth century, over a middle-class academic—indeed, an academic with a specialization in genetics. Whereas eugenics is sometimes conceived as the doctrine of a small group of right-wing extremists who died off in the 1920s, Hooton did not even begin producing pop eugenics until the mid-1930s. And though he was undeniably conservative on many matters, he took liberal positions on others and was one of the most highly regarded academics in the country.[50] As his example indicates, eugenics continued to be a normal discourse at least into the 1940s—not an extremist doctrine but a topic about which dentists and readers of the *Atlantic Monthly* and *Life* wanted to hear more. Hooton's example further indicates the existence of a eugenics culture, at least among middle-class professionals and the reading public—a set of interests and expectations that created a demand for the pop eugenics discourses in which he excelled. During World War II, Hooton vociferously opposed the Nazis, whom he regarded as degenerate monsters. Because it did not occur to him that he might have anything in common with them or their doctrines, he felt no need to repudiate his own eugenics after the war and remained a eugenicist until his death. For him, eugenics never became an embarrassment. Indeed, he considered evolutionary decline the most pressing issue in the modern world, for "if the human dentition breaks down, it will carry with it in its fall the human species."[51]

Notes

1. Hooton had at least two predecessors in his efforts to associate dental degeneration with social degeneration. One was Eugene S. Talbot, a Chicago-area physician and dentist whose *Degeneracy: Its Causes, Signs, and Remedies* (New York: Charles Scribner's Sons, 1899), includes two chapters on the degeneration of lip, palate, teeth, and jaws. The other was Cesare Lombroso, the Italian criminal anthropologist who studied anomalies of the teeth, among a host of other degenerative traits; see, for example, Cesare Lombroso and Guglielmo Ferrero, *Criminal Woman, the Prostitute, and the Normal Woman* (1893), newly edited by Nicole Hahn Rafter and Mary Gibson (Durham, NC: Duke University Press, 2004). Although Hooton may have been unfamiliar with Talbot's work, he knew that of Lombroso well because he used it as a basis for his own research on criminal anthropology.

2. In addition to the writings discussed here, Hooton produced scholarly material on teeth, as in his textbook *Up from the Ape*, rev. ed. (New York: Macmillan, 1946). Here, I focus exclusively on his eugenic writings.

3. Nicole Rafter, "Earnest A. Hooton and the Biological Tradition in American Criminology," *Criminology* 42, no. 3 (August 2004): 735–72. Hooton published two books on criminal anthropology: *The American Criminal* (Cambridge, MA: Harvard University Press, 1939), and *Crime and the Man* (Cambridge, MA: Harvard University Press, 1939).

4. For the scope and contents of this collection, see http://www.peabody.harvard.edu/archives/hooton.html.

5. There is no full-scale biography. Biographical information can be found in Stanley M. Garn and Eugene Giles, "Earnest Albert Hooton, November 20, 1887–May 3, 1954," National Academy of Sciences, *Biographical Memoirs* 68 (1995): 167–79; Earnest A. Hooton, "Hooton, Earnest Albert," in *Current Biography*, 1940: 397–400; and "Memorium: Earnest Albert Hooton," *American Journal of Physical Anthropology* 12 (1954): 445–53.

6. "The Wages of Biological Sin," one of Hooton's best-known articles on eugenics, originally appeared in the October 1939 issue of the *Atlantic Monthly*. He reprinted it as the final chapter of his book *The Twilight of Man* (New York: G. P. Putnam's Sons, 1939), 284–305.

7. Gabriel W. Lasker, *Happenings and Hearsay: Experiences of a Biological Anthropologist* (Detroit, MI: Savoyard Books, 1999), 46.

8. Hooton, *Up from the Ape*, viii.

9. Hooton's résumé can be found in Correspondence Files "E. A. Hooton—Vitae, Appointment Letters, etc.," Box 13, Hooton Papers, Peabody Museum, Harvard University (hereafter cited as Hooton Papers). The résumé lists "The Evolution of the Human Face and Its Relation to Head Form," *Dental Cosmos* 58 (1916): 272–82, and "Observations and Queries as to the Effects of Race Mixture upon Certain Physical Characteristics," *Eugenics* 2 (1922): 74–[final page number missing in original].

10. Earnest A. Hooton, "Anthropometry and Orthodontics," *American Journal of Orthodontics and Oral Surgery* 32 (1946): 673.

11. Hooton, *The American Criminal*, vii.

12. Hooton, *Apes, Men, and Morons* (New York: G. P. Putnam's Sons, 1937), 227.

13. On changing ideas about race in anthropology, see C. Loring Brace, "The Roots of the Race Concept in American Physical Anthropology," in *A History of American Physical Anthropology, 1930–1980*, ed. Frank Spencer (New York: Academic Press, 1982), 11–29; Lasker, *Happenings and Hearsay*; George W. Stocking Jr., *Race, Culture, and Evolution* (Chicago: University of Chicago Press, 1982), esp. chap. 9; Alice Littlefield, Leonard Lieberman, and Larry T. Reynolds, "Redefining Race: The Potential Demise of a Concept in Physical Anthropology," *Current Anthropology* 23 (1982): 641–55.

14. Hooton, *Crime and the Man*, 181.

15. Earnest A. Hooton, "Oral Surgery in Egypt during the Old Empire," *Harvard African Studies* 1 (1917): 29–32.

16. Earnest A. Hooton, "Apes, Men and Teeth," *Scientific Monthly* 38 (1934): 24–34.

17. Earnest A. Hooton, "Man as Director of Human Evolution," originally a lecture delivered at the Tercentenary Conference of the Harvard Dental School on September 15, 1936, printed in the *Harvard Dental Record* (1937), and reprinted in Hooton, *Apes, Men, and Morons*, 248–70.

18. Hooton, *Apes, Men, and Morons*, 76–92.

19. Earnest A. Hooton, "Change and Decay in Americans," originally a talk delivered at the University of Iowa, June 24, 1938, printed in *Twilight of Man*, 193–226; Earnest A. Hooton, "The Lantern of Diogenes," originally a talk delivered at the Annual Meeting of the Associated Harvard Clubs, Chicago, IL, May 21, 1938, reprinted in *Twi-*

light of Man, 31–59. On "The Wages of Biological Sin," see note 6. Hooton's résumé indicates that he produced one other article on teeth during the 1930s: "The Malocclusions of Science," published in the *Angle Orthodontist* 8 (1938) [no page numbers given].

20. Earnest A. Hooton, "On the Relationship of Physical Anthropology to Dental Science" (1952), in Correspondence Files, Box 13, Folder 9.4, Hooton Papers.

21. Material on "An Anthropologist Ruminates on Dentition and Devolution," a speech of September 1940 delivered in Cleveland, OH, can be found in Correspondence Files, Box 1, "American Dental Association," Hooton Papers. The "Ode," originally a peroration to the graduating class of dental hygienists at Forsyth Dental Infirmary, Boston, July 1942, appears in *Subverse* (Paris: Finisterre Press, n.d.), 18. "Anthropometry and Orthodonics" was originally a talk to the Forty-third Annual Meeting of the American Association of Orthodontists, Colorado Springs, CO, 30 September–3 October 1946; it was published in the *American Journal of Orthodontics and Oral Surgery* 32 (1946): 673–81. "The Evolution and Devolution of the Human Face," a second talk that Hooton gave at the Forty-third Annual Meeting of the American Association of Orthodontists, was published in the *American Journal of Orthodontics and Oral Surgery* 32: 657–81. "On the Relationship of Physical Anthropology to Dental Science," dated 1952, can be found in manuscript form in Correspondence Files, Box 13, Folder 9, Hooton Papers.

22. Hooton, *Apes, Men, and Morons,* 76–77.

23. Hooton, *Twilight of Man,* 296.

24. Hooton, *Apes, Men, and Morons,* 88.

25. Hooton, "The Eskimo," in *Subverse* (Paris: Finisterre Press, n.d.), 32.

26. Hooton, *Apes, Men, and Morons,* 88.

27. Earnest A. Hooton, "Homo Rhodesiensis," in *Subverse* (Paris: Finisterre Press, n.d.), 47. In his introduction to this poem, Hooton explained that Rhodesian man evidently suffered from an abscess of the inner ear (otitis media) as well as from tooth decay. This analysis had significance beyond its contribution to the poem's rhyme scheme, for Hooton's eugenic argument pivoted on the contention that diseased teeth infected the rest of the body.

28. Hooton, *Apes, Men, and Morons,* 28.

29. Hooton, "On the Relationship of Physical Anthropology to Dental Science," 3–4.

30. Hooton, *Apes, Men, and Morons,* 89.

31. Ibid., 90.

32. Hooton, "On the Relationship of Physical Anthropology to Dental Science," 4.

33. Hooton, *Apes, Men, and Morons,* 92.

34. Hooton, "On the Relationship of Physical Anthropology to Dental Science," 4.

35. Hooton, *Apes, Men, and Morons,* 90.

36. Hooton, *Twilight of Man*, 39.

37. Hooton, "Their Master's Voice," in *Twilight of Man*, opp. 48.

38. Ibid., 298.

39. Ibid., 222–23. This passage echoes Hooton's poem entitled "The Fat-Buttocked Bushman," who has perfect dentition until "he encounters Christianity" and "sacrifices dental sanity." This poem concludes on a racy eugenic note: "But though his teeth begin to soften, / His gonads function well and often"; see *Subverse*, 33–34.

40. Hooton, *Twilight of Man*, 296.

41. Hooton, "Mother Love May Survive, but Mother's Milk Has Vanished," *Twilight of Man*, opp. 296.

42. Hooton, *Twilight of Man*, 305.

43. For example, see Hooton, *Apes, Men, and Morons*, 266.

44. Ibid., 256.

45. Hooton, "On the Relationship of Physical Anthropology to Dental Science," 5.

46. Hooton, *Twilight of Man*, 303.

47. Hooton, *Apes, Men, and Morons*, 76.

48. Ibid., 77.

49. Hooton, "Going to School, 1900–1939," *Twilight of Man*, opp. 222. One of *Twilight*'s cartoons (217) is captioned, "As the education of women has become broader, their figures have become narrower." Another (259), showing naked men, women, and children attacking one another, is captioned, "The male parent is dominant, if he can manage it, over his mate and his young. If he cannot manage it, she generally does." And several other illustrations, such as "Mother love may survive" and "Going to school, 1900–1939," depict the kind of women Hooton loathed—car-driving, unmotherly, style-conscious battle-axes.

50. On the range of Hooton's political positions, see Rafter, "Earnest A. Hooton and the Biological Tradition in American Criminology."

51. Hooton, *Apes, Men, and Morons*, 77.

ELEVEN

Classical Bodies versus the Criminal Carnival

Eugenics Ideology in 1930s Popular Art

Kerry Soper

ABSTRACT

In this chapter, Kerry Soper examines a key trope that runs throughout much of the visual culture of the decade: the classical Nordic type as eugenic ideal contrasted against what Soper calls the "criminal carnival," the plethora of non-Nordic racial and criminal character types threatening the demise of the nation, made visually manifest through exaggerated stereotypical facial features or other bodily stigmata. Soper's text and illustrations give visual form to themes previously mentioned in this anthology, such as the widely accepted eugenic notion that inner genetic worth correlated with external appearance; verbal descriptions of criminals, such as those made by Faulkner (Ladner's chapter); the flawed notion of the criminal and racial "type" as determined by composite measurements and artistic techniques (Coffey's chapter); and Far Right political views, such as Alexis Carrel's, espousing speedy elimination of the "unfit" (Reggiani's chapter). Soper exposes the classical-versus-criminal/eugenic-versus-dysgenic trope through careful, reflective analysis of common influences, ideas, and visual techniques across four different types of sources.

He begins his essay discussing late-nineteenth-century, Lombrosian criminal anthropology drawings, which served as the visual equivalent of a "founding father" for the criminal imagery of the later sources Soper examines. To show the ongoing relevance of Lombrosian stereotypes and visual techniques into the 1930s, Soper turns to contemporary criminal anthropology illustrations from Earnest A. Hooton's *Crime and the Man* (1939), which generally attempted to negate such stereotypes yet sometimes significantly slipped back into their usage. He then moves to more popular imagery of the decade, in the form of posters on display at the Chicago World's Fair (1933–1934), selecting almost at random (since there were so many to choose from) a Bauer and Black display advertising "Purity" in cotton medical fabric, symbolized by a classically profiled, blonde, white nurse in a white uniform. He compares this display to a promotional poster for the fair, which clearly foregrounds, both visually and evolutionarily, the classical female (symbolizing Anglo-European Chicago) over the disappearing, savage Native American, and also to imagery of criminals on the marquee of the midway's Thrill House of Crime. Finally, Soper examines 1930s segments from Chester Gould's *Dick Tracy* comic strip to show the continuing use of the visual trope and to discuss its relevance—and also its ambivalence—to contemporary eugenic debates.

As the introduction to this book asserts, it has been commonly assumed until recent years that the popularity of eugenics theory in the United States had died out by the 1930s. This view can, indeed, be supported if one looks only at the apparent decline in the theory's legitimacy among respected scientific circles in the 1920s.[1] This essay acknowledges that decline but suggests that because the broader cultural ideology of eugenics developed at the intersection of official and popular texts, one also has to look at the realms of semiofficial texts and popular visual culture to gauge the actual breadth of a larger and lingering—albeit ambivalent—societal embrace of eugenic philosophies.

The mediums of posters, caricatures, and cartoons offer a rich field in which to identify this persistent, though conflicted, cultural engagement with eugenic ideologies in the 1930s. In particular, an analysis of images in three venues—in the quasi-academic books of the Harvard anthropologist E. A. Hooton, at the Chicago World's Fair, and in the comic strip *Dick Tracy*—highlights the varied ways that creators of popular texts drew on the movement's assumptions or popularized its ideology. To be specific, they did this in the following ways: by visually identifying and categorizing individuals into racial, pauper, or criminal classes; by promoting or rationalizing the sterilization or extermination of insane, defective, or criminal classes through demonizing caricature; and by justifying societal divisions between "superior human stock," and degenerate (often racially based) classes through a contrast between idealized, "classical" bodies and distorted, "defective" bodies.

It is important to emphasize at the outset that, to varying degrees, these images were ideologically conflicted. Although they served to amplify in dramatically visual ways core tenets of a eugenic worldview, they also at times expressed competing paradigms or were used and interpreted in ways that ran counter to a eugenic social agenda. This point is critical for two reasons. First, when identifying eugenic philosophies in the popular realm during a period of cultural tumult—where and when artists and entertainers were often merely channeling or popularizing ideas without acting as official apologists or advocates—one has to identify ideological currents as they intersected with related or even competing paradigms. For example, some of the cartoon images of insanity, criminality, and degeneracy highlighted in this study were also influenced, again to varying degrees, by constructs such as Freudian theory, modernist art, or long-lived aesthetic practices that would not necessarily affirm a eugenic worldview. Second, because the creators of popular texts were generally under no obligation to toe an ideological line, they were unreliable tools for promoting a consistent or coherent ideological agenda. Dominant cultural forces may have attempted to shape the meanings and uses of their texts (through censorship, economic pressures, incorporation, institutional filters, and so forth), and promoters of a particular ideology such as eugenics may have tried to harness cartoon images to their causes. But in most cases, the visions of idiosyncratic artists and the preferences of freethinking audiences could wrest away much of the creative or interpretive power and thus play significant roles in determining the richly conflicted meanings and uses of an image.

Although I emphasize the ideological complexity of these images, it is still my contention that the emotional appeal of both positive and negative eugenics was amplified in popular art in the 1930s. Borrowing heavily from dated but persistently useful conceptions of criminal anthropology, racial ranking, and mythical connections between Anglo and Nordic races and classical Greek culture, cartoonists such as Hooton, the creators of imagery at the Chicago World Exposition, and Chester Gould created vivid caricatures of both perfection and degeneracy—markers that were then harnessed, with varying degrees of intentionality, to the celebration or justification of a eugenic worldview. To elaborate, American society in the 1930s was faced with a set of complex cultural crises—including the social tumult of the Depression, the lingering discontent over the rise of a multicultural society in the wake of mass immigration in the 1910s and early 1920s, and the wave of organized crime in the early 1930s—that were most simply (and simplistically) addressed through reductive images of good classes versus criminal classes and types.

Before analyzing the varying ways that each set of images both align and diverge from a eugenic worldview, some discussion about the history, construction, and social uses of caricatures and cartoons of criminality is in order. Exaggerated images of criminal types in the first decades of the twentieth century emerged at the intersection of two visual traditions: earnest Lombrosian-style depictions of atavistic or abnormal criminal types and political cartoons that often conflated degenerate, unruly social types with ethnic classes. In the late nineteenth century, Cesare Lombroso had argued that criminals were a biological atavism—a throwback to an earlier stage in human evolution. According to him, criminal types and classes had a physiognomy and physiology similar to those of animals lower on the evolutionary scale. Thus, "criminals, savages and apes [exhibited] enormous jaws, high cheek-bones, prominent superciliary arches, solitary lines in the palms, extreme size of the orbits, handle-shaped or sessile ears . . . [as well as an] insensibility to pain, extremely acute sight, tattooing, excessive idleness, love of orgies, and the irresistible craving for evil for its own sake, the desire not only to extinguish life in the victim, but to mutilate the corpse, tear its flesh, and drink its blood."[2]

According to Lombroso, one could visually identify these "born criminals" according to an incriminating physiognomy or some other abnormal "stigmata," such as excessive tattooing or cosmically inflicted injuries or scars.[3] Promoters of his ideals included hand-drawn images of deformed criminal types that appeared to the contemporary eye as caricatures because of the obvious way that they amplified or distorted features and proportions (fig. 11.1). American criminal anthropologists popularized Lombroso's ideas in the first decades of the twentieth century to such a degree that a persistent image of the archetypal criminal was established in the popular imagination: the troglodytic thug with a low brow, squashed nose, massive neck and torso, hairy exterior, stunted intellect, and incriminating scars, deformations, or tattoos.

Caricatures of biological criminality existed independently of the eugenics movement, and Lombroso's ideas and methods were effectively discounted in serious scientific circles in the first decades of the twentieth

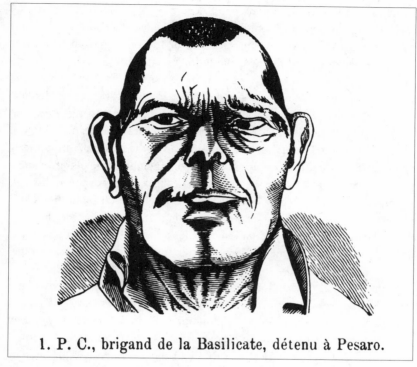

1. P. C., brigand de la Basilicate, détenu à Pesaro.

Fig. 11.1. Drawing of a Lombrosian criminal type from the 1880s. From *The Mismeasure of Man* by Stephen Jay Gould. Copyright ©1939 by Stephen Jay Gould. Used by permission of W. W. Norton & Company, Inc.

century—most impressively by Charles Goring in 1913. But the positivist, deterministic thrust of biological and racial explanations of criminality were too useful to eugenicists and American nativists to die easily. As a result, they were adopted as both official and unofficial devices for promoting the agenda of negative eugenics into the 1930s. For example, as Nicole Rafter's study of the relations between criminal anthropology and eugenics indicates, in the first three decades of the twentieth century in the United States, half of the promoters of biological, Lombrosian-style views of criminality also promoted a eugenic agenda.[4]

Anglo nativists from the 1910s through the 1930s also adopted the theories of visual, criminal anthropology to justify exclusionary immigration laws, describing different racial groups as atavistic, unruly classes that would taint the American gene pool. According to a 1923 *Collier's* article, each immigrant group was supposedly genetically predisposed to commit particular crimes (sloth and intoxication for the Irish, pickpocketing for Jews, and violence and illicit sexuality for Italians and Slavs). To provide emotional, pseudo-scientific weight to these claims, the immigrant male of the Slavic and Italian races was described in vivid caricature. "His face was unchangeable—the heavy, brutal jaw; the surly lowering brow; the dull, cruel eyes; the defiant, dishonest glance; the vulgar gluttonous mouth; the pimpled, pitted skin; the thick, bull-like neck; the guttural, unmannerly speech."[5] Eugenics fueled xenophobia by convincing people that these new immigrants would damage the United States in a variety of ways: through the introduction of disease; the overcrowding of mental institutions and prisons; and a gradual intermarrying among the races that would leave Americans "darker in pigmentation, smaller in stature, more mercurial . . . [and] more given to crimes of larceny, kidnapping, assault, murder, rape, and sex immorality."[6]

These visual descriptions of criminal and racial classes drew on the specious claims of phrenology, physiognomy, and social Darwinism, and they were meant to be objective and literal in their claims. However, they were obviously distortions and exaggerations and had much in common with the comic ethnic caricatures that had thrived in American popular culture from the 1880s well into the mid-twentieth century. In the decades straddling the turn of the twentieth century, cartoonists in magazines such as *Judge, Life,* and *Puck* had established similarly reductive ethnic types that played into fantasies of white superiority. By amplifying physical traits supposedly common to all members of a racial class (traits also drawn largely from social Darwinian concepts), political and gag cartoons could demonize entire immigrant groups, helping to justify passive neglect or active abuse.

But as exaggerated, comic constructions, these visual types were ideologically unstable. Homi Bhabha provides a starting point for discussing this instability: "The stereotype . . . is a form of knowledge and identification that vacillates between what is always 'in place,' already known, and something that must be anxiously repeated . . . as if the essential duplicity of the Asiatic or the bestial sexual license of the African that needs no proof, can never really, in discourse, be proved . . . [and so they are always done in] excess of what can be empirically proved or logically construed."[7] The hysterical distortions and exaggerations in caricatures of ethnic degeneracy gave them, on the one hand, an emotional weight and power that could be exploited by the eugenics movement. If they were true—if particular ethnicities or social classes were really no different from cartoons that equated them with vermin or reduced them to an unreformable, quasi-comic, demonic type and if such qualities were in fact hereditary—then the extreme solutions of negative eugenics were justified. On the other hand, this instability that Bhabha describes would eventually make them unreliable devices for promoting such an overwrought ideological agenda as eugenics.

The cultural weight and power of these ethnic caricatures accrued over the first decades of the twentieth century in part because they were not founded on observable reality or scientific truth. Cartoonists publishing in humor periodicals were supposed to be popular truth tellers who observed politics and culture and then reduced what they saw to an essence—a distortion or simplification that carried greater essential truth than more literal representations. And at times, this truth-telling ability may have been achieved when the target was an individual such as a powerful and corrupt politician; the cartoonist could objectively base his or her caricature on a specific set of features, amplifying those physical traits that indicated the individual's character flaws. But when this authority was transferred to the caricaturing of entire races or social classes, the objective perceptions of the cartoonist no longer undergirded the construction of these images. Cartoonists still drew upon the truth-telling authority of the caricature, but as they reduced an entire race or social class to a physical stereotype—and in the process ascribed a set of inherent, internal flaws—they were basing their images not on observable reality but rather on constructed, racist ideology. Evidence of this flimsy constructedness can be found in a cartooning guide published in 1910 that counseled cartoonists to "go beyond the possibilities of nature and produce already known, accepted, distinctive racial or national expression when drawing foreign characters."[8] In sum, as Bhabha suggests, and as the Italian root word of caricature—*caricare*—implies, the ideological construction of these images made them "overloaded" or "burdened," unstable because they were called on to carry so much social and political weight.[9]

These ethnic caricatures marked early-twentieth-century American culture profoundly, embedding themselves deeply in the cultural vocabulary and imagination. But the overly constructed nature of these images of ethnic and class degeneracy also made them open to flux and movement. The comic characters that were established in racist political cartoons in the late nineteenth century eventually played roles other than scapegoating and demonization. As the types made their way into less racist mediums embraced by immigrants and working-class audiences, such as popular theater and comic strips, exaggerated ethnic types were often as likely to invite ambivalent sympathy or active identification as cruel denigration.

To state it another way, these images of cultural "grotesques," as viewed through Mikhail Bakhtin's conception of the carnival, fulfilled shifting, ambivalent functions.[10] On the one hand, the distorted, animalistic bodies of caricatured immigrants could reinforce the dominant culture's prejudiced, eugenics-influenced conceptions of the difference between normative, classical, white bodies and visages and the unruly, degenerate stock of ethnic and pauper classes. (As Betsy Nies pointed out in *Eugenic Fantasies*, the fecund, earthy representations of ethnic others were indeed used in eugenic propaganda to justify negative eugenic policies; if the ethnic/criminal/pauper classes reproduced like vermin, then the purity of the less fertile, pure, physically transcendent races had to be protected.)[11] On the other hand, the carnival also celebrated these grotesque bodies as joyful, liberating alternatives to the repressed nature of classical, white bodies and the rigidity of social strictures and racial and class divisions. Many of the early-twentieth-century artists, entertainers, and publishers who created or restated ethnic caricatures were ethnic immigrants themselves, and they often held antagonistic or ambivalent feelings toward genteel norms and the authority of racist cultural guardians. As a result, the grotesque ethnic clowns they created in stage shows and comic strips often served as representatives of a more liberating carnival, one that was earthy, democratic, sensual, and unapologetically nonwhite.

By the start of the 1930s, the culture had inherited these ideologically unstable and ambivalent caricatures of degenerate ethnic types, images that had great cultural weight but were ideologically top-heavy and subject to movement and change. The United States of the Depression era was also ambivalent about eugenics. As this collection of essays illustrates, the ideology of eugenics had, by the early 1930s, embedded itself deeply in the popular imagination; for two decades, educational programs in schools, state fairs, medical conferences, and propaganda in the mass media had explained to Americans that the health of the national gene pool was in se-

rious decline and in need of both protection and cleansing. These campaigns were so effective that a large swath of the public accepted many of the
rationalizations and methods of negative eugenics. For example, *Fortune's*
poll in 1937 indicated widespread American support for the compulsory
sterilization of habitual criminals and mental defectives.[12] The pervasive
poverty of the Depression years fueled some of this enthusiasm for sterilization campaigns; indeed, influential public figures including college
professors, grade school principals, mental health workers, and religious
leaders endorsed this method of limiting the poorer, supposedly degenerate classes.[13]

Nevertheless, advocates of an all-out campaign of negative eugenics
were stymied by the general acknowledgment that basic human, democratic rights protected all American peoples.[14] Eugenicists decried the way
that these democratic protections coddled the supposedly weak and defective individuals in society, but they were hard-pressed to find broad support
for such antidemocratic, extreme measures. In light of these obstacles, it
is no wonder that advocates of sterilizing and incarcerating societal "defectives" were eager to ascribe qualities of inherent criminality to entire classes
and ethnicities. If people were biologically or culturally predisposed to dangerous, criminal behavior, then they did not have the protection of civic
rights or public sympathy.

Advocates of eugenics faced an additional challenge: among sociologists
and many in the general populace, there was a rise in the popularity of explanations of criminality that pointed to nonbiological or nonracial causes
such as Freudian theory, environmental factors, or systemic problems that
did not place blame exclusively on individuals, classes, or types. Further, the
multicultural society was undergoing great collective stress as a result of
economic depression, large-scale ethnic assimilation, and the physical and
psychic displacement caused by the tumult of modern society. Although
public opinion was sometimes shaped by the overwrought logic of a eugenic worldview, many people from ethnic and working classes may have
felt targeted by its propaganda—and thus been inclined to sympathize and
identify with the targets of eugenics propaganda: the imperfect, mentally
anguished, occasionally rebellious types that often resembled themselves
in spirit, if not appearance.

Within this cultural tumult, we can look at three sets of cartoon images and identify conflicting ideological currents in the ways that they were

created, received, and used. In each case, there is evidence of the persistent power of eugenic philosophies and outdated conceptions of race, class, and criminality. But contradictions and ambivalence are also present. In particular, there are two fundamental contradictions in each case. First, claims of progress and modernity are juxtaposed with regressive, outmoded representations of criminality and biology, and second, the construction and reception of the images alternates between scapegoating denigration (affirmations of eugenics theories and practices) and sympathetic identification (accompanied with implied rejections of a eugenic worldview).

The Cartoons of Earnest A. Hooton

The cartoons of the Harvard anthropologist Earnest A. Hooton are perhaps the least conflicted of those under consideration here, for he was himself an outspoken advocate of both positive and negative eugenics in the 1930s. As a result, his caricatures of criminality were intentionally and tightly harnessed to that ideological agenda. Nevertheless, because they were caricatures—comically distorted and ideologically unstable—they belied both the flimsy constructedness of Hooton's arguments and the regressive nature of the movement's worldview.

In the 1930s, Hooton was a tireless popularizer of eugenic theory and notions of biological criminality, giving numerous public lectures on the decline of the collective intelligence and physical vitality of the American populace. He publicly declared that the educated American man was "selling his biological birthright for a mess of morons" and urged the nation to engage in some "biological housecleaning" or a "biological purge."[15] In vivid language, he also called for voluntary participation in a broad-scale campaign of negative eugenics, urging "a sit-down reproductive strike of the busy breeders among the morons, criminals and social ineffectuals of our population."[16] In addition, he decried the way that other medical sciences were actually damaging the collective national health by prolonging the lives of inferior or defective individuals.[17] To bolster his arguments, he claimed to have exhaustively studied the connections between race, biology, and crime for over a decade, discovering solid, depressing evidence of a national decline into imbecility and depravity.[18] Playing the role of eugenics missionary and public scholar (in some settings even describing himself as an Old Testament prophet calling the nation to genetic repentance), he published two books, *Up from the Ape* (1931) and *Crime and the Man* (1939), that outlined his evidence, diagnoses, and prescriptions.

Hooton's testy, defensive tone in these books suggests that eugenics was indeed under attack at this time within scientific communities. For example, in *Crime and the Man,* one of his principal objectives was to chart patterns of criminality in the United States according to the prevalence of particular crimes among various ethnic groups. Seemingly aware that this project could be seen as a form of racist propaganda, he assured readers in his introduction that his theories were based on objective science and thus that the images of ethnicity that he would use would be free from exaggeration and stereotype: "I wanted the criminals to be as good-looking as is compatible with the prescribed combination of features."[19] And indeed, some of the illustrations in the book—particularly those done by an artist Hooton hired, Elmer Rising—deliver on this promise; Rising's clinical profiles of ethnic criminal types, such as the Dinaric man (in fig. 11.2), are fairly bland in comparison to Lombroso's earlier criminal grotesques. It was as if Hooton was trying to err on the side of understatement and restraint in order to atone for the exaggerations of earlier eugenicists, such as those made by H. H. Goddard in 1912. In photos that were supposed to highlight physical evidence of the "moronic," genetically flawed features of

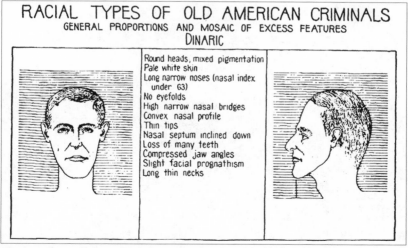

Fig. 11.2. Elmer Rising, "Dinaric Criminal Types." Reprinted by permission of the publisher from *Crime and the Man* by Earnest Albert Hooton, 225 (Cambridge, MA: Harvard University Press, 1939). Copyright ©1939 by the President and Fellows of Harvard College. Copyright renewed 1967 by Mary C. Hooton.

the Kallilkak family, Goddard made the members into caricatures of degeneracy by manually drawing on the photos, making heavy eyebrows indicate evil, vacuous eyes dullness, and overripe lips degeneracy.[20]

Hooton may have been able to deliver on the appearance—if not the actual substance—of objectivity if he had only included these clinical profiles in his book. But as if unable to resist the gravitational pull of foundational, racist stereotypes, he also included his own racist, amateurish cartoons in vividly bizarre charts comparing crime rates among ethnic groups (fig. 11.3). In these images, Hooton abandoned scientific restraint and revived and reinforced all of the ugliest ethnic stereotypes from the previous fifty years. For example, notice the harsh exaggeration of the Dinaric man's nose, brow, and eyes (fig. 11.3). In these images charting rates of sexual deviancy in particular, Hooton resorted to the anxious lies about ethnic depravity that had circulated in eugenic propaganda for years. In another cartoon of deviant sexuality, an Italian man, a "Near Easterner," and Irishman visually articulate one of the eugenic movement's most emotionally powerful weapons: the claim that the American gene pool was in danger of being tainted through miscegenation and the sexual predations of degenerate, ethnic men (fig. 11.4).

To summarize, the disconnect between Hooton's claims to progressive and objective scientific inquiry and the regressive, unapologetic racism of

Fig. 11.3. Earnest A. Hooton, "Offense Rankings of Racial Types: Sex." Reprinted by permission of the publisher from *Crime and the Man* by Earnest Albert Hooton, 251 (Cambridge, MA: Harvard University Press, 1939). Copyright ©1939 by the President and Fellows of Harvard College. Copyright renewed 1967 by Mary C. Hooton.

Fig. 11.4. Earnest A. Hooton, "Offense Rankings of Insane Criminals: Sex." Reprinted by permission of the publisher from *Crime and the Man* by Earnest Albert Hooton, 265 (Cambridge, MA: Harvard University Press, 1939). Copyright ©1939 by the President and Fellows of Harvard College. Copyright renewed 1967 by Mary C. Hooton.

these cartoons effectively reveals the emotional anxiety driving the push for negative eugenics. Proponents such as Hooton wanted to point calmly to statistics to prove their points, but they could not resist using overdone caricatures to give emotional weight to a classist and racist agenda.

Idealized White Bodies versus Criminal Grotesques at the Chicago World's Fair

Now we turn to a second set of images drawn from the Century-of-Progress Exposition held in Chicago between 1933 and 1934: official fair imagery that celebrated an idealized, "classical" conception of the American body and face and caricatures of criminal grotesques featured on the marquee of the midway's Thrill House of Crime. Before comparing the images and exploring the conflicted ideological codings coursing through their construction and uses, a word about the official presence of eugenics at the fair and similar public sites is in order.

As Robert Rydell describes in *World of Fairs*, some of the most effective venues for popularizing eugenics to a broad audience from the 1910s through the 1930s were state fairs, world expositions, and museum displays.

KERRY SOPER

Charles Davenport, head of the Eugenics Record Office, and his assistants created elaborate displays for museums, eugenic world congresses, and state fairs that promoted the movement. These displays included genetic charts, alarming statistics on the reproductive rates of the so-called degenerate classes, plaster casts of fetuses from different races, and so on. Especially captivating to popular audiences were the "fitter families" competitions sponsored by these displays at fairs throughout the country in the 1920s. These contests were constructed on the idea that human stock—like animal stock—should be bred for quality and excellence (an excellence that, of course, accorded with Anglo and Nordic physiognomies). State officials, local doctors, and fitness experts participated in the judging (thus giving official sanction to the eugenics campaign), and the winning families were put on display like living dioramas of genetic excellence.[21] The freak shows featured on the midways of most of these fairs could have served as an unofficial counterpoint to these fitter families displays, presenting a lurid, cautionary exhibit of the grotesques and degenerates that could emerge on the other end of the genetic spectrum.

At the Chicago World's Fair, the official presence of the eugenics movement was muted because of opposition from some fair organizers and scientists critical of the inherent racism of the movement. But in the end, the movement was able to secure a space next to the genetics exhibits within the Hall of Science (figs. 8.5–8.8). Revealing that organizers were embarrassed by this regressive, racist relative who somehow crashed the respectable party, none of the official photos of the scientific and medical displays highlighted or even acknowledged the eugenics exhibit, but maps of the building clearly marked its location.[22] The eugenics movement also participated in the exposition by sending scientists to do statistical and observational studies of the fairgoers themselves. Hooton, for example, was given permission to question and measure over 2,342 fairgoers, looking for evidence to support his ranking of individuals and groups according to intelligence, genetic quality, and potential for criminal behavior.[23]

The unofficial voices or images affirming a eugenic worldview at the exposition were perhaps louder or more striking than these official advocates, but they were more conflicted in their meanings and may have been received in varying ways. First, I will look at celebrations of idealized, classical, white bodies in the official art of the fair, and then I will turn to caricatures of criminal grotesques featured on the midway. There is not

necessarily anything inherently racist in the ubiquitous images of classical, stylized bodies in the architectural motifs, promotional posters, and
scientific displays at the exposition; neoclassical imagery can evoke notions
of perfection, stability, and democracy, and at this fair in particular, the art-
decoesque stylizations of classical Greek sculpture that adorned the exterior and interior of the Hall of Sciences were meant to connote a sort of
progressive humanism. Nevertheless, because social Darwinists in the late
nineteenth century and eugenicists in the early twentieth century had appropriated the conceptions and imagery of classicism to serve their ideological agendas, these images also began to carry additional cultural baggage.
Notions of perfection and progress, in fact, had become so intertwined with
Darwinian notions of evolution and eugenic conceptions of biological and
genetic purity in the first decades of the twentieth century—effectively becoming part of the collective cultural vocabulary or imagination—that artists
and designers may have shaped their imagery to affirm these ideologies.

To add some historical perspective, connections between classicism and
racism were established at Chicago's previous world's fair, the World's
Columbian Exposition in 1893. At this fair, overwrought neoclassical architecture and classically coded statues advertised the arrival of a world-class
culture in the United States. The imagery evoked the promises of Greek
democracy and the sophistication of Old World arts, but it also intimated
that the United States, like imperial Rome, had become a world power. Participants and organizers were unapologetic in their celebration of the manifest destiny of the United States to subjugate not only its native peoples
and frontiers but also other world provinces. Justifying this national hubris
and ambition were heady intellectual discussions of the integral role a
frontier played in keeping the United States exceptional (Frederick Jackson Turner's frontier thesis was unveiled at the exposition), as well as anthropological exhibits that made Native Americans and African tribes into
living dioramas of primitive life, to the extent that social Darwinian theory was incorporated into the very structure of the fair. Visitors were encouraged to see the progression from the midway, with its raucous ethnic
entertainments, to the elevated "White City" as a journey up the ladder of
evolution or race ranking. The blatant racism and hypocrisy of these constructions prompted Frederick Douglass to challenge the meanings of the
White City as a symbol of progress and democracy; to him it was instead
a "whited sepulcher" masking a deep racial divide, racist representations

of blacks at the exposition, and myriad social ills and inequalities of the Gilded Age.

Moving into the first decades of the twentieth century, eugenicists, like their social Darwinist forebears, appropriated classical ideals and imagery for their own purposes. For example, Madison Grant, in his seminal eugenics text, *The Passing of the Great Race* (1916), argued that Nordic types were descended from ancient Greeks and that vestiges of that race's noble physical traits, as relayed in classical sculpture, could be identified in the best (white) genetic stock in the nation. He contrasted this ideal with the degenerate, dark, "fecund" bodies of ethnic immigrants who would dilute the purity of the classical American race.[24] Other eugenicists, such as John H. Kellogg in 1915, made similar connections, calling for Americans to "obey" biological law in order to raise up a "real aristocracy" of "Apollos and Venuses."[25]

Understanding the history of these associations between white superiority and classical ideals, we can look at the first example from the 1933 fair—a corporately sponsored medical display promoting the purity of a cotton fabric used by doctors and hospitals (fig. 11.5). To reinforce the claims

Fig. 11.5. Bauer and Black display at the Chicago World's Fair, 1933. From *The Official Pictures of a Century of Progress Exposition, Chicago, 1933* (Chicago: Reuben H. Donnelley, 1933), 139.

to whiteness and purity in the product, the company, Bauer and Black, created an icon that looked like a classical goddess, sculpted in marble and
dressed as a nurse. The blinding whiteness of the visage and hair, the crisp
and stylized lines in the face and uniform, and the refined shading all
combined to create an image that conflated white racial purity or perfection with pure qualities of a purportedly progressive medical fabric.

The second example, a poster promoting the fair, might fit Rydell's description of the "overdetermined symbolism" used by promoters of the
fair—imagery that was forced to carry a great deal of cultural baggage (fig.
11.6).[26] The female goddess in this image, a personification of Chicago,
looks similar to the representations of Columbia and "the Republic" that
stood in the fountain at the center of the White City during Chicago's 1893
World's Fair. As an image of progress, democracy, and the determination
of Chicago's first white settlers, she is not intrinsically racist in her construction. However, the way in which nativists and eugenicists historically
had appropriated her and similarly idealized classical icons to represent
their causes pushed the codings in that direction. Contributing, perhaps,
to the meanings embedded in the 1933 poster were ideas such as those put
forward by Madison Grant in 1913. Grant asserted that when "two distinct
species are located side by side history and biology teach that but one of
two things can happen; either one race drives the other out, as the Americans exterminated the Indians . . . ; or else they amalgamate and form a
population of race bastards in which the lower type usually preponder-
ates." Moreover, the fact that earlier social Darwinists saw the demise of
Indian nations as a natural, welcome result of racial competition and the
fact that later eugenicists launched a campaign in 1924 to classify Native
Americans as a "black" or "mongrel" race, further reinforces the racist implications of this poster.[27] To summarize, the creators of this poster may
not have been aware of the full implications of the chosen imagery and
juxtaposition of the contrasting visages, but because of the ideological baggage that these icons had accumulated in the previous half century, eugenic
ideals were articulated: a noble but primitive and swarthy race had given
way, in the course of racial and cultural progress, to a white civilization
that aspired to both the principles and the purity of idealized bodies of a
classical, golden age.

The carnival section of the Chicago World's Fair in 1933 contained a
second set of images that could be seen as supporting popularized, though

Fig. 11.6. Promotional poster, Chicago World's Fair, 1933. Reprinted by permission of the Chicago Historical Society.

ambivalent, concepts of eugenics (fig. 11.7). Like antipodes to the idealized classical bodies in the official fair art and designs, a set of criminal grotesques were prominently featured on the marquee of a major midway attraction, the Thrill House of Crime. On one level, these caricatures were descendants of Lombroso's gallery of deviant types; the obvious implication was that each particular crime tended to be committed by individuals with a distinctive physiognomic profile. And drawing from the well of existing, popular stereotypes, several of the visages, such as the bomber and white slaver, were ethnically coded. These were the types of faces—swarthy, heavy-lidded, dark—traditionally used by race-rankers and eugenicists to evoke fears of miscegenation, to block immigration, or to justify the harsh treatment of supposedly congenital criminality. Moreover, the vivid distortions in all the faces could have reinforced the idea that insanity, violence, and degeneracy could be determined by a person's physical appearance or external stigmata.

This attraction may have also ostensibly presented itself as a public service—a set of horrific displays that would warn people about criminal types, help "put a stop to kidnapping," and reinforce the eugenic project of identifying and controlling criminal classes. Because of the social disruptions of the Depression and anxiety over a wave of organized crime in the early 1930s, there was a great deal of public hand-wringing over what to do with the "criminal problem." Eugenicists such as Alexis Carrel capitalized on this anxiety in 1935 to aggressively promote extreme forms of negative eugenics:

> Gigantic sums are now required to maintain prisons and insane asylums and protect the public against gangsters and lunatics. Why do we preserve these useless and harmful beings? The abnormal prevent the development of the normal. This fact must be squarely faced. Why should society not dispose of the criminals and insane in a more economical manner? . . . The community must be protected against troublesome and dangerous elements. How can this be done? . . . Perhaps prisons should be abolished. [Violent criminals and the insane who are guilty of criminal acts] should be humanely and economically disposed of in small euthanasic institutions supplied with proper gases.[28]

On a second level, the showcase of gangsters and lunatics in the midway images was unapologetic entertainment—a "thrill" house located in the "Hollywood" section of the midway that celebrated the criminal as a larger-than-life figure who defied social strictures and performed extreme acts worthy of an appreciative audience. As a result of these mixed messages,

Fig. 11.7. The Thrill House of Crime on the midway of the Chicago World's Exposition, 1933, and detail of the marquee. From *The Official Pictures of a Century of Progress Exposition, Chicago, 1933* (Chicago: Reuben H. Donnelley, 1933), 99.

viewers may have looked on these images and the interior displays with mixed feelings or arrived at conclusions other than the extreme prescriptions of negative eugenics. There may well have been revulsion at the deformed, insane otherness of criminal freaks, but at the same time, there could have also been admiration for outlaw heroism or sympathy for—and identification with—individuals driven by powerful emotions or dire circumstances to commit desperate acts. Moreover, like celebrations of the grotesque in the traditional carnival, these types were elevated to celebrity status, like stars on a movie house marquee—alternative, more vivid matinee idols in comparison to the rigid, classical stars in the official portions of the exposition. And as suggested by the teeming crowds around the thrill house, people were perhaps more interested in being entertained in rowdy ways than being lectured about societal ills. The Columbian Exposition of the previous century was again evoked there; newspaper reports of fairgoers in 1893 suggested that patrons preferred the raucous carnival with its ethnic, democratic entertainments to the White City and its built-in civic lessons on gentility, classical ideals, and racial hierarchies.[29]

Finally, some of the faces on these billboards also departed from a strict Lombrosian mode in their shift away from being literal markers of biological criminality toward figurative expressions of a troubled psychic state. Suggesting that Freudian theory also influenced the construction of these cartoons, the artists used stylized distortions, such as agitated strokes and undulating lines, to suggest different forms of internal anxiety, anger, or despair. They also owe a debt to modernist, expressionistic art; there are echoes of Edvard Munch's *The Scream,* in particular, in the gaunt face of the "drug slave."

Chester Gould's Dick Tracy

A final set of images—Chester Gould's cartoons in *Dick Tracy*—at times aligned with a eugenic worldview by contrasting idealized white bodies with caricatures of ethnic criminality and advocating a form of organic, negative eugenics to the problem of criminal classes. But similarly to the caricatures on the fair's midway, these cartoons could also carry complex meanings that could shift readers away from denigration toward sympathy and identification. Gould developed the idea for his strip—a "true, red-blooded American" cop dishing out vigilante justice on ethnically coded criminal gangsters and grotesques—through trial and error and an adept reading of the cultural climate.[30] Throughout the twenties, Gould, an aspiring cartoonist from the Midwest and a descendant of Scottish-English and German immigrants, had pitched, with little success, numerous comic strip ideas to the head of the Chicago Tribune–New York News Syndicate, "Captain" Joseph Patterson. Gould was a staunch conservative with quasi-fascistic views about how to enforce law and order. His politics and art converged when headlines about rampant organized crime violence inspired him to create a new strip called *Plainclothes Tracy*. Gould was incensed by news coverage that seemed to make criminals into celebrities and heroes, and he felt that he should counter this trend by creating a popular strip that clearly vilified criminals and glorified a noble crime fighter.[31]

Gould never openly affiliated himself with the eugenics movement, but his taste in criminological texts, reliance on ethnic typing, and harsh remedies for social ills and crime suggest that during the early years of his strip (the 1930s), he drew on popularly disseminated eugenic concepts in the construction of his characters and story lines. For example, he was an avid reader of crime literature and procedural manuals and tried to model his strip after these texts.[32] Gould's personal library is no longer intact, so it is difficult to identify particular texts that he might have studied, but there is enough information to suggest that in the early 1930s, he was enamored with simplistic, biological explanations—and physiognomic representations—of criminality. For example, he was especially fond of French crime manuals, and into the 1930s, continental crime literature persisted in placing greater confidence than did American texts on biological explanations and physiognomic methods of detection and categorization.[33]

During the strip's first year (1931), Gould also enrolled in an undergraduate course on criminology at Northwestern University. The brief catalog description of the course stated that it would look at "the nature of crime and the criminal in detail," discuss "preventive programs," and investigate "the Chicago crime dilemma in particular."[34] That the words *crime* and the *criminal* are singular—as if easily identifiable categories or types—and that the course focused on the ethnic gang violence occurring in Chicago at the time suggests that the professor may have relied on established criminology textbooks by authors such as Fred Haynes and Robert Gault, authors who acknowledged multicausal theories of crime but who privileged the deterministic explanations offered by the study of the biology of physiognomy. For example, in his 1930 text *Criminology*, Haynes argued that physiognomic methods were still valid because criminals could either acquire the "stigmata of degeneration" or be seen as "organically defective" persons who belonged to an identifiable "pauper class" and who would never be able to adjust to society.[35]

Gould also worked alongside local police departments in these early years of the strip. Police culture in the 1930s apparently found the outdated biological and ethnic constructs to be persistently useful and appealing. Evidence of this can be seen in a complaint lodged by progressive sociologist Arthur Beely in 1935: the "still prevalent view [within police departments across the country is] that criminals are 'hard-boiled' gorilla-like creatures. . . . Twenty years after science refuted this superstition [Lombrosian conceptions of criminal typing], however, it is still possible to find peace officers literally taken off their guard when the bandit is a well-dressed, handsome youth rather than a 'suspicious-looking' character with all the earmarks of the proverbial criminal."[36]

Law enforcement officers were perhaps slow to accept Freudian or systemic, societal explanations of crime for a number of reasons. First, those explanations made the detection of criminal types ambiguous and complex, placing too much blame on abstract or intangible causal factors and advocating soft treatments and reform rather than decisively harsh and final punishments.[37] By contrast, biological and physiognomic theories—an early form of racial profiling—were comfortingly deterministic. Second, police officers and crime writers such as Gould were also influenced by procedural manuals, by the institutional memory of their departments, and by their own engagement with pulp crime fiction, gangster films, and crime comics—all of which tended to reinforce physiognomic representations of criminality and comfortingly simplistic conceptions of how to pursue and punish criminal classes. Finally, as police forces faced the organized crime problem of the early 1930s, eugenic conceptions of the deviant nature of southern and eastern Europeans—the ethnic groups effectively blocked by racist anti-immigrant legislation in 1924—provided a ready-made storehouse of assumptions, stereotypes, and remedies for dealing with these criminals.

It is interesting to note that Gould was also influenced by Colonel Calvin Goddard while studying at Northwestern. Goddard helped to establish a crime lab at the university in 1931, in the wake of the St. Valentine's Day massacre, and was best known for introducing "modern," scientific methods of crime scene investigation into police work, such as fingerprinting and the gathering of other seemingly hidden forensic evidence. Gould became a champion of these methods in his strip, often anticipating various technological advancements. But he still meshed them with archaic notions about the biological or degenerative stigmata that marked criminals in outrageously obvious ways. It is ironic that within the strip, Tracy advocates the need to employ the subtlest methods of discovering the identities of criminals while pursuing villains who loudly advertise their culpability through a variety of grotesque physical deformities, mutations, and scars.

Gould's political convictions may have also led him to privilege biologically based approaches to understanding and depicting crime. In interviews, he exhibited a somewhat paranoid and mildly xenophobic view of embattled "good" classes fighting against inherently degenerate criminal classes. Moreover, he advocated a type of vigilante justice that was supremely confident about its methods of identifying criminality and guilt; he equated criminals with animals (rats and vermin, most often), and he advocated the extreme preventive measures of swift, justice-system-free extermination.[38] In one interview, he stated, "I came from Oklahoma. . . . Justice was quick and severe when they caught a red-handed culprit. . . . I would read in the paper about a continuance and another continuance, and then the judge finds a flaw in the indictment or something. I used to say to myself, 'They know this fellow's a crook. They know he did this. They know that he is dangerous. Why don't they just take him out and shoot him?'"[39]

Another connection between the politics behind Gould's strip and the eugenic ideas that seem to have emerged in its narratives and character typing is Captain Patterson's influence on Gould's work. It is known that Patterson shared Gould's conservative "eye for an eye" philosophy of punishment and insisted that Gould show the criminals (most of which were coded as southern European in Dick Tracy's first years) being physically destroyed in the strip's climaxes. As if wanting to showcase a ritualistic, representative extermination of an entire criminal class, he insisted that readers be able to see bullets literally going into the villains' bodies.[40] The fact that Patterson was one of the leading apologists for the Third Reich before World War II also suggests that he allowed the ideology of the Nazi Party—

its brand of eugenics that advocated the extermination of criminal (ethnic) "rats" and the general advancement of the superior Nordic race—to spill over into his efforts at shaping this articulation of how the United States should combat crime.[41]

The effort to create explicit connections between Gould's politics, education, worldview, and a eugenics-style approach to understanding and depicting crime should be tempered by an acknowledgment that physiognomic representations of criminality also attracted Gould because he, like crime film creators of the era, wanted to use modes of representation that appealed to a broad audience's desire to see crime dealt with in heroic, black-and-white terms. When asked why his criminals were so ugly, he replied that it was so that "anybody can look at the strip and know right away who's the villain."[42] Considering the pressure to cater to the interests of a popular audience and to eliminate complexity in the name of archetypal character construction, it is easy to see why Gould preferred—and perhaps privileged in his studies—the texts and theories that best provided simplistic images and assumptions.

In the strip itself, popular eugenic conceptions can be seen in contrasts between good and criminal classes, with their correspondingly idealized or distorted bodies and visages. Tracy, the protagonist of the strip, is continually celebrated as a "true, red-blooded American hero," suggesting both his devotion to quintessentially American ideologies and his appropriate genetic pedigree.[43] Although he does not have the blonde hair of the heroic Nordic icons celebrated by eugenicists in the 1920s, he does sport their classical, angular features to an exaggerated, almost comical degree. His face, in fact, is perpetually frozen in a rictus of righteous, stoic anger at the criminal riffraff he has to pursue.

Tracy's love interest is coded even more explicitly as an idealized Anglo or Nordic type, with blonde hair, small and "refined" features, and a slight build (fig. 11.8). Even her name, Tess Trueheart, reinforces the idea that one's physiognomy is a direct reflection of one's inner worth. One of the recurring story lines in the first decade of the strip's run had Tess physically and sexually threatened by ethnically coded criminals, such as Stooge Viller, with comparatively grotesque bodies (fig. 11.9). Like the female protagonists in other eugenics-related narratives, including *Tarzan* and *Superman*, Tess, the hero's relatively helpless love interest, must be continually saved by her genetically acceptable lover, Tracy, from the symbolic threat of

Fig. 11.8. Dick Tracy and Tess Trueheart, in Chester Gould's *Dick Tracy* comic strip, January 2, 1932. Copyright, Tribune Media Services, Inc. All Rights Reserved. Reprinted with permission.

miscegenation and ethnic despoilment. In her study *Eugenic Fantasies,* Betsy Nies suggested that these stories settled collective anxieties about the loss of both masculinity and cultural "purity" in American and western European culture.[44] In the case of Tracy, anxieties about rampant crime intersected with these fears of racial mingling and the fading of the archetypal American male.

Comparing images of Tess being threatened by these ethnic criminals also brings to mind eugenics-influenced Nazi propaganda from the same period that amplified racist fears among the non-Jewish population (fig. 11.10). Gould, of course, was not intentionally constructing racist propaganda, but because those types and narrative constructions had become such a part of a cultural imagination shaped by eugenics, he perhaps drew on them unconsciously as default choices to heighten the strip's level of fear and melodrama.

Tracy's sidekick, a bumbling Irish cop named Pat Patton, also supports this reading of the early strip. Forty years before the comic strip began, the Irish had suffered under social Darwinian theory, whose promoters considered them to be a swarthy, degenerate, "Africanoid" race with a cranial structure that gave them a "temperament quite unsuited to English norms of rational behavior and political maturity."[45] English and American cartoonists

Fig. 11.9. Stooge Viller seducing Tess Trueheart, in Chester Gould's *Dick Tracy*. Copyright, Tribune Media Services, Inc. All Rights Reserved. Reprinted with permission.

Fig. 11.10. Nazi propaganda from the mid-1930s, *Die Sturmer*.

such as John Tenniel, Thomas Nast, Joseph Keppler, and Frederick Opper
Burr solidified the visual representation of this stereotype in magazines
such as *Punch*, *Leslie's Illustrated Weekly*, and *Puck*. According to these
artists, the average working-class Irishman had an apelike posture; a low,
slanting forehead (indicating a small frontal lobe—the part of the brain
that gave a person the ability for rational, civilized thought and behavior);
an extended jaw (another sign of evolutionary backwardness); and a small,
upturned nose. However, during the decades around the turn of the twentieth century, Irish cultural and political fortunes changed; the Irish gained
collective cultural power, they created powerful urban political machines,
and second- and third-generation immigrants assimilated to the point of
joining the largely constructed ethnic category of "white." In popular culture, the Irish caricature persisted in comic strips such as *Happy Hooligan*
and *Bringing Up Father*, but it became more of a playful, figurative stereotype of the put-upon everyman rather than a punishing, social Darwinian
marker of racial inferiority. It also helped the Irish that in the first decades
of the twentieth century, the animus of Anglo and Nordic American eugenicists had shifted toward those in the most recent wave of immigrants: Jews,
Slavs, and Italians.

One of the Irish stereotypes that did persist into these more favorable
cultural circumstances, however, was the bumbling Irish cop. He was considered laughable because it was assumed that he had achieved his position through political connections rather than ability or merit.[46] So Tracy's
sidekick, Patton, serves as comic relief by committing physical gaffes or mis-
reading the evidence. Moreover, Patton's physical appearance—a softened
version of old race-ranking caricatures—also works to make Tracy look more
masculine, American, and heroic. In the context of the early thirties, then,
Patton occupies a comic middle ground between the earnest, iconic ideal
of the American Tracy and the southern and eastern European criminals
who are the strip's initial villains. Having assimilated enough to no longer
be threatening to the American stock, he is allowed to join in the effort of
protecting the dominant culture against these new threats—albeit with a
comical ineptness and no chance of being considered a serious rival for
Tess Trueheart's affections (although he does try, with comically disastrous
results, to court her early on in the strip's run) (fig. 11.11).

Finally, much like in the Chicago World's Fair, we find idealized white
bodies contrasted with criminal grotesques in Chester Gould's strip. His

Fig. 11.11. Pat Patton calling Tess Trueheart, in Chester Gould's *Dick Tracy*, January 24, 1932. Copyright, Tribune Media Services, Inc. All Rights Reserved. Reprinted with permission.

array of deformed criminal types reads as a sort of exaggerated reflection of the more literal mapping of physical criminal types by American and European police departments in the late nineteenth and early twentieth centuries. This practice was first introduced in 1872 by Alphonse Bertillon. According to his model, criminal types could be identified according to signature physical (often racial) characteristics by creating photographic composites of individuals committing similar unlawful acts. This anthropometric system of classifying criminals according to image and measurement was introduced in the United States at the Chicago World's Fair in 1893 and was widely used by police departments into the 1920s.[47] Though contested as being simplistically unhelpful and racist by the mid-1920s, the model persisted into the 1930s in semiofficial criminology textbooks such as Hooton's and, in exaggerated form, in Gould's strip.

Because Gould's criminals acquired their grotesque appearance by accident as often as they did by genetic inheritance, it is tempting to see them as a complete departure from a strict biology paradigm; however, scarification or acquired deformity could still conform to this ideological construct. Nicole Rafter, in *Shots in the Mirror: Crime Films and Society*, explained that popular crime films borrowed from Lombroso the idea that criminals can often be identified by a wound, deformity, or mark of degeneration that serves as an easily identifiable stigmata—a sort of divine marker for recognizing those who should be punished for their sins or evil nature. The visual and psychological appeal of this concept—that criminals bring an incriminating visual condemnation on themselves—helps to explain why, to this day, creators of crime-oriented films, comic strips, and comic books tend to mark their villains with physical imperfections and deformities.[48]

Later in his career, Gould used increasingly more bizarre stigmata for his criminals and began to rely less and less on a literal eugenic depiction of criminal types (shifting to more Freudian treatments of criminals as socially or psychologically maladjusted). But he was relatively straightforward in the 1930s in the melding of caricature and race in his criminal gallery (fig. 11.13). His first villains are repeats of the visual stereotypes that had come to dominate crime films in the early 1930s: troglodytic thugs and southern European gangster types (fig. 11.12). For example, Steve the Tramp, one of

Fig. 11.12. Some of the early 1930s ethnically coded criminal types in Chester Gould's *Dick Tracy. Left to right:* Dan Mucelli, October 12, 1932; Texie Garcia, December 2, 1931; Steve the Tramp, March 4, 1933; Big Boy, April 23, 1932; and Stooge and Maxine Viller (brother and sister), July 7, 1933. Copyright, Tribune Media Services, Inc. All Rights Reserved. Reprinted with permission.

Fig. 11.13. The more complex and bizarre gallery of villains in Chester Gould's post-1930s work. Copyright, Tribune Media Services, Inc. All Rights Reserved. Reprinted with permission.

Gould's most prominent rogues in the 1930s, is of indeterminate ethnicity but has the squat cranium, hairy body, bull-like neck, and thick frame of Lombroso's quintessential criminal type. Most of Gould's other early criminals had stereotypical Jewish, Italian, and Slavic features (large noses, thick lips, flabby physiques, swarthy complexions, heavy-lidded eyes, and so on), and they sported distinctly ethnic names, such as Spaldoni, Mucelli, Villers, Mocco, Meggs, and Salzis. With these names, Gould meant to evoke the monikers of the largely Italian gangster celebrities of the era, but he also added to the tradition of dividing good and evil along racial lines, projecting onto southern and eastern Europeans the criminal traits of being more mercurial, violent, and degenerate. Moreover, by giving them grotesque facial features and deformed physiques, he was playing into the eugenic practice of contrasting the Anglo or Nordic classical body (in the forms of Tracy and Tess) with the supposedly genetically inferior, earthy physicality of the southern Europeans.

The story lines often reinforced these racial divisions. As suggested earlier, Tess was often in peril at the hands of these criminals, and in one especially popular early run, a fictionalized retelling of the Lindbergh baby abduction accentuates the contrast between a genetically pure Anglo victim—"Baby Waldorf"—and the swarthy kidnapping suspects (Mocco, Meggs, and Salzis) (fig. 11.14). By exaggerating physical perfection and innocence—embodied by the little aristocratic boy—on one side, and criminal and working-class deformed bodies and evil intentions on the other, the story appears to tap into anxieties about the larger loss of Anglo and Nordic innocence and genetic purity at the hands of criminal, ethnic immigrants. Gould makes this effort to tap into collective anxieties explicit by

Fig. 11.14. Baby Waldorf kidnapping story resolution, in Chester Gould's *Dick Tracy*, May 22, 1932. Copyright, Tribune Media Services, Inc. All Rights Reserved. Reprinted with permission.

positing that the most sanctified and secure site in the United States—both literally and figuratively—is the home of these wealthy, Anglo aristocrats. Tracy says to the chief of police on hearing about the kidnapping, "The son of John H. Waldorf! Chief, it's hard to believe." To which the chief responds, "Tracy, this country is in the grip of a plague worse than war! Gangsters are striking at the very foundation of America—the home."

The swift justice meted out in the strip and the strange punishments faced by the deformed criminals also articulated eugenic anxieties. Because the criminal types were so readily identifiable in the strip—their guilt was a foregone conclusion, since one could read the culpability in their outward form—the audience comfortably anticipated their demise. In classic eugenic fashion, Gould also tried to alleviate any lingering sympathy for the criminal-ethnic grotesque by referring to him both within and outside the strip as a "rat" or "vermin" in need of extermination.[49] After thoroughly demonizing and dehumanizing the villain, Gould invited readers to participate in a form of collective, societal aggression as he depicted the freak's dramatic, gruesome death in graphic detail (fig. 11.15). Both Patterson and Gould were unapologetic about showing the villains being shot, skewered, crushed, electrocuted, or extinguished in other creative ways. Patterson liked the idea that readers could actually see the bullets go through the bodies of the criminals, and Gould talked with relish about "snuffing out" his criminal "rats."[50]

The graphic depictions of death were included so that readers would have the satisfaction of seeing evil get its proper punishment. However, the strip also seems to have tapped into the popular appeal of the extreme preventative and punitive methods of negative eugenics. Echoing the sta-

THEY'VE GOT 'STUD'!

tistic cited at the opening of this essay, a writer for *Editor and Publisher* in 1934 defended Gould's swift and extreme punishments by arguing that the strip "does not capitalize on the public's morbid curiosity in crime, but satisfies, to a great extent at least, the inner feelings of a vast majority of people who long to see criminals and crooks caught and severely punished."[51] So the strip provided a graphic public ritual—like a hanging in the civic square—in which, in Michel Foucault's theoretical frame, transgressive acts were symbolically punished and the society was cleansed of nonnormals, subversives, and defective genes.[52] Interestingly, Gould's villains also tended to lose body parts along the path toward their ultimate demise. It was as if Gould was echoing eugenicists' preoccupation with the sterilization of criminals as a way of reducing the physical, virile, and cultural threats that they represented.[53]

Together with this argument that *Dick Tracy* articulated the basic outlines or emotional essence of eugenics in its 1930s images and story lines, it should be acknowledged that other influences, traditions, and ideas flowed into the construction of Gould's worldview, narrative structures, and modes of representation. Further, those influences emerged or faded as Gould and the strip adjusted to changing cultural climates. For example, if one tries to sum up Gould's worldview by looking at the whole of his career—a narrative run that lasted for four decades (from 1931 into the early 1970s)—it is possible to argue that a different ideological system, such as Old Testament conceptions of law and justice or a vaguely Freudian view of the causes of criminality, dominated the strip.

Indeed, Gould's treatment of his criminal types became more complex after 1940; in particular, he began to rely more heavily on a Freudian worldview in his construction of his rogues' story lines. Childhood dysfunction or horrific trauma often replaced ethnicity or degenerate living as the primary cause of the villain's visual stigmata. Gould also began to feature criminals who were victims of technology or modernization—a convention that became increasingly popular in superhero comics and science fiction films during the 1940s and 1950s. A vivid example of this more complexly constructed villain can be seen as early as 1937 in Gould's "The Blank"—a rogue who acquired his grotesque stigmata through an accident in which his face was maimed with a shotgun. In an effort to hide his deformed face—and by extension, in Gould's universe, the outward marker of his culpability—he creates a blank visage with a cheesecloth mask. The iconic emptiness of his image invites vivid reader participation in filling in his identity, past, and intentions; it also tempts one to imagine Gould unconsciously questioning the limitations and implications of his methods of caricaturing criminality.

So even as Gould's caricatures of his rogues became more exaggerated and grotesque, his construction of their criminality became more multicausal and even, at times, more sympathetic. As a result, his caricatures shifted in their meaning from literal representations of a criminal's exaggerated, genetic, and ethnic identity to figurative or symbolic representations of a criminal's core neurosis or modus operandi. In making his rogues more entertainingly vivid and figuratively playful, Gould ironically undermined his original intention of deglamorizing criminals. Since these secondary characters were increasingly complex in their motivations and since most of the character construction and narrative focus was devoted to the development of the dramatic arc of their rise and fall, they became cultural celebrities. In effect, Gould's criminals became, much like the caricatured figures on the marquee of the Thrill House of Crime, the true stars of the strip; they were, after all, much more vivid and sympathetic than the two-dimensional, heroic, and intimidatingly righteous Tracy. Readers who might have relished the demise of two-dimensional thugs in 1932 mourned

Fig. 11.16. Flattop, in Chester Gould's *Dick Tracy,* January 17, 1944. Copyright, Tribune Media Services, Inc. All Rights Reserved. Reprinted with permission.

the death of a vividly complex character such as Flattop in 1944 (fig. 11.16). When Flattop—who was a villainous dandy vaguely similar in appearance and behavior to the film noir characters played by Peter Lorre—died, the public outcry was tremendous. Gould's syndicate received half a dozen telegrams from people offering to claim the body; floral arrangements and stacks of sympathy cards were delivered; a wake was held in a bar in Middleton, Connecticut, complete with coffin and candles; and many personal letters were received containing expressions of people's "deep sense of personal loss," as if they had lost a family member or close friend. One soldier wrote, "Two weeks ago my girl left me and married a sailor. I just about got over that, and then Flattop died. That upset me more than losing my girl." And a West Coast woman complained, "Why did he have to die? All America loved Flattop."[54]

The readers' identification with and sympathy toward the villains Gould created attest to the power of comic strip narratives to build sympathetic and resonant characters but may also point to the fact that some readers were never comfortable with Gould's simplistic construct of the world being divided into the genetically pure and morally righteous Tracy and Tess and the flawed and degenerate villains of the early strip. Many second-generation immigrants, African Americans, and working-class readers may have read Gould's more sympathetic and complex criminal types as underdog everymen—exaggerated representations of their own outsider status. Rather than condemning these characters for their misdeeds, they may

have vaguely attributed their difficulties, as David Ruth suggested in relation to similar audiences of gangster films, to systemic problems or the
"disruptive force of urbanization, racial discrimination, [and] modernization."[55] Moreover, since many outsider audiences in the first half of the
century may have been inclined to view policemen as perpetrators of institutionalized violence and oppression rather than heroic champions of their
interests, it is understandable that notorious criminals could come to be
subversive folk heroes. Even for readers securely situated in dominant cultural positions, the grotesques in Gould's strip may have elicited simultaneous feelings of attraction and repulsion.

In sum, the strip's appeal may have initially been based on several factors: a broad cultural frustration with early 1930s gangsterism, lingering
anxieties among Anglo-Americans that immigrants from southern and
eastern Europe had introduced inferior genetics and criminal tendencies into the American cultural organism, Gould's ability to satisfy cultural
anxieties about crime through visually and narratively simplistic morality
tales, and vivid depictions of vigilante-style justice that ritualistically cleansed
the cultural system or figuratively enacted the extreme measures of negative eugenics. But by the 1940s, it seems that the appeal was the more
complex pleasures of reading open-ended, melodramatic story lines; witnessing Gould's multicausal construction of his criminal types; and reader
sympathy for—or ambivalent fascination or identification with—criminal
underdogs. As a result, the strip became the most popular cultural product in the country, "bought by 13,500,000 people and read by perhaps
twice that many" every day in 1944.[56]

Each of the examples showcased in this study highlights the difficulties in identifying popular eugenic ideology as it mingled with competing
paradigms or persisted, like a cancerous or vestigial organ, in established
narrative patterns, cultural ideals, or graphic traditions. But the fact that visual and narrative contrasts between idealized, white, classical bodies and
degenerate ethnic types or classes persist in popular culture to this day
should also highlight the need to forge ahead in attempting to excise carefully such malignant aesthetic growths from the collective cultural imagination. People may bridle if one identifies in simplistic ways these persisting
ideals and types in fashion catalogs, comic books, Barbie-themed entertainment, *Harry Potter* characters, George Lucas space fantasies, and film adaptations of *The Lord of the Rings* trilogy—they sense, rightly perhaps, that
there is error in only focusing on the regressive ideologies present in the

entertainment or imagery. But if one can highlight, much as this study has attempted to do, the way that these constructions emerge, perhaps unconsciously, from an established gallery of archetypes and how creators and audiences can resist and rework a text's most racist implications, then perhaps some of the power retained by these racist constructs can be removed. And that might open up the possibility, at least, for artists to create and viewers to receive popular art that is freed from—or at least consciously working against—the cultural legacy of eugenics.

Notes

1. Daniel J. Kevles, *In the Name of Eugenics: Genetics and the Uses of Human Heredity* (New York: Alfred A. Knopf, 1985), 114. In addition to Kevles's study, Stephen Jay Gould's *The Mismeasure of Man* (New York: W. W. Norton, 1981), is a good general history of social Darwinism, phrenology, physiognomy, and eugenics in American and European cultures.

2. Sandra S. Phillips, Mark Haworth-Booth, and Carol Squiers, eds., *Police Pictures: The Photograph as Evidence* (San Francisco: Chronicle Books, 1997), 22.

3. Robert H. Gault, *Criminology* (Boston: D. C. Heath, 1932), 363.

4. Nicole Rafter, "Criminal Anthropology in the United States," *Criminology* 30 (1992): 541.

5. David E. Ruth, *Inventing the Public Enemy: The Gangster in American Culture, 1918–1934* (Chicago: University of Chicago Press, 1996), 13.

6. Kevles, *In the Name of Eugenics*, 47, 51.

7. Homi K. Bhabha, *The Location of Culture* (New York: Routledge, 1994), 66.

8. John J. Appel and Selma Appel, *Pat-Riots to Patriots: American Irish in Caricature and Comic Art* (East Lansing: Michigan State University Museum, 1990), 12.

9. Ron Tyler, *The Image of America in Caricature and Cartoon* (Forth Worth, TX: Amon Carter Museum, 1976), 2.

10. Mikhail Bakhtin, *Rabelais and His World* (Bloomington: Indiana University Press, 1984), 25.

11. Betsy L. Nies, *Eugenic Fantasies: Racial Ideology in the Literature and Popular Culture of the 1920s* (New York: Routledge, 2002), 30.

12. Kevles, *In the Name of Eugenics*, 114. *Fortune*'s poll showed that 63 percent of Americans endorsed the compulsory sterilization of habitual criminals and that 66 percent were in favor of sterilizing mental defectives.

13. Ibid., 115.

14. Ibid., 116.

15. "Intelligence Wane Seen by Dr. Hooton," *New York Times*, February 18, 1937, 23; "'Biological Purge' Is Urged by Hooton," *New York Times*, February 21, 1937, 27.

16. "'Biological Purge,'" 27.

17. "Intelligence Wane," 23.

18. "'Biological Purge,'" 27.

19. Ernest Albert Hooton, *Crime and the Man* (Cambridge, MA: Harvard University Press, 1939), ix.

20. Gould, *The Mismeasure of Man*, 202–3.

21. Robert W. Rydell, *World of Fairs: The Century-of-Progress Expositions* (Chicago: University of Chicago Press, 1993), 49–51.

22. Eben J. Carey, *Medical Science Exhibits: A Century of Progress* (Chicago: John F. Cuneo, 1936), 36. For other exhibits with eugenic messages at the Chicago fair, see Christina Cogdell, *Eugenic Design: Streamlining America in the 1930s* (Philadelphia: University of Pennsylvania Press, 2004), 84–91.

23. "Race Preferment Declared Fallacy," *New York Times*, May 1, 1936, 16.

24. Nies, *Eugenic Fantasies*, 30.

25. Rydell, *World of Fairs*, 41.

26. Ibid., 39.

27. Edwin Black, *War against the Weak: Eugenics and America's Campaign to Create a Master Race* (New York: Four Walls, Eight Windows, 2003), 177.

28. Alexis Carrel, *Man the Unknown* (New York: Harper and Brothers, 1935), 318–19.

29. John Kasson, *Amusing the Million* (New York: HarperCollins, 1978), 23–26.

30. Herb Galewitz, ed., *Dick Tracy: The Thirties—Tommy Guns and Hard Times* (New York: Chelsea House, 1978), x.

31. Garyn G. Roberts, *Dick Tracy and American Culture: Morality and Mythology, Text and Context* (Jefferson: North Carolina Press, 1993), 5.

32. Ibid., xiv.

33. "Dick Tracy's Creator a Mild Man: Trims Hedges and Plays Violin," *Editor and Publisher* (July 7, 1934): 11.

34. Professor Byron, "Criminology Course Description," *Undergraduate Course Catalog, Northwestern University*, Northwestern University, Special Collections Library, Evanston, IL.

35. Fred E. Haynes, *Criminology* (New York: McGraw-Hill, 1930), 33.

36. Arthur L. Beely, *Social Planning for Crime Control* (Salt Lake City: University of Utah Press, 1935), 13.

37. Ruth, *Inventing the Public Enemy*, 16, 34; Hooton, *Crime and the Man*, 5.

38. Jay Maeder, *Dick Tracy: The Official Biography* (New York: Plume Books, 1990), 22.

39. Jay Maeder, "Dick Tracy: The Story behind Crimefighter Shows He's a Man of the Times," *Austin American Statesman*, June 10, 1990, E1.

40. Galewitz, *Dick Tracy*, viii.

41. Maeder, *Dick Tracy: The Official Biography*, 7.

42. Eric Pace, "Dick Tracy and Mugs: A Rogue's Gallery of Art," *New York Times*, September 17, 1982, C17.

43. Galewitz, *Dick Tracy*, x.

44. Nies, *Eugenic Fantasies*, 10, 13.

45. Perry L. Curtis Jr., *Apes and Angels: The Irishman in Victorian Caricature* (Washington, DC: Smithsonian Institution Press, 1997), 20, 95. For a history of the changing social status of the Irish in politics, society, and popular culture, see Noel Ignatiev, *How the Irish Became White* (New York: Routledge, 1995).

46. Christie Davies, *Ethnic Humor around the World: A Comparative Analysis* (Indianapolis: Indiana University Press, 1990), 82.

47. Phillips, Haworth-Booth, and Squiers, *Police Pictures*, 7, 20.

48. Nicole Rafter, *Shots in the Mirror: Crime Films and Society* (New York: Oxford University Press, 2000), 51.

49. Maeder, *Dick Tracy: The Official Biography*, 16, 22.

50. Galewitz, *Dick Tracy*, viii; "Dick Tracy's Creator a Mild Man," 11.

51. "Dick Tracy's Creator a Mild Man," 11.

52. Stephen Brauer, "An Aesthetics of Crime," *American Quarterly* 53, no. 3 (September 2001): 537.

53. Maeder, *Dick Tracy: The Official Biography*, 26.

54. John Bainbridge, "Chester Gould: The Harrowing Adventures of His Cartoon Hero, Dick Tracy, Give Vicarious Thrills to Millions," *Life Magazine*, August 14, 1944, 44.

55. Ruth, *Inventing the Public Enemy*, 2.

56. Bainbridge, "Chester Gould," 43.

TWELVE

Scientific Selection on the Silver Screen

Madcap Eugenics in *College Holiday*

Karen A. Keely

ABSTRACT

Karen Keely's essay shifts the discussion of the visual culture of eugenics away from sculpture, X-rays, industrial design, posters, and drawings to 1930s films, examining in close detail the Paramount Studios comedy *College Holiday* (1936). This film is a madcap comedy that depicts eugenics as a farcical cult with ludicrous aims and methods. In its goal of casting eugenics as comic, the film studiously attempts to avoid the subjects of race, nationality, class, and mental and physical health in a deliberately apolitical depiction of the eugenics movement. At the same time, however, the film ultimately argues for a "natural" eugenics in which beautiful, healthy, upper-class, intelligent whites are inherently drawn to each other as suitable partners, whereas lower-class whites are depicted, at times, as racially stigmatized and less suitable for marriage.

The film, starring Jack Benny, George Burns, Gracie Allen, and Martha Raye, centers on the "Eugenic Mating Headquarters" for the creation of "a Greek-like Super Race." The script includes references to Charles Atlas, to the tradition of eugenics pageantry, and to the supposed eugenic practices of ancient Greek gods. The movie had to warily skirt the subject of sex itself, since the Production Code Administration was concerned that the very subject of eugenics was dangerously risqué for a Hollywood film. Yet, as Keely's nuanced analysis makes clear, despite its attempts to poke fun at eugenics and avoid censorship from the Production Code, *College Holiday* ultimately fails to seriously challenge—and, in fact, even reifies—some of the major tenets of the contemporary eugenics movement.

Eugenics was an intrinsic part of early movie culture. Film studios and directors used their medium to argue the merits and deficits of eugenic theories and policies, ranging over the full spectrum from eugenics advocacy—as in Pathé's *The Second Generation* (1914) and the Rex film *The Power of Heredity* (1913)—to antieugenics activism, including two Thanhouser films: the drama *A Disciple of Nietzsche* (1915) and the comedy *The Eugenic Boy* (1914). Comedy, especially farcical exaggeration, became a powerful tool for antieugenics filmmakers in particular, beginning in 1904 with Thomas Edison's *The Strenuous Life, or Anti-race Suicide,* a four-minute film satirizing contemporary pushes for increased fertility among the white, educated upper classes. As historian Martin S. Pernick has pointed out, "Early filmmakers quickly discovered that attacks on eugenics had great entertainment potential. The eugenic belief that rational science should outweigh passionate love as the motive for mating made eugenics a tempting target for comedic ridicule." Early farces included *Eugenics at the Bar "U" Ranch* (Selig, 1914), *Wood B. Wedd and the Microbes* (Edison, 1914), *Eugenics versus Love* (Beauty, 1914), and *Snakeville's Eugenic Marriage* (Essanay, 1915).[1]

Even comedic treatments of eugenics, however, soon came under the growing censorship movement, as did all films that, implicitly or explicitly, dealt with sexuality. In 1918, the Pennsylvania State Board of Censors released new regulations for films that included banning all "incidents having to do with eugenics" or "race suicide," standards that were then picked up by other film regulatory boards.[2] In the face of such censorship from various state boards and religious and civic groups around the country, as well as the imminent possibility of federal oversight, Hollywood producers and studios formed the self-regulating Motion Picture Producers and Distributors Association (MPPDA) in 1922, under the leadership of Will Hays. In 1930, the MPPDA ratified the Production Code, which detailed what was and was not acceptable in films. There were significant glitches in administering the Code, but in 1934, the MPPDA established the Production Code Administration, headed by Joseph Breen, which regulated sexuality and violence in filmmaking.[3]

Under the Code, both "positive" and "negative" eugenics—referring to the proposed methods of improving the human race through breeding choices—were problematic topics for motion pictures. Proponents of positive eugenics focused their efforts on those whom they considered fit potential parents, urging white, middle-class, healthy individuals to choose their partners wisely—inquiring into ancestors who were alcoholics, criminals, and the like—and then to have many children. Positive eugenics was at its height in the 1930s due to widespread and well-publicized eugenic concerns over the falling birthrate, which dropped below the replacement level during the Great Depression, a new phenomenon in American history.[4] Because of its emphasis on promoting increased childbearing, positive eugenics was seen as inherently a sexual topic that might easily run afoul of the Code's prohibition against overt sexuality, although the Code did allow for "scenes of passion" if they upheld "the sanctity of marriage and the home" and could be shown "without arousing dangerous emotions on the part of the immature, the young or the criminal classes."[5]

Negative eugenics, by contrast, referred to limiting reproductive options of those considered "unfit"; such efforts included restricting immigration and institutionalizing or sterilizing criminals and mentally ill or developmentally disabled people, a practice that occurred with increasing frequency during the 1930s.[6] Negative eugenics was even more problematic from the Code's perspective, for it was folded into the larger category of "sex hygiene and venereal diseases," which were deemed "not subjects for motion pictures."[7] The 1934 melodrama Tomorrow's Children, for example, ran into censorship difficulties because of its treatment of negative eugenics. Producers of the film, which attacked compulsory sterilization, lost a three-year court battle against the New York State censors, who successfully argued that eugenics was a "disgusting" topic that had no place in movie theaters.[8]

In 1936, Paramount Studios and director Frank Tuttle faced censorship challenges in producing the film College Holiday, a comedy that explicitly grappled with eugenics while relying on farce to escape some censorship difficulties. Paramount and Tuttle tried to avoid the manifold troubles of Tomorrow's Children by focusing on positive eugenics and choosing the hybrid genre of the slapstick musical comedy revue for College Holiday. They studiously ignored negative eugenics and depicted eugenics extremists as a ridiculous cult, laughable in their aims and posing no threat to anyone. By carefully avoiding the difficult issues inherent in the eugenics movement, such as race, nationality, class, and physical and mental health, the film challenged only the surface trappings of extremist eugenics programs while upholding the underlying ideology of the mainstream eugenics movement. The film's criticism of involuntary and overly intrusive eugenics programs was based on the possibility that they could actually interfere with what otherwise would be a "natural" process by which the "fit" would inevitably find one another and the "unfit" would choose not to reproduce at all. Interestingly, contemporary film reviewers all mentioned the eugenics movement as the movie's "hook" for audiences but never discussed the politics of the film's treatment of this movement, apparently finding the underlying eugenic ideology commonplace enough as to be unworthy of mention.[9]

The film follows the musical genre conventions of the time by centering on a song-and-dance stage show, in this case, one designed to save a hotel, the Casa del Mar in Santa Teresa, California, that is about to be repossessed by its mortgage-holder, Carola Gaye. Gaye, played by Mary Boland, is a wealthy older woman who flits from fad to fad. When the narrative begins, she is entranced by the possibilities of the "Bodies Beauteous" movement of scientific sexual selection and has taken up with eugenicist Professor Hercules Dove. Both characters spend the movie dressed in ancient Greek garb as a statement of their devotion to purity and the classical ideal (and, of course, as an ongoing source of physical comedy for the film).

Eugenics is introduced in the film before any of the characters is ever on screen. The movie begins with a standard exposition technique as the camera provides a close-up of a newspaper headline that reads, "Carola Gaye to Produce Greek-like Super Race—Eccentric Heiress Leaves with Professor Hercules to Found Eugenic Mating Headquarters." The opening sentences of the newspaper story are also shown on screen: "'Bodies Beauteous' is the latest fad of Miss Carola Gaye, the chewing gum heiress, whose eccentricities have kept newspaper readers convulsed with laughter for lo, these many months. Carola's latest fad is eugenics—the founding of a super race through scientific eugenic selection. In an announcement today she made known her purpose of joining with Professor Hercules Dove, whose street attire consists of a glorified gunny sack, in establishing a headquarters for a cult whose aim will be . . ."[10] Eugenics was so well established by the 1930s that the film audience did not need to have the term defined beyond the tautological explanation that it was about "scientific eugenic selection." Moreover, the newspaper text fades to black just as the story scrolls down to the specific aims of the movement, thus not specifying those aims any more clearly than the vague utopian desire for a "super race." Scientific eugenic mating is portrayed from the beginning as an activity requiring a millionaire-funded headquarters and resulting in a "Greek-like super race," thus removing eugenics programs from the realm of the everyday and assuming that ordinary people who are not "eccentric" would have nothing to do with such programs of their own accord.

The Greek costumes—"glorified gunny sack[s]"—adopted by Carola and Hercules make eugenicists look like crazy quacks, a view that is strengthened when Professor Hercules Dove explains how his scientific selection works: his daughter Calliope (played by Gracie Allen), possessor of "the perfect mind in the perfect body" and a "perfect blossom in a eugenic garden," stands between a man and a woman, closes her eyes, and waits for a certain feeling that tells her that this couple is eugenically perfect.[11] If the "vibropsychic" Calliope does not receive such a feeling, she replaces one of the partners with a new candidate and tries again. This process continues until she experiences an intuitive thrill, indicating that she has found a "scientific" match (fig. 12.1). Eugenic matchmaking has been ludicrously debased from a practice based on at least pseudo-scientific principles to one in the realm of the mystic, the irrational, the inexplicable, with no pretenses to the detective work of tracking down hereditary strengths and weaknesses.

Calliope is supposedly suited to her task because she is, according to her father, "the perfect product of a perfect eugenic union."[12] Although we never see or hear of Calliope's mother, Hercules is laughable as a eugenically perfect father. Named after the Greek hero celebrated for his strength and courage, our Hercules is frail and weak; at one point, he is dragged away by four white horses that his daughter had effortlessly driven earlier. Moreover, Hercules' last name is Dove, with its peaceful and gentle associations quite the opposite of those adhering to the Greek strongman. The character is played by Etienne Girardot, a small, slight actor whose spindly and definitely dysgenic legs are constantly in view because of his short Greek robe.

Hercules has raised his daughter to believe in his eugenic principles, and he explains to Carola that "Calliope will never marry until she finds a man who measures up to Apollo's perfection." To this end, she carries around a postcard of "the Apollo Belvedere, the ideal of masculine beauty," with the statue's measurements printed on the card, so that she will rec-

Fig. 12.1. Publicity still from *College Holiday,* showing Calliope Dove (played by Gracie Allen) "vibropsychically" testing the eugenic fitness of potential couples. Courtesy of the Academy of Motion Picture Arts and Sciences and of Universal Studios Licensing LLLP.

ognize the perfect man when she meets him.[13] The Greek god Apollo and the muse Calliope were mythological lovers, and our modern Calliope may have taken her cue from her ancient counterpart. More likely, however, she has chosen, under her father's direction, to adopt a traditional and ongoing ideal of the eugenics movement. The Race Betterment booth at the 1915 Panama-Pacific Exposition in San Francisco included plaster casts of Atlas, Venus, and "Apollo, Belvedere type" in an effort "to advertise the human race at its best, and get that race interested in its glorious past and possible future."[14] Similarly, in 1929, a *Popular Science Monthly* article on eugenics and physical anthropometry featured in its leading illustration the Apollo Belvedere, "long considered the acme of physical perfection."[15] In Calliope's search for a husband, she is constantly looking for a man who meets the Apollo Belvedere's perfection; she therefore chases all men she sees and takes their measurements to compare with those on her postcard. She is so inept, however—with all of the nervous laughter and silliness with which Gracie Allen could imbue a role—that every measurement she takes, be it waist or neck or chest or wrist, is always thirty-two inches, which happens to be one of the ideal measurements.

Thirty-two inches is also the circumference of the bodybuilder Charles Atlas's waist, a measurement so famous in the 1930s that Atlas is implicitly an embodiment of the ideal for which Calliope is searching. The body of "America's Most Perfectly Developed Man" (a title Atlas won in 1922) was considered so perfect that his measurements are on file with the New York Public Library and are buried in a vault in Oglethorpe University in Georgia. Atlas worked for a while as an artist's model (his body stood in for the American ideal in almost seventy-five statues throughout the United States, including that of George Washington in New York's Washington Square); as he later boasted, "When I used to walk into a studio on Mac-Dougal Alley in Greenwich Village, they would holler 'Here comes the Greek God.'"[16] Moreover, Atlas was himself involved in a "Bodies Beauteous" movement; Carola and Hercules' movement shares the name of *Physical Culture* publisher Bernarr Macfadden's health movement. In 1921, Macfadden named Atlas the "Most Beautiful Man in America," claiming him as "the living realization of my lifelong battle for the body beautiful." Atlas himself declared, "All I want is to build a perfect race, a country of perfect human masterpieces."[17] He is therefore an appropriate choice for Carola, Hercules, and Calliope to take as their implied ideal man.

Although claiming the Apollo Belvedere/Charles Atlas as an ideal figure was thus standard for 1930s eugenic ideology, Calliope's miraculously consistent measurements undercut forced adherence to this ideal. Because, according to her measurements, all men are thirty-two inches and are therefore equally perfect, she is ultimately free to choose whomever she likes as her ideal Apollo figure. The man she finally decides on is her long-suffering companion George Hymen, played by Allen's husband and artistic collaborator, George Burns, a pairing that provides plenty of opportunities for classic Burns-Allen shtick. George Hymen may be named after the Greek god of marriage, but George Burns looks nothing like the Apollo Belvedere, and the name Hymen, feminine and virginal by implication, certainly does not fit a masculine ideal. In this respect, Calliope's "perfect" marriage falls short of her father's standards, but because Burns and Allen were already a beloved husband-and-wife comedy team in real life, movie viewers would embrace this relationship. The movie thus overtly disdains eugenics programs, preferring romance to science and claiming that ideals cannot be measured objectively but are rather in the eye of the beholder.

Hercules does not believe this platitude, however, and he is anxious to put his theories and his daughter's vibropsychic talent into practice with a systematic eugenics experiment. Carola offers for this purpose the Casa del Mar, which will be hers in a few days when the mortgage comes due; the hotel will then serve as the Eugenic Mating Headquarters. But they also need subjects for their "Bodies Beauteous" experiment, which is where destitute hotel partner J. Davis Bowster (played by Jack Benny) steps in. Bowster, who is fleeing creditors and the police because of the hotel's debt, seizes the opportunity to placate Carola while attempting to save the hotel. He suggests that he collect college students from around the country and bring them to the Casa del Mar for mating experiments. Adopting Hercules' classical emphasis, Bowster tells Carola and Hercules that he will deliver "Vassar Venuses—Wellesley Wenches—He-men from Harvard—Amherst Apollos—Georgia Junos . . . Swarthmore Sirens!" Catching his alliterative excitement, Carola asks for "Princeton Profiles" as well.[18] Bowster promises Carola and Hercules that they can use the students in their eugenics program, but he also secretly plans to employ the students in an entertainment extravaganza that will raise enough money to meet the mortgage obligation. Bowster covers his ruse by telling Carola and Hercules that the students will refuse to come if they realize that they are to be subjects in an experiment—apparently, none of them will have read the newspaper story about Carola and Hercules' "cult headquarters" that begins the film—but that they will be delighted by the opportunity to sing, dance, and act in a large hotel show.

Bowster guarantees to keep the men and women collegians from forming romantic attachments during the trip to the hotel so that they will be receptive to their scientifically determined partners once they arrive. He finds it difficult to keep the promise, however, as young adult hormones rage on the train ride west in some of the movie's funniest scenes. He tells the participants in his "Youth and Beauty Special" that this production runs by three Ns—"No Necking—Not Now—and Nuh-huh!"—but they all find ways of pairing off with members of the opposite sex anyway.[19] Once the college group arrives, they rehearse two different musicals: a stately Greek pageant, designed to show off their physical perfection and their approximation to classical ideals, which they practice whenever Hercules or

Carola is present, and a rousing, tap-dancing number that Bowster intends to present to a paying audience. The latter routine must be kept a secret from Hercules and Carola, who naturally want the hotel to fail financially so that they can use it permanently for their eugenics headquarters. The variety of song-and-dance numbers required between these two musicals was clearly intended to be one of the selling points of the film, although this approach backfired with several reviewers who found the film overly reminiscent of a vaudeville stage show; *Time*, for example, brushed off the movie as "one of those enormous, uninspired amalgamations of specialty numbers which Paramount issues periodically in the hope that sheer quantity will assure every cinemaddict of finding at least one item to his special taste."[20]

Bowster's ostensible use of "a Greek pageant . . . to illustrate [Hercules'] theory of scientific selection" draws on an established tradition of eugenics pageantry.[21] For example, on August 7, 1915, the last day of the week-long National Conference on Race Betterment—held in conjunction with the 1915 Panama-Pacific Exposition (the same exposition at which the Apollo Belvedere was held up as an ideal at the Race Betterment booth)—the five thousand conference attendees were treated to a performance of "Redemption: A Masque of Race Betterment," which allegorically portrayed the triumph of eugenics. As befits an allegorical drama, all of the characters were portrayed by actors in Greek costumes. The two hundred University of California, Berkeley, students who performed the masque depicted Mankind and Womankind neglecting their duty to overcome "disease, vice and other personal and community ills that make for race deterioration." As a result, their son, Neglected Child, became diseased and died "through their own neglect and excesses." But then Hope appeared with a new child, Fortunate, and Mankind and Womankind promised to devote themselves to this new daughter, "pledg[ing] their future to bring up a race physically perfect and mentally enlightened." As Mankind, Womankind, and Fortunate—a family newly committed to the ideals of eugenics—exited the stage, the chorus remained, "chanting of a time of peace and plenty for humankind."[22] Thus, the pageant proposed for the Casa del Mar in *College Holiday* was well within the tradition of dramatic representations of youth and beauty by American eugenicists.

In the arrangements for the Greek pageants, *College Holiday* explicitly ridicules eugenics programs while it implicitly supports eugenic ideology.

As rehearsals continue for both the ostensible and the illicit pageants, Calliope is vibropsychically matching up the male and female college students (fig. 12.1). Bowster explains to the puzzled youths, who still do not know the real reason Carola and Hercules have invited them to the hotel, that the eccentric Calliope is merely selecting dance partners for the show. Her supposedly scientific process becomes even crazier when, during the matchmaking session, an inept stagehand (played by Ben Blue) who is wiring the stage for the show accidentally shocks her in the leg repeatedly; the resulting stimulation—apparently an exaggerated version of her vibropsychic thrills—causes her to pair men and women who are uniformly unhappy with their assigned partners. Once the selection is finished, Hercules and Carola stage a moonlight promenade, designed to cement romantically the "scientific" pairings. The couples wander around the moonlit gardens as perfumed breezes waft through the air. It turns out, however, that the entire setting is a fake; the stagehand is spritzing perfume in front of a fan, and when Carola demands more moonlight, he lights up a second moon in the artificial sky. Moreover, all of the unhappy couples have realigned themselves according to their own wishes, so that none of the pairs now clinging together amorously is "scientific" at all. As one character comments to Hercules, all of his "eggs look pretty scrambled" in this "love incubator."[23] Of course, by blaming Calliope's bizarre pairings on the electric shocks she receives, the movie implies that there might be something to the notion of eugenic pairings when the process is not interfered with by stray electricity. This is one of many telling moments in which the film mocks the extremism or inaccuracy of involuntary and overly intrusive eugenics practices but also upholds the eugenic theories underlying these practices.

The eugenics experiment comes to a crashing halt when Carola and Hercules realize that everyone has switched partners during the moonlight promenade. Outraged, Hercules cries, "Our experiment is ruined! These guinea pigs have revolted!" to which one student replies, "Hey, who's a guinea pig!" Carola then lets the cat out of the bag, screaming, "You might just as well know you were all brought here for an experiment in eugenic selection."[24] Her pronouncement naturally leads to confusion and anger among the youths, who are furious that they have been manipulated. Hercules tells them all to pack their things and go home, which means that there will be no tap-dancing show to bring in revenue and pay off the mortgage and that Carola will own the hotel outright the next week. But the college students talk among themselves and decide to support the hotel owners, especially since one of the owners has a daughter who is a college student like themselves; they plan to stage their own show, the "Inter-Collegiate Minstrel Show," to earn money to pay the mortgage and thus keep Carola from seizing the hotel. It is not clear why they change show ideas, since they have only a few days to prepare and have already rehearsed their tap-dancing Greeks routine. It may well be that their rejection of extremist eugenics manipulation leads them to reject all things ancient and Greek or at least the uses to which these attributes have been put. Although the students do not explicitly say so, moreover, their move from notions of classical purity and idealism to the deliberately degraded appearance (via blackface) of minstrelsy is an additional slap in the face to the goals of Hercules' "Bodies Beauteous" movement and his "Youth and Beauty" special.

Carola and Hercules learn of the students' plans for a minstrel show and get a court injunction to stop the performance (on what legal grounds is never clear) and therefore to keep the hotel for themselves. The college entertainers respond by kidnapping the two eugenicists and the policemen who have accompanied them and locking them up for the duration of the show in the hotel's meat freezer (providing a fur coat for Carola, the only woman in the crowd, so that she will not get cold); also locked into the freezer is an Indian Hindu mystic who has come to the hotel in search of Carola's financial sponsorship. The college show goes on to an appreciative audience, raising enough money for the mortgage, and by the time the chilled group has escaped their temporary prison, Carola has thrown over eugenics for the new fad of astral bodies, thanks to her Indian cell-mate. As Bowster humorously assures the movie audience in the final moments of the film (looking directly at the camera and addressing the viewer), the happy ending is complete: "I hope you've noticed our attempt in this picture to maintain the spirit of Classic Greek tragedy throughout. Whenever the story interfered with art, we did not compromise—we gave up both! So boy got girl—girl got hotel—and I got nothing!"[25] Bowster indeed remains romantically unattached at the end of the movie, but he is also out of debt and no longer on the lam, so only Hercules Dove is left unhappy and unfinanced, an ending that the viewer willingly embraces.

The embrace of the MPPDA, however, was not as immediately forthcoming. Although the emphasis on positive rather than negative eugenics and the film's comedic tone helped it avoid some of the censorship difficulties of *Tomorrow's Children,* it still ran into problems because of the implied threat of overt sexuality, a dangerous threat indeed in 1936 Hollywood. When John Hammell of Paramount Studios first submitted the unfinished script of *College Holiday* to Joseph Breen of the Production Code Administration in September of that year, the Code had been effectively in place for less than two years and was being very strictly enforced. Breen warned Hammell, "The material so far submitted contains an element which we believe to be very dangerous from the standpoint of the Production Code. I refer to the frequent references to 'Eugenic mating.' Any attempt at comedy elaboration or wisecracks on such a subject would, we believe, constitute a violation of the Production Code, and its inclusion in your picture would make it unacceptable under the provisions thereof."[26] Dialogue that Breen specifically condemned included: "When you vibrate then you must mate," "And physique meets physique," "Scientific mating will save the world," and references to "perfect mating" and "great physical development"—dialogue that makes explicit eugenicists' concerns with sexual activity.[27] Over the next couple of months, Hammell continued to submit revisions of the script and to be warned by Breen that care had to be exercised in certain scenes (particularly episodes in which the college men and women were embracing) and in certain references to "mating."[28]

Also of concern for Breen was Calliope's sexuality. He immediately insisted that her character's original name, Aphrodisia, be dropped, and he noted as particularly worrisome the scene in which her body received shocks from the stagehand's wiring, giving her the "vibrations" by which she matched up prospective lovers erroneously. Breen said no more than "Care will be needed with this scene of the electric wires coming in contact with Calliope's leg" and did not explain the specific nature of the problem.[29] Calliope's thigh was entirely covered by her Greek garb, so nudity was not the issue; rather, Breen was no doubt concerned with the implied sexuality of a woman's feeling vibrations in her upper thigh, particularly since such electrical thrills would have a specific referent for viewers. The electromechanical vibrator for female genital massage had been invented in the 1880s as a medical treatment for "hysteria," and vibrators for "self-treatment" at home were available for consumer purchase after 1899. Vibrators were widely advertised with the rhetoric of medical rejuvenation to refer obliquely and decorously to orgasm.[30] By about 1930, however, vibrator

advertisements had disappeared from respectable magazines; historian
Rachel P. Maines speculated that this phenomenon was due to "the growing understanding by both men and women of female sexual function,
making it difficult to disguise the use of vibrators by either physicians or
consumers as a mere therapeutic measure."[31] This newly clarified sexual
context for electrical vibration meant that Calliope's exaggerated and delighted responses to her electrical vibropsychic thrills were certainly read
as sexual excitement and thus came under Breen's censure. It is difficult
to judge from the film's original and final scripts how much "care" was
taken in the staging of the scene, but certainly, the idea of vibrations that
inspired matchmaking, one of the fundamental humorous notions of the
movie, was inherently sexual, no matter what staging changes were made.
In the original script, Calliope is thrown into George's arms by the electric
shock and squeals, "Oh, George, it never felt like that before. Let's do it
again," but these lines were cut in the final script.[32] Even in the final version of the movie, however, each time that Calliope feels a shock, the sheer
electricity of it propels her out of her seat (that is, the stage throne that is
being wired) and into the arms of George, whom she has not, at that point,
chosen as her ideal Apollo. The fact that the audience watches Gracie Allen
being thrown into the arms of her real-life husband, George Burns, miti-
gates the licentious thrill; this fact may have helped the scene eventually
pass muster with Breen.

Despite Breen's continued supervision and critiques of the manuscript,
he wrote to Will Hays, head of the MPPDA, about the movie as early as
September 30, 1936, commenting, "The first script submitted presented
some difficulties, in that the subject dealt in a farcical manner with eugenic marriage, but as a result of a number of script changes, we believe
the finished picture will be acceptable."[33] Breen explicitly noted that the
subject of the film was "eugenic marriage"—that is, positive eugenics—
which was clearly an issue of automatic concern because of sexuality but
which at least potentially fell within the realm of the Production Code's
emphasis on "the sanctity of the institution of marriage."[34] The film may
also have more easily been approved because its title, which did not even
hint at eugenics, positioned it clearly in the roster of madcap campus
comedies for which Paramount Studios became well known in the 1930s:
College Humor (1933), *She Loves Me Not* (1934), *College Swing* (1938), *Campus
Confessions* (1938), *Million Dollar Legs* (1939), and *$1,000 Dollars a Touchdown*

(1939), among others.[35] The film was not set on a campus, of course, and the role of the college students as subjects of eugenics experimentation would seem to work against its classification as a campus comedy romp, but both the title and the eventual marketing of the film highlighted the singing and dancing college students rather than the story itself. The final version of the movie was granted "the Production Code Certificate of Approval" on November 21, 1936.[36]

Even before the mandated cuts of explicit sexuality were made in the original script, the eugenic ideology presented in the film was intentionally mild, focusing on positive rather than negative eugenics, although both were in full swing during the 1930s. The film's emphasis on positive eugenics ignored the reality of involuntary sterilization, which was of particular importance in California, the explicit setting for *College Holiday*. After Indiana became the first state to sterilize the mentally disabled in 1907, California followed suit, passing its first sterilization statute two years later. California quickly took and retained the national lead in numbers of sterilizations, and by 1926, that number had grown so large that E. S. Gosney, founder of the Human Betterment Foundation in Pasadena, California, decided to launch a formal study of the state's sterilization program.[37] According to the journal *Eugenics,* which hailed Gosney as a "philanthropist," "the problem of eugenic sterilization had been well worked out in theory; but a score of states which had adopted sterilization laws in moments of enthusiasm, and foreign countries which had only talked of adopting them, were waiting for some one else to try it first. California, which had been practicing it systematically since 1909, had the only body of real evidence in the world to offer to students on the subject."[38]

Gosney hired his Pasadena neighbor Paul Popenoe, the former editor of the *Journal of Heredity* and a leading author on eugenics, to supervise the study, and the two men collaborated in reporting their findings in a 1929 book entitled *Sterilization for Human Betterment: A Summary of Results of 6,000 Operations in California, 1909–1929.* This number of sterilizations was so large as to be unbelievable, and the coauthors were eventually forced to bring in Robert L. Dickinson of New York, secretary of the Committee on Maternal Health, to verify their results because, according to Popenoe, eastern surgeons refused to believe their report, imagining it to be "another of those California stories."[39] The numbers were real, however, and one of the "foreign countries" that *Eugenics* noted as watching the

California results with interest was Germany. When Nazi Germany enacted its own sterilization law in 1933, German eugenicists declared that
they owed a great deal to their American counterparts, singling out Gosney and Popenoe's report on the California program (translated into German in 1930) for special mention.[40]

Given the widely publicized history of eugenic sterilization in California, a "Bodies Beauteous" headquarters designed to create a "Greek-like
Super Race" might well have raised alarm for some *College Holiday* viewers concerned about the well-being of the college student "guinea pigs."
The film eliminates that possibility, however, by telling the audience from
the beginning (via the newspaper story that opens the film) that they
should be "convulsed with laughter" by Carola's antics.[41] Only the involuntary aspects of Hercules' program, plus the inevitable connection in the
1930s between California and sterilization, might have raised audience
anxieties about the fate of the students if not for the film's comedic reas-
surance and the fact that the student subjects could walk out of the experiment once they discovered its eugenic nature. Rather than reflecting the
reality of eugenics in California, therefore, this comedic treatment actually
deflects from that reality, perhaps indirectly aiding the eugenics project in
California by minimizing its impact.

Indeed, the film consistently ignores most of the vexed issues that surrounded contemporary discussions of eugenics, remaining ostensibly apolitical. The students who congregate at the hotel are already deemed fit by
eugenics standards—the perfect candidates for positive eugenics encouragement—so that there need be no question of screening the applicants
before they are "scientifically" matched. All of the students who arrive for
the summer are white, apparently native-born, intelligent enough to be in
college, and healthy enough to be dancers. Most of the colleges mentioned
are exclusive private schools dominated by upper- or middle-class Anglo-
Saxon Protestants—schools that actually did contribute many student volunteers and researchers to the eugenics movement—so the poorer classes
of potentially "hybrid" ethnic backgrounds did not have the opportunity to
enter this particular mating game.[42]

None of the eugenics movement's assumptions about race, nationality,
mental and physical health, and class is ever made explicit in the movie,
although they are markedly there by implication. This absence helps keep
the movie a light comedy rather than a serious political drama, and it also

enables the film to maintain that eugenics extremism is ridiculous but merely a harmless fad—"curious, cultish whims" (in the words of the *New York Times* review)—whose greatest explicit evil is that a fine hotel run by nice people may be closed.[43] Hercules' eugenics is referred to consistently as a "cult" in the reviews of the film and in Paramount's internal documents—the studio's "prepared reviews" sent to newspapers included phrases such as "crack-pot cultists," and reviewers frequently adopted this language—but the language implied no danger, cueing the viewers to laugh at rather than fear extremist advocates of eugenics.[44] However, the film maintains this stance only by actually conceding the major arguments of eugenic ideology. That is, eugenicists such as Hercules look foolish because they are trying to force what already happens "naturally": good-looking, intelligent, healthy, white, middle-class people inevitably fall in love with one another, and those who do not fit this definition, to the extent that they even seem to exist, are essentially neutered. For a movie that explicitly satirizes eugenics institutions and practices, *College Holiday* upholds eugenic ideology to a significant degree.

Such mixed treatment of eugenics renders the Inter-Collegiate Minstrel Show all the more fascinating (fig. 12.2). *College Holiday* attempts so strenuously to be apolitical that the minstrel scenes at the end of the movie are the first explicit mention of race in the film. There are no nonwhite characters other than black porters and messengers until the final stage show, at which point the collegiate cast produces not only the stereotyped portrayals of blacks requisite in a minstrel show but also a short skit in which Chinese characters (that is, white students made up and costumed to appear Chinese) are presented as humorous by virtue merely of their appearance. In a certain way, of course, the hotel is saved by the Indian "swami" who is introduced near the end of the film and changed Carola's allegiance from eugenics to astral bodies, but he, too, is considered humorous in appearance—Calliope makes fun of his headcloth—as well as slightly threatening in a vague, "oriental" way. There is a decided social ugliness about college students' appearing in blackface while sporting college letter sweaters; in the 1930s, many colleges' doors remained virtually closed to African Americans, and there is certainly no mention by Bowster, Hercules, or Carola of recruiting their "guinea pigs" from historically black colleges. Indeed, although race never arises in their discussion of recruiting the college students, the assumption is clearly that they will all be white.

Fig. 12.2. Publicity still from *College Holiday,* showing Daisy Schloggenheimer (played by Martha Raye) in blackface in the Inter-Collegiate Minstrel Show. Courtesy of the Academy of Motion Picture Arts and Sciences and of Universal Studios Licensing LLLP.

However, the film's fascinating treatment of one character in particular denounces formal eugenics programs and their racial assumptions as inherently flawed even as it maintains the accuracy of eugenic ideology. The star of the minstrel show is Martha Raye's character, Daisy Schloggenheimer from Cornucopia College in Corn City, who is one of the "guinea pigs" but is alone among the college entertainers in being emphatically depicted as rural poor; her clothes, her accent, and the appearance and conduct of her mother all give her away. Her last name is "foreign"—possibly German Jewish—although her ethnicity is never made explicit. She is also the only female character who is not beautiful by Hollywood standards of the day and who is not interested in romantic attachments; on the train ride west, as the other collegians are wildly flirting, she cuffs any young men she thinks may take a shine to her. Class carries eugenic implications in the 1930s, given prevailing concerns that middle-class, college-educated couples, presumably most "fit" to be the parents of a new generation, had fewer children than did poorer couples; as a *Los Angeles Times* columnist noted in 1936, "In poverty the breeding is prolific."[45] Daisy is attending college, but the fact that she is poor, not purely Anglo-American, and below the status of the rest of the cast is a combination of factors that, according to mainline conservative eugenic ideology, would make her less desirable for motherhood. And yet Hercules and Carola have apparently included her in Calliope's vibropsychic selection, for she appears in the moonlight promenade that is supposed to be cementing the "scientific" relationships. This intrusive eugenics program, therefore, would have forced her into a sexual relationship with one of the male college students. Hercules and Carola's inclusion of Daisy in their "Bodies Beauteous" movement, designed to promote childbearing, thus undermines the ideals of eugenic selection, since one of their "guinea pigs" is clearly less suitable by strict eugenic standards. Despite Hercules' and Carola's efforts, we never see Daisy in a romantic situation, and her assigned partner is never identified. Instead, the movie matches her up with actor Ben Blue's inept stagehand, who is not even given a name and is the only other working-class character in the movie. The film thus upholds class division by assuming that social and economic status is a significant determiner of romantic attraction. Moreover, left to her own devices and not forced into a eugenics program, Daisy is essentially asexual, which is reassuring to those viewers who feared working-class or foreign sexuality; her courtship with the stagehand, such as it is, is carried out through the childlike mechanism of mocking, pinching, and hitting each other rather than kissing and hugging as the other couples do. Since the two characters never do have a moment on camera in which their fighting

transforms into erotic tension, the viewer is not presented with the certainty that these two will actually embark on a romance. Therefore, the
film minimizes the possibility of Daisy's potentially dysgenic progeny, and
so, her role in the film remains as comic relief and proof of the success of
"natural" eugenic selection rather than as the specter of out-of-control
breeding, which ironically is associated in the film with eugenics programs.
Daisy is metaphorically sterilized, in keeping with the California tradition,
but this comes about as an apparently inevitable result of "natural" characteristics and attraction rather than at the hands of eugenicists. *College Holiday* thus once again maintains the validity of eugenic ideology as personal
choice while criticizing the harmful interventions of extremist eugenics
programs.

This argument is pushed even further in Raye's minstrel act, such an
unusual scene that it must be read as an attack on notions of racial purity
(fig. 12.2). As Daisy Schloggenheimer—already not "pure white," at least
as implied by her name—sings "Who's That Knocking at My Heart?" her
skin color changes from black to white and back to black as the stagehand
changes the filter on the light he has aimed at her. The entire number is a
romantic song about being willing to take a chance on love, and the scene
begins with Cupid, played by an African American child (actually black,
rather than made up to look so), shooting one of his arrows at Raye. Since
there is no suggestion that the person "knocking at [her] heart" changes
race between verses as she seems to do, the possibility of miscegenation is
strongly implied, although not explicitly enough to flout the Production
Code's prohibition that "[m]iscegenation (sex relationships between the white
and black races) is forbidden."[46] Daisy's apparent racial changes during
her musical number are further emphasized by the fact that *College Holiday*'s minstrelsy is missing a component that political scientist Michael
Rogin sees as "a primal scene in every blackface musical: it shows the per-
former blacking up."[47] Daisy simply appears on stage in blackface, and
since the Inter-Collegiate Minstrel Show is the end of the film, the viewer
never again sees Daisy without her burned-cork makeup. Therefore, her
racial changeability brought about by the spotlight filter is the movie's final
word on the character of Daisy.

The interracial love implied by the staging of the song is not portrayed
as shocking or even titillating. The blackface scene is clearly intended to be
humorous without being racially offensive to its original audience, and

Raye's changing skin tone takes on the excitement of a technologically impressive special effect rather than a social or political statement. The *Variety* review credited "Martha Raye's coon-shouting" in "the lavish minstrel
show finish" as one of "the saving graces" of the movie, and none of the
reviews indicated any anxiety about the racial politics of the film.[48] Nevertheless, Daisy's performance, coupled with her inclusion in the "Bodies
Beauteous" movement, insists on the impossibility of defining strict racial
boundaries and criticizing eugenics programs for their ineffectiveness at
policing these ambiguous boundaries. Although Daisy's racial impurities
are not made manifest until the minstrel show at the end of the film, the fact
that she was rural, poor, and named Schloggenheimer should have already
made her an unsuitable romantic partner for any of the good-looking,
young male college students at the hotel, thus making clear how invalid
the movement's assumptions were. Once the minstrel show makes clear
just how racially impure Daisy actually is, however, the film's emphasis on
her apparent asexuality also has the effect of rendering her blackface character essentially infertile. The "natural" eugenics that comes from leaving
young people to their own devices thus keeps "unfit" characters such as
Daisy from reproducing, whereas the "Bodies Beauteous" movement would
have led to the racially ambiguous progeny that such programs are designed to prevent.

The minstrel show, one of the final scenes of the film, characterizes the
dual nature of the entire movie. *College Hòliday* explicitly ridicules eugenics programs, punishing eugenics advocate Hercules and rewarding those
who have battled against him. It simultaneously and implicitly upholds eugenic ideology, keeping the "unfit"—such as Daisy Schloggenheimer—
from reproducing while pairing up "fit" young men and women—that is,
the other collegians, all of whom find romantic partners on their own,
without benefit of Calliope's vibropsychic help. In an era in which negative
eugenics was categorized with venereal disease as "not subjects for motion
pictures" and film censors worried that the very topic of positive eugenics
was too inherently sexual for this popular medium, Paramount and director Tuttle tackled a vexed subject with what the *New York Times* called a
"good-humored informality which protects the piece against too biting a
review." Although the *Times* reviewer's comment was specifically about
the film's artistic and entertainment merit, the criticism also aptly characterizes the film's goal in its handling of eugenics. *College Holiday* strives to

remain an apolitical musical college romp that simply happens to use eugenics as its audience hook, but both its complicity through silence with negative eugenics programs and its assumption of a "natural" positive eugenics undercut its surface critique of excessive eugenics programs by accepting a fundamental eugenic ideology. The *Times* reviewer continued, "Being trivial, unpretentious and nonsensical on its own admission, the picture demands nothing of the beholder," and indeed, this refusal to demand anything of the viewer—outrage, concern, political action—is central to *College Holiday*'s overt critique but implicit collusion with the eugenics movement of the United States in the 1930s.[49]

Notes

1. Martin S. Pernick, *The Black Stork: Eugenics and the Death of "Defective" Babies in American Medicine and Motion Pictures since 1915* (New York: Oxford University Press, 1996), 130–33; quotation on 130. See 117–41 for a complete discussion of the history of eugenics films, including Pernick's extensive and useful catalog of these movies, many of which no longer exist in complete copies.

2. Ibid., 123–24.

3. For more detailed discussion of the MPPDA and the Production Code, see Stephen Vaughn, "Morality and Entertainment: The Origins of the Motion Picture Production Code," *Journal of American History* 77, no. 1 (June 1990): 39–65.

4. Wendy Kline, *Building a Better Race: Gender, Sexuality, and Eugenics from the Turn of the Century to the Baby Boom* (Berkeley: University of California Press, 2001), 96–97.

5. Motion Picture Production Code [1930], appendix in Leonard J. Leff and Jerold L. Simmons, *The Dame in the Kimono: Hollywood, Censorship, and the Production Code from the 1920s to the 1960s* (New York: Grove Weidenfeld, 1990), 291.

6. Kline, *Building a Better Race*, 100.

7. Motion Picture Production Code, 285; Pernick, *The Black Stork*, 124. The MPPDA's authority extended only to Hollywood films shown in theaters; "non-theatrical" films about eugenics included the 1934 Nazi Party film *Erbkrank* (Hereditary disease), which eugenicist Harry Laughlin imported to the United States and advertised to over three thousand high school biology teachers in 1936; see Pernick, *The Black Stork*, 124, 138, 164–65.

8. Pernick, *The Black Stork*, 124.

9. See, for example, Frank S. Nugent, "College Holiday" [review], *New York Times*, December 24, 1936, 21, reprinted in *The New York Times Film Reviews*, vol. 2 (New York: New

York Times and Arno Press, 1970), 1348; "College Holiday" [review], *Variety,* December 30, 1936, reprinted in *Variety Film Reviews, 1907–1980,* vol. 5 (New York: Garland, 1983), n.p.; "College Holiday" [review], *Time,* January 4, 1937, 22; and collected reviews in the *College Holiday* press book, Paramount Collection, Special Collections, Margaret Herrick Library, American Academy of Motion Picture Arts and Sciences, Beverly Hills, CA.

10. *College Holiday,* Reel 1:9. Quotations from the movie are taken from the final script of December 17, 1936, in the Paramount Collection. The film itself has never been re-released; the copy I watched is held in the Film and Television Archives of the University of California, Los Angeles. Universal Studios now owns the rights to the film.

11. *College Holiday,* Reel 2:5; Reel 4:2.

12. Ibid., Reel 2:5.

13. Ibid.

14. Frank Morton Todd, *The Story of the Exposition,* vol. 4 (New York: G. P. Putnam's Sons, 1921), 38. Martha Banta discusses the Apollo Belvedere as the ideal racial type in nineteenth-century social and scientific thought in *Imaging American Women* (New York: Columbia University Press, 1987), 104–7.

15. Arthur A. Stuart, "Someday We'll Look Like This," *Popular Science Monthly* 115, no. 1 (July 1929): 47. My thanks to Christina Cogdell for bringing this illustration to my attention.

16. Charles Gaines and George Butler, *Yours in Perfect Manhood, Charles Atlas* (New York: Simon and Schuster, 1982), 12, 49. See also John D. Fair, "Atlas, Charles," in *American National Biography,* ed. John A. Garraty and Mark C. Carnes, vol. 1 (New York: Oxford University Press, 1999), 719–20; "Muscle Makers," *Time* 29, no. 8 (February 22, 1937): 75.

17. Gaines and Butler, *Yours in Perfect Manhood,* 59, 65.

18. *College Holiday,* Reel 2:8.

19. Ibid., Reel 2:13.

20. "College Holiday" [review], *Time,* 22.

21. *College Holiday,* Reel 5:1.

22. Calvin Brown, *Official Proceedings of the Second National Conference on Race Betterment* (Battle Creek, MI: Race Betterment Foundation, [1916]), 143, quoted in Kline, *Building a Better Race,* 17. See also "Morality Masque Pictur[e]s the Triumph of Eugenics," *San Francisco Examiner,* August 8, 1915, 59.

23. *College Holiday,* Reel 6:8.

24. Ibid., Reel 7:5.

25. Ibid., Reel 9:8. This ending is consistent with Jack Benny's character's regular bad luck in the romantic arena in his radio show (which ran from 1932 to 1946, overlapping

his work on *College Holiday*), earning him the nickname "America's boy friend who can't get a date." See Margaret T. McFadden, "'America's Boy Friend Who Can't Get a Date': Gender, Race, and the Cultural Work of the Jack Benny Program, 1932–1946," *Journal of American History* 80, no. 1 (June 1993): 127–28.

26. Letter from Joseph Breen to John Hammell, September 9, 1936, in *College Holiday* File, Paramount Collection.

27. Ibid.

28. Letters from Breen to Hammell, September 14, September 16, and September 21, 1936, *College Holiday* File; September 10, 1936, memorandum of meeting among Hammell, producer Harlan Thompson, and others, *College Holiday* File, Paramount Collection.

29. September 1936 memorandum of meeting among Hammell, Thompson, and others, *College Holiday* File; letter from Breen to Hammell, October 2, 1936, *College Holiday* File, Paramount Collection.

30. Rachel P. Maines, *The Technology of Orgasm: "Hysteria," the Vibrator, and Women's Sexual Satisfaction* (Baltimore, MD: Johns Hopkins University Press, 1999), 11, 100, 107–8. For example, a 1916 advertisement for the White Cross Vibrator promised, "Every nerve, every fibre of your whole body will tingle with force of your own awakened powers. All the keen relish, the pleasures of youth, will throb within you. Rich, red blood will be sent coursing through your veins and you will realize thoroughly the joy of living." See *American Magazine* 75, no. 7 (1913): 127, quoted in Maines, *Technology of Orgasm*, 108.

31. Maines, *Technology of Orgasm*, 108–9.

32. *College Holiday* original script, G-16, *College Holiday* File, Paramount Collection.

33. Letter from Joseph Breen to Will Hays, September 30, 1936, *College Holiday* File, Paramount Collection.

34. Motion Picture Production Code, 291.

35. Bernard F. Dick, *Engulfed: The Death of Paramount Pictures and the Birth of Corporate Hollywood* (Lexington: University Press of Kentucky, 2001), 24.

36. Letter from Breen to Hammell, November 21, 1936, *College Holiday* File, Paramount Collection.

37. The California law was repealed in 1913 but amended and reinstated in 1917. California Statutes 1909, chap. 270; California Statutes 1913, chap. 363; California Statutes 1917, chap. 489; E.S. Gosney and Paul Popenoe, *Sterilization for Human Betterment: A Summary of Results of 6,000 Operations in California, 1909–1929* (New York: Macmillan, 1929), 159–60.

38. "The Human Betterment Foundation," *Eugenics* 2, no. 3 (March 1929): 17, 19.

39. Ibid.

40. Daniel Kevles, *In the Name of Eugenics: Genetics and the Uses of Human Heredity*, rev. ed. (Cambridge, MA: Harvard University Press, 1995), 118; Stefan Kühl, *The Nazi Connection: Eugenics, American Racism, and German National Socialism* (New York: Oxford University Press, 1994), 42–44. Moreover, in 1934, the Nazi eugenics exhibit, Eugenics in New Germany, opened in California and was on display for several months in Pasadena, Los Angeles, and Stockton; see Robert Rydell, Christina Cogdell, and Mark Largent, "The Nazi Eugenics Exhibit in the United States, 1934–43," in this collection.

41. *College Holiday*, Reel 1:9.

42. On university and college researchers and volunteers in eugenics programs, see, for example, Diane B. Paul, *Controlling Human Heredity: 1865 to the Present* (Atlantic Highlands, NJ: Humanities Press, 1995), 54–55.

43. Nugent, "College Holiday" [review], 1348.

44. *College Holiday* press book, 6.

45. Fred Hogue, "Social Eugenics," *Los Angeles Times Sunday Magazine,* November 29, 1936, 31, quoted in Kline, *Building a Better Race,* 97.

46. Motion Picture Production Code, 285.

47. Michael Rogin, *Blackface, White Noise: Jewish Immigrants in the Hollywood Melting Pot* (Berkeley: University of California Press, 1996), 182. See 29–30 for Rogin's succinct summary of leading theories of the meaning of blackface.

48. "College Holiday" [review], *Variety,* n.p.

49. Nugent, "College Holiday" [review], 21.

THIRTEEN

Monsters in the Bed

The Horror-Film Eugenics of
Dracula and *Frankenstein*

Angela Marie Smith

ABSTRACT

Angela Smith's discussion of the ways in which eugenic narrative structures and tropes gained a new and powerful visual form in the immensely
popular horror films of the 1930s offers a dark counterpart to Keely's
analysis of comedies of the decade. Smith's essay draws on the eugenic
publications of Charles Davenport, Madison Grant, and Henry Fairchild,
among others still influential in the 1930s, as well as on discussions of eugenic matters in American newspapers, to trace narrative and aesthetic
practices shared by eugenic texts and horror films. Her essay identifies in
Dracula and *Frankenstein* (both 1931) three particular eugenic elements.
First, the "reproduction narrative" plays out the eugenic obsession
with the threat of various monsters to the sanctity of the ideal reproductive white couple. Second, the "inheritance narrative" both asserts
the rise of professional middle classes against a decaying and inbred
aristocracy and expresses fears that modern life enervates and renders
impotent the "desirable" classes, opening the floodgates for the degenerate progeny of the fertile masses. Third—and adding to Soper's analysis of criminal stigmata—is the visual code of "character," an aesthetic
politics closely related to eugenic rhetorical strategies in which physical deviance testifies to aberrant procreation, degenerate systems of inheritance, and inner immorality. Even as classic horrors exploited
these eugenic precepts to sensationalistic effect, however, they revealed
contradictions in and offered a popular critique of eugenic logic.
For example, Smith shows that *Dracula* both puts in play a eugenic
narrative of the defective immigrant and then undermines it with meta-

phors of blood and contagion that contradict eugenic science. In *Frank-enstein*, eugenic ideas about genetic predestination to criminality and immorality are introduced, but they are undercut with critiques of parental neglect and uncharitability. In this way, while confirming some eugenic concepts, these films also complicate simplistic hereditarian eugenic views through the inclusion of strong environmental factors. Inevitably, however, their critique of eugenics is most powerfully conveyed in rendering eugenic scientific representatives monstrous, as in the enervation of Frankenstein. This reliance on a eugenic physiognomic code, even used in critique of eugenics, became entrenched in the horror-film formula and indicates classic horror's facilitation of the endurance of eugenics in the American popular imagination.

In their exploration of physical deviance and its relation to criminality and immorality, nineteenth-century Gothic novels such as Mary Shelley's *Frankenstein* (1816), Robert Louis Stevenson's *Strange Case of Dr. Jekyll and Mr. Hyde* (1886), and Bram Stoker's *Dracula* (1897) often drew overtly on contemporaneous scientific theories about reproduction and physiognomy.[1] As the sciences and pseudo-sciences of the nineteenth century became the eugenics of the twentieth, Gothic fictions were refigured in cinematic form. In particular, the early 1930s classic horror films of Hollywood, such as *Dracula* and *Frankenstein* (both 1931), adapted Gothic conventions to the eugenic thought so familiar to their American audience. In these films, themes of reproduction, inheritance, and physical revelation of inner character traits illuminate the eugenic impulse that shaped the horror-film genre in its early days, demonstrating the persistence in popular culture of eugenic imagery and assumptions.[2] Simultaneously, the films' nuanced presentation of these themes also discredits "mainline," biologically deterministic eugenics. In this way, the films reflect the movement of many 1930s eugenicists toward a more moderate eugenics attuned to environmental influence. They also, however, suggest a more general distrust of all expert efforts to "improve" the population through alterations of reproductive behavior, indicating the conflicted and contradictory ways in which eugenic thought entered into American popular culture.

Eugenic Narratives: Reproduction, Inheritance, Character

The concerns about the degeneration of certain classes and races expressed in nineteenth-century anthropology, criminology, and social Darwinist discourses were channeled into eugenic form by the late-nineteenth-century work of Sir Francis Galton and given scientific validation by the twentieth-century adoption of Gregor Mendel's theories about the role of dominant and recessive factors in heredity. In the United States, these concepts shaped the so-called mainline eugenics that predominated until the 1930s, which moved away from the belief of scientist Jean-Baptiste Lamarck that environment could influence hereditary traits, arguing instead that physical, psychological, and behavioral traits were determined by biology alone.[3] Through a variety of institutions, organizations, legislation, publications, and lectures, eugenicists sought to convince the "fit"—middle-class, white, physically and mentally healthy Americans—to reproduce in greater numbers, while proposing immigration restrictions, institutionalization, and sterilization to reduce the numbers of the "unfit"—racial and ethnic minorities, immigrants, the physically or mentally disabled, and the poor.[4]

Early 1930s American horror films adapt the themes of Gothic literature through certain consistent uses of the eugenic rhetoric permeating early-twentieth-century American culture. Three themes in particular illustrate the commonalities of the classic horror film and American eugenics: reproduction, inheritance, and the bodily encoding of character traits. First, horror films draw on the Gothic genre's concern with obstacles to heterosexual romance and marriage in foregrounding dramas of reproduction. But in so doing, the films dramatize a particularly eugenic obsession with the threat of various monsters to the sanctity of the family unit, usually represented by a young, white, heterosexual couple on the verge of marriage and consummation. As David J. Skal comments, the monsters in films from 1931 "all revolved around fantasies of 'alternative' forms of reproduction."[5] *Dracula* and *Frankenstein* model apparently eugenic warnings against tampering with normative and "healthy" reproductive practices.

Second and relatedly, horror films exhibit an interest in themes of inheritance. As Fred Botting states, Gothic literature often focused on the legitimate bestowal of power, social standing, and wealth and on fears over the corruption of normative processes of inheritance: "By nefarious means Gothic villains usurp rightful heirs, rob reputable families of property and reputation while threatening the honour of their wives and orphaned daughters." Gothic plots indicate a simultaneous fascination with "past forms of power," such as "the aristocratic legacy of feudalism," and an effort to bolster bourgeois values and family structures over traditional social structures and against fears of "complete social disintegration" and political revolution.[6] Similarly, classic Hollywood horror films, with their British actors (and in the case of *Frankenstein,* a British director) and British or western European settings, represent European aristocracy and feudalism as sterile or decaying systems of inheritance. Filtering their narratives through the lens of eugenic injunctions against inbreeding and mimicking eugenic conflation of social and biological heredity, the two films disavow the bloodsucking aristocracy of Count Dracula and question the capacity of the House of Frankenstein to produce an heir.

Third, classic horror films such as *Dracula* and *Frankenstein* are preoccupied with bodily manifestations of "character" that represent, in condensed, visible form, physical and intellectual caliber, physiological and psychological traits, and moral fiber. In the Gothic search for familial history and individual identity, as Eve Sedgwick noted, the face and body become interpretable symbols, given that "character" designates both "personality and personal qualities" and "a graphic symbol."[7] Horror cinema gives potent visual form to this physiognomic manifestation of character, but it reconfigures it along eugenic lines, presenting disability, deformity, and "feeble-mindedness" as the inevitable result and mark of nonnormative reproduction and associating such defects with specific "undesirables" targeted by eugenicists: in *Dracula,* the deficient immigrant, and in *Frankenstein,* the violent criminal.

Emerging in the wake of thirty years of American eugenics, these films thus rework Gothic novels' visions of science and heredity with a specifically eugenic sensibility. At the same time, the films question the biological determinism of eugenics. *Dracula* undoes the hereditarian logic of eugenics through eugenicists' own rhetoric of blood, depicting contagion and infection as environmental influences stronger than germ plasm; *Frankenstein* affirms the determinative effect of nurture over nature and locates monstrosity in the figure of the eugenic scientist. In this way, these horror films embody the ambivalent popular negotiation of eugenic concepts: they simultaneously revel in the fears of difference exploited by mainline eugenics; reflect the 1930s shift toward a more moderate, environmentally attentive eugenics; and ultimately express distaste for any scientific or medical intervention in the act of reproduction.

Dracula

Although it is not one of the 1930s horror films that most explicitly engages images of science, *Dracula* (dir. Tod Browning, Universal) draws readily upon the rhetoric and imagery of eugenics. In particular, it offers strong resonances with the period's eugenic debates over immigration and American racial identity, shot through with the inflammatory language of blood. *Dracula* depicts an assured, gentlemanly vampire (Bela Lugosi) who inhabits a Transylvanian castle complete with creaking doors, sweeping staircases, and copious cobwebs. Ignoring the warnings of superstitious villagers, British realtor Renfield (Dwight Frye) takes a wild coach ride to the castle, where he completes a transaction enabling Dracula to buy Carfax Abbey in London. Drugged by the vampire, Renfield falls unconscious. Dracula's brides, who approach the realtor's unconscious body, are waved away by Dracula, who himself moves in on Renfield's exposed neck. Made insane by the vampire's attack and lusting for the blood of small creatures, Renfield accompanies Dracula to England on a boat, guarding his master, who hides by day in his coffin.

When the boat arrives in England, Dracula disembarks unseen, leaving behind the dead crew members and Renfield, who is taken to Dr. Seward's lunatic asylum. Making himself at home in London, Dracula meets his neighbors, Dr. Seward (Herbert Bunston), his daughter Mina (Helen Chandler), her fiancé John Harker (David Manners), and Mina's visiting friend, Lucy (Frances Dade), who later expresses an attraction to Dracula. That night, Lucy is visited and bitten by the vampire, and she soon dies, returning as a vampire. A Dutch scientist, Professor Van Helsing (Edward Van Sloan), faces skepticism when he asserts that vampirism is at work. Unknown to her father and fiancé, Mina is also bitten by Dracula and grows ill, at one point trying to bite Harker. She is eventually kidnapped by Dracula and taken to the abbey, but Renfield, escaping from the asylum, unwittingly leads Van Helsing and Harker to them. Finding Dracula asleep in his coffin, Van Helsing drives a stake through the vampire's heart and thus saves Mina, who is led off in Harker's arms.

Billed as "the strangest love story of them all," *Dracula* depicts an attractive monster who invades England with an aberrant sexuality and reproductive practice.[8] That monster thus bypasses the normative, marital, heterosexual reproductive relations advocated by eugenics as a means of creating healthy blood or protoplasm and goes directly to the veins. In the thirty years prior to *Dracula* and *Frankenstein,* American eugenics increasingly rejected Lamarckian ideas about environmental influences on heredity, concentrating on "germ plasm" and reproduction as the sites through which the health and racial unity of Americans would be maintained. In *Heredity in Relation to Eugenics* (1911), for example, Charles Davenport, biologist and founder of the Eugenics Record Office, presented heterosexual reproduction as the primary point of access to the all-determining makeup of blood or protoplasm: "The general program of the eugenist is clear—it is to improve the race by inducing young people to make a more reasonable selection of marriage mates; to fall in love intelligently. It also includes the control by the state of the propagation of the mentally incompetent."[9] Davenport's eugenic creed thus aspired toward the reproduction of only nature's "best blood" against the incursions of "crime, disease, and degeneracy," as embodied by those populations for whom the nation had to provide: "half a million insane, feeble-minded, epileptic, blind and deaf, 80,000 prisoners and 100,000 paupers at a cost of over 100 million dollars per year."[10]

The healthy matings envisioned by Davenport depended on a vehement subscription to racial unity and uniformity and an abhorrence of anything hybrid; "a hyberdized [sic] people are a badly put together people and a dissatisfied, restless, ineffective people."[11] The key to protecting the dominant race from the incursions of inadequate or racially "tainted" germ plasm was the construction of both white women and white families as sacred sites of racial propagation. Racial purity relied on the sexual purity and wisdom of white women. Harry H. Laughlin, director of the Eugenics Record Office, feared that "if men with a small fraction of colored blood could readily find mates among the white women, the gates would be thrown open to a final radical race mixture of the whole population."[12]

Through dialogue, story lines, and characterizations that reference degeneration and heredity, classic horror films thus adopt eugenic fears surrounding reproduction, foregrounding the threat posed to a white hero and heroine by a monstrous figure. Repeatedly, horror films offer scenes in which a monster enters a female space, often a bedroom, and physically and sexually menaces or attacks the heroine. The films thus sensationally dramatize the consequences of neglecting the roles of marital consummation and reproductive health in the biological future of the nation and race.[13]

In *Dracula,* the threat to healthy procreation is explicit and is emphasized in the scenes in which the vampire slowly and menacingly approaches Lucy and, later, Mina as they sleep at night. The location of Dracula's encounters with women in bedrooms and beds emphasizes his displacement of normative reproduction in usurping its privileged site. Dracula's sexual practices are nongenital, promiscuous, and bisexual. Rather than inseminating, he withdraws; rather than impregnating, he vitiates.[14]

According to a eugenic reading, Dracula's abnormal sexual and reproductive practices are explained, in part, by his foreignness. The actor playing Dracula, Hungarian immigrant Lugosi, was "an obscure political refugee scratching for work in a new country" prior to his success in the Broadway version of *Dracula,* and he brought to this talking film a slow, thickly accented dialogue, a product of his limited grasp of English.[15] As southeastern Europeans, both Dracula and Lugosi represent the "new" kind of immigrant that concerned American eugenicists of the early twentieth century. Eugenic lore held that the predominantly western European origins of immigrants to the United States in the colonial period formed the basis for a specifically American nationality, grounded in a homogeneity of racial origin and cultural beliefs. However, from the Civil War onward, immigration began to constitute what Henry Pratt Fairchild, American Eugenics Society (AES) president between 1929 and 1931, called the "New Menace," in the form of immigrants from Italy, Austria-Hungary, and Russia. Although the addition of "Mediterranean" and "Alpine" stock to the predominantly "Nordic" population was not seen as a major problem, the racial purity of immigrants from eastern and southeastern Europe was suspect, due to that area's history of invasion by "Mongoloid stocks such as the Avars, the Bulgars, Magyars, and Turks." The result of such "racial contact," Fairchild declared, was inevitably dysgenic mating and reproduction, for "the sexual impulse knows no racial boundaries."[16] Impelled, in part, by eugenic activism, the 1921 Emergency Quota Act and the National Origins Act of 1924 imposed extensive restrictions on immigration from Asia and eastern and southern Europe.[17]

Frequently, eugenic rhetoric presented the threat of such immigration in terms of the mixing and tainting of American blood, as in Davenport's condemnation of "the great influx of blood from South-eastern Europe."[18] Hungarians such as Lugosi thus had the potential to "introduc[e] into the American population considerable strains of Mongoloid germ plasm," to

inhibit the continuation of the specialized "English . . . and American type,"
and to contribute to a general "mongrelization" and a backward evolutionary step: "The result to be looked for in the offspring is . . . a primitive, gen-
eralized type—often spoken of as a 'reversion,' 'atavism,' or 'throwback.'"[19]
Dracula picks up on these rhetorical strands, with Van Helsing lamenting
that Dracula has "fused his blood" with that of Mina, while Harker likens
the vampire, momentarily cornered, to "a wild animal."

At the same time as he embodies a national and racial origin threatening to the "specialized" blood strains of "English and American type[s],"
Dracula also connotes a "throwback" to a different economic and political
order that, most importantly, enacts a different system of inheritance. Again,
the classic horror film draws on the nineteenth-century Gothic genre, which
was characterized by the desire of an emergent middle class to assert its
power against older forms of inheritance.[20] Such antipathy conflates biological and social inheritance; for Thomas Doherty, early-nineteenth-century
Gothic "expressed the loathing that a vital new middle class felt toward the
tired blood of a dying aristocracy."[21] If Gothic offered a literary form for
this desire, Galton's eugenics gave it doctrinal shape. As Daniel J. Kevles
shows, Galton was dismissive of both the manufacturing or commercial
classes and the "hereditary aristocracy," which he thought "a 'disastrous institution' for 'our valuable races.'" In particular, he found the aristocratic
system of primogeniture wasteful of procreative capacity: "The younger
sons of the peerage, unable to afford a family and simultaneously maintain their position, inclined either not to marry at all or to wed heiresses, who
were likely to come from families that were not notably prolific." Against
these classes and the working classes, Galton championed the professional
classes as "the prime repository of ability and civic virtue" and "made them
the keystone of a biological program designed to lead to the creation of a
conservative meritocracy."[22]

In the United States, this fear of reproductive decline among the nation's best "stock," encapsulated in the term *race suicide,* had held cur-
rency at least since its public invocation by President Theodore Roosevelt.
It remained in prominent circulation well into the 1930s in eugenic publications, lectures, and newspaper columns, usually presented alongside
visions of the fertile and expanding "undesirables." For example, an October 19, 1930, editorial in the *Washington Evening Star* summarized the
thesis of Professor Corrado Gini of the University of Rome regarding the

imminent decline of superior races by hybrid, marginal populations: "Some of the supposedly inferior races are displaying an unexpected biological resistance—and this means eventually every other sort of resistance."[23] In an American Eugenics Society exhibit displayed at state fairs throughout the nation during the 1920s and 1930s, flashing lights indicated the difference in birthrate between the desirables and the so-called unfit (Figure 9.2).[24] Eugenicists urged those of good stock to produce large families, and they conducted "fitter families" contests at the fairs to reward positive examples. Simultaneously, they asserted that "defectives" were rapidly increasing in institutions and jails and advocated sterilization as a primary measure to address the birthrate differential, along with the spread of birth control information to the poor and laboring classes.

Dracula develops the Gothic demonization of older forms of inheritance in relation to these American eugenic visions of decaying aristocracies and the dangers of procreative inadequacy among social elites. Skal has represented Dracula as a "sanguinary capitalist," and Marxists have found vampire imagery valuable for their depictions of capitalism.[25] However, as a feudal figure fresh from exploiting and terrorizing the peasants of Transylvania, Count Dracula more clearly embodies both the system of primogeniture and the incestuous aristocracy that bourgeois capitalism and the American meritocracy purport to have overthrown and that eugenics disavows. He incarnates "the decadent feudalism of Continental Europe" condemned by William Starr Myers in 1930.[26] Davenport referenced social structures as one of the factors that contribute to consanguineous marriages and thus the sterility and concentration of peculiar negative traits. He offered as an example the inbreeding of Europe's royal families: "The Barrier of the Clan with its pride of blood leads to self-satisfaction and not infrequently to a desire to concentrate wealth and power." Davenport's statement conflates insular practices of biological and economic inheritance and presents such practices as both attractive to and dangerous for "America's grand families."[27] In Dracula's seduction of Lucy and Mina and Mina's attempted seduction of Harker, that very fascination and danger plays out in an upper-class English family. In using the figure of the immigrant, *Dracula* thus invokes racial and ethnic intermixing; in employing the figure of the decayed and parasitic aristocrat, it summons consanguinity and inbreeding. In so doing, the film mimics the contradictory impulse of eugenics against *both* heterogenous miscegenation and incestuous closeness, as well as the different kinds of biological defects they ostensibly produce.

Finally, in addition to its eugenic representations of reproduction and inheritance themes, *Dracula* offers visual, bodily evidence of the defective character or characteristics produced by this penetration of foreignness and decadent insularity into Western families and nations. American eugenics had a conflicted relationship to the bodily exterior, struggling to align older physiognomic doctrines of a bodily surface that reflected individual, social, and biological identity with the newer eugenic science. Eugenicists understood that defects within the determinative germ plasm might not necessarily be manifest in an individual's physical appearance or behavior. The Immigration Act of the United States upheld eugenic notions of national health by excluding the feebleminded, insane, diseased, and mentally or physically "defective," but Davenport insisted on the need to examine not just immigrants' obvious defects but also individual biological histories, enabling the exclusion of "those with a germ plasm that has imbecile, epileptic, insane, criminalistic, alcoholic, and sexually immoral tendencies."[28] He felt that even apparently normal individuals might possess or lack genetic materials that would produce defective offspring.

Nevertheless, constrained by their inability to see and interpret genetic material, American eugenicists were often limited to an empirical method, a reading of the bodily exterior to determine genetic truth. Marouf A. Hasian notes of the field-workers sent out to gather family histories for Davenport's Eugenics Record Office, "After a few weeks' training, [they] were thought to be able to tell at a glance whether someone had pure or tainted germplasm."[29] Eugenic tracts of the period thus provoked fears about hidden degeneracy in the bodily interior or germ plasm of certain groups and individuals, but they also warned—or reassured—of degeneracy's eventual revelation in the physical structure or appearance of the body.

The visual representation of horror-film characters is closely allied with these eugenic beliefs about physical appearance as an index to biological, intellectual, and moral health. The appearance, traits, and behavior of horror's heroes, heroines, and monsters signify flaws embedded in their parents, in the means of their creation, and in certain systems of inheritance; more broadly, they reference racial "inferiority" and moral and ethical failings. The monster's physical or behavioral deviance, usually accompanied by a lack of moral responsibility indicated by physical violence toward others, testifies to an aberrant method of procreation or a degenerate system of inheritance, whereas the physical enervation and ineffectuality of white male "heroes" conjure the dilemma of the middle and upper classes as they falter in the face of the proliferating defective classes and races.

Dracula thus explores the fear that degeneracy, though embedded deep within, may not be self-evident. Count Dracula is perceived as handsome and charming, and as already noted, it is only his foreign and aristocratic histories that proffer warnings of inner defects. He is an immigrant who conceals his innate degeneracy, as Davenport fears, and is free to wreak havoc on the blood purity and healthy reproduction of the Anglo-Saxon race and its nation-state. Still, attentive characters observe glimpses of Dracula's inner deviance: Mina finds him not quite "normal," and in a moment of confrontation, he appears to Harker "a wild animal" and to Seward "a madman." But the defects embedded within Dracula are most obviously revealed in his victims. The film's object lesson against ethnic mixing and aristocratic intermarriage plays out across the bodies of Lucy and Mina, drained of their vitality and willpower and imbued with abnormal sexual desires, and in the hapless Harker, we find an enervated impotence that supports eugenic fears about the diminishing reproductive capacity of the desirable classes and their inadequacy against the fertility of "degenerate" groups.

In Renfield, in particular, we most easily recognize a visibly deviant character from eugenic narratives. He is "feeble-minded" or deranged and must be contained within an asylum. Already feminized prior to his encounter with Dracula—Michael Brunas, John Brunas, and Tom Weaver describe him as "a bit of a queen . . . with his effeminate look and prissy manner"—Renfield regresses mentally and physically, ranting maniacally, consuming flies and spiders for their blood, and spending a great deal of time in cowering, hunched positions, as if to convey his evolutionary reversal.[30] His (implicitly erotic and sexual) encounter with perverse foreign and aristocratic practices of reproduction thus engenders a visible process of atavism and degeneration in this representative of the bourgeoisie.

Certainly, then, Dracula appropriates eugenic ideas, dramatizing the dangers of any method of procreation other than that of heterosexual, marital sex between young, attractive, and healthy couples. Also like eugenic texts, the film portrays the degeneracy of overthrown systems of feudalism and aristocracy in favor of bourgeois dominance and warns of the risks of upper-class enervation and low fertility. Finally, like eugenic works, the film exploits audiences' fascination with and fear of bodily difference to dramatize the dangers presented by various monsters to the procreation of healthy, white, middle- or upper-class generations.

But *Dracula* and other early horror films also offer a popular recasting of eugenic logic, asserting the power of nurture and environmental influence over that of germ plasm and genes. Thus, even as a "eugenic" interpretation of *Dracula* constrains vampirism as an abnormal sexual/reproductive practice, an outgrowth of foreign and aristocratic customs that produces monstrous and deranged offspring, the film's dynamics of blood and contagion subvert an exclusive focus on reproduction as the key to bodily and mental form. In *Dracula,* the eugenic effort to locate and contain degeneration within the bodies of specific groups is disrupted by metaphors of contamination and disease, facilitated by the eugenicists' own rhetoric of blood.

Even as the twentieth century proceeded and the mechanisms of chromosomes and cells were perceived and understood more clearly, the rhetoric of blood and protoplasm retained emotive value for eugenicists, as noted previously. Early in the century, botanist and university president David Starr Jordan maintained that "[t]he blood of a nation determines its history. . . . The history of a nation determines its blood." He asserted the relevance of the rhetoric of blood even within a Mendelist understanding: "[T]he old word well serves our purposes. The blood which is 'thicker than water' is the symbol of race unity. In this sense the blood of the people concerned is at once the cause and the result of the deeds recorded in their history."[31] Such conflation of "character," blood, and racial and national traits remained salient in eugenic discourse at the time of *Dracula*'s release. In 1930, historian and anti-immigration exponent Lothrop Stoddard declared, in a statement that also entangled reproductive and sanguinary metaphors, that "[t]he 'Slavic' peoples who occupy most of Eastern Europe are all impregnated with Asiatic Mongol and Turki blood."[32]

Certainly, eugenicists sought to represent the threatened penetration of foreignness into the United States in primarily sexual terms, as in the statement of Madison Grant, Stoddard's eugenicist mentor, that "[i]nstead of a population homogenous in race, religion, traditions and aspirations, as was the American nation down to 1840, we have—inserted into the body politic—an immense mass of foreigners, congregated for the most part in the large cities and in the industrial centers."[33] But such concerns also shaded into a notion of disease revealed at skin level, as in author Kenneth L. Roberts's representation of Mexican immigrants, "sizzling with disease," as an "acute plague sore on the body politic."[34] The image of disease in turn invoked that of infection, as in the words of Albert Johnson, chairman of the Immigration Committee of the House of Representatives in 1931: "How shall the Republic endure if there be steady deterioration of standards by ever-recurring new foci of infection, arriving in the land?"[35]

The imagery of disease that undermines strictly genetic understandings also permeates and unsettles the apparently eugenic narratives of Dracula. In the first cinematic portrayal of Stoker's novel, F. W. Murnau's silent Nosferatu (Prana-Film, 1922), the "nosferatu"—etymologically, "plague-carrier"—brings plague and pestilence from Transylvania to mid-nineteenth-century Bremen. Although the proliferation of disease in Nosferatu is recast in Dracula as a limited outbreak of vampirism, brought under control by the rational, scientific deductions and the violent act of Van Helsing, the infiltration of the foreign element into the body by means other than reproduction both challenges the official narrative of eugenics and emphasizes that narrative's frequent lapse into a metaphorics of metonymy and contagion. Dracula infects, rather than impregnates, his victims with physical and behavioral dysfunction. Even as the sage scientist of Dracula disposes of the source of this infection and reunites the engaged, upper-class couple, the threat of disease persists: in a maid whom Renfield has implicitly attacked; in the undead Lucy; and in Mina herself.[36] As Rhona Berenstein comments, Mina's anguished cry of pain as Dracula is staked suggests that "threats of monstrosity endure in women who survive narrative closure."[37]

The biological model of eugenics, in which the monster is a metaphor for foreignness and decadence and miscegenation the vehicle of his infiltration into the American national and racial body, thus breaks down under the weight of its own symbolism. Though eugenicists continued to employ the rhetoric of blood as a valuable propagandistic tool, Dracula demonstrates how such imagery escapes purely biological understandings of disability and defect, how blood inevitably spills over into a metonymics of fluid exchange other than that of normative sexual reproduction and invokes a notion of contagion and psychological influence that disrupts a model of eugenic inheritance. Noel Carroll notes that this "horrific metonymy" shapes representation of Dracula: "[T]he horrific being is *surrounded* by objects that we antecedently take to be objects of disgust and/or phobia. . . . Dracula, both in literature and on stage and screen, is associated with vermin" (emphasis in original).[38] In the film, he is variously linked to wolves, bats, and rats, and although this association with animals can fall within a devolutionary eugenic narrative, it also underwrites a politics of proliferation and contamination that transgresses normative categories.

This is not to suggest that notions of disease and contagion are innocent of racist ideologies; quite the opposite, for as Botting points out, the vampire myth emerges from "fears of the Plague, thought, since the Middle Ages, to have emanated from the East."[39] As Judith Halberstam also comments, referencing Max Nordau, author of *Degeneration* (1893), "[P]redisposition to diseases like syphilis or the possibility of degeneration were ascribed to certain races (such as the Jews), to their genealogy and their lifestyles, in order to give moral structure to the seemingly random process of infection."[40] The rhetoric of contagion is thus complicit with the effort to contain the threat of disease and bodily vulnerability within xenophobic narratives about foreigners. Nevertheless, when Dracula's influence over Lucy, Renfield, and Mina diminishes a simplistic, eugenic model of biological reproduction and inheritance in favor of a model of contamination, it opens the way for a kind of uncertainty and boundary-crossing that defies the positivist interpretations and distinct categories of eugenics. Indeed, . Hasian notes that African American reformists of the period responded to eugenic ideas of racial inferiority with invocations of disease, with one writer observing that "germs of disease have no race prejudice."[41] Eugenic narratives are thus contaminated and deformed by their own metaphors of blood, metaphors that undermine biological claims to racial superiority and enable popular and environmentalist revisions of eugenic concepts.

Frankenstein

James Whale's *Frankenstein* (Universal) similarly employs a set of eugenic narratives that horrify with the spectacle of monstrous reproduction; it also similarly complicates and contests eugenicists' biological determinism. In this film, the obsessive work of Henry Frankenstein (Colin Clive) toward the Monster's creation keeps him from his fiancée Elizabeth (Mae

Clarke). In the novel, the scientist works alone, but the film supplies him with a hunchbacked assistant, Fritz, played by *Dracula*'s Renfield, Dwight Frye.⁴² We first encounter Henry and Fritz lurking around a fresh gravesite, from which they disinter a body. They also cut down a man who has been hanged but whose broken neck necessitates a further search for a suitable brain. Soon thereafter, Fritz eavesdrops on a lecture by Professor Waldman (Van Sloan, *Dracula*'s Van Helsing), Henry's former mentor, at Goldstadt Medical College, and when alone, he steals the "normal" brain that Waldman was discussing. When the jar slips and breaks, Fritz grabs the brain labeled "abnormal" and absconds with it.

Meanwhile, Elizabeth, concerned by Henry's obsession, accompanies her friend Victor (John Bowles) on a visit to Professor Waldman. They discover that Henry's research in "chemical galvanism and electrobiology" was becoming too advanced and dangerous and that Henry left the university because it refused to provide him with cadavers. All three proceed to Henry's laboratory, a watchtower in the Tyrolean mountains, and find him on the verge of creating life. The pieced-together body in his laboratory is winched skyward, where a bolt of lightning engenders life in it. But the creature's monstrosity is confirmed when it kills Fritz, who taunts it with fire. Henry agrees to its sedation and death and accompanies Elizabeth back to the village to organize their marriage.

As Waldman prepares to dissect the creature, it awakens and kills him, gaining its freedom. The Monster then accidentally kills a little girl and soon after enters Elizabeth's room as she awaits the wedding. He prepares to attack her, but when interrupted, he flees, pursued by villagers. He captures Henry and arrives at an old mill, where he is cornered. As the mob sets the mill ablaze, the Monster hurls Henry toward the ground from the top of the structure, before it collapses in flames around him. The script penned by the film's initial director, Robert Florey, called for Henry to die, thus rendering punishment for the Monster's creation. However, although Whale originally envisaged a similar demise, he eventually appended a conclusion in which we glimpse Henry recovering in bed, with Elizabeth at his side, while his father, Baron Frankenstein, makes a toast with his servants: "Here's to a son, to the House of Frankenstein!"⁴³

As in *Dracula*, then, the normative process of marriage and heterosexual reproduction is supplanted by an aberrant act of procreation. In *Frankenstein*, this act takes dead bodies as its materials and is enabled by the unnatural collaboration of two men: a hubristic and apparently psychologically unstable scientist and his "deformed" male assistant. In accordance with eugenic thought, such a deviant act of reproduction produces a monster, and where Colin Clive's Henry is weak and ineffectual, the Monster he creates is potent and forceful. The film thus stages a version of the evolutionary drama in which the civilized and socially upstanding are faltering in the face of modern life, while the degenerate take on monstrous form and threaten to inject their deviance into the very wombs of white women.

The sexual and reproductive threat posed by the Monster is literalized in a climactic bedroom scene. While *Frankenstein* seemingly replaces the act of heterosexual reproduction with the laboratory and artificial, scientific acts of creation, it also dramatically foregrounds the site of the bedroom, uncovering the sexual act as the site at which eugenics really seeks to intervene. When the Monster enters Elizabeth's bedroom, Elizabeth is attired in her wedding dress and awaiting the marriage ceremony. Henry has locked her in the room, ostensibly to protect her but in effect rendering her vulnerable to the Monster and further delaying the marital union. Seeing the Monster, Elizabeth faints onto her bed, her hair and arm hanging down, her throat exposed. Despite its fleeting nature and the subordinate role of Elizabeth in the rest of the film, this scene has been deemed one of the film's most enduring: "[T]he image of the monster lurking ominously in the background with Elizabeth sprawled on the bed [is] an image profoundly phallic and profoundly violent, an unacceptable alternative to and consequence of the act of conception in the laboratory."[44] For Elizabeth Young, the scene proffers a staging of miscegenation and rape: "Although the monster's crime is officially the penetration of the room, not the woman, his actions are framed precisely according to the stereotype of interracial rape."[45] However, given the film's employment of eugenic tropes and narratives, we must also see this scene more broadly, as a multilayered vision of degeneracy encroaching on the virtuous national and racial body.

Just as *Dracula* disparages a bloodsucking aristocracy, so *Frankenstein*, in its concerns over inheritance, exhibits a eugenic and bourgeois criticism of the nobility and its processes of inheritance. Baron Frankenstein, noble overlord of simple peasants, is presented as a buffoon, persistent in his belief that only "another woman" could explain his son's behavior and obsessive in his desire for a male heir to perpetuate "the House of Frankenstein."

The Monster thus emerges as a product of the stifling, aristocratic house, and he embodies its violent relationship to the local commoners in the murder of the peasant girl.

As the representative of the House of Frankenstein, Colin Clive's Henry is weak, ineffectual, and nervous, confirming the eugenic belief in the eventual sterility or defectiveness of the insular aristocracy. Clive's character picks up on the type portrayed by David Manners's John Harker in *Dracula* and prevalent in subsequent horror films: the enervated male "hero" who cannot prevent the Monster from gaining access to his bride-to-be. Henry is thus afflicted with neurasthenia, a disease diagnosed by George Beard in his *American Nervousness: Its Causes and Consequences* (1881), defined as "deficiency or lack of nerve force."[46] In Nordau's *Degeneration*, as Kelly Hurley describes, neurasthenia was defined as a "modern hysteria," engendered in one generation by "such new and stressful phenomena as crowded urban living, railway travel, and daily newspapers" and inherited, as Lamarck theorized, by that generation's offspring.[47] The concept of neurasthenia spoke to the concern that the process of civilization had overly repressed the "primitive" masculine virility and physicality of white upper- and middle-class men. As illustrated in Gail Bederman's discussion of the work of G. Stanley Hall, a close friend of Beard's, neurasthenia thus recast a cultural anxiety as a medical condition, symptomized by white men's fatigue and effeminacy.[48]

Neurasthenia, as a Lamarckian disease, thus combined environmental and biological heredity. Consequently, though Henry's nervousness and lack of willpower testify to the decaying impotence of the aristocracy, they cannot help but also confirm fears about a more general decay triggered by the stresses of modern life. One of the elements of modernity to which Beard attributed American nervousness was "the sciences," and it is only moments after his feat of scientific prowess, the animation of the Monster, that a raving Henry collapses and appears to faint. Beard also mentions "the mental activity of women" as a modern cause of neurasthenia, and it is when confronted with Elizabeth, who has determinedly come to take him back to civilization, that Henry collapses a second time.[49] The implications of impotence and effeminacy that surround both neurasthenia generally and Clive's Henry more particularly also indicate the fears of early-twentieth-century thinkers about modern bourgeois life's feminizing effect on men. Thus, even as Henry's enervation supports a mainline eugenic

critique of the failure of upper classes to reproduce adequately, it also ges-
tures toward a conflicted popular understanding of eugenics in which, as
Lamarck had proposed and as some still believed, environment, more than
biology, might determine character and health.

The physical manifestations of Henry's weakness, emphasized in the
closing scene in which he is bedridden, also concur with eugenic notions
about the bodily revelation of character traits. The consequences in *Frankenstein* of abnormal reproduction and the aristocratic systems of inheritance
are written across the bodies of both the protagonist and his Monster.
Henry's aristocratic and professional impotence contrasts with the Monster's vitality, which connotes the proliferation of degeneracy. If the Monster's entry into Elizabeth's room embodies the threat of the unfit masses
to healthy reproduction, such an embodiment is enabled by visual and
physical codes that denote the Monster's degeneracy. Boris Karloff's Monster differs considerably from his literary forefather. Although the novel's
Monster is merely hideous and abnormally large but also articulate, rational, and learned, the filmic Monster embodies the "manifestly unfit"
decried by eugenic proponents.[50] His "imbecility" is revealed in his lurch-
ing awkwardness, his crude attempts at speech, and his simple-minded
behavior.[51]

Such characteristics had long been presented by eugenicists as indicators of low social status and criminality. Publications about poor, degenerate, and criminal families as burdens on state and taxpayer were intimately
familiar to Americans in this period. Henry Goddard's *The Kallikaks* (1912),
Arthur H. Estabrook's *The Jukes in 1915* (1916), and texts on families such
as the Nams, the Hill Folk, the Pineys, and many others emphasize the
role of heredity in mental defects and criminality and the need for "permanent custodial care and sterilization."[52] The dissemination of stories about
such families and of statistics on feeblemindedness, mental illness, and
physical defects encouraged an easy association between apparent physical or intellectual attributes and racial, sexual, and social reproductive
threats. Thus, in *Frankenstein*, when Waldman advises Henry to kill the
Monster "as you would any savage criminal," he uses criminological discourse to position the Monster as defective and to advocate his euthanasia.
Simultaneously, as Robin Wood notes, the Monster's laboring attire characterizes him as a member of the working class, those masses eugenicists
feared more than the overthrown aristocracy.[53] Finally, as Young suggests,

the Monster also functions as a Gothicized figure for the phantasmatically potent and sexually aggressive black man. The Monster's physical difference thus makes him available for interpretation as any one of several "degenerate" groups feared by eugenicists.

The film *Frankenstein* makes even more explicit its eugenic narrative of biologically determined character by providing its monster with an abnormal brain.[54] Commenting on the degenerate brain, Professor Waldman declaims, "Observe, ladies and gentlemen, the scarcity of convolutions on the frontal lobe as compared to that of the normal brain. And a distinct degeneration of the middle frontal lobe. All of these degenerate characteristics check amazingly with the history of the dead man before us, whose life was one of . . . violence and murder."

Waldman's monologue draws on eugenic terminology about criminality and degeneracy, asserting the legible and interpretable truth of the brain's physical tissue. The film's addition of Fritz's theft of the abnormal brain has been criticized. Martin Tropp finds it *Frankenstein*'s "most absurd and unnecessary sequence," and Skal presents it as "a major subversion of Shelley's intended moral; it is not Henry's divine presumption that sets in motion the catastrophe, but a deception and cover-up by a handicapped employee."[55]

However, Waldman's speech and Fritz's theft of the brain constitute a deliberate positing of eugenics, updating *Frankenstein*'s concerns with monstrous creation, both by introducing a disabled figure into the act of reproduction and by ostensibly putting in motion a biologically deterministic theory. Chris Baldick critiques this determinism, asserting that "the pickled brain . . . offers a crudely simple 'explanation' for the monster's motives" and is thus evidence that "the story's several possibilities have been narrowed and reduced by the sheer visual impact of Karloff's performance."[56] But any easy assumption that the abnormal brain is the sole cause of the Monster's ugliness and violent behavior is undercut, as in the book, by the film's attention to the mistreatment that shapes the Monster from the moment of his birth. The film thus sets up the eugenic theory so as to partially contest it; the visual and verbal iconography of eugenics used in this scene, juxtaposed with the themes invoked as the film proceeds, gesture toward the film's complicated interrogation of a broader understanding of eugenics.

First, as we have seen, *Frankenstein* undercuts the biological focus of eugenics in the neurasthenic depiction of Henry Frankenstein, locating degeneration and sterility not in biological causes but in the modern way of life and normative social systems. Indeed, rather than the aristocracy, it may well be the institution of marriage itself that enervates Henry. For Walter Evans, "Henry is only ready for marriage when his own body is horribly battered and weakened, when he is transformed from the vigorous, courageous, inspired hero he represented early in the film to an enervated figure approaching the impotent fatuity of his father and grandfather."[57] Whether it is his aristocratic heritage, the pressures of modern life, the heteronormative paradigm, or the institution of marriage that renders Henry impotent, the film's mobilization of neurasthenia across his body and behavior inevitably undermines any coherent eugenic message to a 1930s audience.

In fact, neurasthenia's obscuring of the relation between biological, inherited disorders and conditions caused by environmental factors renders *Frankenstein*'s eugenics comparable to conflicted popular understandings of heredity. Recent scholars in eugenics have emphasized more general, public interpretations of eugenics that conflated it with more environmental notions of heredity and that defined it in relation to both biological material *and* parental upbringing: "By this definition of 'heredity,' 'eugenics' meant not just having good genes, but being a good parent."[58] Such popular notions about eugenics were paralleled in the scientific world of the late 1920s and 1930s, as "reform" eugenicists expressed increasing skepticism about elements of mainline eugenics. Social scientists asserted the unknown and dynamic impact of culture on human behavior, and geneticists and mathematicians challenged some eugenicists' simplistic and erroneous assumptions about the operation of heredity. Consequently, reform eugenicists minimized discussion of eugenic notions such as racial superiority and absolute biological determinism, instead advocating both increased genetic knowledge and environmental and social improvements to achieve healthy reproduction.[59]

Classic horror films such as *Frankenstein*, then, mirror this modification to eugenic doctrine in the 1930s. Concepts of nurture over nature shape *Frankenstein*'s most significant revision of biological determinism. Although the condemnation of Frankenstein's parenting skills is less overt in the film than in the novel, largely because the Monster cannot articulate his feelings of abandonment, the film nevertheless makes clear that his violence takes form initially in self-defense, in response to Fritz's torture of him and Waldman's attempt to murder him, and then in ignorance, when he drowns a peasant girl after playing happily with her, not realizing that she cannot float like flowers thrown into the water. By the time the Monster attacks Elizabeth, he is expressing both vengeance toward the maker who created and then abandoned him and rage at the normative (and thus "eugenic") family from which he is excluded.

Therefore, the apparently eugenic moral of the story—which dramatizes the monstrous results of all but conventional, marital reproduction, implicitly censuring the homosexuality suggested by the reproductive collaboration of two men and similarly condemning the participation of the physically deformed, mentally ill, and feebleminded in acts of reproduction—is mitigated by audience sympathy for the Monster as neglected and abused child. He is violent not only because he is made artificially from dead bodies but also because his father fails to provide a proper upbringing. That this reading struck home is suggested in Karloff's contention that he and Whale strove to depict the creature as innocent (rather than neurologically criminal) and that there were "fantastic numbers of ordinary people that got this general air of sympathy. I found all my letters heavy with it. Many also wanted to offer help and friendship. It was one of the most moving experiences of my life."[60] The sympathy elicited by the Monster in Whale's *Frankenstein* thus undermines Lennard Davis's contention that horror films "remove the element of pity in the visual transaction between 'normal' viewer and disabled object" and opens up more complicated understandings of the "racism" and eugenics of horror films.[61] It also denotes *Frankenstein* as a text through which popular negotiations of both mainline and reform eugenics are filtered.

The earliest films of the classic horror cycle thus exploit eugenic concepts to stage sensationalistic scenes in which monsters threaten pure women, ostensibly confirming the eugenic injunction against nonmarital reproduction, miscegenation, and the reproduction of the unfit. At the same time, these films extend notions of heredity beyond the purely biological, to incorporate environmental, parental, and social influences on both physical and moral health. The simultaneous mobilization and complication of eugenic narratives and themes also characterizes other classic horror films of the early 1930s. For example, *Frankenstein*'s sequel, *Bride of Frankenstein* (James Whale, Universal, 1935), counters genetic determinism with the charitable nurture of the old, blind hermit (O. P. Heggie), who recalls Catholic critics of eugenics, and *Dr. Jekyll and Mr. Hyde* (Rouben Mamoulian, Paramount, 1931), in depicting a chemical as the determinative element in

Jekyll's transformation into Hyde (both played by Fredric March), invokes contemporaneous ideas about "race poisons" such as alcohol, which again confuse environmental and biological factors in heredity.[62] At the same time, in the movement from the wise scientist of *Dracula* to the hysterical scientist of *Frankenstein*, the first two films of Hollywood's golden age of horror foreshadow what would become the genre's routine demonization of medical and scientific experts, suggesting a popular distrust of even reformists' visions of eugenic utopias achieved through interventions in the reproductive act.[63]

Rather than simply reflecting either mainline or reform eugenic concepts, then, *Dracula* and *Frankenstein* take their place among what Hasian terms the "*rhetorical* fragments" that constitute eugenics, "representing the ideologies of multitudes of social actors who at different historical junctures have reconfigured these ideographs to legitimate a plethora of political, social, and economic agendas."[64] Classic horror movies offer a contradictory legacy in relation to eugenics: in adopting eugenic visualizations of inherited defect in bodily form, they facilitate the endurance of eugenics in the American imagination, even as they bear witness to popular revisions and obfuscations of eugenic determinism.

Notes

1. On the relationship between Gothic fiction and nineteenth-century sciences and social sciences, see, for example, Daniel Pick, *Faces of Degeneration: A European Disorder, c. 1848–c. 1918* (New York: Cambridge University Press, 1989), esp. chap. 6; Judith Halberstam, *Skin Shows: Gothic Horror and the Technology of Monsters* (Durham, NC: Duke University Press, 1995); and Kelly Hurley, *The Gothic Body: Sexuality, Materialism, and Degeneration at the Fin de Siècle* (New York: Cambridge University Press, 1996).

2. This essay focuses on these films primarily in terms of themes and narratives. For an extended version of this analysis, which also considers the eugenic aspects of classic horror films' formal elements and reception discourses, see Angela Marie Smith, *"Hideous Progeny": Eugenics, Disability, and Classic Horror Cinema* (PhD diss., University of Minnesota, 2002).

3. The distinction between "mainline" eugenics and a later, modified "reform" eugenics was first presented in Daniel J. Kevles, *In the Name of Eugenics: Genetics and the Uses of Human Heredity* (New York: Alfred A. Knopf, 1985).

4. Along with the Kevles work, a plethora of texts provide histories of American eugenics, including, among others, Donald Pickens, *Eugenics and the Progressives* (Nashville, TN: Vanderbilt University Press, 1969); Kenneth Ludermerer, *Genetics and American Society: A Historical Appraisal* (Baltimore, MD: Johns Hopkins University Press, 1972); Elazar Barkan, *The Retreat of Scientific Racism: Changing Concepts of Race in Britain and the United States between the World Wars* (New York: Cambridge University Press, 1992); Diane B. Paul, *Controlling Human Heredity: 1865 to the Present* (Atlantic Highlands, NJ: Humanities Press, 1995); Stefan Kühl, *The Nazi Connection: Eugenics, American Racism, and German National Socialism* (New York: Oxford University Press, 1994).

5. David J. Skal, *The Monster Show: A Cultural History of Horror* (New York: Norton, 1993), 159.

6. Fred Botting, *Gothic* (New York: Routledge, 1996), 4, 5–6.

7. Eve Kosofsky Sedgwick, *The Coherence of Gothic Conventions* (New York: Methuen, 1986), 152.

8. Michael Brunas, John Brunas, and Tom Weaver, *Universal Horrors: The Studio's Classic Films, 1931–1946* (Jefferson, NC: McFarland, 1990), 18.

9. Charles B. Davenport, *Heredity in Relation to Eugenics* (New York: Henry Holt, 1911), 4–5.

10. Ibid., 2, 4.

11. Davenport, quoted in Pickens, *Eugenics and the Progressives*, 57.

12. Harry H. Laughlin, quoted in Pickens, *Eugenics and the Progressives*, 67.

13. This eugenic representation of threats to the normative family and healthy reproduction came to constitute the central element of the horror-film genre, as elucidated in Robin Wood, "An Introduction to the American Horror Film," in *Planks of Reason: Essays on the Horror Film*, ed. Barry Keith Grant (Metuchen, NJ: Scarecrow Press, 1984), and Tony Williams, *Hearths of Darkness: The Family in American Horror Film* (London: Associated University Press, 1996).

14. Or, as noted by Skal and Elias Savada, Dracula's "sexuality can never be satisfied in a conventional manner—vampires are in a sense 'castrated,' their libidos displaced to a mouth that becomes an all-purpose sex organ, penetrating and engulfing simultaneously"; see David J. Skal and Elias Savada, *Dark Carnival: The Secret World of Tod Browning, Hollywood's Master of the Macabre* (New York: Anchor Books, 1995), 156.

15. Brunas, Brunas, and Weaver, *Universal Horrors*, 8.

16. Henry Pratt Fairchild, *The Melting-Pot Mistake* (Boston: Little, Brown, 1926), 107, 110–11, 114.

17. Other factors also contributed to the immigration restrictions of the 1920s, including organized labor's fears that an influx of immigrants would lower wages and

deprive Americans of employment. Mae Ngai notes that the "racial and ethnic remapping of the nation in the 1920s," of which the Immigration Act of 1924 was one part, "took place in mutually constituting realms of demography, economics, and law"; see Ngai, "The Architecture of Race in American Immigration Law: A Reexamination of the Immigration Act of 1924," *Journal of American History* 86, no. 1 (June 1999): 67–92, quote on 71. Nevertheless, in the move toward restrictions, economic and other concerns were repeatedly presented through or alongside eugenic rhetoric and imperatives, as in the 1911 report of the Dillingham Immigration Commission, which incorporated and approved Johann Blumenbach's racial hierarchy; further, eugenicists were extremely influential in the development and realization of the restrictions, as in the case of Harry H. Laughlin's submissions to the House Committee on Immigration and Naturalization. For more on the prominent role of eugenicists in the creation of immigration restrictions, see Matthew Frye Jacobson, *Whiteness of a Different Color: European Immigrants and the Alchemy of Race* (Cambridge, MA: Harvard University Press, 1988), esp. 78–83.

18. Davenport, *Heredity in Relation to Eugenics,* 219.

19. Fairchild, *Melting-Pot Mistake,* 110, 123.

20. Botting, *Gothic,* 4–5.

21. Thomas Doherty, *Pre-Code Hollywood: Sex, Immorality, and Insurrection in American Cinema* (New York: Columbia University Press, 1999), 307.

22. Kevles, *In the Name of Eugenics,* 9.

23. "The Fate of Races," *Washington Evening Star,* October 19, 1930, 2.

24. AES Scrapbook, American Eugenics Society Records, American Philosophical Society, Philadelphia, PA.

25. Skal, *The Monster Show,* 159. On Marxism and vampire imagery, see Chris Baldick, *In Frankenstein's Shadow: Myth, Monstrosity, and Nineteenth-Century Writing* (Oxford: Clarendon Press, 1987), esp. chap. 6.

26. William Starr Myers, "Political Aspects of Immigration," in *The Alien in Our Midst,* ed. Madison Grant (New York: Galton, 1930), 201. That the vampire is a vital metaphor for both the aristocracy and capitalism suggests the ways in which the new capitalist order, from the point of view of its critics, adopted and adapted the exploitative excesses of the inequitable feudal system that it displaced.

27. Davenport, *Heredity in Relation to Eugenics,* 198.

28. Ibid., 220, 224.

29. Marouf A. Hasian Jr., *The Rhetoric of Eugenics in Anglo-American Thought* (Athens: University of Georgia Press, 1996), 82.

30. Brunas, Brunas, and Weaver, *Universal Horrors,* 16.

31. David Starr Jordan, *The Blood of the Nation: A Study of the Decay of Races through the Survival of the Unfit* (Boston: American Unitarian Association, 1902), 7, 9.

32. Lothrop Stoddard "The Permanent Menace from Europe," in Grant, *The Alien in Our Midst*, 227.

33. Madison Grant, "Closing the Floodgates," in Grant, *The Alien in Our Midst*, 16.

34. Kenneth L. Roberts, "Mexican Immigration in the Southwest," in Grant, *The Alien in Our Midst*, 214, 218.

35. Albert Johnson, "The Opponents of Restricted Immigration," in Grant, *The Alien in Our Midst*, 10.

36. The unresolved status of both the maid and Lucy was due to edits; see Skal and Savada, *Dark Carnival*, 153. These elisions nevertheless contribute to an uncertainty that counters eugenic determinism.

37. Rhona J. Berenstein, *Attack of the Leading Ladies: Gender, Sexuality, and Spectatorship in Classic Horror Cinema* (New York: Columbia University Press, 1996), 119.

38. Noel Carroll, *The Philosophy of Horror or Paradoxes of the Heart* (New York: Routledge, 1990), 51.

39. Botting, *Gothic*, 146.

40. Halberstam, *Skin Shows*, 78. The encoding of Max Schreck's Nosferatu as a Jewish plague-carrier thus seeks to domesticate the uncertainties of disease by locating it in certain racial identities.

41. Quoted in Hasian, *The Rhetoric of Eugenics*, 67.

42. Much to his chagrin, Frye was from this time on "typecast as morons, ghouls, and hunchbacks," despite his 1933 plea for comic roles "before I go screwy playing idiots, halfwits and lunatics on the talking screen!"; see Brunas, Brunas, and Weaver, *Universal Horrors*, 15.

43. Ibid., 26–27.

44. George Levine, "The Ambiguous Heritage of *Frankenstein*," in *The Endurance of Frankenstein*, eds. George Levine and U. C. Knoeplfmacher (Berkeley: University of California Press, 1974), 9. For the relationship between this scene in the *Frankenstein* novel and Henry Fuseli's painting *The Nightmare* (1781), see also Gerhard Joseph, "Frankenstein's Dream: The Child Is the Father of the Monster," *Hartford Studies in Literature* 7, no. 2 (1975): 97–115, and Anne K. Mellor, "Possessing Nature: The Female in *Frankenstein*," in *Romanticism and Feminism*, ed. Anne K. Mellor (Bloomington: Indiana University Press, 1988), 220–32. For the relationship between the painting and this scene in the *Frankenstein* film, see Susan Wolstenhulme, *Gothic (Re)Visions: Writing Women as Readers* (Albany: SUNY Press, 1993).

45. Elizabeth Young, "Here Comes the Bride: Wedding Gender and Race in *Bride of Frankenstein*," in *The Dread of Difference: Gender and the Horror Film*, ed. Barry Keith Grant (Austin: University of Texas Press, 1996), 309–37.

46. George Beard, *American Nervousness: Its Causes and Consequences* (New York: Arno Press, 1972), vi; the first edition was published in 1881. See also Tom Lutz, *American Nervousness, 1903: An Anecdotal History* (Ithaca, NY: Cornell University Press, 1991).

47. Hurley, *The Gothic Body*, 74. Colin Clive's unfortunate off-screen life modeled a dysgenic narrative of neurasthenic behavior and eventual degeneration, aided by one of the race poisons eugenics feared. James Curtis documents Clive's anxiety, alcoholism, and premature death in *James Whale: A New World of Gods and Monsters* (Boston: Faber and Faber, 1998).

48. Gail Bederman, *Manliness and Civilization: A Cultural History of Gender and Race in the United States, 1880–1917* (Chicago: University of Chicago Press, 1995), 77–120.

49. Beard, *American Nervousness*, vi. To be fair to Beard, it seems that "the mental activity of women" was meant to be understood as a factor in *women's* potential neurasthenia: "If the brain of the average American is tenfold more active than the average Athenian, the contrast in the cerebral activity of the women must be even greater"; see Beard, *American Nervousness*, 137.

50. The phrase *manifestly unfit* was used by Justice Oliver Wendell Holmes in justifying the 1927 U.S. Supreme Court decision to sterilize Carrie Buck, deemed "feeble-minded" by experts from the Eugenics Record Office. See *Buck v. Bell Superintendent*, in *Eugenics: Then and Now*, ed. Carl Jay Bajema (Stroudsburg, PA: Dowden, Hutchinson and Ross, 1976), 156–208.

51. Indeed, Lennard J. Davis has suggested that the movie's Monster is, in fact, "disabled," insofar as "disability" constitutes "a disruption in the visual, auditory, or perceptual field as it relates to the power of the gaze," for he "is inarticulate, somewhat mentally slow, and walks with a kind of physical impairment"; see Davis, *Enforcing Normalcy: Disability, Deafness, and the Body* (New York: Verso, 1995), 129, 144.

52. Pickens, *Eugenics and the Progressives*, 90. See Arthur H. Estabrook, *The Jukes in 1915* (Washington, DC: Carnegie Institution, 1916); Henry Goddard, *The Kallikak Family: A Study in the Heredity of Feeble-Mindedness* (New York: Macmillan, 1912); and the collection of family studies edited by Nicole Hahn Rafter, *White Trash: The Eugenic Family Studies, 1877–1919* (Boston: Northeastern University Press, 1988).

53. Wood, "An Introduction to the American Horror Film," 171.

54. Skal credits screenwriter John Russell with this emendation; see Skal, *Screams of Reason: Mad Science and Modern Culture* (New York: W. W. Norton, 1998), 128.

55. Martin Tropp, *Mary Shelley's Monster: The Story of Frankenstein* (Boston: Houghton Mifflin, 1976), 87; Skal, *Screams of Reason*, 128.

56. Baldick, *In Frankenstein's Shadow*, 5.

57. Walter Evans, "Monster Movies: A Sexual Theory," in Grant, *Planks of Reason*, 59.

58. Martin S. Pernick, "Defining the Defective: Eugenics, Aesthetics, and Mass Culture in Early-Twentieth-Century America," in *The Body and Physical Difference: Discourses of Disability*, ed. David T. Mitchell and Sharon L. Snyder (Ann Arbor: University of Michigan Press, 1997), 98. See also Pernick, *The Black Stork: Eugenics and the Death of "Defective" Babies in American Medicine and Motion Pictures since 1915* (New York: Oxford University Press, 1996); and Hasian, *The Rhetoric of Eugenics*.

59. On social sciences' increasing environmentalism, see Pickens, *Eugenics and the Progressives*, 203. For more general discussions of the move from mainline to reform eugenics, see the most recent histories of eugenics, including Kevles, *In the Name of Eugenics*; Paul, *Controlling Human Heredity*; Kühl, *The Nazi Connection*; and Anne Kerr and Tom Shakespeare, *Genetic Politics: From Eugenics to Genome* (Cheltenham, UK: New Clarion Press, 2002).

60. Boris Karloff, quoted in Skal, *Screams of Reason*, 129.

61. Davis, *Enforcing Normalcy*, 76n, 183.

62. On Catholic responses to eugenics, see, for example, Kevles, *In the Name of Eugenics*, 118–19, and Hasian, *The Rhetoric of Eugenics*, chap. 5. On "race poisons" and eugenics see Hasian, *The Rhetoric of Eugenics*, and John Kobler, *Ardent Spirits: The Rise and Fall of Prohibition* (New York: Putnam, 1973).

63. To name but a handful, 1930s horror films featuring scientists or doctors made monstrous by their search for biological improvement include (along with *Frankenstein*, *Bride of Frankenstein*, and *Dr. Jekyll and Mr. Hyde*) *Island of Lost Souls* (Erle Kenton, Paramount, 1932); *Doctor X* (Michael Curtiz, First National/Warner Bros., 1932); *The Invisible Man* (James Whale, Universal, 1933); *Mad Love* (Karl Freund, MGM, 1935); and *The Invisible Ray* (Lambert Hillyer, Universal, 1936).

64. Hasian, *The Rhetoric of Eugenics*, 22.

FOURTEEN

The Nazi Eugenics Exhibit in the United States, 1934–43

Robert Rydell, Christina Cogdell, and Mark Largent

ABSTRACT

In this chapter, Robert Rydell, Christina Cogdell, and Mark Largent return to an "official" eugenics display that toured parts of the country between 1934 and 1943, an exhibition called Eugenics in New Germany that was sponsored by the American Public Health Association in collaboration with other social hygiene groups and science museums and that gave de facto approval to mainline hereditarian views of eugenics. Rydell begins the essay by recapping the history of eugenics displays at state and world's fairs and eugenics congresses from the turn of the twentieth century into the 1930s, in order to establish a context for displays of this nature. Cogdell then analyzes the exhibition itself—the origin of its idea, the required cooperation between Nazi and American public health officials, its major themes and visual displays, and its strong political message of state control over reproduction—and traces its path through California in 1934. Largent picks up the show at the state line, marking its progress into Oregon, where the state legislature was then in session considering an amendment to the state's sterilization law that would broaden the number of people eligible for involuntary sterilization. The exhibition thus became a political tool used to garner public support for the amendment, which passed three months after the exhibition had traveled on; in the fall of 1935, to its home at the Buffalo Museum of Science in New York. Rydell concludes the chapter with a brief summary of the exhibition's life in Buffalo through 1943, at which point it was destroyed for being a political liability to the museum.

As the final chapter in this anthology, this essay drives home one main point. Wendy Kline's chapter on the Cooper-Hewitt sterilization trial opens the collection, focusing its attention primarily on the ways in which environmental influences were being co-opted by the eugenics movement as strict hereditarian views were under fire. "Fit" motherhood thus became a focus of eugenicists, the media, and the public alike. This shift in focus—onto environmental factors and onto white, middle-class American women as bearing the burden of race improvement—is a theme that runs throughout a number of essays in the collection. Yet this final essay, homing in on the tightening of Oregon's sterilization law, due in part to the influence of a Nazi eugenic display, shows the ongoing power of and official backing for eugenic beliefs and policies. This was true in the Pacific Northwest as well as in other parts of the country, since the number of state sterilization laws as well as the number of actual involuntary sterilizations increased throughout the decade. The complexities of the written and spoken debate over nature versus nurture is thus brought into perspective; while anthropologists, writers, artists, and filmmakers were debating the relative influence of environment over heredity, people were being sterilized against their will. It is thus fair to say that a deep acceptance of eugenic principles trumped the decade, as individual rights were sacrificed for the goals of the state and society.

Considering the number performed in the mental hospitals of the state, California takes the lead in approximately three-fourths of all such operations for sterilization in the United States which also means probably the majority done in the entire world.

F. O. BUTLER, MEDICAL DIRECTOR, SONOMA STATE HOME, ELDRIDGE, CA, 1933[1]

Taking a tip from Nazi Germany, Oregon today considered embarking on a far-reaching program of sterilization of its unfit citizens.

Oregon Journal, AUGUST 9, 1935[2]

I abominate Hitler's general policies, but if I am correctly informed in regard to his campaign for sterilization of the unfit, I prophesy that Germany will do more for the uplift of her society in the next 50 years, through sterilization, than we have done in 85 years through public education.

LYNN BANKS MCMULLEN, PRESIDENT OF EASTERN MONTANA NORMAL COLLEGE, BILLINGS, MT, 1935[3]

Between 1934 and 1943, an exhibit organized by the Deutsches Hygiene Museum (DHM) in Dresden, a leading center for popularizing the Nazis' eugenics program, traveled across the American cultural landscape. Sponsored by the American Public Health Association (APHA) and variously called Eugenics in New Germany or the Deutsches Hygiene Exhibit, the show opened in California in 1934, moved north to Oregon in 1935, and found a home at the Museum of Science in Buffalo, New York, until 1943, when, in the midst of World War II, museum officials decided the exhibit had become a liability. The show was intended to popularize Nazi eugenics in the United States and to encourage state legislatures to pass laws permitting more eugenically based sterilizations. Thousands viewed the exhibit, and it generally received positive reviews in the media. Understanding its history begins with the recognition that Nazi eugenicists, like their American counterparts, shared a conviction that sterilizations, not expanded social welfare programs, were a cost-effective way to relieve society of the expense of caring for those deemed "defective" or "unfit." As Ernest Carroll Moore, former provost of the University of California, Los Angeles, and Harold Doolittle, chief consulting engineer of Southern California Edison, reportedly told a crowd in 1936, the United States needed a "Republican New Deal" based on a plan that called for the "forcible expulsion of unemployed from relief roles, sterilization of the unfit, and war on radicals."[4] The Nazi eugenics exhibit helped make the case that eugenics provided an economically viable and scientifically valid alternative to the social welfare programs initiated by Franklin D. Roosevelt.

Eugenics Exhibits in the United States: A Brief History

To appreciate the centrality of exhibits to the eugenics movement, it is essential to understand the broader "exhibitionary culture" that swept Europe and the United States from the middle of the nineteenth century to the onset of World War II. Sociologist Tony Bennett coined the phrase *exhibitionary culture* to describe the network of museums and international expositions, often called world's fairs, that came into being after the 1851 Crystal Palace Exhibition.[5] Spurred by the success of this spectacle of Victorian England's industrial and imperial progress, other nations followed suit, building a series of world's fairs that attracted tens of millions of people (the 1900 Paris Universal Exposition, for instance, attracted fifty million visitors during its six-month run). However ephemeral, these "dream cities" were serious educational endeavors (the University of Chicago offered college credit to students who took a course offered in conjunction with the 1904 St. Louis fair) and often had the effect of creating some of the world's great museums. For instance, London's Victoria and Albert Museum, Chicago's Field Museum and the Museum of Science and Industry, Dresden's Deutsches Hygiene Museum, and San Diego's Museum of Man were all the direct by-products of fairs held in these cities. To be sure, fairs were fun, but their blend of serious didacticism with pleasure attracted the multitudes, as well as people and organizations seeking to influence them. Like anthropologists, who saw world's fairs as unsurpassed opportunities for gaining public support for their young profession, eugenicists recognized the opportunity the fairs afforded for reaching the multitudes with their messages of better health care for mothers and infants, immigration reform, and sterilization of the socially and racially unfit.[6]

Between 1884, when British eugenicists established a eugenics display at the British International Health Exhibition, and 1915, when the Race Betterment Foundation of Battle Creek, Michigan, organized a eugenics exhibit at San Francisco's Panama-Pacific International Exposition, displays dedicated to eugenics had become important nodes in the spreading exhibitionary webwork of the Victorian era. But these shows were only the warm-up acts for what came next. Between the onset of World War I and the close of the 1939–40 New York World's Fair, eugenics exhibits became increasingly commonplace at international, national, and local fairs in the United States and were instrumental in eugenicists' efforts to shape the American body politic according to the dictates of "race betterment."

The 1915 eugenics exhibit at the San Francisco fair was the catalyst. Organized by John H. Kellogg's Race Betterment Foundation, the exhibit offered a brief for enacting eugenics-based legislation that would support sterilization of "defectives" and limit immigration to northern Europeans. In addition to attracting crowds of onlookers, the exhibit became the model for an international eugenics conference organized in conjunction with the fair. Supported by Stanford University chancellor David Starr Jordan, Harvard University president emeritus Charles W. Eliot, and conservationist Gifford Pinchot, this conference inspired a eugenics-suffused exhibitionary complex that would radiate across the nation for the next quarter century.

Prime movers behind the American eugenics movement's newfound emphasis on exhibits included Charles B. Davenport, his protégé Harry

Laughlin, and women's health advocates Mary T. Watts and Florence Brown Sherbon. Together, they developed a plan to inject eugenics exhibits into state fairs under the guise of improving health care for rural women and their children. By 1920, they had organized a "fitter families for future firesides" movement at state fairs that Sherbon claimed would help in "the strengthening of the family as the organic racial and social unit." Families deemed the fittest received silver trophies and blue ribbons that were sometimes awarded by prominent politicians, and winners of "better babies" contests were showered with blue ribbons and praised in newspaper headlines. As Sherbon reflected on her work, eugenics "must be made to function in the lives of the people. This can only come about through the use of disciples from among the people who will receive the bread of science from the hands of research—Christ-men—and break it again to their fellow creatures."[7]

At the same time that eugenics' popularizers sought to win over the multitudes with their emphasis on health care and social reform, they also opened a second front and sought to win support for national legislation that would address one of the eugenicists' primary concerns: the immigration to the United States of those considered racially unfit. To make this case, Laughlin and Davenport, in cooperation with the American Museum of Natural History, drew on the precedent of the 1915 fair, and in 1921 and 1932, they turned the museum into the site for two major eugenics exhibitions and one of the most important international meetings of eugenicists ever held.[8] The eugenics exhibits, drawn each time from the museum's own collections and over one hundred private exhibitors, consisted of "mainly embryology and racial casts and models, photographs, pedigree charts and tables, biological family histories and collective biographies, graphical and historical charts on the character and analysis of population, material showing the principles of heredity in plants, animals, and man, maps and analytical tables demonstrating racial vicissitudes, anthropometric instruments, apparatus for mental measurements, and books and scientific reprints on eugenical and genetical subjects."[9] During its month-long run in 1921, the exhibit attracted teachers and their students and between five and ten thousand visitors; in 1932, over fifteen thousand people viewed the displays.[10]

Adding another layer of meaning and authority to the exhibits were the attendant meetings and speeches of the Second and Third International Congresses of Eugenics. The proceedings of the 1921 meeting, in particular, deserve the attention of every student of eugenics, for they give ample testimony to the claims by museum officials that this had been one of the most important scientific meetings ever held. Participants included statisticians, anthropologists, and representatives from eugenics societies in England, Europe, Latin America, and the United States. Papers included examinations of "racial alteration" and an assessment of the impact of World War I on France's birthrate. Charles Darwin's son, Leonard, praised the eugenics exhibit and was so enthusiastic about the whole affair that he confidently predicted, "We may be sure that the seed sown in New York will spring up in many distant cities."[11] He was absolutely right, but even Darwin might have been surprised at how quickly and where this seed produced fruit.

Three months after the eugenics show-and-tell ended in New York, Laughlin, who had acquired the position of "expert eugenics agent" for the House of Representatives Immigration Committee, had portions of the exhibit that pertained directly to immigration mounted on the walls of the room where U.S. congressional representatives were conducting hearings on the need to impose restrictions on immigrants to the United States. With the exhibits providing seemingly irrefutable evidence for restriction based on alleged racial attributes, the committee drafted the National Origins Act in 1924, which would remain the law of the land into the 1960s.[12]

Eugenicists had scored a major victory in shaping the new immigration restriction laws, but they did not rest on their laurels. Indeed, a growing body of criticism from geneticists, Catholic clergy, literary intellectuals, and civil libertarians began to challenge the basic tenets of the eugenics creed. Confronted, on the one hand, by intellectuals' mounting suspicion of the moral and scientific legitimacy of eugenics and, on the other, by eugenicists' realization that increased public support would be necessary for sustaining and widening the scope of sterilization legislation, eugenics supporters in the APHA sought and received support from Nazi Germany in 1934. Specifically, they enlisted the support of the German government to bring to the United States an exhibition organized by the DHM, which toured part of the United States before becoming a permanent, albeit short-lived, exhibit at the Buffalo Museum of Science in New York. The show's tour and especially the legislation its contents supported attest to the power of the exhibit medium and illustrate the overlay of Nazi and American eugenics in the United States in the 1930s. The fact that the show was incorporated into the permanent exhibits of the Buffalo museum underscores the tenacity of American eugenic thought and feeling, whereas the exhibit's destruction in

1943 points to the primary importance of World War II for decoupling eugenics from patriotism and for setting in motion the painfully slow process of reversing eugenics-based legislation in the postwar period.

Eugenics in New Germany in the United States

The exhibit, Eugenics in New Germany, was curated by Bruno Gebhard, scientific secretary and curator at the DHM in Dresden, and arose specifically from American public health professionals' interest in the sophistication of Germany's health and hygiene programs, as evidenced partially in their museum exhibits. Various members of the APHA visited the International Hygiene Exhibition in Dresden in 1930, an exhibition sponsored by the DHM that was intended to educate the public about contemporary health knowledge and concerns through highly engaging, interactive exhibits. That same year, the APHA had formed a committee that included Homer Calver, Louis Dublin, Victor Heiser, and Evart Routzahn to pursue the establishment of the American Museum of Hygiene, based largely on German and British precedent. Routzahn, who was also director of the Department of Surveys and Exhibits for the Russell Sage Foundation and who had worked on various social health exhibits at the Philadelphia Sesqui-Centennial Exhibition of 1926, traveled to Dresden in 1930, where he was impressed by the German exhibits as well as by Gebhard, a recent medical school graduate who had helped officials at the DHM create the Transparent Man sculpture, made of clear cellon plastic showing the ideal man's physique and internal organs, for the exhibition. In their conversations, Routzahn encouraged Gebhard to enter the health museum profession rather than start a private practice, advice that Gebhard followed and that later proved hugely influential on the health museum movement in the United States.[13]

Concurrently, between 1928 and 1931, members of the American Medical Association (AMA) were working toward the establishment of a major public health exhibition at Chicago's Century-of-Progress Exposition between 1933 and 1934. In March 1931, Eben Carey, chief of the Medical Section of the fair, traveled to Dresden with $25,000 provided by the Oberlaender Trust (OT) to meet with Gebhard at the DHM in order to arrange for the purchase of copies of displays from the museum, which were to become the nucleus of the fair's exhibition.[14] The Oberlaender Trust funded research projects that promoted German and American exchange, and during the 1930s, it supported the travel of a number of Americans inter-ested in German eugenics. Haven Emerson, president of the APHA in 1934, and Louis Dublin, on the APHA Committee of the American Mu-seum of Hygiene with Homer Calver, were both trustees of the Oberlaen-der Trust and avid supporters of eugenics. It is therefore not surprising that the trust served as a crucial link between the APHA, the Medical Sec-tion at the Chicago World's Fair, Gebhard and other officials at the DHM, and the creation of the exhibition Eugenics in New Germany, which trav-eled through six U.S. cities between 1934 and 1935.

In late fall 1933, William W. Peter, assistant secretary of the APHA and a longtime public health worker, traveled to Germany for a six-month tour under the auspices of the APHA and the Oberlaender Trust to visit Ger-man health museums and meet with government officials to gain a full comprehension of Germany's public health and race hygiene programs. In July 1933, Germany had passed its compulsory sterilization law, which was scheduled to go into effect January 1, 1934, and American officials wanted firsthand knowledge of the effects of the law and the context in which such far-reaching legislation would be enacted. Peter described his findings in "Germany's Sterilization Program," an article published in the March 1934 issue of the *American Journal of Public Health,* the official jour-nal of the APHA. He described the intentions of the law and stated it had been his "privilege to meet some of the leaders in the present political regime who are responsible for new undertakings in reconstruction of the social order."[15] That same month in Berlin, Peter received a letter from Calver, who also chaired the Committee on Scientific Exhibits for the APHA, asking Peter to use his powerful contacts to try to convince Gebhard, the DHM, and the German government to send an exhibition documenting Public Health and Eugenics in New Germany; it was to be displayed at the upcoming annual convention of the APHA, to be held in Pasadena, from September 3–6, 1934.

Peter was excited by the possibility and immediately went to work, drafting and presenting a proposal for the organization of the exhibition, which he reported was, without exception, well received. German officials were eager to have an opportunity to "promote the new Germany through scientific channels abroad."[16] Peter responded to Calver: "I wasted no time with small fry but took the matter directly to the big shots in the fields of medicine and public health who will be able to put it through at this end if that is possible for anyone to do at this time," due to Germany's dire financial straits.[17] These men included Gebhard, George Seiring (president of the DHM), Falk Ruttke (of the German Health Education Service), Helmut Unger (editor of the Educational Office for Population Problems and Race Hygiene), Hans Reiter (president of the German Federal Health Service), and Arthur Gütt (minister director for the Ministry of the Interior of the NSDAP and the man in charge of all medical and public health activities in Germany). Five of these men then formed the German committee in charge of the exhibition.[18]

Peter and the men he selected chose the themes of Germany's population problems arising from differential birth and death rates and issues of race hygiene with regard to hereditary disease, costs of institutionalization, sterilization, and governmental attempts to foster an increase in the number of eugenic births. The committee agreed with Peter's suggestion that, since the exhibition would likely travel to other venues besides the Pasadena convention, it should fill between 300 and 500 square meters and consist of approximately fifty translated displays from the race hygiene and population problems section of the 1934 exhibition in Berlin, Deutsche Volk–Deutsche Arbeit, on which Gebhard had worked (fig. 14.1).

Fig. 14.1. Photo of installation at Deutsche Volk–Deutsche Arbeit, Berlin, 1934, showing Bach's lineage on the left and panels pertaining to sterilization in the center. Photo GF-4-150b (Folder 3), Bruno Gebhard Papers. Courtesy of the Dittrick Medical History Center, Case Western Reserve University.

In turn, the American committee for the exhibition, known as the Committee on Scientific Exhibits of the APHA and headed by Calver, was responsible for finding other venues for the show in the United States and Canada, as well as for raising the necessary funds for the transport of the exhibition within the states. Peter suggested the Chicago World's Fair as a possible venue, since it was open again in 1934 and already contained health exhibits from the DHM. Although this never materialized, the converse did, as some of the materials from the fair, including twelve celluloid models of reproductive fertilization and maturation and the Transparent Man, did, in fact, travel with the Eugenics in New Germany exhibition up the West Coast, as various newspapers promoting the exhibition made clear.[19]

When the exhibit opened in Pasadena, Gebhard was in attendance, having flown to the States to oversee its installation and to mingle with his American colleagues (fig. 14.2).

Installed by Japanese American workers and occupying 3,000 square feet in the Civic Auditorium, the exhibition was arranged in four general sections.[20] The first contained charts graphing German population changes,

Fig 14.2. Installation and viewers at the Eugenics in New Germany exhibit in Pasadena's Civic Auditorium, early September 1934. Gebhard is second from the right facing the camera, and the posters on the wall show recent German migration patterns. Photo GF-5-24a, Bruno Gebhard Papers. Courtesy of the Dittrick Medical History Center, Case Western Reserve University.

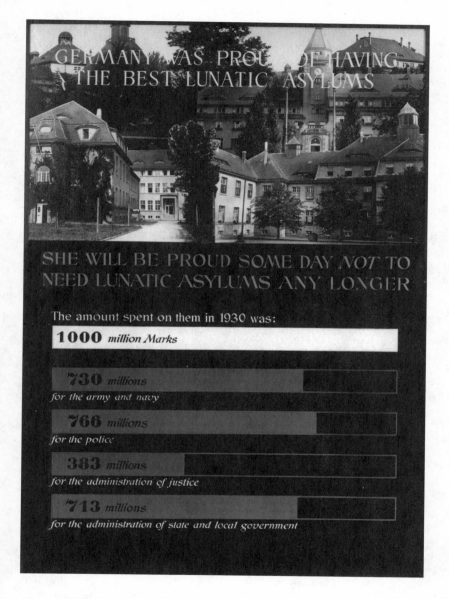

GERMANY WAS PROUD OF HAVING THE BEST LUNATIC ASYLUMS

SHE WILL BE PROUD SOME DAY *NOT* TO NEED LUNATIC ASYLUMS ANY LONGER

The amount spent on them in 1930 was:

1000 *million Marks*

730 *millions*
for the army and navy

766 *millions*
for the police

383 *millions*
for the administration of justice

713 *millions*
for the administration of state and local government

Fig. 14.3. "Germany was proud of having the best lunatic asylums. . . . She will be proud some day *not* to need lunatic asylums any longer." Panel included in the Eugenics in New Germany exhibition. Photo GF-5-18, Bruno Gebhard Papers. Courtesy of the Dittrick Medical History Center, Case Western Reserve University.

including birth and marriage rates, predominantly between 1930 and 1934, at times comparing German trends to those of other European nations. Overall, these showed declines in population and births since World War I. The next section opened with celluloid models displaying the "wonders of hereditary transmission," followed immediately by posters explaining Mendelian laws of hereditary transmission and dominance; the heredity of eye color, hair color, body build, and such unfavorable characteristics as the Habsburg lower lip; and the difference between identical and fraternal twins.[21] This knowledge of the principles of heredity was then applied to the hereditary transmission of physical, mental, and behavioral defects, concluding with posters showing the recent increase in the number of mental cases and the large amount of federal funds spent on their care, funds that could be reduced significantly by the implementation of sterilization (fig. 14.3).[22]

The third section elaborated on the structure and policies of Germany's race hygiene program. It began with the law intended to prevent hereditary diseases for posterity, which, it explained, would be accomplished through sexual sterilization.[23] A racist illustration of a poor, black man portrayed him as a carrier of *all* types of hereditary disease, claiming that "if this man had been sterilised, then there would not have been born . . . 12 hereditarily diseased" children, bearing social, physical, and mental abnormalities (fig. 14.4).

To volunteer oneself for sterilization, especially if one possessed a "hereditary inclination for crime," one put in an application to the Court of Heredity, which then rendered a decision.[24] In reality, doctors and relatives did most of the "volunteering" for targeted individuals. The following panel then explained that a criminal could be incarcerated and even castrated "to eradicate the morbid sexual desire of the criminal pervert," should his crime have been sexual and a repeat offense.

The panels then shifted from such negative content to displays showing how Germany was, at the same time, trying to encourage desirable births. State subsidies were given out in increments of 25 percent to young married couples having children, ensuring that to receive their full government subsidy, the couple would have at least four children. Berlin in particular changed its policies from "indiscriminate[ly]" caring for all infants, thereby preserving "worthless lives," to "intentional[ly]" furthering only "hereditarily sound off-spring." It offered as well more selective marriage

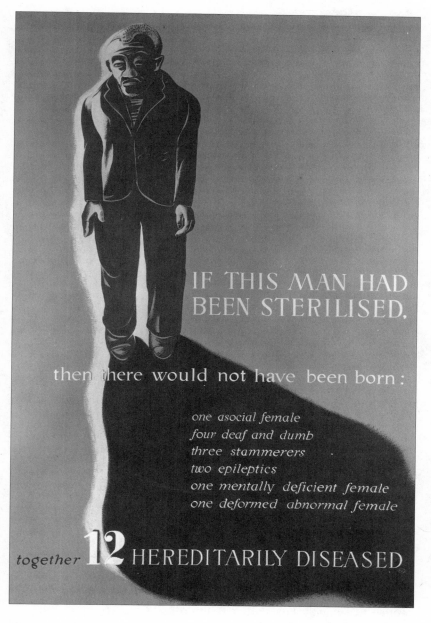

IF THIS MAN HAD
BEEN STERILISED,

then there would not have been born:

one asocial female
four deaf and dumb
three stammerers
two epileptics
one mentally deficient female
one deformed abnormal female

together **12** HEREDITARILY DISEASED

Fig. 14.4. "If this man had been sterilised. . . ." Panel included in the Eugenics in New Germany exhibition. Courtesy of the Buffalo Museum of Science, Buffalo, New York.

advice to achieve the "high biological standard" of a "new race nobility" (fig. 14.5).

The third section concluded with an explanation of Germany's Central Register for "hereditarily diseased or suspect people," which consisted of a record bank of entire families that officials consulted when offering marriage advice or for other reasons. Finally, the last section of the exhibit contained miscellaneous displays of general trends in the German birthrate (including the fact that more children were born in rural and agricultural areas than in urban areas and industrial regions), as well as Hitler's and Bach's genealogies and the historical migrations made by Germans into other parts of Europe and beyond, thus showing the extension of German influence across the "civilized" world.

Pasadena residents warmly received the exhibit, which an editorial in the *American Journal of Public Health* described as having "unusual interest."[25] Many years later, Gebhard lamented that he could participate in only a few of the formal sessions because "there was a constant stream of visitors at my exhibition." "Naturally," he added, "I was questioned about how far the Nazi government had changed the practice of medicine. I was surprised how many of my questioners were in favor of Adolf Hitler—they hated Franklin D. Roosevelt just as much as I hated Hitler."[26] One evening at a conference social gathering, Walter Mangold, who worked for the Los Angeles County Health Department, asked Gebhard and Calver if his organization could offer the first traveling venue of the exhibition by showing it for thirty days at the Los Angeles County Museum. They agreed and displayed it in the large exhibit hall for two months instead of one, owing to high media publicity and popular demand.[27] Early in January 1935, the exhibit was transferred for two weeks to the Armory in Stockton, California, at the request of the Women's Auxiliary of the San Joaquin County Medical Society and John J. Sippy, director of the San Joaquin County Health District. "Famous Exhibit from Germany Seen in Armory" proclaimed the front page of the *Stockton Record* in an article that encouraged the public to attend for free, especially high school and college students in "biological and social science classes." "The unmistakable message of the display is an urge for the building up of a virile, healthy race," the journalist explained. "Through a large portion of the exhibit is apparent the Hitler ambition for an increased birth rate for Germany. Not only from a hygienic and health education standpoint but from political insight into the German

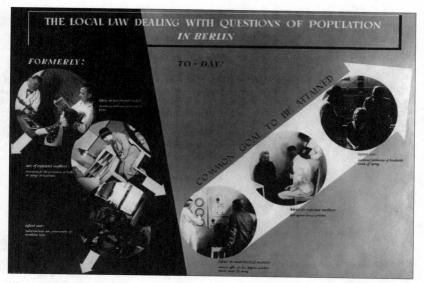

Fig. 14.5. "The local law dealing with questions of population in Berlin." Panel in-
cluded in Eugenics in New Germany exhibition. Photo GF-5-11, Bruno Gebhard
Papers. Courtesy of the Dittrick Medical History Center, Case Western Reserve
University.

program the exhibit is deeply interesting."[28] From Stockton, the exhibit traveled to Sacramento briefly in mid-February, and after a failed attempt to get
it shown at the New York Academy of Medicine, it was immediately transferred to Salem, Oregon, in care of Vernon Douglas, Marion County health
officer. It arrived at an opportune moment—just as the state legislative session was considering revisions to Oregon's sterilization statute.[29]

The Deutsches Hygiene Exhibit in Oregon

The exhibit arrived at the Salem Young Men's Christian Association (YMCA)
on February 11, 1935, and the *Capital Journal* and the *Oregon Statesman*,
Salem's two newspapers, covered its arrival and explained Gebhard's role
in bringing it to the United States.[30] Reports about the exhibit emphasized
the fine craftsmanship of its models as well as its intended use in educating the public on Mendel's law of heredity, trends of populations in Europe, and the hereditability of "epilepsy, habitual drunkenness and mental

disorder."[31] The display was open for public inspection during afternoon and evening hours through February, and classes of students from Willamette University viewed it. After it had been on display for two weeks, newspaper reports began to more fully explain the exhibit's basic argument: "The exhibit is a part of the great German program to eliminate undesirable types of persons through a carefully worked out sterilization program."[32] Increasingly, Salem-area newspapers mentioned the exhibit's promotion of sterilization of "groups with hereditary and mental defects" and explained that when the problem was "attacked at its source," the Germans would bring about "racial improvement and fewer defectives to be cared for at public expense."[33] The connection the exhibit made between the use of coerced sterilization and the public's anxieties about the high cost of prisons and mental health facilities was not at all new to Oregonians, so the papers' references to the subject would have been fully understood by their readers.

At the end of February 1935, after the exhibit had been at the YMCA for several weeks, Douglas oversaw its move to the state capitol, where he anticipated even more local residents would see it. Two weeks later, as health officials made stereopticon slides of the exhibit's charts and models for use by state hospital staff, Douglas estimated that more than six thousand people had viewed it at the YMCA, in the corridors at the capitol, and during a brief visited to the Salem High School.[34] By the time it left Salem in mid-March, Douglas claimed that between seven and eight thousand Salem-area residents had viewed the exhibit before health officials crated the show and transferred it to Reed College in Portland, then to the Portland YMCA.[35]

In sharp contrast to the Salem newspapers, the *Oregonian* covered the exhibit's showing in Portland with a small announcement indicating it would open at the YMCA on April 24, 1935. The article briefly described the health exhibit as consisting of "celluloid models, posters, charts, graphs and pictures," but it failed to detail its contents or message.[36] Fred Messing, executive secretary of the Oregon Social Hygiene Society, took the exhibit to Portland and advertised its arrival in letters to area institutions. On May 21, a portion of the exhibit was shown to students at Reed College.[37] In a letter to Carlos Cummings at the Buffalo Museum of Science, Messing claimed that about forty thousand visited the exhibition when it was shown in the Portland area.[38] Added to the nearly eight thousand that Douglas claimed to have visited it in Salem, then, if their numbers are accurate, approximately one out of every twenty Oregonians saw the Deutsches Hygiene Exhibit in 1935.[39]

Long before the exhibit arrived in Oregon in 1935 and traveled from Salem to Portland, proponents of involuntary sterilization had convinced the state legislature to condone their plan to improve the state's citizenry.[40] One of the state's most celebrated women, Bethenia Owens-Adair, had first called for the legalization of coerced sterilization in 1904. Owens-Adair was the first female medical doctor in the Pacific Northwest and an ardent supporter of progressive reform measures, including women's suffrage and eugenic sterilization. In a letter to the *Oregonian,* she claimed that "the greatest curse of the races comes through our vicious criminal and insane classes." Mental health patients and convicted felons, she believed, ought to be "dealt with, not by chloroform or strangulation, but by the science of surgery, for if their power to reproduce themselves were rendered null a tremendous important step in advance would have been taken, not only without injury to life, but often with positive benefit to the victims them-selves."[41] Encouraged by Owens-Adair and her growing number of support-ers, which included the *Oregonian* and the *Oregon Journal,* state legislators passed the state's first involuntary sterilization bill in 1909. The passage of the bill began a nearly decade-long fight in which successive legislatures passed sterilization bills that were vetoed by the governor, rejected by a public referendum, and declared unconstitutional by a county court. Finally, in 1923, the legislature passed a sterilization bill that the governor sup-ported, the courts accepted, and the public overlooked.

Legal involuntary sterilization began slowly in Oregon, with one man sterilized in 1912, a woman sterilized a year later, and another woman in 1917. In 1918, the numbers jumped dramatically to seventeen when the leg-islature created the State Board of Eugenics to analyze the cases of patients and prisoners to determine those "who are persons [with the] potential to produc[e] offspring who, because of inheritance of inferior or antisocial traits, would probably become a social menace, or ward of the State."[42] In 1922, when at least eighty-three people were forcibly sterilized, the Marion County Circuit Court nullified the law because it violated the patients' and prisoners' right to due process, as they were sterilized as a result of their incarceration. A separate trial or administrative proceeding, the court ex-plained, would be necessary to overcome this problem. The legislature moved quickly to change the process by which sterilizations were ordered, which effectively addressed the problems identified by the court, and between twelve and twenty-five involuntary sterilizations were performed each year throughout the 1920s and early 1930s.[43]

In practice, the particular types of sterilization procedures performed on Oregon's mental health patients and prisoners demonstrated that the medical community was interested in far more than merely improving the genetic quality of future generations. Despite claims from historians that castration was far too brutal a procedure and was not regularly performed in the United States, at least 163 Oregonians were castrated between 1912 and 1945.[44] The 1917 law required that "no person shall be emasculated under the authority of this Act except that such operation shall be found to be necessary to improve the physical, mental, neural or psychic condition of the inmate."[45] Given these constraints, the castration of men declared feebleminded or convicted of either sexual offenses or three or more felonies could have been justified only on therapeutic grounds. Therefore, to some extent, the practice of coerced sterilization in Oregon was at least sometimes motivated or justified by supposedly therapeutic ends.

When the Deutsches Hygiene Exhibit arrived in Salem in February 1935 and toured the area through the spring of that year, Oregon's Board of Eugenics had been meeting regularly for almost two decades and had already ordered the coerced sterilization of approximately one thousand mental health patients, convicted felons, and people accused of being "sexual perverts."[46] There is no direct evidence that the exhibit influenced Oregon's sterilization policy, but there is considerable circumstantial evidence that, just as Laughlin's use of eugenics exhibits influenced passage of the 1924 National Origins Act, the Nazi eugenics exhibit powerfully motivated the legislature's expansion of the use of coerced sterilization in Oregon. When the exhibit first arrived in Salem, the *Capital Journal* explained that its appearance was particularly appropriate at the time "due to the introduction in the legislature of measures to check the spread of mental disease."[47] Similarly, the *Oregon Statesman* quoted Willamette University sociologist S. B. Laughlin's claim that the exhibit was "very valuable and of great interest in Oregon now."[48]

Oregon, like most other American states and like Germany, experienced severe economic hardships during the 1930s, and newspapers often parroted claims made in the exhibit that coerced sterilization would bring about lower welfare and institutional costs. The regular session of the state legislature met through the first several months of 1935 and was recalled for a special session in the fall to debate and pass dozens of bills, many of them relating to the funding of state agencies.[49] Among the more than seventy bills passed into law during the special session was an extension of the range of people eligible for coerced sterilization.[50] Chapter 39 of the 1935 Special Session provided "for the inclusion of additional classes of persons as subject to sterilization" and specifically required the superintendents of the state training school for boys and the state industrial school for girls to join the heads of the state hospitals, the institutions for the feebleminded, and the state penitentiary in submitting to the Board of Eugenics the names of patients and prisoners for review. Some juvenile wards of the state had already been subject to involuntary sterilization, which had prompted a nineteen-article series on the commitment and sterilization of children by *Oregonian* reporter Margaret Skavlan in the early 1930s. The 1935 revision specifically called for the sterilization of unfit children housed in boys' and girls' training schools, as well as the review of files from anyone convicted of performing or attempting a sex crime, including rape, incest, sodomy, contributing to the delinquency of the minor by sexual act or act of sexual perversion, or a crime against nature, the legal framework used to prosecute men convicted of committing acts of homosexuality.

On August 9, 1935, only three months after the Deutsches Hygiene Exhibit had toured the area, the *Oregon Journal* reported that state leaders were "taking a tip from Nazi Germany" by considering "a far-reaching program of sterilization of its unfit citizens."[51] Comparing Oregon's plan positively to the Nazi program, the article explained that state officials considered sterilization a useful and appropriate tool for reducing the state's expenditure on unfit citizens. Emphasizing the economic nature of the state's concerns, State Treasurer Rufus C. Holmes and Secretary of State Earl Snell discussed with the governor the need to increase the number of sterilizations performed on residents of the state's charitable and penal institutions. The goal was to "take more drastic steps to halt the increase in numbers of criminally and mentally diseased persons who are responsible for an alarming growth in the population of institutions."[52] When the exhibit was first moved to the state capitol, Prince W. Byrd, an assistant superintendent of the Oregon State Hospital, had explained that by adopting a sterilization program, "there will be racial improvement and fewer defectives to be cared for at public expense."[53] Governor Charles H. Martin signed the revisions into law on November 15, 1935, and began offering prisoners convicted of sex crimes parole if they would volunteer for sterilization. The numbers of Oregonians sterilized spiked in the mid-1930s to rates nearly double what they were only a few years earlier. Involuntary sterilization remained a common tool for the maintenance of Oregon's wards of the state until 1983, when the state legislature officially closed the last avenue for state officials to sterilize mental health patients and prisoners against their will. In 2002, outgoing Governor John Kitzhaber formally apologized to the nearly three thousand Oregonians forcibly sterilized in the twentieth century.

Conclusion

The German exhibit cost about 15,000 DM ($6,000), no small sum in the early 1930s, yet the German government made no provision for its return to the DHM. Gebhard had hoped that his work would find a permanent home in the New York Academy of Medicine, but a critical review in a British medical journal suggesting that portions of the exhibit seemed "designed rather to support a political conviction than to illustrate natural law" led the academy's directors to decline the exhibit.[54] But all was not lost. Carlos Cummings, a medical doctor and naturalist at the Buffalo Museum of Science, saw the New York Academy's loss as a long-term gain for his museum, presenting it with, as one of Gebhard's associates put it, "the nucleus of the first American museum exhibit of this kind."[55] By March 1935, arrangements were made to ship nine cases of the Nazi eugenics material from Portland to Buffalo, where they were intended to be part of the museum's permanent collections. Cummings could scarcely contain his enthusiasm for his acquisition. "What is the astounding eugenics program upon which Chancellor Hitler has launched the German people?" asked *Hobbies,* a museum-based magazine for young people that was edited by Cummings. "As a matter of public interest, without endorsement," the magazine announced, "the Museum will display in the Central Hall, throughout this final quarter of 1935, a set of fifty-one posters and charts, a gift from the Deutsche Hygiene-Museum of Dresden, which gives Americans a graphic explanation of German's campaign to rear in posterity 'a new race nobility.'"[56]

That was 1935. By August 1942, with the United States deeply involved in a war to defeat Nazi Germany, the exhibit had become a distinct liability for the museum, and Cummings sought permission from the insurance firm that had bonded the exhibit and from U.S. Customs to destroy "certain German propaganda charts" that had become "perfectly useless material." One year later, the museum incinerated "certain propaganda pamphlets, etc.," and sought and evidently received additional permission to destroy "models of fertilization and maturation, made of celluloid, wood, etc., which we have had on permanent display in our Hall of Heredity."[57] The Nazi eugenics road show was finished—except, perhaps, in the minds of those who saw it and in the memories of those who experienced its message most directly in the form of coerced sterilization.

Notes

1. F. O. Butler, "Utility of Sterilization for the Mentally Deficient," c. 1933, Box 28, Folder 6, Ezra S. Gosney Papers, Cal Tech Archives, Pasadena, CA.

2. "Far-Reaching Sterilization Plan Studied," *Oregon Journal*, August 9, 1935.

3. "Montana Man Lauds One of Hitler's Moves," *Great Falls Leader*, August 17, 1935.

4. "Sterilization of Workers Urged by Cal. Men," *United Progressive News*, May 4, 1936.

5. Tony Bennett, *The Birth of the Museum* (London: Routledge, 1995), 59.

6. For a fuller account of American eugenics exhibits, see Robert W. Rydell, *World of Fairs: The Century-of-Progress Expositions* (Chicago: University of Chicago Press, 1993), chap. 2.

7. Florence Brown Sherbon, "Popular Education," *Eugenics* 1, no. 1 (October 1928): 33.

8. The Third International Congress of Eugenics, held at the American Museum of Natural History in 1932, attracted fewer eugenicists from the international community due to the limited availability of funds during the international economic depression.

9. Harry Laughlin, *The Second International Exhibition of Eugenics . . . An Account of the Organization of the Exhibition, the Classification of the Exhibits, the List of Exhibitors, and a Catalog and Description of the Exhibits* (Baltimore, MD: Williams and Wilkins, 1923), 13–18.

10. *A Decade of Progress in Eugenics: Scientific Papers of the Third International Congress of Eugenics, Held at American Museum of Natural History, New York, August 21–23, 1932* (Baltimore, MD: Williams and Wilkins, 1934), 489–509.

11. Leonard Darwin, "Reports of the International Congress of Eugenics Held at New York in September 1921," *Eugenics Review* (undated clipping), Eugenics Education Society Library, London.

12. Frances Janet Hassencahl, "Harry H. Laughlin, 'Expert Eugenics Agent' for the House Committee on Immigration and Naturalization, 1921 to 1931" (PhD diss., Case Western Reserve University, 1970).

13. Cedric Dover, "Welfare Museums in Germany," *Museums Journal* 35 (December 1935): 325, and letter from Homer Calver to the editor of the *Health Museums Journal*, July 31, 1962, in Folder 2-36, Bruno Gebhard Papers, Dittrick Medical History Center, Case Western Reserve University, Cleveland, OH (hereafter cited as BG Papers). Calver recounted his role in the origin of health museums in the United States. He described the APHA Committee on American Museums of Hygiene, founded in 1930, as including Evart Routzahn, Dublin, himself, and three others. He mentioned that the Oberlaender Trust (OT) approached this committee in the mid-1930s through OT's representatives, Haven Emerson and Wilbur K. Thomas, to fund travel research on English and German health museums in order to aid in the establishment of the American Museum of Health after the 1939–40 New York World's Fair. This research was completed by September 1936; see Folder 2-48, "Homer N. Calver: American Museum of Health," BG Papers, and also mimeographs entitled "Russell Sage Foundation, 1907–1946," and another untitled one dated 1944, Box 2, Folder 24, "Evart G. Routzahn, Chairman American Public Health Association," BG Papers. Gebhard credited the Routzahns with convincing him to work in health museums rather than enter private practice in the early 1930s after finishing medical school. See also Rosmarie Beier and Martin Roth, *Leibesvisitation* (Berlin: Deutsches Historisches Museum, 1990), for more information on the Transparent Man.

14. Letter from Eben Carey to Bruno Gebhard, August 1, 1945, Box 3, Folder 2-47, BG Papers. William Pusey, at a meeting of the American Medical Association in 1928, came up with idea of medical, dental, and pharmaceutical exhibits at Chicago, and he began to develop these ideas subsequently until 1931. In March 1931, Carey was appointed chief of the Medical Section by the Executive Committee of the Fair (Rufus Dawes, Lenox Lohr, and Pusey) and was told by them to visit the Deutsche Hygiene Museum (DHM) in Dresden, as well as other museums, to purchase exhibits to be built by the DHM. Carey stated that part or all of this money came from the Oberlaender Trust. A clipping in the BG Papers entitled "American Museum of Hygiene," dated October 10, 1933, Folder 2-36: "American Museum of Health," stated that in 1933, Calver and Heiser of the APHA committee met with fair officials to install an exhibit on hygiene but instead were directed to Carey's medical exhibits. The eugenic intentions of Calver's and Heiser's work on the fair exhibits in Chicago and later in the decade in New York, as part of their goal to establish the American Museum of Health, were stated in the "Report of the Committee" at the Pasadena convention: "As an added help in visualizing the contents of such

a museum, we are also fortunate in having this year in connection with this meeting an exhibit directly from the German Hygiene Museum, which was arranged for by the Committee on Scientific Exhibits of the Association." See "American Museum of Hygiene," Folder 2-36: "American Museum of Health," BG Papers.

15. William W. Peter, "Germany's Sterilization Program," *American Journal of Public Health* 24 (March 1934): 187–91, and Stefan Kühl, *The Nazi Connection: Eugenics, American Racism, and German National Socialism* (Oxford: Oxford University Press, 1994), 54–55. Kühl mentioned that Peter also published a highly propagandistic visionary article in the *Neues Volk* publication of the Nazi Party.

16. Memo sent to the Ministry of the Interior announcing the exhibition, May 4, 1934, copied to W. W. Peter by Gebhard, in Folder 2-54: "American Public Health Association: Pasadena Exhibit, 1934, American Museum of Health 1937," BG Papers.

17. Letter from W. W. Peter to Homer Calver, late April 1934, included behind a translation of "Nonbinding Proposals by W. W. Peter MD Regarding a German Hygiene Exhibit at the Annual Meeting of the APHA," in Folder 2-54: "American Public Health Association: Pasadena Exhibit, 1934, American Museum of Health 1937," BG Papers.

18. The German committee for the exhibition consisted of Gebhard as executive secretary, Seiring, Klein (of CMO Berlin), Ruttke, and Gütt. See letter from W. W. Peter to George Seiring," Folder 2-54: "American Public Health Association: Pasadena Exhibit, 1934, American Museum of Health 1937," BG Papers.

19. "'Transparent Man' Sensation of Chicago Fair Will Be Exhibited Here Next Week," *Pasadena Post*, September 1, 1934, and "Famous Exhibit from Germany Seen in Armory," *Stockton (California) Record*, January 16, 1935, both in Oversize Box 8: "Clippings, 1930s, German and English," BG Papers. It is unclear from these news articles if the Transparent Man traveled beyond Pasadena, although it did end up at the Buffalo Museum along with the rest of the exhibition. The celluloid models are described in a letter from Mrs. Karl E. Wilhelm of the Buffalo Museum of Science to the Collector of Customs in Los Angeles, May 3, 1947, when she requested them to be destroyed; the letter is in Folder A-01/2(3), F3, Archives of the Buffalo Museum of Science, Buffalo, NY (hereafter cited as BMS).

20. A description of the items in the exhibition in German, entitled "Austellungsgegenstände Pasadena," can be found in Box 3, Folder 2-47: "History of World's Fairs," BG Papers. Gebhard's archive, Folder GF-5, contains photos of many of the exhibition panels, some of which are in English and some in German (these were the prototypes from Deutsches Volk-Deutsches Arbeit exhibition). However, Folder A-042 (3), F3, BMS, contains a list of the "American Public Health Exhibits to Be Destroyed," September 1, 1942. Our description of the sections is drawn from these two lists. The photo of the

installation at Deutsches Volk-Deutsches Arbeit is in Box 3, Folder GF-4, BG Papers. Information about the installation is from Gebhard's autobigraphy, "Two Lives," 181, in Box 1, Folder 1, BG Papers.

21. The list of exhibits to be destroyed from Buffalo omitted items B-8 through B-18 on the list in German that Gebhard saved, which are the celluloid models, the descriptions of Mendel's laws, the heredity of eye and hair color, body build, the Habsburg lip, and the difference between fraternal and identical twins. Homer Calver to Mr. Chauncey Hamlin (president of the Buffalo Museum of Science), February 16, 1935, Folder A-042(3), F3, BMS, described a case of exhibition materials that failed to be included in the Pasadena exhibit: "The material consists of nine cases, of which eight are now, according to my information, in Salem, Oregon, in charge of Dr. Vernon A. Douglas, Health Officer of Marion County. . . . The ninth case is in the custody of the James Louden Company, Commercial Street, Los Angeles, California. This case was received too late to be unpacked in time for the exhibit in Pasadena and I do not know what it contains." There is a chance this case contained the materials omitted on the destruction list; if so, these may not have shown in Pasadena; the *Stockton Record* article, however, mentioned the inclusion of the celluloid models.

22. The defects displayed were harelip, hand and foot deformities, schizophrenia, manic depressive insanity, St. Vitus's Dance, epilepsy, mental deficiency, criminality (through a comparison of criminal twins), and chronic alchoholism.

23. No photo of the panels "Law for the Prevention of Hereditary Diseases in Posterity" and "What Is Sterilization" remain in Gebhard's papers. However, in the photo of the Deutsche Volk–Deutsche Arbeit installation (fig. 14.1), the central section contains a panel showing the process of sterilization for the male and female reproductive systems. As most, if not all, of the panels in Eugenics in New Germany were translated versions of those from the German exhibition, this piece may be the prototype for that panel.

24. The panel discussed stated: "How does the hereditarily diseased protect him- or herself from producing hereditarily diseased offspring? He or she puts in an application. The Court of Heredity deliberates on the application." See W. W. Peter's article, "Germany's Sterilization Program," for an in-depth discussion of the law and its enactments.

25. "The Pasadena Meeting," *American Journal of Public Health* (October 1934): 1075.

26. Gebhard, "Two Lives," 182. Although Gebhard wrote these comments long after World War II, there is little reason to doubt the sincerity of his hatred of Hitler. Gebhard was a Christian Socialist who had decided to leave Germany because of Nazi policies. Nevertheless, it is important to stress that neither his doubts about eugenics nor his hatred of Hitler was evident during the exhibit's U.S. tour—no doubt because a Schutzstaffel (SS) officer accompanied him on the tour. Indeed, if we take him at his word when he

said that he "hated" Hitler, we can appreciate his surprise at finding so many Hitler enthusiasts in the United States.

27. Memo by Walter Mangold to Bruno Gebhard, May 30, 1969, recounting the events at the conference, in Folder 2-54: "American Public Health Association: Pasadena Exhibit, 1934, American Museum of Health 1937," BG Papers. A letter from Gebhard to W. W. Peter mentioned that the exhibition went to the Los Angeles County Museum by way of the Los Angeles County Fair, so perhaps it showed at the fair as well; see letter dated February 16, 1935, in the same folder. The strength of the eugenics movement in Southern California is evident in the E. S. Gosney Papers, Cal Tech Archives, and in Molly Ladd-Taylor, "Eugenics, Sterilisation and Modern Marriage in the U.S.A.: The Strange Career of Paul Popenoe," *Gender and History* 13 (2001): 298–327.

28. "Famous Exhibit from Germany Seen in Armory."

29. *The Lancet,* a British publication, ran an unfavorable review of the exhibition in September 1934. Partially because of this review, as well as the influence of Jago Galdston (according to Gebhard), the New York Academy of Medicine refused to show the exhibition, despite strong support from Robert Louis Dickinson. See letter from Gebhard to W. W. Peter, February 16, 1935, BG Papers.

30. "Hygiene Exhibits to Come Monday," *Oregon Statesman,* February 10, 1935, 7.

31. "Hygiene Exhibit of Dresden, Germany on Display at Y.M.C.A.," *Capital Journal,* February 2, 1935, 7.

32. "Hygiene Exhibit Viewed by Class," *Oregon Statesman,* February 22, 1935, 14.

33. "Health Exhibit Is Placed in Capital," *Oregon Statesman,* March 1, 1935, 2.

34. Ibid., and "Part of Hygiene Exhibit Taken to High School," *Oregon Statesman,* March 12, 1935, 3.

35. Vernon Douglas to Homer Calver, March 22, 1935, Folder 042(3), F3, BMS.

36. "Exhibit at Y.M.C.A. Tells Health Story," *Oregonian,* April 24, 1935, 2.

37. "Fred Messing to Reed College," n.d., Special Collections, Eric V. Hauser Memorial Library, Reed College, Portland, OR.

38. Fred Messing to Carl E. Cummings, June 22, 1935, A-042(3) F3, BMS.

39. The one in twenty figure is based on the 1930 U.S. Census report of Oregon's population as 953,786.

40. For a detailed history of eugenic sterilization in Oregon, see Mark A. Largent, "'The Greatest Curse of the Race': Eugenic Sterilization in Oregon, 1909–1983," *Oregon Historical Quarterly* 103 (2001): 188–209.

41. Bethenia Owens-Adair, "Letter to the Editor," *Oregonian,* March 11, 1904. See also Owens-Adair, *Human Sterilization* (Warrenton, OR: n.p., 1910).

42. Chapter 279, *General Laws of Oregon* (Salem: State of Oregon, 1917), 519.

43. Total sterilization numbers were assembled by analysis of records found in "Eugenics Records, 1918–1945," Oregon State Archives, Salem, OR.

44. Philip Reilly made this argument in *The Surgical Solution: A History of Involuntary Sterilization* (Baltimore, MD: Johns Hopkins University Press, 1991).

45. Chapter 279, *General Laws of Oregon*, 519.

46. "Far-Reaching Sterilization Plan Studied," *Oregon Journal*, August 9, 1935, 11.

47. "Hygiene Exhibit of Dresden, Germany," 7.

48. "Health Exhibit to Remain This Week," *Oregon Statesman*, February 24, 1935, 5.

49. A fire at the state capital, which caused nearly $3 million in damage, a looming social security problem, and Governor Martin's worries that his party would soon lose its majority in the house motivated the special session; see "Special Session May Be Called," *Oregonian*, April 21, 1935, 1; "Flames Raze Oregon Capital," *Oregonian*, April 26, 1935, 1; "$3,000,000 Loss Seen at Capital," *Oregonian*, April 27, 1935, 1.

50. "Governor Balks on Capitol Bill," *Oregonian*, November 16, 1935, 1.

51. "Far-Reaching Sterilization Plan Studied," *Oregon Journal*, August 9, 1935, 11.

52. Ibid.

53. "Health Exhibit Is Placed in Capitol," 2.

54. "United States of America," *Lancet* (September 29, 1934): 729. See also Gebhard, "Two Lives," 170, 184.

55. Frederick L. Henning to C. E. Cummings, January 4, 1935, Folder A-042 (3), F3, BMS.

56. "Museum News," *Hobbies* 16, no. 1 (October 1935): 14–15. For years, rumors (still unsubstantiated by hard evidence) circulated at the Buffalo Museum of Science that Cummings possessed a photograph that Adolf Hitler inscribed to him. Museum officials deny the truth of these reports.

57. Karl E. Wilhelm to Collector of Customs, May 3, 1947, Folder A-042 (3), F3, BMS.

ABOUT THE CONTRIBUTORS

Mary K. Coffey, PhD, is assistant professor of art history at Dartmouth College. Her research concerns the intersection of exhibition, social governance, and discourses of race, nation, and gender. She is the author of "From Nation to Community: Museums and the Reconfiguration of Mexican Society under Neo-liberalism"; "Angels and Prostitutes: José Clemente Orozco's Catharsis and the Politics of Female Allegory in 1930s Mexico"; and, with coauthor Jeremy Packer, "Hogging the Road: Cultural Governance and the Citizen Cyclist."

Christina Cogdell, PhD, is assistant professor of art history in the Thaw Art History Center, Department of Art, at the College of Santa Fe in Santa Fe, New Mexico. She is the author of *Eugenic Design: Streamlining America in the 1930s;* "The Futurama Recontextualized: Norman Bel Geddes's Eugenic 'World of Tomorrow'"; and "Products or Bodies? Streamline Design and Eugenics as Applied Biology."

Susan Currell, PhD, is lecturer in American literature at the University of Sussex, England. She is the author of *The March of Spare Time,* which examines the cultural reconstruction of leisure during the 1930s. She is currently working on a biography of self-improvement writer Walter B. Pitkin, in the context of the self-help literature of the 1930s.

Stephen Fender, PhD, is research professor in the humanities in the Graduate Research Centre for the Humanities at the University of Sussex, England, and is a founding coeditor of *Atlantic Studies.* He has written on early American exploration and discovery, American Puritan literature and culture, emigrant writing, American western travel, the American 1930s, and modern American poetry. His books include *The American Long Poem, Plotting the Golden West: American Literature and the Rhetoric of the California Trail, Sea Changes: British Emigration and American Literature,* and the Oxford World's Classics edition of Thoreau's *Walden.* Most recently, he has published on the Works Progress Administration Writers' Project, and he is now working on a book about the New Deal and the country poor, supported by a fellowship from the Leverhulme Foundation.

KAREN A. KEELY, PhD, is assistant professor of English at Mount Saint Mary's University, Emmitsburg, Maryland. She received her doctorate from the University of California, Los Angeles. Her recent publications include "Poverty, Sterilization, and Eugenics in Erskine Caldwell's *Tobacco Road*" and "Teaching Eugenics to Children: Heredity and Reform."

WENDY KLINE, PhD, is associate professor in the Department of History at the University of Cincinnati, Ohio. She is the author of *Building a Better Race: Gender, Sexuality, and Eugenics from the Turn of the Century to the Baby Boom.*

BARBARA LADNER, PhD, is professor of English and coordinator of general education at West Virginia State University. She received her doctorate in American studies from Yale University in 1987. She has published on Appalachian literature and 1930s regionalist painting and is currently at work on a book project, "Region and Remembering: The Body and Folk Imagery in 1930s Regionalism." She has presented frequently on William Faulkner, Thomas Hart Benton, and gender and body imagery in World War II–era film.

MARK LARGENT, PhD, is a historian of science and assistant professor at James Madison College at Michigan State University. The focus of his research is the history of biology in the United States in the late nineteenth and early twentieth centuries, with special interest in the development and application of evolutionary biology.

BETSY NIES, PhD, is assistant professor of American literature at the University of North Florida in Jacksonville. Her book *Eugenic Fantasies: Racial Ideology in the Literature and Popular Culture of the 1920's* examines the presence of eugenic rhetoric in the works of Hemingway, Fitzgerald, and H.D.

NICOLE HAHN RAFTER, PhD, professor at Northeastern University, is the author of *Creating Born Criminals*, a history of eugenic crime control

programs in the United States, and *White Trash: The Eugenic Family Stud-
ies, 1877–1919.* She has also authored works on feminist criminology and
Shots in the Mirror: Crime Films and Society. Recently, she retranslated the
major criminological works of the Italian criminal anthropololgist Cesare
Lombroso. In 2004, she published "Earnest A. Hooton and the Biological
Tradition in American Criminology."

ANDRÉS REGGIANI, PHD, is professor of history at the Universidad Tor-
cuato di Tella in Buenos Aires. He has completed a biographical study of
Nobel laureate and eugenicist Alexis Carrel, entitled *God's Eugenicist: Alexis
Carrel and the Sociobiology of Decline.* He has also published on population
and medicine in American, French, German, and Latin American journals
and is currently working on the formation of international networks of eugenics experts in the period between 1910 and 1940.

MICHAEL REMBIS, PHD, is visiting assistant professor in the Department
of History at the University of Arizona, where he earned his doctorate. He
has published numerous encyclopedia entries and several journal articles,
including "Breeding Up the Human Herd: Gender, Power, and the Creation
of the Country's First Eugenic Commitment Law," which the editors at the
Journal of Illinois History named "best article published in 2002," and "'I
ain't been reading while on parole': Experts, Mental Tests, and Eugenic
Commitment in Illinois, 1890–1940." His dissertation, "Breeding Up the
Human Herd: Gender, Power, and Eugenics in Illinois, 1890–1940," won
the Florence Hemley Schneider Prize for promise of outstanding scholarship in a dissertation appropriate to women's studies.

ROBERT RYDELL, PHD, is professor and chair of history and philosophy
at Montana State University. He is a specialist on world's fairs and the
author of many books and articles, including *All the World's a Fair, World
of Fairs: The Century-of-Progress Expositions,* and most recently, with Rob
Kroes, *Buffalo Bill in Bologna: The Americanization of the World, 1869–1922.*

KERRY D. SOPER, PHD, is assistant professor in the Department of
Humanities, Classics and Comparative Literature and coordinator of the
American studies program at Brigham Young University. He is author of
"From Rowdy, Urban Carnival to Middle-Class Pastime: Reading Richard
Outcault's *The Yellow Kid* and *Buster Brown*" and "Performing 'Jiggs': Irish

Caricature and Comedic Ambivalence towards Assimilation and the American Dream in George McManus's *Bringing Up Father, 1913–1930*." He also publishes as a cartoonist and satirist.

ANGELA SMITH, PHD, is assistant professor of English and gender studies at the University of Utah. She is the author of "Shriveled Breasts and Dollar Signs: Material(ist) Subjects and the Body of the Prostitute in Myra Page's *Moscow Yankee*," and "Impaired and Ill at Ease: New Zealand's Cinematics of Disability." She is working on a book on eugenics and disability in classic horror cinema.

INDEX

Page numbers in italics denote illustrations.

Father Abraham, 165–69, 174; *Flags in the Dust*, 165, 169, 176, 174; *The Hamlet*, 165, 168–69, 172, 174–75; *Light in August*, 175; *The Mansion*, 165; *Mosquitoes*, 165; *Sanctuary*, 175; *Sartoris*, 165–66; *The Sound and the Fury*, 136, 174; *The Town*, 165; *The Unvanquished*, 169
Federal Arts Project, 142, 161
Federal Writers Project, 140–61
feebleminded, 2–3, 19, 21, 24, 27, 33, 50, 59, 77–78, 80, 123–24, 153, 170–71, 207, 270–71, 277, 289, 310, 321, 334–35, 337, 341–42, 349, 352, 357n50, 370, 371, 375–77
feminism, 78, 105–6, 207–8, 210, 238. *See also* "new woman"
Fender, Stephen, 8, 140
fertility, 3, 24, 39, 78, 101, 147, 149, 155, 157, 164, 166, 218, 227–28, 233, 268n39, 276, 309, 325, 327, 332, 342–43, 348
Field Museum of Natural History (Chicago), 213n19, 362
films, 63, 102, 235, 291, 293, 297–98, 304; comedy, 10, 308–28, 332; with eugenic themes, 5, 6; horror, 5, 10, 50, 332–53; industry, 10
"Finley, Clem," 160
Firestone Company, 85
Fisher, Dorothy Canfield, *Learn or Perish*, 58
Fisher, Irving, *How to Live: The Nation's Foremost Health Book*, 228
Fishes and Their Ways of Life (Roule), 237
Fisk, Eugene, *How to Live: The Nation's Foremost Health Book*, 228
fitness, 17, 44, 51, 58, 79, 92, 99–101, 106, 111, 113–14, 194, 198, 206, 230, 233, 313, 322, 325. *See also* unfit
fitter families contests, 214n42, 240, 241, 282, 340, 363. *See also* better babies contests; typical American family
Flags in the Dust (Faulkner), 165, 169, 176, 174
Flexner, Simon, 72
Florey, Robert, 346
folklore, 142–43

food, 258, 260, 261
Ford, Henry, 85
Ford Motor Company, 239
"forgotten man," 45
Forster, W. O., 159
Fortune, 122; survey about sterilization, 37, 277, 301, 305n12
Forum, 218
Fosdick, Raymond, *The Old Savage in the New Civilization*, 79
Foucault, Michel, 301
Fourtner, August, 34, 36
Frankenstein, 10, 332–53
freak, 1, 282, 289, 300
French Canadians, 135
French Foundation for the Study of Human Problems, 86
Freudian theory, 271, 277, 289, 291, 298, 302
Fruit of the Family Tree, The (Wiggam), 180n41
Frye, Dwight, 336, 346, 356n42
Functional Disorders of the Large Intestine (Buckstein), 228

Gallagher, Nancy, 93
Galton, Sir Francis, 94, 198, 207, 334, 339
Garren, Lester, 154, 158
gas chambers, 81, 287
Gasser, Herbert, 85
Gault, Robert, 290
Gebhard, Bruno, 365, 367–68, *368*, 373, 380n13, 382n26
Gellhorn, Martha, 52
gender roles, 12, 17, 27–28, 54, 78, 80, 83, 91–114, 189, 249–51, 256, 258, 260, 262, 263, 268n49, 360
geneticists, 19
genetics, 2. *See also* Mendelian genetics.
Germany, 196, 239, 248n70; Central Register, 372; Court of Heredity, 370, 382n24; Educational Office for Population Problems and Race Hygiene, 367; Federal Health Service, 367; Health Education Service, 367; Hereditary Health Courts, 81; Ministry of the Interior, 367. *See also* National Socialists, German

Index

Saraka laxative exhibit, 229
Sartoris (Faulkner), 165–66
Saturday Evening Post, 222
Savage, Kirk, 190–91, 194; *Standing Soldiers, Kneeling Slaves*, 190
Scally, Mary, 29–30, 32
Schreck, Max, 356n40
Schwesinger, Gladys, 23
science fiction, 6,
Science News Letter, 101
"science of man," 79
Scientific Monthly, 249, 254
Scopes monkey trial, 169, 173
sculptural exhibitions, 185, 187, 191, 238, 365. *See also* exhibitions
Second Generation, The, 309
Sedgwick, Eve, 335
segregation, 50, 95, 98, 149
Seiring, George, 367
Selden, Steven, 93
self-control, 6, 49, 56, 102
self-help, 6, 48, 50, 54, 57, 59, 61–62
self-improvement, 5, 44–64, 85, 251
Semites. *See* Jews; anti-Semitism.
sermons, 221, 224, 228
sexuality, 13n3, 25, 35–36, 56, 131, 136, 319–21, 325, 336, 354n14
sharecroppers, 121–22, 134, 151, 156–57, 159
She Loves Me Not, 320
Shelley, Mary, 333, 350; *Frankenstein*, 333
Sherbon, Florence Brown, 363
Sherman, Mandel, 140; *Hollow Folk*, 140, 145–48, 150, 152, 154, 156, 160
Short Introduction to the History of Human Stupidity, A (Pitkin), 45, 57, 61
Shots in the Mirror (Rafter), 297
Sinel, Joseph, 237
Sippy, John J., 372
Skal, David J., 334, 340, 350
Skavlan, Margaret, 377
Slavs, 274, 296, 299, 338, 343
slums, 60
Smith, Angela, 5, 10, 332
Smith College, 104, 198
"Smith" family, 151
"smooth flow," 9, 220, 227, 240, 242
Snakeville's Eugenic Marriage, 309

Snell, Earl, 377
Snelson, David M., 158
Social Darwinism, 149, 261, 274, 283–85, 294, 333
social planning, 6
social reform, 2, 4
social scientists, 18, 19, 50–51, 53, 60, 351
Social Security, 47, 51, 52
socialism, 207
sociology, 6, 20, 47, 52, 53, 132, 143–45, 150, 158, 161, 201, 277, 291, 376
Sonoma (California) State Home for the Feebleminded, 19, 34, 360
Soper, Kerry, 9, 269, 332
Sound and the Fury, The (Faulkner), 136, 174
South, the, 1, 7–9, 120–36, 140–61, 164–76; dysgenic, 7–8. *See also* Southern Agrarians; Southern aristocracy
Southern Agrarians, 8, 55, 120–136, 165
Southern aristocracy, 8, 132–33, 164–65, 168, 174
Southern California Edison, 361
speed, 6, 55, 59, 218, 228, 234–35-7, 239–40, 242
Spencer, Herbert, 260–61
Spengler, Oswald, 74
Stahnke, Herbert L., 110
Standing Soldiers, Kneeling Slaves (Savage), 190
Stanford University, 362
Station for Experimental Evolution, 189
Steel, Ernest, 153
Steinbeck, John, 201
stereotypes, 347; criminal, 273, 279, 288, 297–300, 302–4; ethnic, 9, 269, 273, 274–76, 279–81, 280, 281, 284, 287, 289–91, 293–94, 295, 299, 323, 324, 350; of poor whites, 123; of the South, 120. *See also* physiognomy; "poor white trash"
sterilization, 52, 59, 98, 101, 124–26, 174, 225, 250, 260, 270, 277, 301, 310, 326, 334, 340, 349, 367, 367, 370, 371, 374, 377; and class, 17, 121, 132; committee on, 75; compulsory, 2, 81, 124, 182n54, 321, 359, 375, 379; cost-effective, 19, 361, 369; and the

403